The Uprooted

The Uprooted

Improving Humanitarian Responses to Forced Migration

Susan F. Martin, Patricia Weiss Fagen,
Kari Jorgensen, Lydia Mann-Bondat,
and Andrew Schoenholtz

LEXINGTON BOOKS
A Division of
ROWMAN & LITTLEFIELD PUBLISHERS, INC.
Lanham • Boulder • New York • Toronto • Oxford

LEXINGTON BOOKS

A division of Rowman & Littlefield Publishers, Inc.
A wholly owned subsidiary of The Rowman & Littlefield Publishing Group, Inc.
4501 Forbes Boulevard, Suite 200
Lanham, MD 20706

PO Box 317
Oxford
OX2 9RU, UK

British Library Cataloguing in Publication Information Available

Library of Congress Cataloging-in-Publication Data

The uprooted : improving humanitarian responses to forced migration /
Susan F. Martin . . . [et al.].
   p. cm. — (Program in migration and refugee studies)
   Includes bibliographical references and index.
   ISBN 0-7391-0816-6 (cloth : alk. paper) — ISBN 0-7391-1083-7 (pbk. : alk. paper)
   1. Forced migration. 2. Refugees-International cooperation. 3. Humanitarian
assistance. I. Martin, Susan F. II. Series.
HV640.U67 2005
362.87—dc22   2005013129

Printed in the United States of America

⊗™ The paper used in this publication meets the minimum requirements of American
National Standard for Information Sciences—Permanence of Paper for Printed Library
Materials, ANSI/NISO Z39.48–1992.

Contents

Acknowledgments

This book has been a collaborative project from the very beginning. We are grateful to the John D. and Catherine T. MacArthur Foundation for providing a multi-year grant that enabled us to bring together a research team from four continents: the Institute for the Study of International Migration at Georgetown University and the Brookings-SAIS Project on Internal Displacement in Washington, D.C., the Refugee Studies Centre at Oxford University, the Centre for the Study of Forced Migration at the University of Dar es Salaam in Tanzania and the Regional Centre for Strategic Studies in Colombo, Sri Lanka. These organizations were soon joined by researchers in Colombia, Georgia, Australia and Denmark, who engaged with us in site visits in Sri Lanka, Tanzania and Burundi, Georgia, Colombia, and East Timor and headquarters studies in New York and Geneva. The case studies are being published separately as *Catching Fire: Containing Complex Displacement in a Volatile World*.

Our thanks, in particular, to Stephen Castles, Nicholas van Hear, Roberta Cohen, Khoti Kamanga, Christopher McDowell, Matthew Karanian, Amelia Fernandez Juan, Finn Stepputat, Roberto Vidal Lopez, Darini Rajasingham-Senanayake, R. A. Ariyaratne, and Trish Hiddleston who participated in headquarters and field visits. Appreciation also goes to a number of hardworking research assistants who provided invaluable legal and policy research, including Laura Sheridan, Laila al Baradei, Joe Cutler, David Fisher, and John Warner.

Georgetown University assumed responsibility within this collaborative project for policy analysis and recommendations. To help us formulate the issues we convened an advisory board. The members served in their personal capacity. We thank Arthur Eugene Dewey, Julia Taft, Princeton Lyman, James Purcell, and Richard Smyser for their insightful advice. While the end result is ours alone, we hope that our advisors see that we have taken seriously their comments. Erin Mooney, Walter Kalin, and Francis Deng reviewed earlier drafts of some chapters of this book.

Support from the Andrew W. Mellon Foundation and the Fritz Institute for Georgetown University's Program on Refugee and Humanitarian Emergencies gave us the resources and opportunity to transform our research into this volume. Our thanks as well go to Serena Krombach, our editor at Lexington Books.

An earlier version of chapter 3 was published in the Journal of Refugee Studies (Susan Martin, "Making the UN Work: Forced Migration and Institutional Reform" vol. 17 no. 3: 301–318). Our appreciation goes to the peer reviewers for their very helpful comments and suggestions.

Our final appreciation goes to the refugees and displaced persons and humanitarian aid workers whom we interviewed and from whom we learned so much. This book is dedicated to them.

1

Introduction

By conservative estimates, about 50 million migrants are living outside of their home communities, forced to flee to obtain some measure of safety and security. Forced migration has many causes and takes many forms. People leave because of persecution, human rights violations, repression, conflict, and natural and human-made disasters. Many depart on their own initiative to escape these life-threatening situations, although in a growing number of cases, people are driven from their homes by governments and insurgent groups intent on depopulating or shifting the ethnic, religious, or other composition of an area. This definition of forced migrants includes persons who cross international borders in search of refuge as well as those who are internally displaced. Also of concern are persons who are at high risk of forced migration, particularly war-affected civilian populations and stateless persons.

The legal and institutional system created in the aftermath of World War II to address refugee movements is proving inadequate to provide appropriate assistance and protection to the full range of forced migrants needing attention today. Although there has been some progress within the United Nations in coordinating responses to emergency movements, particularly with the establishment of the Office for the Coordination of Humanitarian Affairs (OCHA), and some greater willingness of such agencies as the United Nations High Commissioner for Refugees (UNHCR) to move beyond their traditional activities, gaps remain in the capacity of the international community to assist and protect the full range of forced migrants in need of humanitarian assistance and protection.

Chapter 1

Forced migration is an inevitable and increasing consequence of conflict, especially internal and ethnic conflict. Addressing humanitarian crises involving mass migration is integral to maintaining international security and promoting sustainable development. This is particularly the case post-September 11, when it has become apparent that such countries as Afghanistan that experience prolonged humanitarian emergencies can too easily become breeding grounds for terrorism.

The nature and scale of forced migration makes clear the need not only to broaden current approaches to humanitarian assistance, but also to reassess longstanding assumptions about the international humanitarian regime overall. This collaborative project examines the progress and the persistent shortcomings of the current humanitarian regime in addressing the needs of millions of people. That progress has been made is unquestionable. Indeed, the very fact that terms such as "internally displaced person," "environmental," and "development induced" migrants have entered the international vocabulary indicates growing awareness of the phenomenon.

However, the gaps and inefficiencies of international and national agencies to reach entire categories among the growing numbers of forced migrants demonstrate organizational, political, and conceptual shortcomings. While there is a growing acceptance for extending international mechanisms to protect people who are mistreated by their governments or whose governments are unable to provide protection, in nearly all cases, it is still the nation state that governs international access to its internally displaced persons. Access has been a problem in all the cases studied.

Even where there is political will to assist and protect forced migrants, organizational mandates and national structures are often impediments to doing so effectively. The militarization of refugee and displaced persons camps remains a major problem, and all sides in civil conflicts increasingly use the displacement of civilians for strategic purposes. Serious disagreements have been aired about the effects of humanitarian assistance for refugees and other forced migrants—as to whether they facilitate or impede prospects for peace and economic development. Finally, as this study will demonstrate, the persistent notion that forced migration is a temporary phenomenon—a notion derived from experience with natural disasters and previous successes in resettling refugees—is now untenable in most cases and is detracting from needed attention to longer-term solutions.

This book examines the current humanitarian regime, in the context of these developments, and makes recommendations to improve international, regional, national, and local responses. It assesses the international response to forced migration induced by conflict, ethnic cleansing, other human rights repression, natural disasters, and development, focusing on situations where there are complex mixes of refugees, internally displaced persons, returnees, and other uprooted people.

Documenting the very complexity and interconnections among the various categories of forced migrants is a major contribution of the study. Forced migration is far more fluid than considered by the international humanitarian system that still utilizes a categorization system based largely on whether forced migrants cross international borders or remain within their own territory. Rather, people are forced to flee because of a complex combination of circumstances and they seek safety in a variety of locations. Moreover, they often move from one status to another during the period of their displacement. For example, it is not uncommon for repatriating refugees to find they are unable to return to their home communities and become internally displaced persons.

This book urges the development of more comprehensive and cohesive strategies to address forced migration in its complexity. There are many barriers to such an approach, however. Many of these barriers have been identified in other studies as well, but they bear repeating because they remain persistent foes of effective humanitarian aid and protection:

- The legal system to address protection and assistance of forced migrants is inadequate to comprehensively protect today's broad range of forced migrants.
- Gaps in international, regional and national responses to forced migration lead to gross inconsistencies in assistance and protection afforded to different categories of forced migrants, and they impede efforts to implement comprehensive approaches to humanitarian emergencies.
- Inadequate financial resources resulting from both underfunding and maldistribution of funds harm the aid efforts that can be undertaken.
- Prolonged insecurity renders forced migrants and humanitarian aid agencies subject to attack and undermines efforts to reach large numbers of refugees and internally displaced persons.
- The inability to achieve durable solutions prevents millions of forced migrants from returning home or integrating into new communities.

The solutions to these problems are also not new, but they are needed today more than ever before:

- Reforming the international legal system to include protection for the full range of forced migrants needing international attention;
- Implementing new institutional arrangements for assisting and protecting forced migrants, particularly by the creation of a UN High

Commissioner for Forced Migrants that would assume responsibility for refugees and displaced persons and by improving coordination mechanisms within the United Nations and between the UN and other actors;
- Increasing and better directing financial resources available for humanitarian operations, particularly by improving donor responses and using the Consolidated Appeals Process (CAP) as a mechanism for strategic planning and identification of funding priorities;
- Improving the safety and security of forced migrants, including through the deployment of international police forces to protect humanitarian aid operations; and
- Renewing efforts to find durable solutions for forced migrants, which require improved coordination between the humanitarian assistance regime and the political, peacekeeping, and development agencies that address the causes of these crises.

With a study team composed of researchers and policy analysts from the Institute for the Study of International Migration at Georgetown University, the Refugee Studies Centre at Oxford University, the Centre for Development Research in Copenhagen, the Project on Internal Displacement at the Brookings Institution, the Centre for the Study of Forced Migration at the University of Dar es Salaam in Tanzania, and the Regional Centre for Strategic Studies in Sri Lanka, this project provides a unique opportunity to develop and test various models for reform through a collaborative effort by experts on four continents.

The project began with an intensive effort to document the efficacy of current mandates and capacities at the headquarters and field levels. We have conducted extensive interviews with officials in the principal humanitarian, human rights, and development agencies in New York and Geneva and with representatives of the major donor governments. We have also reviewed the "gray" literature of documents produced by and for the international organizations but generally not broadly published.

In the field, we used a case study approach in which the multidisciplinary research team focused on institutional roles, responsibilities and relationships. The five sites—Burundi, Colombia, East Timor, Georgia, and Sri Lanka—allowed the team to assess the effectiveness of the humanitarian response to forced migration at different stages in the humanitarian emergencies. The case studies also cover a broad range of situations, in terms of the causes of forced migration; geographic location; institutional arrangements for assigning and coordinating responsibilities; assistance and protection mechanisms used; nature of governmental capacities for assistance and protection; and degree of access and security. We have examined throughout the impact of these programs on the actual recipients of international aid and protection. Those interviewed included the full array of actors involved in humanitarian relief operations: international organization officials; national government officials; local, national, and international nongovernmental organizations; and the displaced themselves. By interviewing informants at the various levels of policymaking and implementation, we have been able to identify where major differences exist and, in some circumstances, ways to address these conflicting perspectives. To supplement these field visits, we have also used desktop studies of international responses in Afghanistan, the former Yugoslavia, and the Sudan, which provide the team with additional relevant information based on existing evaluations and assessments.

The research team organized intensive workshops in the Americas, Europe, Africa and Asia in which participants drawn from international and regional organizations, national authorities, nongovernmental agencies, and the research community discussed the findings and options presented. These workshops provided feedback on the study team's options and stimulated debate and discussion of improvements needed in the humanitarian regime. With the results of the workshops, the study team authored two books, one of case studies (*Catching Fire: Containing Complex Displacement in a Volatile World*) and the other, this volume, outlining our recommendations for change.

NATURE OF FORCED MIGRATION TODAY

This book focuses on a range of migrants who share a common situation— they have been forced to flee their homes. They do not, however, share the same status or rights in the international humanitarian system. Refugees are a subset of forced migrants who have a special status in international law, coming under the terms of the 1951 UN Convention and 1967 Protocol Relating to the Status of Refugees. The UN High Commissioner for Refugees (UNHCR) has special responsibilities as the international organization mandated to protect and assist refugees. UNHCR estimates that there were about twenty million persons under its mandate, as of January 2002, of whom twelve million were refugees and the remainder fit into other categories of forced migrant. Under the 1951 Convention, a refugee is a person outside of his or her country who has a well-founded fear that he or she would be persecuted on return. Refugee status has been applied more broadly, however, to include other persons who are outside their country of origin because of armed conflict, generalized violence, foreign aggression, or other circumstances that have seriously disturbed public order, and who, therefore, require international protection and assistance.

The number of refugees—that is, persons outside of their home country— is at its lowest level in years. Increasingly, people in life-threatening situations are finding avenues of escape closed to them. Even when they are able to leave, an increasing number find no country willing to accept them as refugees.

The decrease in the number of refugees does not mean that the number of forced migrants has reduced. There is a growing number of conflicts in which civilians are targets of military activity as well as war crimes and crimes against humanity. At the same time, there has been a large increase in the number of internally displaced persons in need of international protection. While there is no international convention similar to the 1951 refugee convention for internally displaced persons, the United Nations has promoted *Guiding Principles on Internal Displacement*, drawn from existing human rights and humanitarian law, to provide a more comprehensive framework for protecting and assisting internally displaced persons. The *Guiding Principles* offer the following descriptive definition of internally displaced persons: "persons or groups of persons who have been forced, or obliged to flee or to leave their homes or places of habitual residence, in particular as a result of armed conflict, situations of generalized violence, violations of human rights, or natural or human-made disasters, and who have not crossed an internationally recognized state border."[1] In the late 1990s, the internally displaced outnumbered refugees by two to one. The Norwegian Refugee Council's Global IDP Project estimates that there are about twenty-five million IDPs.[2] UNHCR considers about six million of the IDPs to be under its mandate.

The decrease in the number of refugees reflects a second phenomenon as well, the repatriation of millions of refugee returnees to their home countries. During the 1990s, large-scale return occurred to a wide range of countries. In Africa alone, repatriation occurred in Angola, Burundi, Eritrea, Ethiopia, Liberia, Mali, Mozambique, Namibia, Rwanda, and Somalia. Other prominent repatriation destinations were Cambodia, Afghanistan, El Salvador, Nicaragua, Guatemala, and Bosnia-Herzegovina. In some cases, the movements are voluntary and secure because hostilities have truly ended, and with peace could come repatriation and reintegration. Too often during the past decades, though, refugees along with their internally displaced cousins returned to communities still wracked by warfare and conflict. A range of factors induces such return. Countries of asylum may be weary from having hosted the refugees and place pressure on them to repatriate prematurely. Donors may also reduce their assistance in the expectation that return will soon take place. The refugees themselves may wish to re-stake their claim to residences and businesses before others take them, or they may wish to return in time to participate in elections. Families split by hostilities may be anxious for reunification.

Forced repatriation because of emergencies in host countries occurs among non-refugees as well. For example, when Iraqi forces invaded Kuwait, massive numbers of foreign workers fled the country. Although most of the economic migrants could avail themselves of the protection of their home countries, the logistics of their return overwhelmed Jordan, the principal country of transit, as well as the international community. Because many of the foreign workers were returning to countries that had their own political and economic problems, concerns that the returnees would have destabilizing effects were well founded.

Statelessness is both a cause and consequence of forced migration. Stateless persons generally enjoy fewer rights than those who are citizens of a sovereign state. When they are also distrusted minorities within the country in which they reside, stateless persons often experience discrimination and may be the targets of violence and repression. These factors may cause them, in turn, to take flight. Statelessness is a consequence of forced migration in situations where refugees lose their former nationality but do not qualify for a new one. This may occur for seemingly benign reasons. For example, their country of origin may confer citizenship through "jus solis," birth on its territory, whereas the country of asylum may confer citizenship through "jus sanguine," that is, by descent. The children born to refugees will qualify for neither citizenship, not having been born in their parents' home country and not sharing the nationality of the host country.

Environmental degradation and natural disasters uproot another type of forced migrant. Unlike the refugees and displaced persons described above, environmental migrants generally do not need protection from persecution or violence, but like refugees and internally displaced persons, they may be unable to return to now uninhabitable communities. Most environmental migrants move internally, some relocating temporarily until they are able to rebuild their homes and others seeking permanent new homes. Some environmental migrants, however, cross national boundaries.

Development projects may also cause large-scale migration of what are referred to as development-induced migrants. Involuntary relocations occur, for example, as a result of the building of dams for irrigation or hydropower, highway construction, and urban renewal. Some governments have tried to redistribute residents from over to underpopulated regions, sometimes compelling relocation through force.[3]

Not all environmental- or development-induced migrants are of concern to the international community. In many cases, national governments are willing and able to assist and protect those displaced because of environmental factors or induced to move because of development projects. They have policies and procedures in place to consult with the victims and help those forced to move to relocate. They provide compensation for property taken in the interests of development.

In other cases, however, governments are overwhelmed and request aid from outside to help with this process. In still further cases, the international community becomes concerned because the national government is unwilling to provide aid or its policies are instrumental in causing harm to its population. An important subgroup of these migrants shares the characteristics of refugees and internally displaced persons because aid is withheld on the basis of their nationality, race, religion, or political opinion. Sometimes, the location for a project resulting in mass displacement is chosen to lessen political opposition or to repress an ethnic or religious minority. These situations may differ little from displacements caused by more overt political factors and conflict.

NEW CHALLENGES AND OPPORTUNITIES

In some respects, the increasing number of forced migrants reflects the limitations of globalization. At the same time that supranational mechanisms for economic and political cooperation are taking hold, extreme nationalism is re-emerging in many parts of the world. Some countries have split peacefully into component national groups (e.g., the Czech Republic and Slovakia) with each part then negotiating access to such regional conglomerates as the European Union (EU) or the North American Treaty Organization (NATO). Far too often, however, nationalism has turned rabid with ethnic group pitted against ethnic group in determining the national identity (e.g., Rwanda or the former Yugoslavia). In certain extreme cases, sovereignty itself has been compromised as no group can amass the strength or legitimacy to maintain order (e.g., Liberia or Somalia). Intense fighting erupts, with targeted attacks on civilians, massive population displacements, "ethnic cleansing" of opposing nationalities, and even genocide.

Many of the institutions created to assist forced migrants, particularly the UN High Commissioner for Refugees, emerged in the post World War II era as the Cold War intensified. Built around traditional notions of sovereignty, the refugee system assisted and protected individuals who could not or would not claim the protection of their own governments. The focus was particularly on those who sought refuge outside of their countries, with the sites of many conflicts off limits to outside intervention. The refugee regime also served important geopolitical and strategic interests since many refugees had fled Communist countries or surrogate Cold War conflicts supported by the superpowers.

In the post-Cold War era, the opportunities to respond to humanitarian crises are greater than ever before though still difficult. While the international community could provide aid and sometimes protection to those who left their countries in the decades after World War II, addressing root causes or bringing aid to victims still inside their countries was limited. That surrogate Cold War conflicts triggered many humanitarian emergencies only complicated matters. At the height of superpower rivalry, intervening in the internal affairs of a country allied with either the United States or the Soviet Union could have provoked a massive military response from the other. It was unlikely that the Security Council would authorize such actions.

Today, humanitarian intervention has taken place in countries as diverse as the Sudan, Iraq, Bosnia, Somalia, Haiti, Kosovo, East Timor, and Afghanistan. The forms of intervention range from airlifted food drops to outright military action. The results have been mixed. Aid reached heretofore-inaccessible people in many of these cases. The deployment of peacekeepers lessened immediate reasons for flight and permitted some repatriation to take place. The root causes of displacement have not generally been addressed, however, and internally displaced populations often remain out of reach. Moreover, safe havens established to protect civilians have too often been vulnerable to attack.

Yet, the willingness of countries to intervene on behalf of internally displaced and other war-affected populations represents major change, seen no less in day-to-day activities than in these heralded interventions. Classic notions of sovereignty are under considerable pressure if they are used to prevent humanitarian assistance from reaching populations in acute need of aid. International human rights and humanitarian law have growing salience in defining sovereignty to include responsibility for the welfare of the residents of one's territory. To quote Francis Deng, the Representative of the UN Secretary General on Internally Displaced Persons, and his colleague Roberta Cohen, in arguing for greater international attention to internally displaced persons:

> Since there is no adequate replacement in sight for the system of state sovereignty, primary responsibility for promoting the security, welfare and liberty of populations must remain with the state. At the same time, no state claiming legitimacy can justifiably quarrel with the commitment to protect all its citizens against human rights abuse. . . . Sovereignty cannot be used as justification for the mistreatment of populations.[4]

Nonintervention clearly does not prevail when the actions of a sovereign state threaten the security of another state. What is new is the recognition that actions that prompt mass exodus into a neighboring territory threaten international security. In a number of cases, beginning with Resolution 688 that authorized the establishment of safe havens in northern Iraq, the Security Council has determined that the way to reduce the threat to a neighboring state is to provide assistance and protection within the territory of the offending state. Even more significant, the international community has also determined that massive human rights abuses merit international action, even if other states face no security threats. As the threat of terrorism became more apparent in the aftermath of September 11, routing out the roots and strongholds of terrorism has become another base for intervention, leading, as in the case of Afghanistan, to the return of millions of war-affected persons.

This emerging redefinition of sovereignty has led the United Nations to think anew about its role in other respects. As Kofi Annan, the UN Secretary General, describes:

> The United Nations is increasingly called upon to adopt a comprehensive approach aimed not only at keeping the peace but also at protecting civilian populations, monitoring human rights violations, facilitating delivery of needed humanitarian assistance, and promoting lasting solutions that include reintegration, development, and transitions to democracy.[5]

The very complexity of forced migration today—which means that the United Nations must go well beyond traditional refugee-focused humanitarian assistance—presents special challenges to the United Nations and its humanitarian partners.

CASE STUDIES

The study team undertook site visits in five countries with significant levels of displacement, some internal and others international. The cases showed a wide range of experiences in addressing the situation of forced migrants, with the international, national, and local responses in certain countries far exceeding those in others. The cases were chosen as well to ensure geographic diversity, allow the team to examine issues at different stages of the humanitarian emergency, and to examine different strategies undertaken by the United Nations in assigning responsibility for forced migrants. Briefly, the findings from the sites are as follows:

Burundi

Conflict in Burundi has lasted over thirty years, the most recent crisis developing in 1993. During this period, more than 200,000 Burundians lost their lives; many fled abroad and many more were displaced, some temporarily and some more long-term. At the time of the site visit in October 2000, there were approximately 340,000 Burundians in Tanzanian refugee camps, an estimated 170,000–200,000 living in Tanzanian settlements, most since 1972, and an estimated 300,000 who spontaneously settled in Tanzanian villages along the border with Burundi.[6] There were approximately 330,000 IDPs living in camps for internally displaced persons and approximately 170,000 men, women, adolescents, and children who were otherwise dispersed in Burundi.[7]

In 1998, negotiations for peace were initiated. A Peace Agreement was signed by most, but significantly not all, of the parties to the conflict in August 2000.[8] No cease-fire was agreed upon although negotiations on a cease-fire continue. The peace agreement remains fragile and could collapse at any time. In fact, fighting intensified following the signing of the Peace Agreement, as a result of which refugee flows to Tanzania, which had been decreasing steadily between January and July 2000, increased again. Civilians continue to be caught in the middle and the numbers of deaths continue to rise. Both rebel forces and extremists within the Burundi military are implicated in attacks against civilians and humanitarian aid organizations. Regional instability and conflict also complicates prospects for peace in Burundi.

The deterioration in the security situation inside the country, and the inability to forecast when peace will be established and what will happen in the meantime, have made operating conditions for humanitarian aid agencies particularly difficult. Inevitably, therefore, the quality and level of planning and humanitarian assistance that can be provided is adversely affected. Of particular concern is the often-desperate situation of the large internally displaced population. Should peace come, and repatriation significantly increases, the needs of returnees from Tanzania and within Burundi will also require significant new attention.

Broadly, three categories of IDPs, with some movement between the categories, are referred to in Burundi: the displaced in IDP camps, the regrouped in regroupment or former regroupment camps (camps established when the military removed the local population to facilitate their military operations), and the dispersed who do not live in camps but rather live in the forests and marshes or have sought refuge with relatives or friends. In addition, some of the refugee returnees have subsequently become internally displaced. Urban street children and other homeless populations have grown in size because of the conflict although they tend not be considered IDPs. The terminology employed can lead to confusion. For instance, references to IDPs or displaced persons can sometimes refer only to those in IDP camps.

Many factors constrain effective delivery of humanitarian assistance and the protection of the internally displaced. Security is the principal constraint on assistance and protection to war-affected populations, including internally displaced persons. As the peace process has progressed, rather than the fighting decrease, it in fact has increased and continues to this day. Since aid operations have been targets of attack, not just collateral damage, it has been particularly difficult to reach vulnerable populations. In some cases, aid agencies have little information about displaced populations because it is too dangerous to reach them. When asked, for example, how the formerly regrouped population are doing, several humanitarian agencies that had provided services in the camps said that they had not been able to return home with the regrouped because of security concerns.

A further impediment to effective humanitarian assistance to IDPs and other war-affected populations was the weakness of the UN in Burundi at the time of the site visit. This was due to a number of factors including the security problems described above, as well as demoralization and high turnover of staff after the 1999 murders of several senior UN staff. No UN agency had taken on responsibility for assistance or protection of the massive number of internally displaced or other populations affected by the conflict. UNHCR played a limited role in relationship to refugee returnees, but the agency had no plans to take on a broader responsibility for IDPs.

Lack of information about the situation of the large number of dispersed and formerly regrouped also hinders effective assistance and protection. Many, if not most IDPs, are effectively out of sight and out of mind of the international system. Finally, the donors contribute to the inadequate response by narrowly defining the scope of assistance activities that will be permitted, allowing only emergency services. Although fighting continues in Burundi, there are safer areas that could be stabilized by the injection of resources for education, income generation, psychosocial and other programs that will help displaced populations move toward greater self-reliance.

The situation of longer-term Burundian refugees in Tanzania is also problematic. Long known for its hospitality toward refugees, the Tanzanian government shows clear signs of "host fatigue." Concerned about diminished financial support from the international community, Tanzanian authorities have encouraged that repatriation take place as soon as possible. Yet, with conflict continuing in Tanzania, premature return is unsafe and unsustainable. In the meantime, there are no opportunities for local integration or self-reliance programs for refugees in Tanzania, leaving the refugees highly dependent on humanitarian assistance and local communities bearing much of the burden of their support.

Colombia

For more than forty years, Colombia has experienced conflict, and the rural population has suffered displacement. Nevertheless, the identification of internally displaced persons as a category of national concern dates only from the early 1990s, as the conflict significantly expanded the areas from which people have been forced to flee.[9] Just how many Colombians have been forcibly displaced is much debated. Estimates range from approximately 750,000 to a little over two million people since 1995.[10] Different humanitarian actors—the state, the Church, nongovernment organizations and the international agencies[11]—have different definitions of who is an internally displaced person. These definitions vary according to whether only those whose flight is due to violence are counted, whether only those formally registered with the government are counted, how long ago the migration took place and whether the IDPs choose to identify themselves.

The Colombian conflict has also produced international forced migration, but in much smaller numbers. Colombians have sought refuge in Venezuela, Ecuador, Panama, and Costa Rica. Until the closing of the demilitarized zone, the outflow from Colombia has been smaller than anticipated, probably due both to problematic conditions in the two neighboring countries and the difficulties encountered in attempting to cross either of the borders. By early 2002, border crossings were on the rise. In addition, Colombians have fled to the United States, where several thousand have filed for and been granted asylum. There have also been repeated calls, not yet heeded by the U.S. government, that Colombians be granted Temporary Protected Status (TPS), which is available to persons who cannot return home safely because of conflict or other civil disturbances.

The vast majority of forced migrants remain within Colombia. The Colombian government has tried to put in place a system that operates on the state, departmental, and local levels to meet the challenges of displacement in all its phases. Comprehensive legislation has specified the rights of the displaced and the responsibilities of government entities at all levels. The system is coordinated by a single entity, the Network of Social Solidarity (RSS), created in 1994 for programs that addressed poverty and helped the most vulnerable sectors, including displaced persons. IDPs have the right to health, education, and basic services that span the emergency and stabilization phases of displacement. The IDPs receive the services free of charge during the three months they are receiving emergency assistance and thereafter are obliged to pay a small amount.

Although Colombia has the most comprehensive structures in the world for IDPs, a closer look uncovers a system that is grossly underfinanced and understaffed, in which responsibilities are undefined and officials are rarely if ever held accountable. The obstacles are largely institutional and financial, but the problems are exacerbated by a lack of political will among the key policy actors and, obviously, the failure to win concessions from the armed groups toward "humanizing" their methods of warfare. The assistance system is additionally weakened by the tension between its centralized management and decentralized operation with municipal authorities having the principal responsibility for implementing assistance programs.

The major international organizations now operating in Colombia have oriented their humanitarian programs to take account of the situation of massive nation-wide displacement. On the UN side, the agencies involved in working on displacement have come together in Thematic Group on Displacement, led by the UN High Commissioner for Refugees (UNHCR) and supported by the Office for Coordination of Humanitarian Affairs (OCHA).[12] Several of the large international NGOs have made responding to displacement a priority, while an unknown but very large number of smaller, international and national NGOs work with one or more IDP communities.

The reach of the UN in assisting and protecting IDPs is limited both geographically and in time. Even in the regions where displaced persons are concentrated, it is difficult to reach more than a small percent of the population. The combined operational budget of UN agencies for attending to IDPs is a mere $17 million,[13] inadequate in the face of the large numbers requiring assistance and protection. Although the UN system in Colombia has achieved a reasonable level of cooperation, there is little formal coordination and few mechanisms for interagency action in priority areas. In some areas, nearly all the agencies were present; in others, equally impacted, only one or two are found, or none at all. Neither the international agencies nor the Colombian government has targeted programs in a systematic way with respect to gender, ethnicity, or age. The links between the UN system and grass roots entities, including IDP organizations and the groups in civil society that work on behalf of IDPs, require more systematic attention as well.

East Timor

In September 1999, as violence increased in the aftermath of a positive referendum in support of independence, more than 500,000 people (out of a total population of 700,000) were displaced in East Timor. Almost 200,000 were reportedly forcibly evacuated to refugee camps in West Timor that were under the control of the militias behind the communal violence. On September 15, as conditions deteriorated, the International Force in East Timor (INTERFOR), under the leadership of Australia received authority from the Security Council to intervene militarily and secure the territory. By September 18, the Office for Coordination of Humanitarian Affairs had established an office to coordinate the humanitarian relief operation. One of OCHA's first tasks, with the support of UNHCR, was to assess the humanitarian needs in

East Timor, and this included an audit of the humanitarian capacity in Darwin and East Timor and an assessment of NGO capability. In addition, it shared with UNHCR the responsibility for liaison with the military, particularly over the issue of reserving space on flights for relief supplies and personnel.

The humanitarian crisis in East Timor has gone through several phases, from emergency response to stabilization to a transition to reconstruction and development. The initial phase of the emergency response to East Timor was characterized by a dynamic mixture of formal and nonformal arrangements based to a large extent on frequent, dense, and well-managed contact between and within UN agencies, government aid departments, and NGOs. Four factors help explain the success of the early emergency phase: (a) strong leadership from the onset and setting of clear objectives; (b) excellent on-the-ground coordination; (c) commitment and dedication of all the humanitarian actors; and (d) quick support by the international community (including quick disbursements of financial resources).

Overall, the East Timor Consolidated Appeals Process was deemed to be a success because donors were quick to pledge funds for the various operations, money was disbursed relatively efficiently, and overall, immediate basic needs were met within the timeframe set. Donors, in particular, regarded the CAP as a useful planning and funding tool, providing, as it did, a list of overall estimated needs set out as fundable projects on a sector basis both for immediate and medium-term programs.

Some problems in implementation and coordination did arise, however, particularly in military-humanitarian coordination. The military was noticeably uncomfortable with the relatively unstructured style of working of the international humanitarian agencies. Though denied by the military, NGOs felt that INTERFET was relegating the distribution of relief and that humanitarian workers were regarded as an encumbrance and impediment to military-defined 'mission success.'

Much of the early humanitarian momentum was lost by mid-2000, despite the continuing need for an emergency response in a number of areas. A Humanitarian Coordinator working through an Inter-Agency Committee should have been in place to ensure that the focus on humanitarian needs was not lost prematurely. This would have been particularly useful in the shelter sector, which experienced greatest unmet need, particularly for internally displaced persons and returning refugees.

One of the greatest challenges facing the UN was to secure access to, and the return of, East Timorese refugees who had been forcibly removed to camps in West Timor. UNSC Resolution 1264 offered no mandate for INTERFET to accord protection to those East Timorese who continued to be forcibly removed from their homes and sent to West Timor or elsewhere in

Indonesia after the multinational force had arrived in Dili. The murders of UNHCR workers in West Timor further reduced international presence in the camps, rendering the refugees even more vulnerable to protection problems. At the time of the site visit, controversy continued to surround the West Timor camps, particularly regarding a proposed amnesty for militia leaders returning to East Timor.

Georgia

The Georgian government and UNHCR report a population of about 270,000 internally displaced people, almost exclusively as a result of the conflicts in Abkhazia and South Ossetia. Population figures for IDPs within Abkhazia and South Ossetia are more difficult to acquire, largely because problems in security impede access to these areas. The capital city of Tbilisi is host to 32.5 percent of the population, and the Samegrelo region, which is adjacent to Abkhazia, is host to 42 percent of the IDPs. IDPs are housed about equally in collective centers and in the homes of host families. The collective centers are public buildings that were once operated as factories, hotels, or offices, and they are often overcrowded with very poor sanitation and heating facilities. It is believed that many of the IDPs in the border region with Abkhazia move back and forth between their old homes and their collective center housing.

Within Georgia is also a population of refugees, who number roughly 6,000. This group consists almost entirely of Chechen nationals who have fled the fighting in Chechnya and who live in the Pankisi Gorge, a region located northeast of Tbilisi. Chechen militants are also reputed to live in this remote region, and the fear that this is true has kept the entire area off-limits to Georgian and international authorities. Georgia is also the source of refugees for some neighboring regions. Ethnic Ossetians from the Georgian region of South Ossetia have in many cases sought refuge in the bordering republic of North Ossetia, which is a constituent part of the Russian Federation. Their migration is attributed to the conflict between South Ossetia and Georgia, and also to the absence of an economy in South Ossetia.

Like Colombia, Georgia has a very progressive legal framework setting out the status and rights of IDPs. The Ministry of Refugees and Accommodation, which has a Department of Refugee Issues, a Department of IDP Issues, and a Department of IDP Registration, has responsibility for coordinating the programs offered to refugees and displaced persons by other agencies. These programs provide cash allowances, housing, and certain social welfare benefits to displaced persons. This department is also responsible for tracking and registering the population.

The government agencies do not tend to be proactive in this effort, however. Georgia's central government has a tenuous hold on political power outside Tbilisi, and the country's economy is crippled. The government does not have the financial means for assistance programs, and it is burdened by the needs of its non-IDP population, as well. The absence of an economy has also made IDPs continually dependent upon humanitarian assistance. There are simply no jobs available, even for skilled workers.

International humanitarian assistance to Georgia has varied over time. At the time of greatest need, when fighting was most intensive, the international aid was swift and generous. The United Nations initiated an inter-agency appeal early in 1993 through which it was able to deliver more than $20 million in direct assistance. UNHCR early on took lead responsibility for assisting and protecting IDPs. Georgia was not alone within the former Soviet Union in needing humanitarian aid. In May 1996, the "Regional Conference on Refugees, Displaced Persons and Other Forms of Involuntary Displacement in the CIS and Relevant Neighboring States" was convened to develop a comprehensive national, regional and international strategy for coping with the problem of forced migration. Although successful in setting out principles and programmatic needs, the international financial response has been less than fully adequate.

Security remains one of, if not the principal barrier to effective national and international assistance and protection of forced migrants. Aid workers are fearful of traveling outside of the capital and other larger cities, making access to displaced persons and refugees very difficult. The only recommended means of accessing Abkhazia is by joining the UN Observer Mission in Georgia (UNOMIG) convoys, highlighting the level of insecurity. High turnover rates among aid personnel further impede aid efforts. These issues tend to override efforts to coordinate assistance activities since agencies understandably base decisions on where they will work on safety rather than a joint assessment of need.

The biggest challenge facing the humanitarian system is the long-term status of the IDPs. The Georgian government has conducted its IDP programs with the expectation that the IDPs will soon return to their homes in Abkhazia, South Ossetia and elsewhere. The IDPs themselves support return as the most desirable solution to their plight. Because of the intractable nature of the conflicts, however, return is unlikely to occur in either the short or long-term. Recognizing the problem, the UN Resident and Humanitarian Coordinator, UNDP, UNHCR, the World Bank, and OCHA have worked together on what is referred to as the New Approach. The plan calls for helping IDPs to integrate in their host communities, and for providing them with small business loans and business counseling. Whether the government and IDPs agree that local integration should be a priority, regardless of whether return eventually occurs, remains unclear, as does the level of sustainability of the projects proposed under the New Approach.

Sri Lanka

Sri Lanka has experienced complex forms of migration within and outside the country over the last three decades as a result of a complex combination of ethnic, nationalist, socio-economic and religious tensions that have contributed to armed conflict. Varying with the intensity of the conflict, between 500,000 and one million people have been displaced within Sri Lanka at any one time. In addition, more than 100,000 Sri Lankans, mostly Tamil, are refugees in India. Canada, Switzerland, the United Kingdom, and other European countries have also seen large numbers of Sri Lankan asylum seekers. At the same time, Sri Lankans, particularly female domestic workers, participate in guestworker programs in the Gulf states, east Asia, and elsewhere. The recent advances in negotiating a peace settlement have prompted an increase in return migration, particularly among IDPs who have ventured back to homes in formerly contested areas.

The government of Sri Lanka is by far the most significant actor in the provision of assistance to the internally displaced and other war-affected people. In 2000, the government is said to have provided food and other assistance to about 690,000 displaced and war-affected people out of a total estimated population of up to 800,000 displaced people. The main form of assistance is a food ration, but there is also a commitment to rehabilitate infrastructure in government-held areas and to provide drinking water, schooling and health facilities to displaced and war affected people wherever they reside, including areas held or controlled by the opposition forces.

While the civilian government has been fairly responsive to humanitarian concerns and appears receptive to initiatives and recommendations made by humanitarian agencies, the military often stymied them. Moreover, policy formulation, decision-making and implementation in the arena of displacement are dispersed among many government departments. There are or were two ministries for handling rehabilitation and reconstruction, one for the north and the other for the rest of the island. Two bodies handle the distribution of relief as well. A wide range of UN organizations, other multilateral and bilateral agencies, and local and international nongovernmental organizations are also engaged in humanitarian operations for forced migrants in and from Sri Lanka.

In recognition of the fragmented nature of relief provision, there have been various government attempts to improve coordination in recent years. The

Framework for Relief, Rehabilitation and Reconciliation (RRR) was set up in July 1999 precisely to address this problem, but a top-heavy command structure has impeded effective coordination of relief agency activities. Various coordination bodies covering UN agencies have also been set up in recent years. The Relief and Rehabilitation Theme Group (RRTG) has been the principal forum for UN agency cooperation and coordination in the capital. The RRTG helps with information sharing and makes joint assessments of the humanitarian situation in Sri Lanka. It is charged with maintaining an adequate level of emergency preparedness, promoting collaborative and complementary programming in the areas of relief, rehabilitation, and recovery, and jointly addressing sensitive issues.

UN agencies also participate in a number of bodies that attempt to encompass the wider relief and assistance/humanitarian community. At the suggestion of representatives of EU member states in Sri Lanka, a Donor Working Group on Relief and Rehabilitation was established at the end of 1999, facilitated by the UN; the Humanitarian Adviser to the UN Resident Coordinator is the facilitator to the group. UN agencies and nongovernmental organizations involved in assistance to the displaced also meet regularly under the auspices of the Colombo-based Consortium of Humanitarian Agencies (CHA).

Despite the seemingly broad international coordination, gaps remain in humanitarian assistance and protection. From the perspective of the displaced, relief and assistance interventions can appear haphazard, overlapping, and sometimes contradictory, involving a great number of humanitarian agencies. The diversity of displacement histories in Sri Lanka is compounded by the diversity of regional coverage of the humanitarian organizations that are involved. The living conditions and life chances of displaced people therefore vary greatly according to the geographical area in which they find themselves, according to the reach of the humanitarian regime, and according to the duration of displacement. As in the other case studies, assistance in Sri Lanka is constrained by the very circumstances that cause forced migration—lack of security in conflict zones. With a serious possibility of peace, the humanitarian agencies are already reaching pockets of displaced persons who had been beyond their reach. They will, of course, also face the challenges of return, reconstruction, and development that have eluded some of our other case studies.

OVERCOMING BARRIERS TO EFFECTIVE HUMANITARIAN RESPONSE

While the case studies show great variation in international responses to complex forced migration, several common problems arise in all of the settings.

These barriers to more effective humanitarian responses to forced migration fall into five areas, discussed in greater detail in the following chapters: gaps in legal frameworks; gaps and inconsistencies in responses within and across countries; resource inadequacies; absence of secure environments in which to protect and assist forced migrants; and difficulties in securing durable solutions for forced migrants.

Gaps in Legal Frameworks

International and national law today is insufficient to address the needs of the wide range of forced migrants seeking international assistance and protection. Laws tend to classify forced migrants by both cause of flight and location of "refuge." The resulting differences in individual rights and state powers reveal both helpful standards and major gaps in enabling the international community to address the protection and assistance needs of displaced persons caught up in complex emergencies. In general, international law provides for the protection of refugees fleeing persecution, though its implementation has been seriously challenged by state practices developed during the last two decades. Only one regional instrument, the Organization of African Unity refugee convention, extends hard-law protection to refugees fleeing civil wars and generalized violence. Displaced persons who remain within their states, often the most vulnerable of forced migrants, are not explicitly protected by either international or regional instruments although progress has been made in setting out their rights through the *Guiding Principles on Internal Displacement*.

Chapter 2 discusses a comprehensive set of tools to address the protection needs of all forced migrants. First, states and forced migrants will benefit when asylum systems provide for meaningful access, are operated fairly and efficiently, and minimize abuse. Second, national and regional approaches based on the OAU Convention definition of a refugee are the best ways to ensure legal protection for the vast majority of today's refugees who flee conflict and other forms of serious harm. Efforts to develop a European law that protects civil war refugees should be strongly encouraged as long as such a law complements, rather than takes the place of, European asylum law. Third, to help ensure the effective protection of refugees in their region of origin, the international community should find ways to get important refugee receiving states to become parties to the 1951 Refugee Convention and 1967 Protocol. Finally, with regard to internal displacement, there is an urgent need to develop national legal frameworks for the protection and assistance of internally displaced persons. Promoting the *Guiding Principles* to all levels of society is the only way to truly change the cultural, legal, and political landscape of IDP law and policy in countries with significant internal displacement.

Gaps and Inconsistencies in Institutional Responses

The institutional system for assisting and protecting forced migrants is extremely complicated. Dozens of international, national, and private agencies play important roles in providing food, shelter, health care, and other services to refugees, returnees and internally displaced persons. Despite—and in some cases, because of—the vast number of agencies, we have found serious gaps, particularly in protection of displaced persons who are still within their own countries. The Burundi site visit highlighted by far the most extreme gaps, with no international or national agency taking responsibility for the vast majority of internally displaced persons at the time of the site visit. However, serious institutional problems could be found in the other cases as well, particularly regarding inconsistent treatment of the various categories of forced migrants—refugees, returnees, internally displaced persons, etc. Moreover, the cases show inconsistencies in responses from one crisis to another, with considerably greater attention to some humanitarian emergencies than to others. Finally, the international system tends to focus most of its attention on crisis response, while protracted refugee and displaced persons situations tend to see diminished attention as solutions fail to materialize

Chapter 3 discusses the evolution of the humanitarian regime, detailing its strengths and weaknesses. Chapter 3 also presents recommendations for improving legal and organizational arrangements to address forced migration around the globe, with the case made for the need for a new UN High Commissioner for Forced Migration. Recognizing that some progress has been made within the UN system for addressing the interconnections between forced migration and peacekeeping, development and human rights, chapter 3 also outlines further steps needed to enhance coordination of responses.

Securing Adequate and Effective Resources

Chapter 4 addresses another major constraint on effective action—lack and mismatch of resources. Throughout our case studies, it was apparent that inadequacies in funding have undermined efforts to assist and protect forced migrants. By mid-year, only 29 percent of the 2002 Consolidated Inter-Agency Appeals had been met, excluding the response to Afghanistan. Even counting Afghanistan, which garnered considerable though now flagging donor attention, less than 40 percent of the appeals were met. Additional problems include a serious maldistribution in funding by country, by types of forced migrants, and by functions. Existing funding mechanisms contribute to maldistribution through short funding cycles, bilateral rather than multilateral funding, and donor preference for certain elements of humanitarian appeals.

This is not to say that improvements have not been made in securing financial resources for complex humanitarian emergencies. The Consolidated Appeals Process (CAP) helps to identify the range of needs in each crisis and outlines in an easily digestible manner what UN agencies propose for their parts of the relief operations. Donors appreciate receiving these appeals in one package at one time, rather than as each agency finishes its own assessment and develops its funding appeal.

Nevertheless, the CAP does not function sufficiently as a planning document that identifies priorities for humanitarian assistance and protection and then assigns responsibilities to UN agencies to respond to these needs. Instead, the CAPs often seem to be agency wish lists, cut and pasted into a single document, but demonstrating relatively little prior consultation or joint assessment of needs and capacities. The exceptions to this general picture prove the rule that the CAP can be a much more effective tool than is currently the case. The East Timor appeal involved substantial cooperation and coordination, not only within the UN but with NGO partners as well, and the CAP gained considerable credibility as a result.

Donors must cooperate as well if the CAP is to become a more realistic planning document. Even when based on good assessments and consultation in the field, CAPs are seldom funded in their entirety. Government donors still pick and choose what they consider to be priorities within the CAP, embracing some activities and ignoring others. Were these decisions to be taken in consultation with other donors, and they resulted in a division of responsibility with all parts of the CAP funded by someone, this process could work. However, too often no donor steps up to the plate to fund important activities while other programs receive pledges in excess of the amount requested.

Improvements are also needed in the aid package provided in complex humanitarian emergencies. Aid should be consistent with the stage of emergency. For example, the needs at the height of a new emergency will differ from those in a protracted conflict where the majority of persons have been displaced for several years. However, even in protracted emergencies, there may be persons who themselves are newly displaced and require emergency assistance and protection. So-called "donor fatigue" often threatens funding for protracted crises even when refugees and displaced persons remain vulnerable because of continuing conflict and instability. In fact, the emergency aid package is too narrowly defined in many humanitarian crises—gaps include education, participation of forced migrants in decision-making, reproductive health care, psychosocial programs, and longer-term shelter. Aid needs to take into account gender and age of forced migrants to assess specific protection and assistance needs and capabilities. Further, aid should be conceived not only to help forced migrants but also help ensure that forced migrants do not become a burden on other vulnerable populations, particularly residents of the communities in which they relocate.

Improving Security of Forced Migrants and Humanitarian Workers

Chapter 5 discusses the current state of security for humanitarian operations and presents recommendations to increase protection of forced migrants and those seeking to help them. Our research has identified lack of security as by far the biggest impediment to effective humanitarian responses, particularly when forced migrants are still within their own countries or remain under the control of military forces in a country of refuge. Burundi, Colombia, Georgia and Sri Lanka are examples of the former whereas East Timor (now Timor Leste) exemplifies the latter situation. Insecure conditions impede access to vulnerable populations for delivery of aid, create protection problems for aid workers as well as their clients, and make it impossible to monitor and evaluate the effectiveness of aid operations. As the Burundi case study demonstrated, forced migrants are too often "out of sight and out of mind" of the very humanitarian system that is designed to assist and protect them.

At the start of each complex humanitarian emergency, a professional security assessment should be taken and repeated periodically thereafter. The vulnerabilities of forced migrants to attack and exploitation are key issues to cover in such assessments, as are the vulnerabilities of humanitarian aid workers seeking to bring assistance and protection to these populations. The assessments should recommend ways to increase access to and protection of forced migrants and reduce risk to aid workers. Sometimes, relatively simple steps can greatly enhance security. In Burundi, for example, one NGO found that identifying itself by name increased security for its workers outside of certain urban areas but reduced it in other locations. The solution was to travel with a banner that could be attached to its vehicles when identification proved useful and removed when it would render its activities too visible to those who would do the agency harm.

We are skeptical that a broad role for peacekeepers in securing access to and protecting displaced populations will be forthcoming. The decision to intervene with military forces even when loss of life is at risk, and to commit peacekeeping troops to maintain security, is a difficult one that political leaders are generally loathe to make. Nevertheless, humanitarian interventions have occurred with some regularity during the past decade and peacekeepers are likely to continue to be deployed during humanitarian emergencies. Military forces, such as NATO and the Australian military, have also been called upon to assist with logistics, construction and other assistance in such places as Kosovo and East Timor. The peacemaking and peacekeeping forces should have clear mandates to protect civilian populations and humanitarian relief operations in such situations. They should have adequate human and financial resources to fulfill this security mandate, and they should negotiate terms of reference for cooperation with humanitarian agencies. Better training of military forces that are likely to come into contact with civilians, particularly displaced persons, could also help improve security for IDPs, returnees and other war-affected populations.

At the same time, civilian capabilities to protect forced migrants should be developed. A welcome step is the decision made by the United Nations in January 2002 to provide funding out of the regular budget for staff safety and security activities. UNSECOORD was provided with a core budget to deploy 100 Field Security Officers (FSOs) in crisis areas. Many times the threat to relief operations comes from bandits and criminal elements or loosely organized militias rather than actual military forces. In such situations, civilian policing may be the appropriate way to gain greater security for displaced persons and humanitarian workers. Many agencies maintain rosters of emergency professional personnel who can be called up for short-term assignments. Such a roster of police may be useful in broadening access to the expertise needed for both assessing security problems and identifying and implementing appropriate remedies. Given the scale of insecurity, though, it may be necessary to develop a standing international police force that is explicitly mandated to protect the humanitarian operations. The UNSECOORD FSOs may form the core of such a group.

Humanitarian organizations must also look to their own programs to reduce the vulnerability of forced migrants to attacks, abuses, and exploitation. Reports of the sexual exploitation of refugees and displaced children in West Africa highlight problems that have long been known or suspected. Dependency on humanitarian aid creates vulnerability to exploitation by unscrupulous officials, military, police, and aid workers. If the aid is insufficient, and no legitimate economic opportunities are available, women and children will be forced to take other measures, including prostitution, in order to feed themselves and their families. These problems arise in all settings, affecting refugees and displaced persons in camps and spontaneously settled in rural and urban areas. Growth in the population of street children in cities may be one indicator that the humanitarian response is failing to provide adequate security for a highly vulnerable group.

Finding Durable Solutions

Chapter 6 tackles one of the most elusive issues—durable solutions to forced migration. As our case studies demonstrate, the transition from war to peace and from relief to development are generally far from the smooth paths that one would hope for these societies. In Burundi, peace negotiations ratcheted up the level of violence and increased displacement. Long-term Burundian refugees in Tanzania remain in camps and settlements, with no opportunities for self-sufficiency and cause financial and other burdens on local communities. In East Timor, the focus of the international community probably turned too quickly to development, leaving urgent humanitarian needs unmet. IDPs in Georgia await a return that may never happen while living in squalid conditions with little prospect for self-support. After decades of conflict, the peace process in Sri Lanka bodes well for return of refugees and displaced persons, presenting new challenges to a war-weary society. Displacement in Colombia grows as a new government puts together plans to resolve the long-standing instability, conflict, and narco-trafficking in that country.

What is clear from the case studies is that these situations do not easily or quickly resolve. From the very beginnings of peace negotiations, the impact of forced migration must be taken into account. We have found gaps in the relationship between the UN Special Representatives responsible for peace negotiations and the UN humanitarian missions. Often, the only UN presence in a war-affected country is the humanitarian agencies, but their staff may not be consulted or participate in the peace negotiations even when they have a better sense than political figures as to the situation on the ground. Certainly, peace agreements themselves must include realistic frameworks for addressing displacement, including plans for return and reintegration of refugees and internally displaced persons. In developing different plans and scenarios for peace, the negotiators should examine the impact on displacement as well as the effects of various displacement scenarios on the likelihood that peace will be achieved.

Forging closer cooperation between the humanitarian and political regimes is not without risks, however. Humanitarian agencies are already vulnerable to attacks by military and political forces that doubt their impartiality or neutrality. At times these attacks are violent, leading to some of the security risks discussed above. Even agencies whose mandates require them to be neutral in dealing with all parties to a conflict, such as the International Committee for the Red Cross, have been subject to such attacks. Should peace negotiators be seen as tipping toward one side over another, or the United Nations as a body imposes sanctions against warring parties or rights abusers, humanitarian agencies that are perceived, even unfairly, as engaged in these political processes may be targeted or refused access to civilian populations. Nevertheless, finding long-term solutions to the causes of humanitarian crises may well require the risks.

The plight of forced migrants is directly related to the situations that cause their flight. Finding durable solutions to forced displacement requires solutions to the conflict, repression, instability and other causes of mass migration. However, it must be kept in mind that political changes, including an end to conflict, though necessary, are not sufficient to resolve large-scale displacement. Forced migrants, along with the communities in which they reside, must have access to economic opportunities, permanent shelter and other necessities of life. Forced migrants also need assurances of legal and property rights. Where property cannot be recovered, some form of compensation should be negotiated. For those living in war-torn societies, solutions mean a transition from dependence on relief to reconstruction and then longer-term development.

The transition from relief to reconstruction and development also requires a long-term commitment by the international community as well as institutional capacity building in public and private sectors at the national and local levels. Collaboration between relief agencies, such as UNHCR, and development agencies, such as World Bank and UNDP, is essential. There has been progress in this regard during the past decade, under such rubrics as the New Approach in Georgia, but more sustained cooperation is needed. The UN agencies, as well as donors, must also explore alternative funding mechanisms in order to ensure sustained support for the transition. At present, reconstruction often falls through the cracks of donors who can provide humanitarian aid and donors who can fund development programs.

A durable solution in the case of refugees and IDPs means that they have been integrated in the place they reside or reintegrated in the communities to which have returned. Integration, at a minimum, implies that there are no significant differences between this population and the previously existing local population in terms of rights, legal status, and access to services and opportunities. In difficult times, the entire population may be in a situation of isolation, misery and insecurity and in this case, the humanitarian assistance and development aid should logically be targeted at the community level. This is the case in situations of both internal and international displacement. On the humanitarian aid side, UNHCR and other relief agencies recognize this and usually try to channel their assistance accordingly. However, the coverage, as noted above, tends to be fragmentary and short term. In Georgia, Colombia, and East Timor, international relief agencies and NGOs limited their activities to short term interventions that ended with their departure. In Tanzania, little if any international assistance goes to the local communities that have long hosted refugees or to self-reliance activities that would help refugees to support themselves.

The key to reconstruction and, hence, durable solutions, involves cooperation among international agencies and donors and better collaboration between relief and development projects. Even more important, the capacity of the state to lead in the process is essential. A durable solution means one that international assistance supports but does not drive. In other words, the objective of international assistance in difficult transition periods is to enable societies to mend, governments to assume responsibilities for the well-being of their citizens, and people to achieve economic sustainability. In other words, the durable solution for forced migrants is a gradual process that begins with restored confidence and ends when "normalcy" can be defined in terms of rule of law and a stake in the future. There are multiple tools in the international basket conducive to building capacities and helping to create the legal, judicial, economic, and political conditions needed, but they require comprehensive planning and programming, and longer-term commitments than most donors are willing to ensure.

The programs that are most often shortchanged are those aimed at capacity building, institutional strengthening, and security sector reforms. Moreover, generosity with humanitarian assistance is rarely buttressed by trade, credit and debt-relief policies that would allow citizens long on the margins of their societies to develop economic stakes for the future. Understandably, donors worry that commitments to support integration, capacity building and institutional strengthening will be open-ended and significant economic support is difficult to achieve politically. The well-recognized irony is that the relatively small monetary cost of investing in such programs in most cases would be less costly and more sustainable than present practices. International post-conflict interventions continue to feature massive investments in weak societies followed by premature departures before the societies are prepared to take the lead and before the populations uprooted by war and crises have achieved stability.

CONCLUSION

More than ten years after exuberance about the end of the Cold War prompted the UN High Commissioner for Refugees (UNHCR) to declare a "decade of voluntary repatriation,"[14] the international community is faced with a significant number of complex emergencies involving the forced movements of millions of persons. Some manage to escape their countries and find temporary or permanent refuge abroad while an alarmingly large number remain trapped inside or are forced to repatriate before the home country conditions change in any significant manner.

Policy makers within and outside of the United Nations have used a classification system that places forced migrants into specific boxes, with the assumption that standards, mandates and programs will follow the designated classification. This pattern has been particularly the case in designating internally displaced persons as a specific classification. To a large extent, this approach has succeeded in raising the visibility of groups of forced migrants who heretofore had been either ignored or fell between the cracks in the international system.

There are limits to the approach taken to date, however. These categories of forced migrants are not mutually exclusive. More often they are overlapping. The victims of humanitarian emergencies may belong to more than one group, either at the same time or in close sequence. In many cases, drawing careful lines between categories of forced migrants hinders rather than facilitates the ability of national, intergovernmental and nongovernmental organizations to offer appropriate assistance and protection. Agencies may too easily avoid responsibility by citing an institutional mandate to serve a specific population. Alternately, agencies interested in intervening on behalf of a particular group may be denied the opportunity because they have no explicit mandate to do so. Even where institutional barriers are overcome, insecurity and inadequate resources constrain the ability to respond comprehensively in assisting and protecting forced migrants.

Addressing humanitarian emergencies involving mass displacement requires new, more comprehensive approaches. This book outlines strategies to improve organizational responses, increase and make more effective the use of financial resources, increase security for humanitarian aid operations and the civilians they assist, and find durable solutions to the longer-term problems of forced migration. With millions forced out of their homes, there is urgent need for reform. A more effective capacity to prevent, respond to and solve complex forced migration crises is in everyone's best interest.

NOTES

1. Representative of the Secretary-General for Internally Displaced Persons, "Guiding Principles on Internal Displacement" (Geneva: UN Office for the Coordination of Humanitarian Affairs, 1999), 2–3.

2. Global IDP Project Norwegian Refugee Council, "Global Overview" http:// www.idpproject.org/global_overview.htm#1 (November 21, 2004).

3. Susan Forbes Martin, "Development and Politically Generated Migration," in *Determinants of Emigration from Mexico, Central America, and the Caribbean*, ed. Sergio Diaz-Briquets and Sidney Weintraub (Boulder, CO: Westview Press, 1991).

4. Roberta Cohen and Francis Deng, *Masses in Flight—The Global Crisis of Internal Displacement* (Washington: The Brookings Institution, 1998), 275–76.

5. Kofi Annan, "Preface," in Cohen and Deng, *Masses in Flight*, xx.

6. United Nations System Emergency Plan for Burundi, "Without Development there Cannot Be Sustainable Peace, from Humanitarian Assistance to Development"

(Bujumbura: UN Country Team in Burundi, 2000), 10; and UNHCR "Briefing Notes: Caucasus, Colombia, Afghanistan/Pakistan, Burundi 13 October 2000."

7. Women's Commission meeting with OCHA officials, New York, November 3, 2000. Regroupment camps are discussed in the section on Internally Displaced Persons below.

8. Arusha Peace and Reconciliation Agreement for Burundi, Arusha, August 28, 2000, referred to as the "Peace Agreement" or "Arusha Peace Agreement" in this report.

9. In 1995, the official planning agency, the National Council of Economic and Social Policy, CONPES, recognized the presence of a crisis of internal displacement caused by violence, and proposed government policies to respond to it. CONPES 2804. CONPES is comprised of the major ministries, banks and syndicates of the state, and answers directly to the President.

10. For example, Presidencia de la República, Red de Solidaridad Social, PrensaRED, February 13, 2002, 6.

11. The government's Network of Social Solidarity, (RSS) is limited to those displaced by violence and based on registration. The Church's Human Mobility Section of the Colombian Episcopal Conference counts persons who have come to the attention of the parishes; the Consultancy on Human Rights and Displacement, CODHES, an NGO devoted to tracking displacement and documenting human rights associated with displacement makes estimates based on Church and NGO sources. The ICRC has its own estimates also based on various sources. International agencies may use government figures for certain programs but their estimates of real numbers are more likely to rely on CODHES.

12. OCHA is present in Colombia through a staff person who sits in the UNHCR office.

13. United Nations Senior Inter-Agency Network on Internal Displacement, "Mission to Colombia, August 16–24, 2001: Findings and Recommendations." (New York: United Nations, 2001), 9.

14. Speech by High Commissioner Sadako Ogata, June 26, 1992.

2

Improving Legal Frameworks

A review of international law reveals both helpful standards and major gaps in enabling the international community to address the protection and assistance needs of displaced persons caught up in complex emergencies. In general, international law provides for the protection of refugees fleeing persecution, though its implementation has been seriously challenged by state practices developed during the last two decades. Only one regional instrument extends hard-law protection to refugees fleeing civil wars and generalized violence. Displaced persons who remain within their states, often the most vulnerable of forced migrants, are not explicitly protected by either international or regional instruments. The *Guiding Principles on Internal Displacement*, particularly when applied through national law, provides the best approach to the protection needs of internally displaced persons.

BALANCING INDIVIDUAL RIGHTS AND SOVEREIGN POWERS

International legal standards for the protection of forced migrants are found in refugee, human rights and humanitarian law. The most developed of these frameworks applies to refugees—persons who have crossed an international border—but there is a growing international consensus about the rights of internally displaced persons and the obligations of states and the international community toward them. In developing these standards, states had to resolve the conflicting interests of sovereigns to retain a considerable degree of authority and individuals to enjoy such fundamental rights as the right to life.

The first modern international document to address rights to move within one's own country or across borders, the Universal Declaration of Human Rights, exhibits this fundamental tension between individual rights and state powers. First, Article 13 establishes the individual right to move and reside freely within one's own country. That article also declares the right to leave any country, including one's own, and to return to one's own country. The Soviet Union wanted to qualify the right to leave to reflect its understanding of a citizen's duty to a state, but the drafting committee determined that to be too statist a position.

Having established a right to leave one's own country, the committee then turned to the problem that to be able to leave one's own country, an individual must enter another one. Member states differed considerably on how to resolve this issue. States such as Lebanon, Uruguay and Pakistan supported a right to asylum. Others, including the United States delegation led by Eleanor Roosevelt, preferred to limit state obligations with regard to refugees. Article 14 affirms only a "right to seek and to enjoy in other countries asylum from persecution." In a very close vote, states rejected any obligation to grant asylum.

The 1951 Refugee Convention

Within just a few years, states addressed this issue again, but in a very different, European-focused context. The 1951 UN Convention Relating to the Status of Refugees emerged in the early days of the Cold War particularly to resolve the situation of some hundreds of thousands of refugees who still remained displaced by World War II and fascist/Nazi persecution.[1] At its core, this treaty substitutes the protection of the international community (in the form of a host government) for that of an unable or unwilling sovereign. The underlying principle is that all individuals must belong to a state—which is at the foundation of our Westphalian state system. The treaty limits this stand-in protection to those who were unable or unwilling to avail themselves of the protection of their home countries because of a "well-founded fear of persecution based on their race, religion, nationality, political opinion or membership in a particular social group." The grounds of persecution match groups targeted by two different totalitarian regimes: certain ethnic, religious, national, and sexual-oriented groups attacked by the Nazis, and political dissent suppressed by the Soviets. The 1951 Convention included time limitations (persons displaced as a result of events occurring before 1951) and an optional geographic restriction (Europe). Just like the statute that officially created the Office of the United Nations High Commissioner for Refugees for a period of three years,[2] the 1951 Convention aimed at dealing with a confined set of refugees.

The Convention refugee definition reflected the rise of individual human rights. The Convention definition "meant that refugees would now be identified not only on a group basis, as had been the case in preceding years, but also on an individual case-by-case basis."[3] Protection was no longer limited to specific national groups, such as Russians or Armenians, as had been the case in the 1920s and 1930s.

The core legal obligation of States pursuant to the Convention is quite narrow: to refrain from forcibly returning (refouling) refugees to countries in which they would face persecution.[4] States do not have the obligation to provide asylum or admit refugees for permanent settlement, and they may relocate refugees in safe third countries that are willing to accept them. However, the Convention has been interpreted to require States to undertake status determinations for asylum applicants at their frontiers or inside their territories in order to determine if they have valid claims to refugee protection. While the only legal obligation to a refugee is *non-refoulement*, in practice this has often meant admission and asylum in the host country.

The Convention drafters recognized that among refugee populations would be found individuals whose actions made them undeserving of international protection. The so-called "exclusion" clauses of the Convention set forth two major kinds of such individuals—human rights violators and serious criminals. Thus those who have committed a crime against peace, a war crime, a crime against humanity, or a serious nonpolitical crime are excluded from international protection. That is, they are not to be granted refugee status and its attendant benefits.

Separately, two exceptions are provided for with respect to a state's *non-refoulement* obligation under Article 33. States may return to a country of persecution an individual regarded "as a danger to the security of the country" of refuge, as well as someone who "having been convicted by a final judgment of a particularly serious crime, constitutes a danger to the community of that country."[5]

The Convention also sets out the rights of refugees who have been admitted into the territory of another country. Certain fundamental human rights such as freedom of religion (Article 4) and access to courts (Article 16) are guaranteed to be at least those accorded to the citizens of the state hosting the refugee. Thus if legal assistance is provided to citizens, the same must be accorded to refugees (Article 16(2)). Elementary education is also accorded to refugees as it is to citizens (Article 22(1)). Refugees lawfully residing in a host country are guaranteed public relief in this way as well (Article 23). In addition, the Convention cannot be applied in a discriminatory way regarding race, religion, and country of origin (Article 3).

Many important rights accorded recognized refugees, however, do not need to match those of citizens. Rights as fundamental as the right of association (Article 15) and freedom of movement (Article 26) are accorded to refugees to the same degree that they are accorded to nationals of other countries. Rights regarding employment (Article 17), property (Article 13), public education beyond elementary school (Article 22(2)), and housing (Article 21) are also accorded to refugees in a manner no less favorable than those accorded to citizens of other countries. However, with regard to wage-earning employment, refugees are accorded national treatment after three years of residence in the host country (Article 17(2)(a)).

Certain legal matters are left completely to the host state. States are encouraged to facilitate the naturalization of refugees, though they are not required to match any naturalization rights provided to other noncitizens (Article 34).

The Convention also ensures that states cannot impose penalties on refugees if they enter or stay illegally, as long as the refugees "present themselves without delay to the authorities and show good cause for their illegal entry or presence" (Article 31).

The Convention includes a dispute settlement provision pursuant to which a party to the Convention may refer any dispute to the International Court of Justice (Article 38). With respect to most of the rights discussed above, states may make reservations at the time of signature, ratification, or accession. The major exceptions are freedom of religion, basic access to courts, and *non-refoulement*.

To come into force, the Convention required adherence by at least six states. This occurred in April 1954, almost three years after the United Nations Conference of Plenipotentiaries on the Status of Refugees and Stateless Persons adopted the Convention in Geneva.[6]

At the time the Convention was adopted, it represented a leap forward in several significant ways. First, it established "an international code of rights of refugees on a general basis."[7] The scope of these rights exceeded those of earlier international agreements:

It is the first agreement which covers every aspect of life and guarantees to refugees—as a minimum—the same treatment as to foreigners not enjoying special favors. None of the previous conventions had such a general provision. Similarly, the scope of rights explicitly established in the Convention is broader than in any of the previous agreements. For instance, the 1938 Convention concerning the Status of Refugees coming from Germany did not contain such important provisions as: the prohibition of penalties for illegal entry into the territories of a state by a bona fide refugee; special stipulations covering the rights of refugees to acquire property or to be engaged, as independent persons, in agriculture, industry or handicraft; the right to enjoy the benefits of rules governing rationing and housing accommodations; the obligation of the state to issue documents certifying the exercise of rights by refugees (for instance, proof of family status, diplomas, etc.).[8]

All preceding conventions generally referred only to European refugees, while states may choose to apply the 1951 Convention to refugees from around the world. In contrast with the more *ad hoc* previous agreements tied to particular groups of refugees, the Convention grants the same legal status to all refugees. The principle of nondiscrimination triumphed after the Second World War.

The Mandate Expanded

Within just a few years of the Convention's entry into force, the world had changed such that the limited conception of a time-bound European protection system for refugees no longer made sense. In fact, it no longer existed. International events superceded it, and the UN General Assembly authorized the High Commissioner to assist refugees who did not come clearly or fully within the Convention definition.

The first limitation that the UN addressed concerned the time restriction. When some 200,000 Hungarians fled their homeland as the Soviet Union suppressed the uprising in 1956, the UN General Assembly instructed UNHCR to take on emergency operational responsibilities.[9] Two months later, Paul Weis, a refugee from Vienna and Legal Adviser to the High Commissioner, argued that UNHCR already had competence under Article 6(B) of the statute creating UNHCR with regard to refugees who have a well-founded fear of persecution whether or not their flight resulted from events occurring before January 1, 1951. This is very clear from the statute. Weis also argued that the Hungarians met the Convention time restriction because the October 1956 uprising and the consequent exodus of refugees were an after-effect of profound political change that occurred when the Communists took over Hungary in the late 1940s.[10]

The General Assembly then further determined that refugees beyond Europe were "of concern to the international community" and expressly authorized the High Commissioner "to use his good offices" to assist them.[11] The first case involved large numbers of mainland Chinese in Hong Kong in 1957.[12] But refugees fleeing liberation wars made this new mandate a permanent expansion of refugees to be assisted. The General Assembly authorized the High Commissioner to use his good offices to assist Algerians fleeing to Tunisia and Morocco in 1958[13] and Angolans to the Congo in 1961.[14] UNHCR's role in assisting Algerian refugees during the war of national liberation marked the beginning of a much wider involvement in Africa. At the beginning of the 1960s, the violence that followed the independence of the Congo, Rwanda and Burundi led to large-scale displacement. Armed struggles for independence from Portuguese-administered Angola, Mozambique, and Guinea-Bissau led to massive displacements as well. Other significant refugee movements resulted from internal armed conflict in Ghana, the Republic of the Congo, the Sudan, Ethiopia, and Nigeria. By the end of the 1960s, about two-thirds of UNHCR's global program funds were being spent in African countries.[15]

The 1967 Refugee Protocol

By 1965, there were about 850,000 refugees in African countries,[16] making it impracticable for UNHCR to assist and protect them in the same way as European refugees. Prima facie group determinations of refugee status replaced individual screening, and UNHCR used its "good offices" to provide emergency relief to meet urgent material needs. By the mid-1960s, the 1951 Convention did not apply to the majority of refugees being assisted by UNHCR.[17]

It just took time for international law to catch up somewhat with international realities. Reflecting the international community's increasing awareness of the global nature of refugee movements, a new Protocol was drafted in 1967 that extended the temporal and spatial scope of the 1951 Convention. Both the time and optional geographic limitations of the 1951 Convention were removed from the treaty. The Protocol was signed by the President of the General Assembly and by the Secretary General on January 31, 1967, and the treaty entered into force less than nine months later.[18] Since 1967, the Refugee Convention has been a universal instrument, applying to refugees from all over the world fleeing persecution.

Regional Expansions of the Refugee Definition

The limits of a treaty focused on persecution as the cause of forced migration reverberated particularly in the developing world.[19] The causes of flight of most Third World refugees were war, generalized violence, and natural disasters.[20] In recognition of the actual forced movements occurring regularly in Africa, the Organization of African Unity (OAU) adopted the Convention Governing the Specific Aspects of Refugee Problems in Africa in 1969. While acknowledging the UN Refugee Convention as the basic and universal instrument regarding the protection of refugees, the OAU Convention broadened the definition and set out other important protection provisions. In addition to protecting one who flees persecution, this regional treaty protects an

individual who "owing to external aggression, occupation, foreign domination, or events seriously disturbing public order in either part or the whole of
his country of origin or nationality, is compelled to leave his place of habitual residence in order to seek refuge in another place outside his country of
origin or nationality."[21]

The OAU Convention explicitly forbids states from rejecting asylum seekers at the frontier. The grant of asylum is declared to be a peaceful and humanitarian act, not to be regarded as unfriendly by other states. The Convention also requires "as far as possible" and "for reasons of security" that
countries of asylum settle refugees at a reasonable distance from the frontier
of their country of origin for security reasons. This regional treaty further explicitly states that no refugee shall be repatriated against his will. Most
African states are parties to the OAU Convention. The OAU Refugee Convention came into effect in June 1974.[22]

In a similar vein, the 1984 Cartagena Declaration on Refugees expanded
the definition of protected refugees in the Latin American region. Like the
OAU definition, it supports the 1951 Convention and adds protection to those
who have fled their country "because their lives, safety or freedom have been
threatened by generalized violence, foreign aggression, internal conflicts,
massive violation of human rights or other circumstances that have seriously
disturbed public order." It emphasizes that repatriation of refugees must be
voluntary, and embodies principles for their protection, assistance, and reintegration. Although a nonbinding instrument, the Declaration has been endorsed by the General Assembly of the Organization of American States, and
most states in Central and Latin America apply the Declaration's broader
definition of a refugee as a matter of practice. Some have incorporated this
definition into their own national legislation.[23]

More recently, the forty-five-member state Asian-African Legal Consultative Organization adopted the OAU refugee definition in its revision of the
Bangkok Principles on the Status and Treatment of Refugees.[24] As with the
Latin American expansion of the refugee definition, the Bangkok Principles
are declaratory in nature.

The United States and European nations have developed more limited policies on protecting civil war refugees and others covered by the OAU Convention and the Cartagena Declaration. Prior to the 1990s, these states generally refrained from returning such refugees, but provided them with minimal
rights. This improved somewhat in the 1990s. Various European states established temporary protection policies in response to movements of large numbers of former Yugoslavian refugees at different times during the 1990s.[25] UN
High Commissioner for Refugees Sadako Ogata first called upon the international community to grant temporary protection to the tens of thousands of

Croats fleeing to neighboring countries during the conflict with Serbia in 1991. Hundreds of thousands of Bosnians fled the civil conflict there starting in 1992. UNHCR and the Europeans hoped that these wars would resolve themselves quickly, and the temporary protection policies looked toward eventual return as the durable solution for those fleeing civil war.[26]

While those who made it to Germany and other European countries did find safety, they experienced different kinds of treatment in terms of rights. Many were not permitted to access the asylum system for several reasons. First, UNHCR considered temporary protection to be a "flexible and pragmatic means of affording needed protection to large numbers of people fleeing human rights abuses and armed conflict, . . . who might otherwise have overwhelmed asylum procedures."[27] By the time Yugoslavia started to collapse, asylum applications in the European Union had raised dramatically from an average of about 110,000 per year in the first part of the 1980s to some 200,000 each year in the latter part of the 1980s. In 1990, European Union states received over 400,000 asylum applications.[28]

Second, the emergency arrivals of large numbers of former Yugoslavs were concentrated in a few states, particularly Germany, which sought and failed to obtain burden sharing among European Union countries to care for the hundreds of thousands of refugees. Some 700,000 Bosnians alone received temporary protection in Western Europe. About three-quarters of the 350,000 Bosnian refugees in Germany resided in five of the sixteen federal states (*länder*).[29] For the European countries most affected by the mass movements of Balkan refugees, the "temporary" nature of the offered protection limited their responsibilities. Third, European Union governments were loathe to reaffirm ethnic cleansing via permanent protection through asylum.

Learning from this mass forced migration experience, the Council of the European Communities adopted a Directive in 2001 on minimum standards for giving temporary protection in the event of a mass influx of displaced persons (Directive).[30] The protection is granted in situations of mass influx if the Council, upon recommendation by the Commission and taking into account reception capacities of the Member States, so decides by a qualified majority. Temporary protection may last up to a maximum of three years and obliges Member States to grant beneficiaries a residence permit, employment authorization, access to suitable accommodation, social welfare and medical assistance, access to education for those under the age of eighteen, and nuclear family reunification.[31] The Directive requires States to allow beneficiaries to lodge an asylum application, but allows States to suspend the examination of such applications until after the end of temporary protection.[32] According to a leading expert, the Directive is, in principle, compatible with the requirements of international refugee law, although much will depend on the quality

of the asylum procedure when temporary protection ends and most beneficiaries can return home in safety and with dignity.[33]

In addition to temporary protection in the event of mass forced migration,
European states apply this type of humanitarian program in individual status
determinations to refugees who are found unqualified for asylum. In 2000–
2002, for example, European states granted humanitarian status, that is, protection complementary to Convention protection, to an average of 70,000
applicants each year.[34] About 57,000 individuals received asylum in those
same states in each of those years.[35]

For some time now, the members of the European Union have been working
on developing consistent policies with regard to subsidiary or complementary
protection.[36] States attach different rights to this humanitarian status that they
define in various ways. In some states, subsidiary protection is simply an obligation not to remove a person, while in others it requires the grant of a residence
permit. Sweden and Finland provide subsidiary protection for those who flee an
environmental disaster.[37] The Commission's Draft Proposal envisaged that subsidiary protection shall be accorded to any person who cannot return to the
country of origin because of a "well-founded fear of being subjected" to "a
threat to his or her life, safety or freedom as a result of indiscriminate violence
arising in situations of armed conflict, or as a result of systematic or generalized violations of their human rights."[38] In April 2004, the Council of the European Union adopted a more restrictive definition in the final Council Directive on the minimum standards for qualification for this type of protection.[39]

The United States version of "temporary protection" is both broader and
more limited than the European version. Temporary Protected Status (TPS)
covers not only refugees fleeing armed conflict, but also those fleeing natural
disasters. While this type of protection is established by statute, Congress
gave the Attorney General significant discretion in determining which nationals qualify for TPS, and these officials have exercised their discretion by
selecting only some of the many countries experiencing conflict for this status. Most important, even when the Attorney General provides TPS to certain
nationals, this status is limited to those who have already reached the United
States at the time of the Attorney General's proclamation. This type of protection regime was not established to handle ongoing mass migration emergencies, which differentiates it significantly from the European use of temporary protection. On limited occasions, however, an Attorney General has
moved the qualifying date forward to allow those nationals who arrived after
the initial qualifying date to become eligible for TPS. Except for a belated use
as the civil wars in Central America were winding down in the early 1990s
and later in connection with natural disasters in that region the numbers provided this type of temporary protection have been relatively small.

Those protected under TPS are allowed to work and attend public school but are generally not eligible for public assistance.[40] TPS status does not provide for family reunification. It is awarded on a group basis. The United States does not offer any complementary humanitarian status in individual determinations, though experts have proposed such policies.[41]

The Undermining of Asylum

The vast majority of persons fleeing conflict and persecution try to find protection and assistance in the developing world. According to the *World Refugee Survey 2004*, between 10 and 11 million of the almost 12 million refugees worldwide reside in Africa, the Middle East, and Asia. While only a limited number of refugees from these regions reach Europe, North America, or Australia, the asylum policies and practices in the developed world seriously affect the protection of the large numbers of refugees who remain in their regions. In fact, experts maintain that one of the important reasons that internally displaced persons do not become refugees is that states more and more try to prevent refugee flows and restrict refugee admissions.[42]

As explained at the outset, no international treaty provides for a right to asylum—only a right to seek asylum. Attempts to secure a right to asylum in the 1960s and 1970s were rejected by the United Nations Conference on Territorial Asylum in 1977. Given the lack of consensus on this issue, the Conference simply recommended that the General Assembly consider its reconvening at a suitable time. The Conference has never been reconvened.[43] Sovereign states have consistently chosen to retain their discretion over asylum, and as detailed below, have made it considerably more difficult for individuals to seek asylum in recent years.

Refoulement and Denial of Access

When States in the developed world violate the core protection obligation provided by the Refugee Convention and Protocol—*non-refoulement*—States in the developing world imitate their misbehavior. During a two-year period from 1992 to 1994, the official policy of the United States was to interdict Haitians on the high seas and return them directly to Haiti without considering any protection needs and rights they might have.[44] This was a period of political repression in Haiti, as the democratically-elected government had been overthrown by a military coup. It was no surprise in 1996, then, when Côte d'Ivoire officials denied entry to a boat, the Bulk Challenge, carrying several thousand Liberian refugees. Despite a long tradition of generosity toward refugees from Liberia, Côte d'Ivoire did not hesitate to turn this boat away, knowing well that a key supporter of UNHCR had recently refouled thousands of Haitians on boats.[45]

Even when developed nations stop short of such open refoulement but deny entry to their territory, the message is clear: find protection elsewhere. Australia adopted a new policy to address boat arrivals of asylum seekers in late August 2001, not long before national elections were to be held. Under the new policy, Australia refuses to allow such arrivals into Australian territory and sends them to other countries in the Pacific, where their refugee claims are assessed. After the number of boat arrivals increased in the late summer, Australia refused entry to a Norwegian freighter, the Tampa, carrying some 430 persons, most of whom claimed to be Afghans. The Australians negotiated temporary refuge for the passengers with the tiny Pacific nation of Nauru and New Zealand. Australia provided Nauru with an aid package worth the equivalent of $10 million in return for hosting the asylum seekers. New Zealand said it would assess the asylum claims of those brought to its territory. The Nauru government asked UNHCR to screen the asylum seekers taken to Nauru, and UNHCR eventually agreed, but only for the group sent to Nauru. UNHCR expressed serious concern that Australia's actions could send a negative message to impoverished nations closer to conflict zones, which often take in hundreds of thousands of refugees.[46]

Visa Practices

Developed states have changed their visa policies to prevent asylum seekers from reaching their territory. During the conflict in the former Yugoslavia, for example, many European states imposed visa requirements that made it considerably more difficult to flee and prevented some people from crossing land borders.[47] Even if individuals qualified for such visas, reaching the embassies to apply for visas was often too risky given the nature of the conflict. North American states use visa policies in the same manner. Until recently, for example, the United States allowed Colombians to transit on their way to an international destination, but stopped that practice as the number of asylum seekers increased.[48]

Pre-Clearance and Pre-Inspection

Departure site and enroute pre-clearance and pre-inspection by destination-state personnel also prevent the arrival of asylum seekers. Many countries deploy immigration officials to work with foreign governments and airline personnel to identify persons traveling with fraudulent documents and to combat smuggling and trafficking operations. In 1996, the European Union adopted a policy allowing states to post "Airline Liaison Officers" (ALOs) abroad for purposes of advising air carriers about the authenticity of specific travel documents.[49] The United Kingdom, Netherlands, Germany, and Denmark have all posted such officers in their embassies in refugee-producing countries.[50] In 2001, more than 22,000 passengers en route to the United Kingdom were denied boarding by carriers at twenty ALO locations.[51] The United States, Canada, Australia, and New Zealand also post ALOs abroad.[52]

Pre-inspection is the forward deployment at airports abroad of the country's immigration control system. The Unites States established pre-inspection sites in Ireland, Canada, and a few other locations. Immigration officials examine airline passengers and their documents while they are waiting to board their flights. While this facilitates travel for many, it restricts the movement of refugees who do not possess valid travel documents.

Domestic law in a number of states requires common carriers (including, in various combinations, sea, air and land carriers) servicing their territories internationally to verify travel documents of all boarding passengers. Developed states impose financial and other serious penalties on airlines that allow individuals who do not possess required documentation to travel on international flights. Since carrier sanctions are imposed worldwide, this directly affects the ability of asylum seekers to board flights from their country of origin unless they are able to obtain valid documentation.

Detention and Lack of Representation

Detention of asylum seekers has been adopted by some states purportedly to discourage arrivals and ensure compliance with legal proceedings. In general, it is used with respect to asylum seekers arriving in boats or at the border. Some European states, Australia, and the United States employ this policy, but no systematic study has evaluated the deterrence effects of detention. No doubt detention ensures compliance with legal proceedings, but a major study has shown that detention at the outset is not an effective or humane use of a limited resource except for those deemed security or public safety risks. For asylum seekers with legitimate claims, the study showed, supervised release, an approach more in keeping with the humanitarian nature of asylum, results in compliance at a much lower cost than detention.[53]

Detention has a deleterious affect on the ability of asylum seekers to assert a good claim for protection by making it very difficult to obtain effective representation.[54] The asylum process in any state is very difficult to navigate for the untrained, let alone for individuals who often do not speak the language of the adjudicators, come from very different legal cultures, and are detained. Moreover, the law itself, with developments from gender-related claims to the

Torture Convention, is complex. Expertise on human rights conditions in many of the world's countries is needed. In the United States, for example, claims are made annually bearing on conditions in some 175 countries. Given the complexity of asylum law and its proceedings as well as linguistic and cultural barriers for most asylum seekers, representation plays a major role in setting forth a good claim for protection. Asylum seekers are four to six times more likely to be granted asylum if they are represented. Two of every three asylum seekers in the United States are unrepresented in the first instance (before an Asylum Officer), and still one of every three lacks representation in formal proceedings before Immigration Judges.[55]

Expedited Processing

European nations were the first to create rapid asylum procedures, which were practiced in the major countries there by 1994. These procedures were aimed particularly at identifying "manifestly unfounded" applications at the airports and other ports of entry. Applicants arriving from "safe states" (discussed more fully below) are screened out of the regular asylum process and into an accelerated determination system. In Germany, for example, the asylum seeker in this situation has forty-eight hours to apply.[56] Rejected asylum seekers are given three days to file an appeal with an administrative court. In the United Kingdom, asylum seekers from "safe" countries are returned within twenty-four hours.[57]

In the United States, the Illegal Immigration Reform and Immigrant Responsibility Act of 1996 created an expedited removal procedure upon entry for those with fraudulent documentation or without documentation. Under these procedures, asylum seekers must demonstrate that they have a credible fear of persecution in order to continue with their asylum application. The law mandates that the "credible fear" determination be made swiftly and requires that the Immigration Judge's review of that determination be completed in no more than one week. Detention is mandated during this period of time.[58]

The effects of expedited processing, particularly the degree to which they prevent forced migrants from accessing fair hearings, are not clear. In Germany, most asylum seekers who use the three-day airport procedure or the rapid border procedure are unsuccessful. At the border, this is particularly because of the safe third country policy (discussed further below). Yet some 90,000 asylum seekers lodged applications in Germany each year on average from 1998 to 2001. In many cases, apparently, applicants tell the German authorities that they do not know what route they took to reach the interior of Germany.[59] In the United States, over 90 percent of those placed in expedited proceedings meet the credible fear requirements and are then placed in the full hearing proceedings before an Immigration Judge.[60] It is not known how many bona fide refugees are removed in this expedited process without being referred by an Immigration Inspector to an Asylum Officer for the credible fear interview.

Safe Third Country and Safe Country of Origin[61]

States developed these two distinct policies to address concerns about abuse of their asylum systems and to facilitate efficient determinations regarding which asylum seekers do not require normal access to a particular state's asylum system and which do not merit protection at all. These policies establish certain countries as "safe" states to which asylum seekers can be returned. States implementing the safe third country policy deny admission if an asylum seeker arrives via a country where she already enjoyed, or could or should have requested, asylum. States using the safe country of origin policy usually place those who originate from a country in which there is generally no serious risk of persecution in expedited processing with a presumption that they do not merit asylum. As implemented, these policies raise serious concerns regarding the return (*refoulement*) of refugees in violation of the core obligation of the 1951 Refugee Convention.

What makes a country "safe" is one of the critical issues in terms of the protection of bona fide refugees. In their 1992 "Resolution on a harmonized approach to questions concerning host third countries," the Ministers of the Member States of the (then) European Communities set out the following requirements to be a safe third country: life or freedom must not be threatened; there must be no exposure to torture or inhuman or degrading treatment; the asylum seeker either has been protected there or has had an opportunity to make contact with the country's authorities in order to seek protection; and the third country provides effective protection against return to the country of persecution. The resolution did not set out particular standards, however, as to just what procedures and laws ensure that asylum seekers have a real opportunity to gain protection or what it takes to meet any of the other requirements.

The Western Europeans developed the safe third country policy initially to prevent asylum seekers from "shopping" for asylum: being denied in one country, and then trying again in another European state. A second goal was to address the practice of asylum seekers "in orbit"—moved back and forth between countries that refused to adjudicate their claims. The Dublin Convention and Schengen Implementation Treaty both identify the member state responsible for making the one and only asylum determination on behalf of all signatories, a determination that all other signatories then pledge to respect.

The assumption made in these arrangements is that all EU countries are safe. But even this assumption has proven to be problematic. Until very recently, for example, Germany denied asylum claims where non-state agents, such as the Taliban, carried out the persecution. Concerned that such asylum seekers who came to the UK via Germany would be returned to their country of origin if the UK determined Germany to be a safe third country, the UK House of Lords refused to make such a determination.

Some states actually name safe third countries in their asylum laws. For Germany, all EU and European Free Trade Association states, as well as Poland and the Czech Republic, are named. At a recent Council Meeting, EU Ministers declared that candidate countries are effectively safe when they accede to the EU. Austrian law states that all countries that signed the Refugee Convention or Protocol are to be considered safe third countries. More than 140 nations have ratified these treaties, including Liberia, Rwanda, Sierra Leone and Yugoslavia. As the notion of "safe" is expanded to include, for example, any signatory state to the Refugee Convention or Protocol, asylum seekers may be returned to countries experiencing conflict, other kinds of very unstable conditions, and even serious human rights problems.

The effect of EU enlargement coupled with the safe third country policy has also raised serious protection concerns. Many of the asylum seekers returned to safe third countries by EU member states are sent pursuant to readmission agreements to the Central and Eastern European states that have only recently adopted the Refugee Convention and established status determination systems. Some of these states have imposed significant access restrictions to their asylum systems. Slovakia reportedly requires asylum seekers to file applications within twenty-four hours of arrival and interpreted this such that asylum seekers who first transit Slovakia and are then returned by their "first choice" asylum country are deemed ineligible for protection. The readmission agreements with these transit states cannot guarantee a fair opportunity for asylum seekers to claim protection. Not surprisingly, the Central and Eastern European states have introduced these very same policies with their neighbors to the east. In such circumstances, some bona fide refugees are not identified and are returned via so-called "chain deportations" to countries of persecution.

The safe third country policy is only now being developed in North America. U.S. law prohibits asylum applications from those who can be returned to a safe third country pursuant to a bilateral agreement. The only bilateral discussions initiated by the United States have involved Canada. The first set of negotiations failed in the mid-1990s, principally due to Canadian concerns that the U.S. asylum system did not provide adequate protection to refugees. The second attempt, part of a broad border security agreement between the two countries in reaction to the September 11 terrorist attacks, resulted in an agreement in December 2002 with respect to asylum seekers who present themselves at the land border between the two countries.

The concept of safe countries of origin, developed first by Switzerland and Germany in 1990 and 1992, respectively, aimed at facilitating the review of manifestly unfounded asylum claims. Such major asylum hosting states believed that many economic migrants were abusing their asylum systems. Again, some state's laws actually list safe countries of origin. This policy is regularly used, but the standards that states use to select safe countries of origin are inconsistent and of concern.

In determining whether a country of origin is safe, conclusions reached by European Immigration Ministers in 1992 noted four factors to be considered: previous number of refugees and recognition rates; observance of human rights; democratic institutions; and stability. However, standards—such as the maximum number of refugees and recognition rates, the level of human rights observance, the meaningfulness of democratic institutions, and the degree of stability—are not specified. It is not surprising, then, that EU member states have interpreted this general guidance in various ways, resulting in different lists of safe countries of origin. Even if everyone agreed on the meaning of safe, the asylum determination system is based on individual cases and particular facts. In recent years, the United States has granted asylum to refugees from more than 150 countries, a reasonable number of which many would consider generally safe.

Independent Review

Developed-nation asylum systems have traditionally permitted some degree of review of the initial asylum decision. This practice, however, is changing, particularly in the United States. The trend in the United States both in terms of administrative and judicial review has been to limit very significantly the role of the review function in the asylum system. The 1996 U.S. law, IIRIRA, made the Immigration Court the final arbiter of the merits in credible fear proceedings.[62] These determinations cannot be appealed to the Board of Immigration Appeals (BIA) or the federal courts, both of which have traditionally had significant review authority over the lower administrative court.

In 1999, the U.S. Attorney General authorized major changes in the BIA review process in order to address an increasing caseload and backlog, including authority to issue summary affirmances, that is, decisions without any analysis, in certain circumstances.[63] Changes initiated by a new Attorney General in 2002 went considerably further in order to speed up adjudication at the BIA in such drastic ways that some experts believe they will render the appeal process meaningless. The Attorney General required the BIA members to clear their current backlog of about 55,000 cases within 180 days—so fast that each appellate judge essentially had to decide thirty-two cases every work day, or one every fifteen minutes.[64] Finally, the Attorney General eliminated eight of the nineteen Board members, a downsizing aimed particularly at the newer members who have come from the practice of asylum and immigration law, advocacy, and academia.

Roadblocks to asylum have become the rule rather than the exception in developed countries during the last two decades. Visa requirements, carrier sanctions, safe country of origin and safe third country rules, expedited processing and removal, filing deadlines, detention, and pre-inspection discourage or bar asylum seekers from receiving protection in developed countries. Many analysts believe that such tools lead asylum seekers into the hands of smugglers, making escape and finding protection far more risky.[65] Such roadblocks are being followed as well by countries just now developing individualized asylum systems. Developed countries like Germany and the United States have advised countries such as Poland and South Africa how to replicate the developed country asylum system.

Policies that limit first asylum as described above send a very strong signal to countries around the world. The intended message is clear—if you're fleeing conflict or persecution, do not try to escape to a developed country. The unintended consequence is equally clear. The states that created the Refugee Convention to correct the inadequate responses to those fleeing Nazi Germany are no longer strong supporters of refugee protection. They may talk to developing nations as if they are, trying to persuade them to protect and assist the vast majority of forced migrants in the world. But developing countries see what is really going on and act accordingly.

Internally Displaced Persons

Only in the past decade or so has there been serious attention to those who are displaced within their own countries as a result of persecution, conflict and instability. Two of the principal barriers to protecting internally displaced persons result from the exercise of sovereignty by states unwilling to assist and protect their own citizens and the reluctance of governments to infringe on the sovereignty of other governments. These problems exist at both ends of the spectrum. In some cases, the offending states are such powerful members of the Security Council as Russia and China that would use their veto if the international community tried to intercede on behalf of those internally displaced from such areas as Chechnya or Tibet.[66] In other cases, such as Somalia and Liberia, there has been no effective sovereign authority within the country willing or able to request or accept international assistance.[67]

International human rights and humanitarian law have helped change the meaning of sovereignty to include responsibility for the welfare and security of the residents of one's territory. In arguing for greater international attention to internally displaced persons, Francis Deng, the Representative of the UN Secretary General on Internally Displaced Persons [the Representative], and his colleague Roberta Cohen, applied the concept of sovereignty as responsibility:

> Since there is no adequate replacement in sight for the system of state sovereignty, primary responsibility for promoting the security, welfare and liberty of populations must remain with the state. At the same time, no state claiming legitimacy can justifiably quarrel with the commitment to protect all its citizens against human rights abuse. . . . Sovereignty cannot be used as justification for the mistreatment of populations.[68]

As the internally displaced continue to reside in their own country, of course, their rights derive from international instruments other than the Refugee Convention: human rights law and, to the extent displacement is caused or affected by war, the Geneva Conventions. With the help of a group of legal experts, the Representative identified two important gaps in the existing protection framework for internally displaced persons. First, as the human rights laws and the Geneva Conventions are laws of general applicability, they were not specifically designed to address the full range of problems that the internally displaced face. Thus, while certain rights can be implied for the displaced, they are not explicit. For example, there is a:

> need for an expressed right not to be unlawfully displaced, to have access to protection and assistance during displacement, and to enjoy a secure return and reintegration. There are also gaps in legal protection relating to personal documentation for the internally displaced or restitution or compensation for property lost during displacement. And although there is a general norm for freedom of movement, there is no explicit right to find refuge in a safe part of the country or an explicit guarantee against the forcible return of internally displaced persons to places of danger.[69]

Second, there are several general shortcomings in the international law that is applicable to IDPs:

> First, in some situations of tensions and disturbances short of armed conflict, humanitarian law is not applicable, and human rights law may be restricted or derogated from; as a result, protections that are critical for the well-being or

survival of the internally displaced are diminished. Second, international human rights law generally binds only states, not nonstate actors, such as insurgent groups, under whose authority large numbers of internally displaced persons reside. Third, some states have not ratified key human rights treaties or the Geneva Conventions and their Additional Protocols and therefore are not formally bound by their provisions unless they are reflective of customary law. And fourth, although some principles of refugee law may be applicable by analogy, the strong and effective protection accorded refugees under the 1951 Refugee Convention cannot apply directly to internally displaced persons, even if conditions are similar.[70]

To apply these international laws explicitly to the situation of internally displaced persons and address the identified general gaps, the Representative and his team of legal experts developed a valuable normative framework for the legal protection of the internally displaced in the late 1990s. The *Guiding Principles on Internal Displacement* sets forth the major rights of the internally displaced and the responsibilities of sovereign authorities and other concerned actors to such individuals prior to, during, and following displacement. The *Guiding Principles* also look to international refugee law by analogy for guidance in certain situations. Although the *Principles* are not themselves a binding document, they restate and interpret existing binding law and have been recognized as a standard for governments, rebel groups, humanitarian organizations, and others regarding their conduct toward displaced persons.

The *Guiding Principles* define the internally displaced as "persons who have been forced or obliged to flee or to leave their homes or places of habitual residence in particular as a result of, or in order to avoid the effects of, armed conflict, situations of generalized violence, violations of human rights, or natural or human-made disasters, and who have not crossed an internationally recognized state border." This definition is descriptive, not legal, as there is no international instrument that defines an IDP. The definition includes not only those displaced by conflict, but those uprooted by floods and earthquakes, by famine and nuclear power plant eruptions like the Chernobyl disaster, and by large-scale development projects. Persons uprooted by natural or human disasters were found to be in desperate need of attention and subject to neglect or discrimination by their governments on political or ethnic grounds. For example, when drought and famine ravaged Ethiopia in the mid-1980s, the government, under the pretext of responding to a natural disaster, forcibly relocated hundreds of thousands of ethnic Tigreans it regarded as political opponents. As for development projects, an increasing number of reports have shown that poor, indigenous, and marginalized groups are often displaced without consultation, respect for their rights, or the provision of adequate resettlement or compensation.[71]

The *Guiding Principles* provide protection against arbitrary displacement, offer a basis for protection and assistance during displacement, and set forth guarantees for safe return, resettlement and reintegration. One of the unique features of the *Guiding Principles* is that they tailor existing laws to the specific needs of internally displaced persons. For instance, after restating general norms of international law on respect for family life, the principles spell out what this means for the displaced—that families separated by displacement should be reunited as quickly as possible. Or, after reiterating the general norm that every human being has the right to recognition before the law, they point out that the authorities must issue the displaced all the documents needed to exercise their legal rights.

To ensure that the *Guiding Principles* are understood and applied in the field by human rights and humanitarian actors, the Representative and the UN Office for the Coordination of Humanitarian Affairs (OCHA), respectively, engaged experts to develop two field guides. The *Handbook for Applying the Guiding Principles on Internal Displacement* spells out the meaning of the principles in nontechnical language to facilitate their practical application by field staff and displaced populations. The *Manual on Field Practice in Internal Displacement* complements the *Handbook* and describes concrete activities that may be undertaken in situations of internal displacement to strengthen the link between assistance and protection activities.

ADDRESSING LEGAL GAPS IN PROTECTING AND ASSISTING FORCED MIGRANTS

As the above discussion demonstrates, universal and regional international laws protect some forced migrants, but many remain subject to discretionary state policies. Below we focus on three important problems. First, the right to seek asylum has been seriously undermined in developed states. Second, universal international law does not protect refugees who can demonstrate a well-founded fear of serious harm other than persecution. Only the regional OAU Convention provides this type of binding protection for refugees displaced in OAU countries. Third, the protection of internally displaced persons under international law needs to be made more explicit and suffers from certain general shortcomings of governing international law. When adopted as national law in states with significant internally displaced populations, the *Guiding Principles* overcome these problems where hard law is most needed. To address identified gaps, then, we propose a package of measures that develops forced migration law comprehensively and from the ground up.

Protecting Convention Refugees in Developed States

As discussed above, states have denied or seriously limited the right to seek asylum in order to control irregular movements. Such movements involve a mix of forced and economic migrants. The challenge to states is to manage such irregular movements while fulfilling humanitarian obligations. Below we recommend laws and policies that better enable states to accomplish these tasks.

Develop a Fair and Efficient Asylum System

States cannot manage irregular movements well unless they develop successful asylum and migration regimes. If the asylum process is the only legal migration door open to irregular migrants, that is the one they will choose. To ensure that asylum systems are not abused by large numbers of economic migrants, states should establish a professional corps of asylum adjudicators, work with NGOs to develop fair and efficient processes, and ensure that policies do not encourage economic migrants to apply for asylum. The experience of the United States serves as a model in this regard.

In the 1980s, adjudicators in local District Offices of the Immigration and Naturalization Service made asylum decisions. These adjudicators mostly handled immigrant petitions and naturalization applications. This locally run system resulted in major lawsuits challenging decision-making that highly favored asylum seekers from certain countries and greatly disfavored others for ideological reasons. The first Bush Administration decided to establish a professional corps of officers to address these and related problems.

Shortly after the creation of the Asylum Corps, the new Asylum Division's limited staff was overrun with significantly increasing numbers of applications and crises (e.g., the Haitian mass exodus in 1992).[72] A backlog of nearly half a million asylum applications developed, and most experts believed that economic migrants took advantage of the system and its growing backlog in order to obtain work permits. At the time, asylum applicants received work permits adjudicated by Asylum Officers ninety days after filing their asylum application.

The INS Commissioner and key Asylum Division staff led an asylum reform effort to address these problems. After extensive internal and external consultations with all interested parties, the INS instituted reforms in January 1995. Generally, its core features were a sufficient number of professional, well-trained decision makers; timely decisions in the first and second instances (three and six months, respectively); and benefits accruing to recognized refugees when asylum is granted rather than at application. The new procedures were implemented on a "last in, first out" basis, while the backlog of pending cases was addressed primarily via legislative action.

These reforms resulted in a well-functioning asylum system. The number of applications decreased dramatically once work authorization was no longer an automatic benefit received by all asylum seekers, and the grant rate increased dramatically over time. In recent years, the United States has granted asylum to more than one-half of those individuals whose claims are decided on the merits. The Asylum Division has made timely decisions on its current caseload for many years now. Indeed, the Asylum Corps not only took care of its annual domestic caseload, but also aided the U.S. resettlement program by adjudicating many refugee determinations overseas.

Part of the strength of this function has been its leadership and professional approach to its responsibilities. The recruitment of Asylum Officers has been a top priority from the very beginning of the Asylum Corps in 1990. Asylum Officers receive solid training both when they are initially hired and throughout their careers. Headquarters has also developed a very good training program for Supervisory Asylum Officers. Training enables Asylum Officers to keep abreast of the developments in statutory and case law so that they correctly apply substantive law. Training also helps prepare Asylum Officers to understand better the cultural behavior of claimants from all over the world. Moreover, information on country conditions is critical in asylum determinations, and the Asylum Division's Resource Information Center has provided Asylum Officers with valuable, up-to-date information on a regular basis.

When a state is able to make credible determinations in an efficient manner, it is not necessary to impose artificial barriers to asylum, such as time limits for applying and expedited procedures. When a fair and timely system does not yet exist or is not yet perceived as effective, states concerned about abuse sometimes impose time limits for individuals to file asylum claims. Turkey requires that applications be lodged within ten days of entering the country. Pursuant to a 1996 law, the United States requires applications to file for asylum within one year of the claimant's arrival in the country. The only exceptions are changed circumstances that materially affect the applicant's eligibility for asylum or extraordinary circumstances relating to the delay in filing. Those who object to such time limits argue that genuine refugees often have good reasons for failing to file their claims immediately or soon after arrival. Many refugees are traumatized. Unless they are in countries that provide them with food and shelter, their first priority is survival—finding relatives, friends, or others who will help them. Language barriers, as well as ignorance of the law, hinder compliance with such limits. Perhaps most important of all, filing a considered asylum application is extraordinarily difficult without help from a lawyer or other professional who specializes in asylum. There is no evidence that the imposition of time limits decreases abusive claims. It is clear, however, that such restrictions limit the access of bona fide claimants to a decision on the merits. The 1996 U.S. law has now limited the rights of tens of thousands of individuals to seek asylum.[73] If an asylum system is effective, the imposition of time limits and expedited processes is not needed to control abuse. States should eliminate such restrictions and focus resources on establishing fair and efficient systems.

Develop Mechanisms to Share Protection Responsibilities

When states interdict asylum seekers on the high seas or impose other barriers to border crossing, they are trying to prevent movements to their territories where individuals would have the right to make asylum claims in full legal proceedings. Under these circumstances, states bear two obligations. First, states cannot return individuals to countries where they have a well-founded fear of persecution. Second, states must respect the right to seek asylum.

These obligations do not equate necessarily with admission. In general, however, developed states should be able to shoulder the responsibility for a reasonable number of such asylum seekers. Those who qualify for protection should be able to remain, while those not qualified at all can be returned.

Mass movements of asylum seekers present greater challenges. In these circumstances, states may determine that they cannot shoulder the responsibility alone and should look to neighboring states to share that responsibility. As noted above, the European Communities has created a mechanism to address responsibilities for mass movements that has yet to be tested. Council Directive 2001/55/EC of July 20, 2001, concerns the "minimum standards for giving temporary protection in the event of a mass influx of displaced persons and on measures promoting a balance of efforts between Member States in receiving such persons and bearing the consequences thereof."[74] The Directive provides for a responsibility-sharing mechanism among member states. States must indicate their reception capacity before the Council takes its decision to establish temporary protection in all member states and may indicate additional capacity afterward (Art. 25.1). If demand is higher than reception capacity, the Council may recommend additional support for affected member states (Art. 25.3). The Directive also establishes a procedure for the voluntary transfer of protected persons from one member state to another (Art. 26) and ensures access to asylum procedures (Art. 17).

Use Limited Resources More Effectively and Efficiently by Developing Alternatives to Detention

States purportedly detain asylum seekers to ensure compliance with legal proceedings and removal orders as well as to deter irregular movements. No empirical study has ever demonstrated that detention deters such movements. It is difficult to imagine that persons fleeing human rights abuses or conflict will be deterred by detention policies.

As a recent study has shown, compliance with legal proceedings and removal orders can be achieved through supervised release programs that rely on detention only when an asylum seeker no longer complies with program requirements. Under a contract with the U.S. INS, the Vera Institute of Justice developed and evaluated an Appearance Assistance Program (AAP) to understand the effect of supervised release on compliance. Prior to the study, INS estimated that about 50 percent of those released from detention do not appear for their hearings. Vera found that 93 percent of those asylum seekers in the intensive supervised release program appeared at all of their hearings, even though they were repeatedly reminded that they would face re-detention in court if they lost their cases. Vera also followed the behavior of asylum seekers released from detention who did not participate in the supervised release program. Seventy-eight percent of that group appeared at all of their hearings. From this, Vera concluded that the most important finding on asylum seekers is that "overall they successfully complete their court cases at very high rates and these rates remain high regardless of any other factors, including participation in the AAP."[75] "Asylum seekers do not need to be detained to appear for their hearings. They also do not seem to need intensive supervision."[76]

Vera was not able to collect systematic information to report about asylum seekers' compliance with final orders of removal. With regard to other types of individuals in immigration removal proceedings, Vera found that participation in the supervised release program almost doubled the rate of compliance with final orders of removal (69 percent v. 38 percent).[77] INS had speculated prior to the study that only 11 percent departed from the United States when required to do so.[78]

Vera also studied the costs of detention versus supervised release and found that the government would save more than half the costs of detention through supervision of asylum seekers.[79]

The Vera study's findings demonstrate that detention is not needed for asylum seekers to appear at their hearings. States would both save funds and treat asylum seekers more humanely by no longer using detention to ensure their appearance at hearings. As supervised release significantly increases compliance of non-asylum seekers with final orders of removal, states may wish to put some of those saved funds into such programs for asylum seekers.

Provide Representation to Asylum Seekers to Ensure Fair and Efficient Legal Proceedings

Representation generally results in three positive effects on asylum systems. First, studies have suggested that represented asylum seekers have a higher rate of compliance with hearing requirements than those who are not represented.[80] In fiscal year 1999, more than 80 percent of those who failed to appear at their U.S. Immigration Court hearings lacked representation.[81] Second, studies have also shown that representation generally ensures a higher level of fairness in a formal adversarial system where the government is always represented. Asylum seekers are four to six times more likely to be granted asylum if they are represented.[82] Finally, many adjudicators and practitioners believe that when noncitizens are represented in proceedings, cases move more efficiently, economically, and expeditiously through the system. Issues presented for decision by the administrative courts and on appeal are more readily narrowed. In addition, the asylum system bears significant costs when claimants cannot find representation, as adjudicators often prefer to proceed only when both sides in an adversarial proceeding are represented.[83]

Today there are basically two different models on representation, and each has its problems. In the U.S. model, asylum seekers placed in proceedings are guaranteed the privilege of being represented by an attorney or other qualified legal representative, but at no expense to the government. Unfortunately, this system results in many claimants without representation, as reported above: two of every three asylum seekers are unrepresented in the first instance (before an Asylum Officer), and still one of every three lacks representation in formal proceedings before Immigration Judges. In a second model, one used by several European states (Denmark, France, Netherlands, Sweden), lawyers are appointed to take up cases at government expense.[84] Where legal aid is provided, however, free legal advice may be limited to the first instance or the appeal, or the amount that the state may spend on financial legal aid may be wholly inadequate. The European Council on Refugees and Exiles, an umbrella organization of refugee NGOs, advocates that legal aid payments should reflect the time and disbursements required for competent representation and be administered by a body independent of the executive arm of government. In both models, quality of representation is very mixed.

Accordingly, governments should create pilot programs that experiment with different ways to develop representation programs that guarantee a fair and efficient asylum process. There are good practices, including pro bono and training programs, established even where representation is not yet mandated.[85] Serious pilot programs should be built on such practices to ensure quality and effectiveness in the system.

In addition to direct representation, one successful program that helps those in removal proceedings understand their chances for relief is the legal orientation program. Developed initially in 1989 by the Florence Immigrant and Refugee Rights Project, the program consists of live presentations for all detained noncitizens before or at the time of their initial administrative court hearing, with follow up screening and case assessment for those without private counsel. Additional legal assistance, referral or representation is provided when available. During fiscal year 1998, the U.S. Department of Justice (DOJ) funded a pilot project to document the benefits of such legal orientations. Based on case data from the pilot, DOJ evaluators found that legal orientations saved both time and money for the government while also benefiting detainees.[86] In addition, they found that such programs were useful management tools that "strengthen the capability of [the government] to operate safer detention facilities." In conclusion, the evaluators recommended that the government should expand legal orientations to all INS detention facilities. The U.S. Congress has provided initial funding for such legal orientation programs at several detention facilities. Experts believe that this model can also address the information needs of non-detained asylum seekers and help make the asylum system more efficient.

Ensure Accurate and Consistent Legal Standards through Independent Review

Accuracy, consistency and public acceptance are among the most important goals of any adjudicative system.[87] Experts believe that the mere prospect of independent review encourages more thoughtful deliberation at the initial hearing stage.[88] Independence can be achieved in various ways. In Europe, for example, the French appellate commission, the *Commission de recours des réfugies*, provides a model with considerable independence. Its members sit in panels of three, composed of a judge, a member of the board of the French Refugee Office (the office that makes first instance decisions), and a representative of the United Nations High Commissioner for Refugees. The judge who chairs the panel may be a member of the *Conseil d'état*, the *Cour des comptes*, an administrative appeal court, or an administrative tribunal.

As discussed above, the U.S. Attorney General, the chief law enforcement officer, has seriously limited review of formal asylum decisions through administrative fiat. In fiscal year 2003, some 33,500 of 198,000 Immigration

Judge decisions (17 percent) were appealed to the Board of Immigration Appeals by either noncitizens or the government.[89] Subsequent to the limited review procedures established by the Attorney General, decisions by Immigration Judges are largely summarily affirmed without explanation by a single member of the Board of Immigration Appeals.[90] Since such decisions do not provide any analysis, they cannot ensure consistent legal standards. Moreover, no one can know whether such decisions are accurate unless they are appealed to the U.S. Courts of Appeal that sit just below the U.S. Supreme Court. To ensure accurate and consistent legal standards in a more efficient manner, the United States should provide for independent review of the formal asylum decisions by establishing the Board of Immigration Appeals as an independent agency, as proposed by the U.S. Commission on Immigration Reform in 1997.[91] States that do not yet have independent review mechanisms also should establish them.

Ensure That Safe Third Country and Safe Country of Origin Laws Are Used Soundly or Eliminate Them

As described above, governments have applied the notions of safe third countries and safe countries of origin in ways that limit access of asylum seekers to fair procedures and at times result in *refoulement*. First, states should be sure from a policy point of view that such policies really address abuses in their asylum systems. Empirical studies should be done to assess the effects of these policies.

Even if such policies are effective in addressing abuse, this must be weighed against the adverse consequences of these policies with regard to bona fide refugees. Determining which countries are safe is complex and changes. Legislating such a list should never be done, given the challenges in keeping such legislation up to date. But even if such determinations are carefully made and updated, they should never eliminate access to a fair opportunity to make an asylum claim. According to experts, "*No* country is 100 percent free of persecution."[92] In effect, an asylum seeker has a higher burden of proof to demonstrate a well-founded fear of persecution in a country that to many appears safe. But that is the only way to ensure that a state does not return bona fide refugees to persecution. Accordingly, states should either not use safe country of origin laws at all (U.S. policy), or they should use them only with regard to the burden of proof.

With respect to safe third countries, it is critical that states that apply this notion find ways to ensure that refugees are not subject to chain refoulement —whereby they are indirectly returned to a country of persecution when the country of intended asylum removes the asylum seeker to a so-called safe country that does return that person to a country of persecution. One expert has proposed the following way to cure such a problem: states should only designate a country as "safe" if it does "(1) not practice persecution itself; (2) provide[s] a full and fair procedure for assessing asylum claims; and (3) [does] not send anyone to other countries unless those other countries *meet this same definition of 'safe.'*"[93]

Develop Methods to Protect Refugees Subject to Visa, Pre-clearance and Pre-inspection Requirements

Several of the restrictive measures (visa practices, pre-clearance and pre-inspection) apply generally to travelers and thus have separate migration policy rationales, even though they have a significant effect on the ability of asylum seekers to reach developed states. States are not about to forego such practices in general if they continue to be seen as appropriate migration management tools. Accordingly, states need to find ways to identify refugees who cannot travel because of these measures and provide them with protection.

This is perhaps the most difficult dilemma to resolve. Interestingly, the United States is the only country that includes in its refugee definition those with a well-founded fear of persecution who still reside in their country of origin.[94] Other states should follow this legal example. But the major problem here is not a legal one. Rather, it is the challenge of successfully identifying refugees without compromising their ability to remain safe while they reside in a country of persecution. States have enough experience to know that the persecuting governments easily observe those who come to their embassies. The successes here have happened quietly and should be encouraged.

There are several options for in-country protection processes.[95] Where it can be safely done, special "refugee" visas should be issued by embassies and consulates to persons who do not qualify for regular visas but who can demonstrate that they are or will be endangered if they do not leave their home countries. A second option is to establish UNHCR offices in countries of origin where would-be asylum seekers could request protection, with the understanding that they would be evacuated to countries willing and able to receive them. Finally, states could broaden the responsibilities of pre-inspection personnel and other immigration officials assigned to overseas locations so that they can assess the asylum claims of persons seeking to board aircraft and other carriers without proper documentation. States would have to be prepared to provide protection for those identified as refugees or to arrange for another state to do so. Given the challenges and inexperience with regards to in-country processes, these various approaches should all be tested in meaningful ways in order to develop good practices.

Protecting Refugees Fleeing Civil War or Generalized Violence

As discussed above, most forced migrants who cross international borders in search of protection flee situations of civil war or generalized violence (civil war refugees).[96] Universal treaty law only protects refugees fleeing very specific kinds of persecution. In practice, most states generally do not return those fleeing civil wars and other disorder to situations of violence. However, decisions not to return such refugees are discretionary rather than mandatory. Moreover, most states limit certain fundamental rights of such refugees in very serious ways.

With regard to providing protection to these refugees, governments prefer to maintain as much discretion as possible. A universal international treaty would oblige them not to return such refugees to countries where they would face serious harm. Like the Refugee Convention, it would set out legal rights for covered refugees. With the exception of the OAU member states, governments have so far opted to establish their own domestic laws and policies to govern how they protect these refugees.

One regional development is noteworthy, however. The European Commission's 2001 proposal on subsidiary protection attempted to establish a "supranational instrument to outline a comprehensive complementary protection regime, moving 'complementary protection' beyond the realm of *ad hoc* and discretionary national practices to formalize it as part of EU asylum law."[97] While member states debated the precise contours of the rights to be associated with subsidiary protection and the ultimate outcome remains unknown, the proposal established eligibility criteria for this type of protection for forced migrants based on state practice and international obligations under human rights instruments.[98] As indicated above, the final Council Directive established minimum standards on eligibility, rights, and benefits. While welcoming certain aspects of the Directive, the European Council on Refugees and Exiles criticized the lack of any provision guaranteeing the right to family reunion and the number of derogations on the content of international protection, particularly concerning benefits afforded to family members, duration of residence permits, provision of travel documents, entitlement to social welfare benefits, and access to health care, and employment.[99] Experts have also expressed serious concern that states may use any new legal regime on subsidiary protection as a substitute for Convention protection in order to minimize obligations under international law.[100] This is a serious problem that must be guarded against. As discussed below, this issue can be addressed and should not prevent the development of a protection system in Europe for civil war refugees.

Even though developed states largely do not return civil war refugees, such forced migrants deserve universal international laws to ensure their legal protection. As it is unlikely that these states would agree to a universal treaty obligation to achieve this, the best way to formalize such protection is to develop sound regional and national laws. In addition to establishing a right not to be returned to a country of harm, such instruments need to ensure that two issues are squarely addressed. One regards the rights attached to the legal status, and the other concerns the relationship between the granting of Convention and subsidiary protection status.

To address what rights should attach to subsidiary protection, policymakers should carefully examine the needs of those who have a well-founded fear of death compared to the needs of those who fear persecution. That examination should focus particularly on the need for a durable solution for these different types of forced migrants. The longstanding practice by most developed states provides a durable solution right from the start for those fleeing persecution. The assumption has been that the root causes of persecution are unlikely to change within a few years time. Rather than keep such refugees in limbo, particularly those who have suffered past persecution, developed states provide such forced migrants at least with the minimal rights set forth in the 1951 Convention. A similar analysis should be done with regard to those fleeing serious harm other than persecution. The answer will not be the same in all cases. To take one example, some civil wars have gone on for decades. A few, though not that many in recent years, have lasted from one to four years. Determining which conflicts are likely to be prolonged and for how long invites problems, but it is reasonable to distinguish between relatively new conflicts whose duration is not known and ones that have already gone on for more than a few years and have no serious peacemaking efforts underway. Under such a distinction, those coming from relatively new conflicts would not necessarily need rights associated with a durable solution immediately. They would if the conflict continues for a few years. Of course, such forced migrants still have many fundamental needs that must be met by any legal regime.

The second issue involves the concern that states will use subsidiary protection as a substitute for Convention protection in order to limit their obligations. To the degree that those granted subsidiary protection need a durable solution and are provided with associated rights, this is not likely to be an issue. But to ensure that subsidiary protection does not become a substitute, the system should develop and rely on a corps of professional decision makers, sound legal standards, accessible human rights and conflict information, and fair procedures. Successful asylum systems have demonstrated that these elements ensure that the rule of law is properly executed.[101]

Ensuring Effective Protection of Refugees in Their Region of Origin

Most refugees seek protection in their region of origin, but the quality of that protection is in dire need of improvement. First, many refugees cross borders into states that are not parties to the Refugee Convention where they are mistreated. Second, many signatory states severely restrict the rights of refugees who manage to cross an international border.

More than forty-five states are still not party to the 1951 Refugee Convention or the 1967 Protocol.[102] These include the following receiving countries hosting more than 100,000 refugees: Pakistan (over one million), Syria, Thailand, India, Lebanon, Saudi Arabia, Jordan, Nepal, Iraq, and Bangladesh.[103] Despite UNHCR's encouragement to become parties, these states have determined not to provide refugees with the rights contained in these treaties. This translates into a range of practices by some of these states that flout the international community's system of protection—established, as noted earlier, in part to ensure the stability of our Westphalian state structure.

The most egregious practice, of course, is refoulement—despite the fact that this is a violation of customary international law.[104] The U.S. Committee for Refugees reports that some of the more troubling cases of 2003 in which states forcibly returned persons who were denied access to a fair refugee determination procedure involved such nonparties to the Convention or Protocol as Thailand, Malaysia, Bangladesh, and Nepal. These forcible returns likely included the refoulement of refugees from Myanmar, Indonesia, and China. Other practices that some nonparties have used toward refugees include imprisonment, eviction, seizure of food and medicine ration books, and threats of physical attack.[105] Such practices need to stop, and one way to move states in that direction is to provide them with incentives to become parties to the Convention and Protocol. The international community should develop a campaign that targets these nonparties with both carrots and sticks. Carrots include aid, while sticks could involve trade and other economic restrictions.

Of course, parties to the Convention and Protocol also forcibly return refugees and seriously restrict their rights. Iran, Venezuela, China, the United States, Yemen, and Panama reportedly forcibly returned some refugees emanating from their region in 2003.[106] Other state practices significantly erode the protection refugees receive in their region of origin. These include placement of camps near borders, restriction of movement, and denial of economic livelihood opportunities.

Two different types of security problems affecting refugees, local populations and host governments, arise from the placement of camps near borders. First, militaries cross borders and sometimes regionalize civil wars when the fighters flee internationally. This presents important security problems for host governments. Combatants use refugee camps not only for rest and medical treatment, but for recruitment as well. Armies cross borders to attack insurgents and sometimes attack camps, as discussed below. Small arms may proliferate in camps sheltering combatants. Security is one of the major reasons that the Tanzanian government asserts as to why it has restricted the rights of refugees during the past seven years after more than two decades of generosity.[107] Unfortunately in this situation, refugees suffer both from physical attacks due to the location of the camps and the host government reaction to restrict their rights.

Second, fighters sometimes create very serious security problems in refugee camps that can spillover into the local communities. One dramatic example of this occurred in West Africa. Several West African states became engulfed in conflicts that crossed borders in the 1990s. Two West Africans (Taylor and Sankoh) trained to fight guerrilla warfare in Gadafy's training camps helped start civil wars first in Liberia and then in Sierra Leone. The civil war in Liberia forced some half million refugees to flee to Guinea and the Ivory Coast. After Taylor became President of Liberia in the mid-1990s, Guinean rebels took cover and were trained in Liberia and formed alliances with the major rebel group in Sierra Leone. Regime changes in 1997 and 1998 in Sierra Leone sent refugees, including rebels, into already overcrowded camps in Guinea and Liberia. In 1999, Guinea and Liberia sent government troops into each other's territory to attack rebels sheltered in each other's country. When attacks continued in Guinean camps sheltering some 400,000 refugees from Liberia and Sierra Leone, many civilians were killed, and Guineans turned on refugees trapped between the rebels and Guinean troops.[108] Finally, when civil strife broke out in the Ivory Coast, Liberian soldiers and former Sierra Leone rebels reportedly helped rebel groups in the area near the Liberian border.[109]

The placement of camps near borders occurs in various parts of the world. The only treaty that recognizes this as a problem is the OAU Convention discussed earlier. Article II(6) states: "For reasons of security, countries of asylum shall, as far as possible, settle refugees at a reasonable distance from the frontier of their country of origin." While this language leaves too much discretion to parties ("as far as possible"), it does require protection of refugees away from borders. This principle should be universally adopted and implemented, as it both provides for the physical protection of refugees and addresses the security concerns of states. States should follow the example of Zambia, which from the very beginning of the Angolan refugee movements three decades ago established camps away from the border.[110]

Chapter 2

Restriction of movement and livelihood rights result in dependency on food aid as well as psychological dependency. As stated earlier, the Refugee Convention provides for both freedom of movement (Art. 26) and employment rights (Art. 17) to the same degree that these are accorded to nationals of other countries. Yet states such as Tanzania restrict refugees from traveling more than very short distances outside of camp perimeters.[111] At the end of 2003, Tanzania hosted one of Africa's largest refugee populations, almost half a million, mostly from Burundi. Nearly all are required to live in ten designated camps near the western border with Rwanda and Burundi. Most have done so for more than ten years. Refugees may not travel more than 2.5 miles from the camps, which seriously reduces their ability to farm or earn income. They have become completely dependent on dwindling humanitarian aid. Moreover, funding shortfalls have resulted in reduced food rations for Burundian refugees many times in the last few years. These restrictions on refugee rights to earn a livelihood are fairly typical. Ethiopia, for example, has denied land to the majority of Sudanese refugees living in western Ethiopia.

The U.S. Committee for Refugees recommends granting Burundian refugees, most of whom are farmers, greater access to agricultural land, which is reportedly plentiful in western Tanzania. This would enable them to become self-sufficient. In one nearby country, Zambia, Angolan refugees have achieved a remarkable level of self-sufficiency by cultivating land that local officials provided them upon arrival in Zambia.[112] Living in settlements as opposed to camps, these Angolans contributed to the national Zambian economy during their protracted stay (some for three decades) and are returning home in relatively good health. Three years after settling in Zambia, refugees no longer received monthly food rations, except for the elderly, orphans and single mothers. In addition to empowering refugees, the land distribution policy benefited the local and national economy such that the Zambian government issued thirty to sixty day permits to refugees so that they could travel outside of the settlements to sell their vegetables. Through partnerships with Zambian businessmen and women, refugees also marketed their products to countries in the region. While land may not always be available to states, many times it is. In such cases, states should be strongly encouraged to respect Articles 17 and 26 of the Convention by following Zambia's model.

Donors can and should play a central role in encouraging effective protection in the region. As the U.S. Committee for Refugees has recommended, donors should facilitate self-sufficiency policies by compensating host countries for some of the costs associated with respecting Refugee Convention rights.[113] Donors can also facilitate the placement of camps away from the border by assisting host countries financially with transportation and related costs.

Finally, most signatories apply the Convention and Protocol to refugees from everywhere in the world. Turkey, however, has limited its obligations to refugees from Europe. Given that Turkey rarely is asked to provide protection to refugees from Europe but often asked to protect refugees from other parts of the world, this treaty obligation should be expanded. This should be required for Turkey to become part of the European Union, as all other EU states, with the sole exception of Malta, have legally bound themselves to protect Convention refugees from everywhere in the world. Malta, too, should be required to harmonize with all other EU member states.[114]

Protecting Internally Displaced Persons

The *Guiding Principles* are the first document to comprehensively and exclusively denote the rights of IDPs and the responsibilities of governments toward them. They mostly restate the requirements of binding international law, such as International Humanitarian Law, the Convention against Torture, the Covenant on Economic, Social and Cultural Rights, and the Covenant on Civil and Political Rights. They also provide some new responsibilities not derived from international legal sources. As the *Guiding Principles* are not binding themselves, however, states are not required to adhere to them *per se*. Of course, states remain bound by the underlying hard law.

The purpose of the *Guiding Principles*, then, is to guide States in bringing "their policies and legislation into line with them."[115] IDP advocates disseminate and encourage the application of the *Guiding Principles*. As Francis Deng wrote in his report to the UN Commission on Human Rights in January 2003:

> The *Guiding Principles* on Internal Displacement, which were presented to the Commission in 1998 (E/CN.4/1998/53/Add.2), consolidate the numerous norms relevant to addressing the specific protection, assistance and development needs of internally displaced persons. They set forth the rights and guarantees relevant to all phases of internal displacement, providing protection against arbitrary displacement, protection and assistance during displacement, and during return or resettlement and reintegration. The Principles provide guidance to all pertinent actors: the Representative in carrying out his mandate; States faced with the phenomenon of internal displacement; all other authorities, groups and persons in their relations with internally displaced persons, including non-State actors; intergovernmental and nongovernmental organizations; and, certainly, internally displaced persons themselves.[116]

Through the work of the Representative of the Secretary-General on IDPs and the Brookings-SAIS Project on Internal Displacement which supports his mandate, the IDP Unit in OCHA, the Global IDP Project of the Norwegian Refugee Council, the Office for Democratic Institutions and Human Rights (ODIHR) of the Organization for Security and Cooperation in Europe (OSCE), and other regional and nongovernmental organizations around the world, efforts at the national level have begun to reach a wide range of actors. Pursued simultaneously, three promising models for the dissemination and integration of the *Guiding Principles* have successfully moved IDP law and policy forward in several nations with significant internally displaced populations.

The first model focuses on introducing new legislation at the policy-making level of the national government to codify and formalize recognition of IDP rights. IDP-specific legislation also formally designates an accountability structure within the government—changing the character of the *Guiding Principles* to enforceable law.

The second model follows the process by which the *Guiding Principles* were primarily formed and aims to illustrate to national governments how their existent national law can be interpreted as protecting IDPs. For example, most countries with constitutions or displacement policy of any kind likely have laws that could be interpreted as affording protection to IDP populations. While this approach relies on interpretation rather than explicit statutes, it appears to be working well in several nations. Its pragmatism and direct dialogue with all levels of national, state, and local government strengthen its effectiveness.

The third model focuses on NGOs and non-state actors like insurgent forces and opposition leaders. One great benefit from this approach for the protective goals of the *Guiding Principles* is that it targets the armed forces that often engage in human rights abuses against IDPs. Because of their focus on the NGOs (who are trying to protect IDPs) and the armed insurgencies (whose activities may place IDPs at risk), workshops with non-state actors offer the promise of influencing those who have the closest contact with IDPs.

Model One: Focus on Passing National Legislation

Several states with internally displaced populations have adopted, or are considering the adoption, of legislation that reflects the rights and responsibilities contained in the *Guiding Principles*. Colombia actually passed its own IDP legislation prior to the issuance of the *Guiding Principles*. Passed on July 18, 1997, IDP Law 387 "provides a relatively comprehensive coverage of the protection and assistance needs of the displaced during the different phases of displacement (emergency phase, long term displacement, return and resettlement)."[117] The following January, Presidential Decree No. 173 created the

National Plan on Comprehensive Assistance of IDPs.[118] This decree divided the institutional responsibilities within the Colombian government for assisting IDPs. The plan failed, however, to specify how the proposed measures were to be implemented.[119] In 2000, Presidential Decree No. 2569 specified in more detail some of the more crucial aspects of Law 387.[120] The primary IDP policy document in Colombia, CONPES 3057, "provides an analysis of the current (1999) IDP situation and the existing mechanisms to attend to IDPs."[121] Most important, it explicitly states its commitment to "promote and respect the implementation of the *Guiding Principles*."[122]

In 2000, Angola became the first nation to explicitly incorporate the substantive norms from the *Guiding Principles* into its legislation on resettlement."[123] Unfortunately, Angolan IDPs are not well protected during the return process, evidencing a significant gap between the tenets of the new law and actual governmental performance.[124] Uganda, after a "wide-ranging consultation process among stakeholders . . . developed a text integrating local needs and international standards."[125] The final draft is pending before the Cabinet.[126] In Peru, "the Congress passed a bill that would lay out a number of rights of internally displaced persons in language very similar to that of the *Guiding Principles*."[127] The President has not yet signed the bill due to lingering concerns about particular "institutional arrangements for dealing with internal displacement, which are also addressed in the bill."[128] In Mexico, "the Government is seeking a constitutional amendment and the development of a policy and legislation in internal displacement based on the *Guiding Principles*."[129] So far, then, Angola remains the only country with legislation specifically incorporating substantive elements of the *Guiding Principles*.

Three other countries have issued sub-legislative policies or declarations specifically referencing the *Guiding Principles* in 2002. In Liberia, the Minister of Justice and Attorney General issued a Declaration of the Rights and Protection of Internally Displaced Persons (IDPs) that specifically referred to the *Guiding Principles* and other documents "guaranteeing every person the right to leave and return to their habitual places of reference."[130] The Philippine National Disaster Coordinating Council issued Policy Guidelines on the Delivery of Basic Services to Displaced Children in Disaster Situations, listing the *Guiding Principles* as one of its legal bases.[131] UNICEF supported the publication of the document.[132] The Sri Lankan Government adopted the "National Framework of Relief, Rehabilitation and Reconciliation, which notes, inter alia, that 'the universally accepted rights of the internally displaced . . . are enshrined in the *Guiding Principles on Internal Displacement* . . . the *Guiding Principles* unquestionably . . . apply to the situation in Sri Lanka."[133] In 2001, the "Government of Burundi signed a 'Protocol for the Creation of a Permanent Framework of Cooperation for the Protection of

Displaced Persons'"[134] with the UN. In it, the government accepted to be "bound by the *Guiding Principles on Internal Displacement*."

As these sub-legislative efforts and the few national laws that are on the books or nearly so demonstrate, the *Guiding Principles* are slowly being integrated into the national legal and political landscape of nations with acute IDP problems. Although formalistic in nature, the model succeeds in garnering legitimacy at the national level for the *Guiding Principles*. Thus far, however, no comprehensive empirical study has documented whether these new laws and policy decrees actually have improved conditions and protection for IDPs.

The adoption of the *Guiding Principles* into national legislation alone will not improve the plight of IDPs. Efforts are needed to guide and train local governments, law enforcement, policymakers, and judges in interpreting and applying such new legislation to the IDP situations for which they are responsible.

Model Two: The Workshop Approach to Interpreting Existent Laws

The second model appears most promising when used in a country that is also willing to formalize its commitments into law (like Colombia). This model focuses on proper interpretation of existent resettlement, displacement, and social treatment laws within the country. For example, the Global IDP Project, run by the Norwegian Refugee Council, sets up and chairs workshops in a particular country, bringing together scholars, national, state, and local government officials, and NGO representatives, to discuss strategies for addressing the needs of IDPs in the country. The Project workshops follow a simple format. First, the Project discusses the history and importance of the promulgation of the *Guiding Principles*, focusing on the way the *Guiding Principles* restate existent international norms and law. Then, the workshop turns to the participants to assist them in interpreting their own national legislation in light of the *Guiding Principles*. The workshops strive to show local leaders that they may not need new, IDP-specific legislation to explicitly protect IDPs. By focusing on primary protective instruments like constitutional provisions, eminent domain laws, and local tort laws, the participants see that their own laws likely prohibit mistreatment of IDPs and require state responsibility for their plight. Finally, where the participants discovered *bona fide* gaps between the *Guiding Principles* and the fabric of existent property, tort, criminal, and immigration law, the workshop will issue recommendations for legislative change or reform.

The Colombian example demonstrates how this model (combined with legislative reform under model one) can result in sound legal measures to protect and assist IDPs. After IDP Law 387 and the Presidential Decrees came into effect, several groups challenged them in Colombia's Constitutional Courts. The Court's decisions in SU-1150 (2000) and T-327 (2001) both suggest that the *Guiding Principles* be used to define the "parameter for any new legislation on displacement as well as for the interpretation of the existing IDP legislation, and the assistance to displaced persons."[135] The Constitutional Court "frequently used the UN *Guiding Principles* as a yardstick when commenting on national norms" in its T-327 decision.[136] The combination of hard legislation and judicial interpretation and support render a particularly strong approach to IDP law in Colombia.

In a workshop conducted by the Global IDP Project in Colombia, "participants were introduced to a group exercise aimed at comparing the coverage of the *Guiding Principles* to the content of the Colombian IDP legislation . . . making them search for the content of the *Guiding Principles* in Law 387 and Presidential Decree 173."[137] The report found that "the comparison between the *Guiding Principles* and the national legislation showed that almost all aspects of the Principles are covered by Colombian IDP legislation."[138]

In States without IDP-specific legislation, the workshops also seem successful. Many countries have laws providing relief for IDP issues that do not necessarily refer to IDPs as such.[139] "Both Ethiopia and Eritrea, for example, have comprehensive disaster-relief laws and programs that handle IDPs (as well as prevention of displacement) along with other vulnerable populations."[140] The challenge of the workshops is to help leaders at all levels of the government to see the IDP-specific issues that these more generic laws cover.

Workshops combined with a legal study helped identify both strengths and gaps in existing legislation on IDPs in the South Caucasus. In a regional workshop convened by the Brookings Institution Project on Internal Displacement, ODIHR, and the Norwegian Refugee Council in November 2000, members of the region's governments, NGOs, and international community representatives convened to assess the situation of internal displacement in the South Caucasus. The workshop facilitated spirited discussion on topics such as physical security, assistance, and the right to vote. Through the dialogue, several gaps between domestic law and the *Guiding Principles* emerged. For example, current Georgian legislation (as of then) did "not allow the displaced to register and vote in local or parliamentary elections without losing their IDP status and benefits. Consequently, many IDPs have lived in one locality for seven years without being able to vote."[141] A two-year study process ensued, culminating in reports and roundtables on national law compliance with the *Guiding Principles*. Some of the major issues addressed include citizenship rights, return or resettlement of the displaced, property restitution and compensation, education, employment, housing, and political participation. Recommendations include providing legal guarantees for the right of IDPs in Georgia to vote without penalty, the development in Armenia of a national law on IDPs, and the elaboration in Azerbaijan of separate laws on IDPs and refugees to clarify and better ensure the legal protection of both groups.[142]

The best solution is to combine the efforts of model one and two. Workshops can best advance the interpretation of existing law when sound legislation already exists. Without the training and guidance of a workshop approach, legislation is less likely to lead to effective implementation. Of course, without government resources and commitment to effectively implement sound law, the IDP protection gap cannot be addressed. Ensuring compliance with the newly enacted laws remains a challenge. Even though Colombia is the country with the most comprehensive and judicially advanced IDP laws,[143] the national government has not yet been able to implement the laws effectively.

Model Three: Outreach and Training of Non-State Actors

A third approach involves the Representative working directly with insurgent groups as well as NGOs. In his 2003 report, the Representative notes that the *"Guiding Principles* are also being acknowledged and used by non-state actors."[144]

The obvious reason for visiting the insurgent groups is to convince them to conduct their insurgencies with respect for the human rights and dignity of the IDPs who reside in areas controlled by them. While meeting with insurgents involves some challenges with regards to host governments, this can work well in certain situations. In his visit to Georgia in 2000, Mr. Deng met with de facto authorities in both South Ossetia and Abkhazia. In both of these instances, the leaders suggested that the *Guiding Principles* be translated into local languages and expressed support for using the *Guiding Principles* in their activities. In the course of meeting with authorities in the Philippines, the Representative also met with "representatives of the Moro Islamic Liberation Front (MLLF) and stressed the relevance of the Principles."[145]

In the Sudan, the Sudan People's Liberation Movement and Army (SPLM/A) currently is considering a draft policy on internal displacement based on the Principles. The policy had been drafted and presented to the Executive Director of the Sudan Relief and Rehabilitation Association, the relief wing of the SPLM/A, in September 2002 at a training workshop sponsored by the OCHA IDP Unit with the assistance and participation of the office of the Representative.[146] The Executive Director indicated at a follow-up seminar in Rumbek, Sudan, in November 2002 that he intended to formally present the draft policy to the SPLM/A leadership and hoped to have the policy adopted.[147]

With regards to NGOs, both humanitarian and human rights organizations can protect IDP populations by serving as watchdogs and advocates. The *Guiding Principles* give them specific and useful tools in defending the IDPs they serve. A particularly strong effort was made in Sri Lanka to educate, monitor, and advocate for IDPs in local civil society. The Consortium of Humanitarian Agencies (CHA), a group of more than fifty NGOs, has been conducting an outreach program based on the *Guiding Principles* for government officials, non-state actors, international organizations, international and national NGOs, and displaced communities. As part of these efforts, it published a "Toolkit" in 2001 on the *Guiding Principles* in English, Sinhala and Tamil, as well as a variety of other training materials for use in ongoing workshops and roundtables.[148] The "Toolkit" explains what rights IDPs have and what they should expect in the way of assistance and protection from national and other authorities. It emphasizes that IDPs are "resources," rather than "recipients," who can take steps to better protect themselves, their families, and their communities if empowered to do so.

As the peace process in Sri Lanka moved forward, CHA also produced a "Practitioner's Kit for Return, Resettlement, Rehabilitation and Development," wherein practitioners are provided with particular ways to address these complex issues in the context of the unique features of the protracted Sri Lankan conflict.[149] The "Kit" adapts international standards for voluntary, safe and sustainable returns to the Sri Lankan experience, providing the many steps needed to bring a successful end to displacement by 2006. It deals with land issues, property claims, minority protection, judicial systems, and the broad range of rights to which displaced persons and all other citizens are entitled.

Both the "Toolkit" and the "Practitioner's Kit" draw not only on the *Guiding Principles* themselves, but on other major documents that explain them or provide for their practical implementation, such as the *Handbook*, the "Modules on Internal Displacement" developed by the Norwegian Refugee Council and the Office of the UN High Commissioner for Human Rights, and the legal *Annotations* written by Walter Kalin. They serve as very useful models of how to translate the *Guiding Principles* into action.

While training insurgent groups and certain NGOs on treating the displaced in accordance with international standards has become quite challenging in the post-September 11 environment, this approach continues to be an important way to encourage respect for the rights of internally displaced persons.

CONCLUSION

International law today is insufficient to address the needs of the wide range of forced migrants seeking international assistance and protection. Two major problems exist. First, international law does not directly and comprehensively address the needs of two of the largest categories of forced migrants today: those fleeing conflict and the internally displaced. Specific measures, such as the *Guiding Principles on Internal Displacement* and the 1969 OAU Convention Governing the Specific Aspects of Refugee Problems in Africa have been significant but insufficient steps. Second, although refugees fleeing persecution are well protected by the 1951 Refugee Convention and its 1967 Protocol, developed states have recently implemented measures that have undermined the right of such refugees to seek asylum. These problems have left significant legal gaps in the ability of the international community to address the protection and assistance needs of forced migrants.

In order to increase legal protection and assistance for forced migrants, and in particular to address the major gaps identified above, a comprehensive set of tools is needed. We propose three steps to develop forced migration law comprehensively and from the ground up.

First, protections for refugees who are fleeing for grounds other than persecution need to be formalized in both national and regional law. These forced migrants need to be granted the right not to be returned to a country of harm, a protection that is fundamental for Convention refugees. Durable solutions for these forced migrants also need to be developed in order to avoid the often multi-year uncertain legal status faced by most non-Convention refugees today. Such durable solutions should be based upon a serious analysis of the situation the migrant has fled (such as the nature, intensity, and duration of conflict, as well as the nature of international diplomatic or military response), with different types of forced migrants requiring different levels of solutions. A refugee who has fled a multi-year conflict that shows no sign of resolution might thus be granted a different durable solution than a recent refugee from a conflict with significant international involvement to end the conflict that motivated flight. Finally, where systems of subsidiary protection are established, the Refugee Convention needs to be protected from derogations. To this end, migration law and asylum systems need to both be undertaken with a corps of professional decision makers, sound legal standards, accessible human rights and conflict information, and fair procedures. National and regional approaches based on the OAU Convention definition of a refugee are the best ways to ensure legal protection for the vast majority of today's refugees who flee conflict and other forms of serious harm. Efforts to develop a European law that protects civil war refugees should be strongly encouraged as long as such a law complements, rather than takes the place of, European asylum law.

Second, the three models discussed above that develop national legal frameworks for the protection and assistance of internally displaced persons deserve to be robustly promoted by the international community. In order to increase protections for the internally displaced, the *Guiding Principles* need to be disseminated and integrated into national and, where applicable, regional law. Such efforts should follow three processes concurrently: first, the introduction of national legislation to codify and formalize recognition of IDP rights, thus designating an accountability structure within the government and bringing the *Guiding Principles* to the level of enforceable law; second, work with national governments to illustrate to them how existent national laws, such as the constitution or any displacement policies, can be interpreted to protect IDPs; and third, outreach and training of non-state actors such as NGOs and armed insurgencies on the protection needs and rights of forced migrants in order to influence the groups that often have the closest contact with IDPs. This three-model process has already seen success in moving IDP law and policy forward in several countries with significant IDP populations. While a regional approach to protecting the internally displaced may develop in time, the national approach is the best way right now to advance a legal framework in the states where it is most sorely needed. Promoting the *Guiding Principles* to all levels of society is the only way to truly change the cultural, legal and political landscape of IDP law and policy in countries with significant internal displacement.

Third, states need to be deterred from denying or limiting the right of forced migrants to seek asylum. Several laws and policies can enable states to accomplish this task. First, the international community should find ways to get important refugee receiving states to become parties to the 1951 Refugee Convention and 1967 Protocol. States also need to develop fair and efficient asylum systems that use a professional corps of asylum adjudicators, follow fair and efficient processes, and encourage only forced and not economic migrants to apply for asylum. Time limits to applying for asylum should also be removed in order to avoid penalizing migrants who are often traumatized, ignorant of local law, and do not speak the local language. While there is no evidence that the imposition of time limits decreases abusive claims, such restrictions do limit the access of bona fide claimants to a decision on the merits. If an asylum system is fair and efficient, the imposition of time limits is not necessary to control abuse. Nations also need to address the causes of forced migration by *not* returning individuals to countries where they have a well-founded fear of persecution and by respecting the right to seek asylum. In addition, limited resources should not be wasted on expedited asylum procedures and restrictive detention policies. Finally, fair and effective legal proceedings can also be attained by measures such as providing representation to asylum seekers, an independent review of legal standards and the asylum process, the use of only sound safe third country and safe country of origin laws (or, alternately, their elimination), and the development of methods to protect refugees subject to visa, pre-clearance, and pre-inspection requirements. States and forced migrants will both benefit when asylum systems provide for meaningful access, are operated fairly and efficiently and minimize abuse. As the Refugee Convention specifies fundamental rights that should be available to all forced migrants, defending it from derogation is an essential component of the effort to protect forced migrants. Donors can play a role by encouraging all states to adopt and implement the safe placement of camps principle found in the OAU Refugee Convention, and by providing incentives for states to respect the rights to freedom of movement and livelihood found in the 1951 Refugee Convention.

Pursuing adherence to the international treaties and the development of national and regional laws and policies regarding the protection of all forced migrants is the most feasible way to accomplish for today's displaced what the 1951 Refugee Convention achieved for persecuted refugees more than a half century ago.

NOTES

1. United Nations High Commissioner for Refugees (UNHCR), *The State of the World's Refugees 2000: Fifty Years of Humanitarian Action* (New York: Oxford University Press, 2000), 17.

2. Annex to the Statute of the Office of the United Nations High Commissioner for Refugees, Chapter 1(5), General Assembly Resolution 428(V) of December 14, 1950.

3. UNHCR, *The State of the World's Refugees 2000*, 24.

4. According to the UN High Commissioner for Refugees, "There is no universally accepted definition of 'persecution,' and various attempts to formulate such a definition have met with little success. From Article 33 of the 1951 Convention, it may be inferred that a threat to life or freedom on account of race, religion, nationality, political opinion or membership of a particular social group is always persecution. Other serious violations of human rights—for the same reasons—would also constitute persecution." See UNHCR, *Handbook on Procedures and Criteria for Determining Refugee Status under the 1951 Convention and the 1967 Protocol relating to the Status of Refugees* (Geneva: UNHCR, January 1992), para. 51.

5. *UN Convention Relating to the Status of Refugees*, Art. 33(2), July 28, 1951.

6. United Nations Treaty Series (UNTS) No. 2545, Vol. 189, 137.

7. Nehemiah Robinson, *Convention Relating to the Status of Refugees: Its History, Contents and Interpretation* (New York: Institute of Jewish Affairs, 1953), 6.

8. Nehemiah Robinson, *Convention Relating to the Status of Refugees*, 6–7.

9. *UNGA Res. 1006 (ES-II)*, November 9, 1956.

10. UNHCR, *The State of the World's Refugees 2000*, 30–31.

11. Gil Loescher, *Beyond Charity: International Cooperation and the Global Refugee Crisis* (Oxford: Oxford University Press, 1996), 71–74. The 1950 Statute of the Office of the United Nations High Commissioner for Refugees had already extended the competence of the Office to refugees without any geographical or temporal limitations.

12. *UNGA Res. 1167 (XII)*, November 26, 1957. See generally Guy S. Goodwin-Gill, *The Refugee in International Law*, 2nd ed. (Oxford: Clarendon Press, 1998), 9–10.

13. *UNGA Res. 1286 (XIII)*, December 5, 1958. The General Assembly renewed this authorization for several years: *UNGA Res. 1389 (XVI)*, November 20, 1959; *UNGA Res. 1500 (XV)*, December 5, 1960; and *UNGA Res. 1672 (XVI)*, December 18, 1961.

14. *UNGA Res. 1671 (XVI)*, December 10, 1961.

15. UNHCR, *The State of the World's Refugees 2000*, 37, 44, 46–47.

16. UNHCR, *The State of the World's Refugees 2000*, 52.

17. UNHCR, *The State of the World's Refugees 2000*, 52–53.

18. UNTS No. 8791, Vol. 606, 267.

19. See Louise W. Holborn, *Refugees: A Problem of Our Time: The Work of the United Nations High Commissioner for Refugees, 1951–1972* (Metuchen, N.J.: Scarecrow Press, 1975).

20. James Hathaway, *The Law of Refugee Status* (Toronto: Butterworths, 1991), 10.

21. OAU, *Convention Governing the Specific Aspects of Refugee Problems in Africa*, UNTS No. 14, Vol. 691 (1969).

22. OAU, *Convention*.

23. UNHCR, *The State of the World's Refugees 2000*, 123.

24. Asian-African Legal Consultative Organization, *Asian-African Legal Consultative Organization Resolution 40/3*, New Delhi (June 24, 2001).

25. Susan Martin and Andrew I. Schoenholtz, "Temporary Protection: U.S. and European Responses to Mass Migration," in *Immigration Control and Human Rights*, ed. Kay Hailbronner and Eckart Klein (Heidelberg: C.F. Muller Verlag, 1999).

26. Goodwin-Gill, *The Refugee in International Law*, 199.

27. UNHCR, *Note on International Protection*, UN Document A/AC.96/815 (1993).

28. UNHCR Population Data Unit, Population and Geographic Data Section, *Asylum Applications in Industrialized Countries: 1980–1999* (November 2001), 2, 26, 53.

29. Martin and Schoenholtz, "Temporary Protection," 20–21.

30. Council of the European Union, "Council Directive 2001/55/EC of 20 July 2001 on minimum standards for giving temporary protection in the event of a mass influx of displaced persons and measures promoting a balance of efforts between Member states in receiving such persons and bearing the consequences thereof," *Official Journal of the European Communities* (2001): L 212/12.

31. "Council Directive 2001/55/EC of 20 July 2001," 8, 12–15.

32. "Council Directive 2001/55/EC of 20 July 2001," Article 17.

33. Walter Kalin, "Temporary Protection in the EC: Refugee Law, Human Rights and the Temptations of Pragmatism," *German Yearbook of International Law* 44 (2001): 202, 220.

34. UNHCR, *Asylum Applications Lodged in Industrialized Countries: Levels and Trends, 2000–2002* (Geneva: UNHCR Population Data Unit, 2003), Table 2.

35. UNHCR, *Asylum Applications*, Table 2.

36. See "Scoreboard to Review Progress on the Creation of an Area of 'Freedom, Security and Justice' in the European Union," http://www.ue2004.ie/templates/standard.asp?sNavlocator=4,20,304 (November 21, 2004).

37. Jane McAdam, *The European Union Proposal on Subsidiary Protection: An Analysis and Assessment*, Working Paper No. 74 (Geneva: UNHCR, December 2002), 9.

38. Commission of the European Communities, "Proposal for a Council Directive on minimum standards for the qualifications and status of third country nationals and stateless persons as refugees or as persons who otherwise need international protection," COM (2001) 510 final (Brussels, September 12, 2001), Article 15(c).

39. Council of the European Union, "Council Directive 2004/83/EC of 29 April 2004 on minimum standards for the qualification and status of third country nationals or stateless persons as refugees or as persons who otherwise need international protection and the content of the protection granted," *Offical Journal of the European Union*, Articles 2(e) and 15.

40. Susan Martin, Andrew I. Schoenholtz, and Deborah Waller Meyers, "Temporary Protection: Towards a New Regional and Domestic Framework," *Georgetown Immigration Law Journal* 12, no. 4 (1998).

41. Martin, Schoenholtz, and Waller Meyers, "Temporary Protection," 569–70.

42. Roberta Cohen and Francis Deng, *Masses in Flight—The Global Crisis of Internal Displacement* (Washington: The Brookings Institution, 1998), 29–30.

43. Goodwin-Gill, *The Refugee in International Law*, 181–82.

44. Martin, Schoenholtz, and Waller, "Temporary Protection."

45. U.S. Committee for Refugees, *World Refugee Survey 1997* (Washington: USCR, 1997).

46. U.S. Committee for Refugees, *World Refugee Survey 2002* (Washington: USCR, 2002).

47. See Norwegian Information Services, *Norwaves* No. 31, October 5, 1993: "The Norwegian Government has announced that as of 2 October it will require visas from Bosnian refugees entering Norway, as the last country in northern Europe to do so," http://www.norwaves.com/norwaves/Volume1_1993/v1nw31.html.

48. United States Embassy, Bogota, Colombia, "New Visa Requirement for Colombians Transiting the U.S. Enroute to Third Countries," (March 29, 2001), http://bogota.usembassy.gov/wwwsvt1e.shtml (November 29, 2004).

49. Council of the European Union, "Joint Position of October 25, 1996 on prefrontier assistance and training assignments," *Official Journal of the European Communities* (October 31, 1996): L 281.

50. John Morrison and Beth Crosland, *The Trafficking and Smuggling of Refugees: the End Game in European Asylum Policy?* Working Paper No. 30 (Geneva: UNHCR, April 2001), http://www.unhcr.ch/cgibin/texis/vtx/home/ opendoc.pdf?tbl= RESEARCHandid=3af66c9b4andpage=research.

51. United Kingdom Home Department, *Secure Borders, Safe Haven: Integration with Diversity in Modern Britain*, CM 5387, (February 2002): 92–93.

52. International Organization for Migration, *International Comparative Study of Migration Legislation and Practice*, (Dublin: Stationary Office, April 2002), 26–28.

53. Eileen Sullivan, Felinda Moltino, Ajay Khashu and Moira O'Neill, *Testing Community Supervision for the INS: An Evaluation of the Appearance Assistance Program: Volume 1* (New York: Vera Institute of Justice, August 2002).

54. Andrew Schoenholtz and Jonathan Jacobs, "The State of Asylum Representation: Ideas for Change," *Georgetown Immigration Law Journal* 16, No. 4 (2002).

55. Schoenholtz and Jacobs, "The State of Asylum Representation."

56. Susan Martin and Andrew I. Schoenholtz, "Asylum in Practice: Successes, Failures, and the Challenges Ahead," *Georgetown Immigration Law Journal* 14, No. 1 (2000): 602.

57. Martin and Schoenholtz, "Asylum in Practice," 602.

58. *Immigration and Nationality Act (INA)*, Section 235(b)(1)(B)(iii)(IV).

59. Martin and Schoenholtz, "Asylum in Practice," 603.

60. Headquarters Asylum Division, Office of Refugee, Asylum, and International Operations, United States Citizenship and Immigration Services, Department of Homeland Security, *Credible Fear Statistics, FY 2000–2003* (on file with the authors).

61. The information reported in this section comes from the following sources: Rosemary Byrne and Andrew Shacknove, "The Safe Country Notion in European Asylum Law," *Harvard Human Rights Journal* 9 (1996):185–228; Maryellen Fullerton, "Failing the Test: Germany Leads Europe in Dismantling Refugee Protection," *Texas International Law Journal* 36, No. 2 (2001): 231–75; Joanne van Selm, "Access to Procedures: 'Safe Third Countries,' 'Safe Countries of Origin,' and 'Time Limits,'" (Geneva: UNHCR Global Consultations on International Protection, 2001); U.S. Committee for Refugees, "At Fortress Europe's Moat: The 'Safe Third Country' Concept," (1997); Sabine Weidlich, "First Instance Asylum Proceedings in Europe: Do Bona Fide Refugees Find Protection?" *Georgetown Immigration Law Journal* 14, No. 3 (2000): 643–72.

62. *INA*, Section 235(b)(1)(B)(iii)(III).

63. *64 FR 56135* (October 18, 1999).

64. *67 FR 54878* (August 26, 2002); Human Rights First, "New Regulations Threaten to Turn Board of Immigration Appeals into Rubber Stamp," http://www.humanrightsfirst.org/media/2002_alerts/0828.html (November 21, 2004).

65. See, for example, European Council on Refugees and Exiles, "The Promise of Protection: Progress towards a European Asylum Policy since the Tampere Summit," (Brussels: European Council on Refugees and Exiles, November 2001).

66. See country profiles, Global IDP Project, http://www.idpproject.org/.

67. See country profiles, Global IDP Project, http://www.idpproject.org/.

68. Cohen and Deng, *Masses in Flight.*

69. Cohen and Deng, *Masses in Flight*, 74.

70. Cohen and Deng, *Masses in Flight*, 74–75.

71. Roberta Cohen, "Nowhere to Run, No Place to Hide," *Bulletin of the Atomic Scientists* 58, No. 6 (November 2002): 37–45.

72. U.S. Immigration and Naturalization Service, *Asylum Reform: 5 Years Later* (Washington: U.S. Immigration and Naturalization Service, 2000). This report provides much of the information discussed in this section.

73. See U.S. CIS Asylum Division, "Asylum by Nationality and Deadline FY 1999–2003," and "1 Year Deadline Rejections by Asylum Office FY 1998–2004" (on file with authors).

74. Council of the European Union, "Council Directive 2001/55/EC of 20 July 2001," L 212/12.

75. Sullivan et al., *Testing Community Supervision for the INS*, 29.

76. Sullivan et al., *Testing Community Supervision for the INS*, 31.

77. Sullivan et al., *Testing Community Supervision for the INS*, ii.

78. Sullivan et al., *Testing Community Supervision for the INS*, 1.

79. Sullivan et al., *Testing Community Supervision for the INS*, 3.

80. Felinda Mottino, "Moving Forward: The Role of Legal Counsel in Immigration Court" (New York: Vera Institute of Justice, 2000—on file with authors), 13–14. This report was based on research performed by Mottino on behalf of the Vera Institute of Justice but was not published. It is used here by permission of the author.

81. Schoenholtz and Jacobs, "The State of Asylum Representation."

82. Schoenholtz and Jacobs, "The State of Asylum Representation," 739–40.

83. Mottino, "Moving Forward," 47.

84. European Council on Refugees and Exiles, "Guidelines on Fair and Efficient Procedures for Determining Refugee Status" (Brussels: European Council on Refugees and Exiles, 1999).

85. See Schoenholtz and Jacobs, "The State of Asylum Representation," 749–64.

86. U.S. Department of Justice, Executive Office for Immigration Review, "Evaluation of the Rights Presentation" (Washington: Executive Office for Immigration Review, 1998).

87. See Stephen H. Legomsky, "An Asylum Seeker's Bill of Rights in a Non-Utopian World," *Georgetown Immigration Law Journal* 14 No. 3 (2000): 619, 622.

88. Legomsky, "An Asylum Seeker's Bill of Rights," 641.

89. EOIR Office of Planning and Analysis, *FY 2003 Statistical Year Book* (Washington: Executive Office of Immigration Review, 2004), Y1.

90. See, for example, EOIR Office of Planning and Analysis, *FY 2003 Statistical Year Book*, U1.

91. U.S. Commission on Immigration Reform, *Becoming an American: Immigration and Immigrant Policy* (Washington: U.S. Commission on Immigration Reform, 1997), 175–83.

92. Legomsky, "An Asylum Seeker's Bill of Rights," 628.

93. Legomsky, "An Asylum Seeker's Bill of Rights," 630.

94. 8 U.S.C. Sec. 1101(a)(42).

95. Susan F. Martin, "Global migration trends and asylum," UNHCR Working Paper No. 41, *Journal of Humanitarian Assistance* (2001): http://www.jha.ac/articles/u041.htm.

96. "In terms of sheer numbers, non-Convention 'refugees' fleeing civil wars, ethnic conflicts, and generalized violence in the Third World or in Eastern Europe are a bigger problem for the international community than Convention refugees. And they are not adequately protected by current international norms," Loescher, *Beyond Charity*, 6.

97. McAdam, *The European Union proposal on subsidiary protection*, 5.

98. Commission of the European Communities, "Proposal for a Council Directive on Minimum Standards," Preamble, 18.

99. European Council on Refugees and Exiles, "ECRE Information Note on the Council Directive 2004/83/EC of 29 April 2004 on minimum standards for the qualification of third country nationals and stateless persons as refugees or as persons who otherwise need international protection and the content of the protection granted" (Brussels: European Council on Refugees and Exiles, 2004), 4, 11–17.

100. McAdam, *The European Union proposal on subsidiary protection*, 7, 15, 23.

101. See Martin and Schoenholtz, "Asylum in Practice," 589; U.S. Immigration and Naturalization Service, *Asylum Reform: 5 Years Later*; Gregg A. Beyer, "Establishing the United States Asylum Officer Corps: A First Report," *International Journal of Refugee Law* 4, No. 4 (July 1992): 453; and Gregg A. Beyer, "Reforming Affirmative Asylum Processing in the United States: Challenges and Opportunities," *American University Journal of International Law* 9, No. 4 (November 1994): 50.

102. UNHCR, "States Parties to the 1951 Convention relating to the Status of Refugees and the 1967 Protocol," as of February 1, 2004, www.unhcr.ch (November 21, 2004); U.S. Committee for Refugees, *World Refugee Survey 2004*, (Washington: USCR, 2004): 16, Table 15.

103. See U.S. Committee for Refugees, *World Refugee Survey 2004*, 5, Table 4.

104. Goodwin-Gill, *The Refugee in International Law*, 167–69.

105. U.S. Committee for Refugees, *World Refugee Survey 2004*, 13, Table 10.

106. U.S. Committee for Refugees, *World Refugee Survey 2004*, 13, Table 10.

107. Human Rights Watch, "Tanzania: In the Name of Security—Forced Round-Ups of Refugees in Tanzania," Vol. 11, No. 4, (New York: HRW, July 1999), http://www.hrw.org/reports/1999/tanzania/index.htm#TopOfPage (April 22, 2004).

108. Guardian Unlimited, "A history of war in west Africa," http://www.guardian.co.uk/westafrica (March 10, 2003).

109. Fabienne Hara and Comfort Ero, International Crisis Group, "Ivory Coast on the brink," *Observer Online—Worldview Extra: Unseen Wars* (2002), http://www.crisisweb.org/home/index.cfm?id=2195andl=1 (November 22, 2004).

110. See UNHCR, *UNHCR Global Report 2002—Zambia* (Geneva: UNHCR, 2003), 267 (map with camp sites).

111. Joel Frushone, "Unevenly Applied, More Often Denied: Refugee Rights in Africa," *World Refugee Survey 2004* (Washington: U.S. Committee for Refugees, 2004), 77. The information on Burundian refugees in Tanzania reported in this paragraph comes from this article at pp. 77–79.

112. Frushone, "Unevenly Applied," 74–77. The information on Angolan refugees in Zambia reported in this paragraph comes from these pages of this article.

113. Merrill Smith, "Warehousing Refugees: A Denial of Rights, a Waste of Humanity," *World Refugee Survey 2004* (Washington: U.S. Committee for Refugees, 2004), 54.

114. UNHCR, "States Parties to the 1951 Convention."

115. United Nations ECOSOC, "Specific Groups and Individuals Mass Exoduses and Displaced Persons," Report of the Representative of the Secretary-General on Internally Displaced Persons, Francis M. Deng, UN Commission on Human Rights 59th Session (January 21, 2003): U.N. Doc. E/CN.4/2003/86, para. 69.

116. United Nations ECOSOC, "Specific Groups and Individuals Mass Exoduses," (January 21, 2003), par. 14.

117. Global IDP Project, "Workshop on the UN *Guiding Principles* on Internal Displacement and the National IDP Legislation in Colombia" (Geneva: Global IDP Project, May 15–17, 2001), 16. http://www.idpproject.org/training/reports/colombia_2001.pdf (November 22, 2004).

118. Global IDP Project, "Workshop on the UN *Guiding Principles*" (May 15–17, 2001).

119. Global IDP Project, "Workshop on the UN *Guiding Principles*" (May 15–17, 2001).

120. Global IDP Project, "Workshop on the UN *Guiding Principles*" (May 15–17, 2001).

121. Global IDP Project, "Workshop on the UN *Guiding Principles*" (May 15–17, 2001).

122. Global IDP Project, "Workshop on the UN *Guiding Principles*" (May 15–17, 2001).

123. UN ECOSOC, "Specific Groups and Individuals Mass Exoduses" (January 21, 2003), para. 23. A copy of an unofficial translation of the Angolan Government's decree is available on the Global IDP Project's website: http://www.db.idpproject.org/Sites/idpSurvey.nsf/AllDocWeb/AF137501A421FADDC1256A41003B2504/$file/Angolanormsdecree.pdf (November 21, 2004).

124. Andrea Lari, "Returning home to a normal life? The plight of Angola's internally displaced," African Security Analysis Programme Occasional Paper 85 (Pretoria: Institute for Security Studies, February 5, 2004) 9.

125. UN ECOSOC, "Specific Groups and Individuals Mass Exoduses and Displaced Persons," Report of the Representative of the Secretary-General on Internally Displaced Persons, Francis M. Deng, UN Commission on Human Rights, 60th Session (March 4, 2004): UN Document E/CN.4/2004/77, para. 17.

126. UN ECOSOC, "Specific Groups and Individuals Mass Exoduses" (March 4, 2004), para. 17.

127. UN ECOSOC, "Specific Groups and Individuals Mass Exoduses" (March 4, 2004), para. 17.

128. UN ECOSOC, "Specific Groups and Individuals Mass Exoduses" (March 4, 2004), para. 17.

129. UN ECOSOC, "Specific Groups and Individuals Mass Exoduses" (March 4, 2004), para. 17.

130. "Republic of Liberia Declaration of the Rights and Protection of Liberian Internally Displaced Persons (IDPs)," Declaration by Minister of Justice and Attorney General Lvely Kobbi Johnson, September 26, 2002.

131. Philippine National Disaster Coordinating Council, "Policy Guidelines on the Delivery of Basic Services to Displaced Children in Disaster Situations," *NDCC Circular* no. 14 (2002): 1, http://www.ocd.gov.ph/POLGUIDE.pdf (April 7, 2004).

132. Philippine National Disaster Coordinating Council, "Policy Guidelines," forward.

133. *National Framework for Relief, Rehabilitation and Reconciliation in Sri Lanka* (June 2002), 11.

134. UN ECOSOC, "Specific Groups and Individuals Mass Exoduses" (January 21, 2003), para. 23.

135. Constitutional Court Decision SU-1150 (August 2000), cited in: Global IDP Project, "Workshop on the UN *Guiding Principles* on Internal Displacement and the National IDP Legislation in Columbia" (May 15–17, 2001), 17.

136. Global IDP Project, "Workshop on the UN *Guiding Principles*" (May 15–17, 2001), 17.

137. Global IDP Project, "Workshop on the UN *Guiding Principles*" (May 15–17, 2001), 7.

138. Global IDP Project, "Workshop on the UN *Guiding Principles*" (May 15–17, 2001), 7.

139. Roberta Cohen, Walter Kalin and Erin Mooney, eds., *The Guiding Principles on Internal Displacement and the Law of the South Caucasus* (Washington: The American Society of International Law and the Brookings Institution-SAIS Project on Internal Displacement, 2003).

140. Brookings Institution-SAIS Project on Internal Displacement, "Conference on Internal Displacement in the IGAD Sub-Region: Report of the Experts Meeting," Khartoum, Sudan August 30–September 2, 2003 (Washington: Brookings Institution, 2003), 17, http://www.brookings.edu/dybdocroot/fp/projects/idp/conferences/IGAD/20030903.pdf.

141. Global IDP Project, "Workshop on the UN *Guiding Principles* on Internal Displacement," Borjomi, Georgia, November 13–15, 2000 (Geneva: Global IDP Project, 2000), 3, http://www.idpproject.org/training/reports/Borjomi_workshop_2000.pdf.

142. Cohen, Kalin, and Mooney, eds., *Guiding Principles*.

143. Global IDP Project, "Workshop on the UN *Guiding Principles* (May 15–17, 2001), 1.

144. UN ECOSOC, "Specific Groups and Individuals Mass Exoduses" (January 21, 2003), para. 28.

145. UN ECOSOC, "Specific Groups and Individuals Mass Exoduses" (January 21, 2003), para. 28.

146. UN ECOSOC, "Specific Groups and Individuals Mass Exoduses" (January 21, 2003), para. 28.

147. Brookings Institution-SAIS Project on Internal Displacement, The Representative of the United Nations Secretary-General on Internally Displaced Persons, and

The United Nations Children's Fund, "Seminar on Internal Displacement in Southern Sudan," Rumbek, Sudan, November 25, 2002 (Washington: Brookings Institution, 2002), 5–6.

148. Consortium of Humanitarian Agencies (CHA), "Guiding Principles on Internal Displacement: A Toolkit for Dissemination, Advocacy and Analysis—What You Can Do" (CHA: Colombo, Sri Lanka, 2001).

149. Consortium of Humanitarian Agencies and The Brookings-SAIS Project on Internal Displacement, "Practitioner's Kit for Return, Resettlement, Rehabilitation and Development" (CHA: Colombo, Sri Lanka, March 2004).

3

Evolving Institutional Responses

Toward a UN High Commissioner for Forced Migrants

INTRODUCTION

The current organizational system for protecting and assisting forced migrants has failed repeatedly to respond effectively to the full range of population displacements seen today. The system is fragmented and based on outmoded concepts about forced movements of people, with an elaborate organizational framework for refugees who cross international borders and makeshift, *ad hoc* institutional responses for other displaced persons. Moreover, coordination within and between the humanitarian relief organizations and other important actors involved in addressing crises resulting in displacement too often fails in its efforts to find coherent, consistent responses to crises. This chapter outlines the evolution of the current system, and makes recommendations for a fundamental rethinking of the organizational arrangements for refugees and displaced persons as well as more effective mechanisms for international, regional, and national coordination of humanitarian responses.

The chapter begins with a discussion of the agency that has the most explicit mandate for assisting and protecting forced migrants: the UN High Commissioner for Refugees. It then discusses the other actors in the system as well as efforts made during the past two decades to improve humanitarian responses, before turning to a detailed discussion of how the United Nations and the humanitarian "system" working to assist and protect forced migrants can be strengthened. It concludes with a proposal for the appointment of a UN High Commissioner for Forced Migrants who would assume responsibility for both refugees and internally displaced persons, with particular focus on those fleeing persecution and conflict.

INSTITUTIONAL ROLES AND RELATIONSHIPS

The UN High Commissioner for Refugees

The first High Commissioner for Refugees was the world famous Norwegian explorer Fridtjof Nansen.[1] The League of Nations appointed Mr. Nansen to negotiate the repatriation of Russian war prisoners.[2] The League limited the High Commissioner's mandate to cover Russian refugees only, although he was soon called upon to help other groups, particularly the Turks, Greeks, and Bulgarians caught up in the massive population exchanges and repatriations of the 1920s.[3] "For most of the interwar period, the international refugee regime ran on extremely limited *ad hoc* budgets, put together without benefit of long-range planning."[4] The League only provided administrative costs—expecting Mr. Nansen to solicit donations from host governments and individual states to cover the actual costs of refugee aid.[5] The most important result of Nansen's activities in these early years included the introduction of a passport system.[6] He persuaded fifty-one governments to recognize travel documents termed 'Nansen passports' for stateless Russians.[7] His passport system foreshadowed the current visa system still used today to track and manage migration.

Nansen died in 1930. The office he created proved unable to address the growing refugee problem precipitated by Nazi persecution and World War II. With little international support for resolving the refugee crisis, James McDonald, the High Commissioner for German Refugees resigned in 1936. The next High Commissioner, Sir Herbert Emerson, found his powers even more constrained, and with the outbreak of World War II, the international willingness and capacity to help would-be refugees declined still further.

The war saw the displacement of millions from conflict and repression. In 1943, the Allies established the United Nations Relief and Rehabilitation Agency to provide relief to those likely to flee the counter-offensive against the Axis powers. Following the war, the agency also assisted the displaced to return to their home countries. UNRRA spent more than $3.6 billion on relief and repatriation assistance until its closure in 1947.

By 1947, the Cold War had begun in earnest and the spreading influence of the Soviet Union in Eastern Europe raised questions about the viability of repatriation as a solution to the situation of refugees unwilling to return to Communist-dominated countries. The International Refugee Organization (IRO) succeeded UNRRA. The IRO was mandated to repatriate refugees, but the "political build-up to the Cold War tilted the balance instead toward resettlement of those who had valid objections to returning home."[8] Despite early success in finding resettlement opportunities for refugees, the IRO found itself with a growing population, with new refugee movements coming from the east, and reduced willingness of States to foot the relief bill.

The UN High Commissioner for Refugees (UNHCR) emerged from negotiations between the United States and most non-Communist European governments;[9] "the United States was tired of financing international refugee programs. With the expensive experiences of UNRRA and the IRO fresh in their minds, U.S. policy-makers were principally interested in limiting rather than expanding their financial and legal obligations to refugees."[10] The governments soon looked for another institutional model to succeed the IRO.

The original mandate of the UNHCR, under its 1950 Statute and the 1951 Convention Relating to the Status of Refugees, focused on protection, with particular concern for repatriation and resettlement, but not direct assistance to refugees. Chapter I of the Statute specifies:

The United Nations High Commissioner for Refugees, acting under the authority of the General Assembly, shall assume the function of providing international protection, under the auspices of the United Nations, to refugees who fall within the scope of the present Statute and of seeking permanent solutions for the problem of refugees by assisting Governments and, subject to the approval of the Governments concerned, private organizations to facilitate the voluntary repatriation of such refugees, or their assimilation within new national communities.

The Statute defined a refugee as:

Any person who, as a result of events occurring before January 1, 1951, and owing to well-founded fear of being persecuted for reasons of race, religion, nationality or political opinion, is outside the country of his nationality and is unable or, owing to such fear or for reasons other than personal convenience, is unwilling to avail himself of the protection of that country; or who, not having a nationality and being outside the country of his former habitual residence, is unable or, owing to such fear or for reasons other than personal convenience, is unwilling to return to it.

In addition, the UNHCR could exercise its mandate on behalf of refugees previously granted status under various international agreements and the IRO Constitution. The UNHCR could exercise its competence on behalf of other refugees under limited circumstances if no other UN body was providing assistance or protection.

The Statute also defined the circumstances under which UNHCR would no longer be mandated to protect refugees, generally because they had returned home, been resettled, or the circumstances that caused them to flee had changed and they could not "claim grounds other than those of personal convenience for continuing to refuse to return to that country." The Statute, as did the Convention adopted in 1951, also excluded from its protection persons undeserving of protection because of the serious crimes they had committed.

The Statute defined the ways in which the "High Commissioner shall provide for the protection of refugees falling under the competence of his Office by:

(a) Promoting the conclusion and ratification of international conventions for the protection of refugees, supervising their application, and proposing amendments thereto;
(b) Promoting through special agreements with Governments the execution of any measures calculated to improve the situation of refugees and to reduce the number requiring protection;
(c) Assisting governmental and private efforts to promote voluntary repatriation or assimilation within new national communities;
(d) Promoting the admission of refugees, not excluding those in the most destitute categories, to the territories of States;
(e) Endeavoring to obtain permission for refugees to transfer their assets and especially those necessary for their resettlement;
(f) Obtaining from Governments information concerning the number and conditions of refugees in their territories and the laws and regulations concerning them;
(g) Keeping in close touch with the Governments and intergovernmental organizations concerned;
(h) Establishing contact in such manner as he may think best with private organizations dealing with refugee questions;
(i) Facilitating the coordination of the efforts of private organizations concerned with the welfare of refugees.

Policy directives and advice within the UNHCR are primarily given by the Executive Committee (EXCOM).[11] The High Commissioner is elected by the UN General Assembly and submits annual reports to the Assembly through ECOSOC.[12] EXCOM is not a governing body, but "does fulfill a number of essential oversight/advisory functions."[13] These quasi-governing functions include:

(a) Approving the High Commissioner's assistance programs in an Annual Program Budget;
(b) Scrutinizing all financial and administrative aspects of the Office's work;

(c) Advising the High Commissioner on the discharge of his/her protection function.[14]

Originally, the executive committee represented only European nations, which caused the resistance to expansion and enlargement of the mandate. Over the years, the executive committee was enlarged. For example, "it was enlarged to fifty-eight members by General Assembly Resolution" in December 2000.[15]

UNHCR was established initially with a three-year mandate and limited funding. Over time, however, UNHCR has been called upon increasingly to provide assistance to persons under its mandate. Through a mechanism dubbed the 'extension of its good offices,'[16] the UNHCR responds to specific assignments from the General Assembly to reach beyond its mandate and assist other forced migrants who did not qualify for refugee status under the Convention.[17] The UN General Assembly eventually formalized the 'good offices' approach by resolution in 1959. It "authorize[d] the High Commissioner, in respect of refugees who do not come within the competence of the United Nations, to use his good offices in the transmission of contributions designed to provide assistance to these refugees."[18] This extension *allows* the UNHCR (with the General Assembly's blessing) to reach non-Convention migrants.[19] The process, however, remains *ad hoc*.[20]

Neither the 1951 refugee convention nor the statute creating UNHCR explicitly covers those who are internally displaced even if they would be refugees if they could cross an international boundary. From at least the 1970s, however, UNHCR has aided persons still within their home countries. Often, implementing programs for returning refugees prompted UNHCR to offer its good offices to the internally displaced as well. This was the case in southern Sudan in the early 1970s when UNHCR assisted about 180,000 returnees and about 500,000 internally displaced persons.[21] The UNHCR also assisted displaced people in Cyprus, in this case, acting as the Secretary General's Special Representative and Coordinator for United Nations Humanitarian Assistance for Cyprus.

Although UNHCR exercises its mandate on behalf of the internally displaced, the agency has considerable discretion in determining if and when to do so unless specifically requested by the General Assembly. The UNHCR itself noted the:

wide-ranging variations in terms of UNHCR's role in assisting and protecting internally displaced persons within comparable phases of conflict and displacement. These include, for example, variations from a one-time relief assistance package in Rwanda to around-the-clock engagement in Bosnia-Herzegovina; or from direct involvement with mixed populations of returnees and internally displaced in Sri Lanka to only very indirect involvement in a similar situation in Sierra Leone or in the Sudan.[22]

In March 2000, UNHCR issued a position paper clarifying its relationship to internally displaced persons. The agency makes clear its interest in this population arises from its humanitarian mandate on behalf of persons displaced by persecution, situations of general violence, conflict, or massive violations of human rights. This mandate places upon UNHCR "a responsibility to advocate on behalf of the internally displaced; mobilize support for them; strengthen its capacity to respond to their problems; and take the lead to protect and assist them in certain situations."[23] Stopping short of asserting an operational responsibility for all internally displaced persons, UNHCR set out six requirements for its involvement: "a request or authorization from the Secretary General or a competent principal organ of the UN; consent of the state concerned, and where applicable, other entities in a conflict; access to the affected population; adequate security for staff of UNHCR and implementing partners; clear lines of responsibility and accountability with the ability to intervene directly on protection matters; and adequate resources and capacity."[24]

The policy paper specifies that UNHCR will be ready to take the lead where its protection and solutions expertise is particularly relevant, or where involvement with the internally displaced is closely linked to the voluntary repatriation and reintegration of refugees. Recognition is given that the linkages between refugees and the internally displaced can be complicated: "Countries of asylum may be more inclined to maintain their asylum policies if something is done to alleviate the suffering of the internally displaced, reduce their compulsion to seek asylum and create conditions conducive to return. On the other hand, UNHCR's activities for the internally displaced may be (mis)interpreted as obviating the need for international protection and asylum."[25]

At present, a majority of internally displaced persons remain outside of UNHCR's mandate. Comparing statistics on "persons of concern to UNHCR" with statistics on the total number of refugees and displaced persons is illustrative. In 2003, for example, UNHCR estimated that about 20.6 million people fell within its mandate; about 11.4 million were refugees and asylum seekers, another 2.4 million were returnees, almost one million were stateless, and almost 6 million were internally displaced persons. At the same time, the Representative of the Secretary General on Internally Displaced Persons estimated a total internally displaced population that was four times as large.[26]

While the role of UNHCR regarding responses and solutions, at least to refugee crises, had evolved fully by the 1960s, its role with respect to prevention is more recent. As late as 1986, the report of a Group of Governmental Experts on International Cooperation to Avert New Flows of Refugees made no specific reference to UNHCR playing a role in this respect. By contrast, the report called upon the development organizations of the United Nations to give greater support to projects that directly or indirectly averted new flows of refugees. By the 1990s, however, UNHCR's participation in prevention activities had been established and the High Commissioner herself gave prominence to this role.

The UNHCR Executive Committee supported the emphasis given to prevention. Recognizing that the refugee experience is closely linked to the degree of respect by States for human rights and fundamental freedoms and the related refugee protection principles, the Executive Committee reaffirmed the importance of educational and other programs to combat racism, discrimination and xenophobia, to promote tolerance and respect for all persons and their human rights, to advance the rule of law and legal and judicial capacity-building, and to strengthen civil society and sustainable development.

Today, the UNHCR engages in large-scale assistance programming in addition to its traditional protection and solutions role. "The implementation of UNHCR's assistance projects is normally entrusted to an implementing partner, in accordance with the Statute of the Office."[27] Implementing partners are "usually specialized government departments or agencies, other members of the United Nations system, nongovernmental and intergovernmental organizations and, in some instances, private firms."[28] UNHCR out-sources much of its work to nongovernmental organizations who "[continue] to provide the most sustained and devoted services to the cause of refugees, returnees and other persons of concern."[29] In some instances, "UNHCR has no option but to provide direct assistance" by implementing refugee assistance itself.[30] This usually occurs in the "initial stages of an emergency involving a sudden influx of refugees, or in a repatriation operation where it is not possible to mobilize other agencies fast enough to respond to the needs of the refugees."[31]

Administrative costs and the costs of "certain core activities of the program are met from the UN's regular budget," which amounts to approximately $20 million per year.[32] "The material assistance programs (which cost close to $1 billion a year in 2002 and may go even higher when new emergencies involving refugees arise) are financed from voluntary contributions."[33] Currently, funding for operational aspects of UNHCR comes from voluntary donors. Until 1999, UNHCR programs "were divided into two broad categories of General Programs and Special Programs. Effective . . . January 1, 2000, all programs have been consolidated into a unified Annual Program Budget."[34] The unified budget aims to add transparency and continuity to the budget—giving donors a view of the 'big picture' in terms of UNHCR's comprehensive work in protection and assistance.[35] "The Annual Program Budget is made up of the following elements: Regional Programs . . . Global Programs . . . [and] Headquarters."[36] The total UNHCR budget amounts to nearly $1 billion—with only $20 million coming from the UN Regular Budget.[37] The remainder comes from voluntary contributions from governments and private donors.[38] The 2004 UNHCR Framework for Durable Solutions focuses on efforts to "empower refugees to end their dependence on humanitarian assistance . . . [which will hopefully attract] funding from development sources."[39]

The budget is normally divided into two large groups: the Annual Program Budget and the Supplementary Programs.[40] Supplementary programs "represent those activities that arise after the approval of the Annual Program Budget and before the approval of the next Annual Program Budget, and which cannot be fully funded from the Operational Reserve."[41] Special earmarked funds from special appeals fund these programs.[42] The 2004 budget grew considerably because several large supplementary programs from 2003 became part of the Annual Program Budget for 2004.[43] The bulk of funds are obtained each December at the annual pledging conference, held in Geneva.[44] As with other organizations, earmarked funds represent the largest funding challenge to the efforts of UNHCR. As discussed in greater detail in chapter 4, when donors limit the use of funds, some important (but unpopular) programs suffer—despite their high priority nature.[45]

Other Humanitarian Actors

While UNHCR has had principal responsibility for forced migrants, other humanitarian agencies play an important role, particularly the International Committee of the Red Cross (ICRC), and the International Organization for Migration (IOM). These organizations are international bodies with independent mandates though they maintain close working relations with the United Nations. The discussion continues with first three new sets of international actors, drawn from the human rights, development and military communities, which have growing involvement in complex humanitarian emergencies, and second institutions at the regional, national, and nongovernmental levels, including forced migrants themselves.

International Committee of the Red Cross

The mandate of the International Committee of the Red Cross (ICRC) covers some but not all forced migrants. ICRC predates the United Nations, having been founded in 1863. It is an "impartial, neutral and independent organization whose exclusively humanitarian mission is to protect the lives and dignity of victims of war and internal violence and to provide them with assistance." It directs and coordinates international relief activities in situations of conflict; promotes adherence to humanitarian law and universal humanitarian principles. ICRC has also served as a neutral arbiter during negotiations for ceasefires and end to hostilities.

ICRC's activities derive from the 1949 Geneva Conventions and Protocols, the principal instruments of humanitarian law. Since most conflicts today are within States, Article 3 common to the four Geneva Conventions is particularly pertinent. It prohibits a range of actions against civilian populations, including violence to life and person, cruel treatment and torture, taking of hostages, and outrages upon personal dignity, in particular, humiliating and degrading treatment. Civilians benefit from this protection as long as they do not take a direct part in hostilities. The displacement of the civilian population may only be ordered if its safety or imperative military reasons require it, and only after all possible measures have been taken to ensure it will be received under satisfactory conditions.

The Geneva Conventions and, by extension, the work of ICRC applies to all civilians affected by conflict, not just to those displaced by it. Some ICRC staff question whether internally displaced persons should receive special attention or be treated equally with other war-affected populations. Marguerite Contat Hickel, for example, fears that an office devoted specifically to internally displaced persons might "reinforce the 'discriminatory' nature of the approach because of the specific mechanisms set up to respond to the needs of a single category."[46] Such concerns underestimate the special problems arising from displacement itself. Moreover, the Geneva Conventions do not serve as vehicles for protection of individuals fleeing their home communities because of other life-threatening situations. Where civil strife or repression creates displacement, but does not rise to the level of armed conflict, ICRC's mandate and the applicability of the Geneva Conventions are limited.

International Organization for Migration

The International Organization for Migration (IOM) plays an increasingly important role in addressing issues arising from forced migration. IOM is involved in all phases of complex forced migration emergencies, providing technical and operational expertise in such areas as transportation, health, and other services for migrants. In particular, IOM's work in post-conflict societies aims to facilitate return and reintegration of affected populations, accelerate restoration to normalcy, avoid further mass outflow of people, empower key local authorities in the management of local resources to reconstruct the social structure, and help create an atmosphere of peace, reconciliation and trust so that national experts and professionals living outside the country may return and help in the overall reconstruction of the country. Typical projects include assistance to vulnerable returnees, including elderly, women and children, reinsertion of demobilized combatants, registration of returnees, tracing and family reunification, migration information and referral services, and support for microeconomic development activities for affected communities. IOM does not, however, have a mandate for protection of forced migrants and generally acts only at the request of the United Nations or a national government.

UN Office for the Coordination of Humanitarian Affairs

The UN Office for the Coordination of Humanitarian Affairs (OCHA) was created in 1997 to replace the Department of Humanitarian Affairs (DHA). An Under-Secretary General for Humanitarian Affairs who is also the Emergency Relief Coordinator (ERC) heads OCHA. As ERC, the head of OCHA is responsible for coordinating humanitarian agencies, which is largely achieved by chairmanship of the Interagency Standing Committee, which brings together all major humanitarian, development and human rights bodies. The Under Secretary is also the Secretary General's principal adviser on humanitarian issues and provides an important interface between the humanitarian community and the intergovernmental organs of the United Nations. This is achieved by the Under Secretary's functions as the Convener of the Executive Committee for Humanitarian Affairs (ECHA) and through the chairmanship of the IASC. The ECHA provides a forum for the humanitarian community and the political and peacekeeping departments to discuss humanitarian crises and issues. Resident in-country humanitarian coordinators all report directly to the Emergency Relief Coordinator.

An important function of the OCHA is that of ensuring that humanitarian issues that fall into the lacunae between existing institutional mandates are addressed. The ERC is, for example, responsible for coordinating the protection of internally displaced persons. OCHA has established a unit with special responsibility for internally displaced persons. The unit has been in operation only since January 2000. It came into being largely because of persistent criticism within and outside of the United Nations concerning gaps in responses to IDPs. The unit is small, nonoperational, and composed of staff largely drawn from other UN agencies; the Unit's terms of reference set out the following activities: promotion and support of advocacy efforts, monitoring of situations of internal displacement in order to identify operational gaps in the responses to internal displacement; provision of training, guidance and expertise to Resident and Humanitarian Coordinators, UN Country Teams and humanitarian organizations on IDP-related issues, and the formulation of strategies to address the protection, humanitarian and durable development needs of IDPs; development of necessary linkages between the humanitarian response to internal displacement and the security, political and development spheres of activity; mobilization of the resources needed to assist IDPs; and further development of interagency policies on IDP issues. The IDP unit works with the Representative of the Secretary General on Internally Displaced Persons to promote the operational application of the *Guiding Principles on Internal Displacement.* See below for evaluation of the role of this office.

Another key role of OCHA is the development of consolidated funding appeals. Under DHA, the UN began to issue consolidated appeals for each emergency, with all of the UN agencies presenting their requests. In a new development, in December 1998, United Nations Consolidated Appeals for Emergencies were jointly launched under the auspices of OCHA. In 2002, the Consolidated Appeals Process (CAP) issued nineteen appeals for individual and regional emergencies. Almost all appeal countries are in the midst of conflict situations or in the immediate post-conflict phase of rehabilitation, reconstruction and reconciliation, and many of the beneficiaries are uprooted people. By simultaneously requesting funds for the principal emergency situations throughout the world, this approach "seeks to provide an enhanced strategic overview and establish the operational goals and activities of the international humanitarian community." Recognizing that the consolidated appeals process takes time to assemble, the United Nations may draw upon an emergency fund in the interim.

Office of the High Commissioner for Human Rights

A newer UN player regarding forced migration issues is the Office of the High Commissioner for Human Rights (OHCHR) OHCHR intersects with forced migrant issues through its monitoring activities and its field-level operations to promote the rights and safety of refugees and displaced persons. The Office also supports the mandates of the Representative of the Secretary General on Internally Displaced Persons and Special Rapporteurs of the Sub-Commission on such related issues as population transfers, freedom of movement and forced evictions.

OHCHR has field presence in numerous countries affected by forced migration, including Burundi, Angola, the Democratic Republic of Congo, Georgia (Abkhazia), Bosnia and Herzegovina, Croatia, the Federal Republic of Yugoslavia, the Former Yugoslav Republic of Macedonia, Colombia, Gaza (Occupied Territories/Palestine), and Cambodia. These field operations in theory could potentially allow for greater monitoring of the rights of returnees and displaced persons. They also support the ability of the country and thematic special rapporteurs, where applicable, to monitor and report on the situation of refugees and displaced persons. A manual on human rights monitoring being developed by OHCHR includes chapters on monitoring in camps of refugees and displaced persons and during the return process.

OHCHR supports the work of the Representative of the Secretary General for Internally Displaced Persons. Appointed in 1992 at the request of the UN Commission on Human Rights, the Representative has a mandate to monitor displacement problems worldwide, undertake country missions, establish dialogues with governments, develop an international legal framework, promote effective institutional arrangements at the international and regional levels, identify preventive and protection strategies, focus attention on the needs of internally displaced women and children, and publish reports and studies in an effort to increase international awareness of the problem. The most noted product of this work is a set of *Guiding Principles on Internal Displacement* that are rooted in existing international human rights, humanitarian, and, by extension, refugee law. Although they do not themselves have the standing of an international convention, the *Guiding Principles* are gaining wide recognition as a framework for increasing the protection of internally displaced persons.

Since 1992, the Representative has engaged in dialogue with governments and human rights, humanitarian and development agencies to raise awareness of the global problem of internal displacement. He has visited twenty-six countries with serious problems of internal displacement, published reports on these situations, and made recommendations for improving the conditions of the displaced. His visits have often mobilized public attention at the national level to the needs of internally displaced persons and in certain cases spurred the creation of mechanisms and institutions to deal with the problem at that end.

The Representative also has launched a series of workshops on internal displacement aimed at improving understanding of the problems confronting internally displaced persons on the ground, and of the strategies needed at the national, regional, and international levels to help address their plight. More specifically, the workshops have facilitated valuable discussion on the promotion and dissemination of the *Guiding Principles*, stimulated steps by regional organizations to integrate internal displacement into their programs, and encouraged civil society to undertake projects on behalf of the displaced.

Other UN Agencies

Other UN agencies also play a role in assisting forced migrants. The United Nations Children's Fund (UNICEF) Executive Board reaffirmed in 1992 that UNICEF should "continue providing emergency assistance to refugee and displaced women and children, particularly those living in areas affected by armed conflict and natural disasters." The work of UNICEF on behalf of displaced populations is grounded in such human rights instruments as the Conventions on the Rights of the Child and the Convention on the Elimination of All Forms of Discrimination against Women.

The United Nations Development Program (UNDP)'s mission is "to help countries in their efforts to achieve sustainable human development by assisting them to build their capacity to design and carry out development programs in poverty eradication, employment creation, and sustainable livelihoods, the empowerment of women and the protection and regeneration of the environment, giving first priority to poverty eradication." UNDP describes itself as having three key roles in reference to mass exoduses: prevention, coping, and recovery. UNDP's special program initiatives seek to attenuate circumstances that may promote flight, for example, through promoting a small arms reduction program in Albania and by supporting preventive diplomacy in the Central African Republic. UNDP works to sustain development during crises and to rekindle development initiatives at the earliest opportunity, through joint planning and implementation with UNHCR and other agencies. However, disparate funding strategies of donors and other factors continue to foster artificial gaps in international assistance that impede a swift transition from relief to development.

The mission of the World Food Program (WFP) is "to provide food aid: to save lives in refugee and other emergency situations; to improve the nutrition and quality of life of the most vulnerable people at critical times in their lives; and to help build assets and promote the self-reliance of poor people and communities, particularly through labor-intensive works programs." Emphasizing that access to adequate food is a basic human right, WFP follows a threefold strategy in situations of forced migration. First, with respect to advance planning for potential emergencies, activities include vulnerability analysis and mapping, contingency planning and assessment of logistical capacities and intervention options. Second, WFP has strengthened its efforts with respect to the inputs required for immediate response to large-scale population movements and other types of humanitarian emergencies. Third, to improve emergency management, WFP has taken steps to decentralize its operations through increased delegation of authority to the field.

UN authorized peacekeeping operations, supervised by the Department of Peacekeeping Operations (DPKO) play a role in assisting and protecting forced migrants. Some peacekeeping operations have a specific mandate to protect displaced persons, as in Rwanda and the former Yugoslavia, and/or are mandated to protect the delivery of humanitarian assistance by UN agencies and other organizations, as in Somalia and former Yugoslavia. Others (like UNIFIL in southern Lebanon) have provided limited humanitarian assistance (help in medical emergencies, dealing with injury and damage caused by fighting and/or natural disasters) to people in the area they cover, although this was not specifically part of their mandate. Mine clearance is another important function performed by peacekeepers.

Other Organizations

International organizations are by no means the only actors involved in assistance and protection of forced migrants. Regional intergovernmental organizations sometimes play important roles.[47] The Organization of African Unity (OAU) adopted its own convention that broadens significantly the definition of a refugee to include not only those fearing persecution but also those fleeing other dangerous situations. Subregional bodies, such as the Economic Community of West African States (ECOWAS), also become involved; in Liberia and Sierra Leone, ECOWAS deployed the Economic Community Monitoring Group (ECOMOG) to serve as a peacekeeping force and ensure delivery of humanitarian assistance. In the Americas, the Cartegena Agreement, though without the force of a treaty, mirrors the broadened definition of a refugee found in the OAU Convention. The Inter-American Commission on Human Rights has taken the lead regarding internally displaced persons, appointing a special rapporteur, a voluntary position that marks the first such appointment at the regional level. In 2002, the Council of Europe appointed a special rapporteur on internal displacement in Europe. The Organization for Security and Cooperation in Europe (OSCE) also focuses on forced migration, for example as a cosponsor of the conference on refugees, displaced persons and other forms of involuntary displacement in the Commonwealth of Independent States (CIS) and meetings in the South Caucasus on forced internal migration. The OSCE has also disseminated the *Guiding Principles on Internal Displacement*.

No less important are national governments and, in certain situations, insurgencies. The *Guiding Principles on Internal Displacement* spell out the responsibilities of governments and insurgencies in these situations. National governments have the principal responsibility for assisting and protecting persons forced to leave their homes because of conflict, natural disasters, and other reasons, but major gaps remain in their ability and willingness to carry out these activities. Some forced migrants are under the control of insurgencies that effectively control the territory in which the forced migrant resides, but the same problems arise in ensuring that they meet their responsibilities. National governments also play important roles with respect to refugees and returnees. Although the UNHCR has a special mandate regarding refugees precisely because they are without the protection of their own governments, international law makes clear that countries of asylum have obligations as well. In reality, assistance and protection, including physical security, is offered by government agencies, military and police forces of the receiving state. Similarly, national governments offer important services to refugees who return to their home countries. Provincial and municipal governments generally augment the work of the national authorities in all of these cases of forced migration.

Nongovernmental organizations (NGOs) are the backbone of the humanitarian system for assisting and, to a lesser degree, protecting forced migrants. As partners with UNHCR and other international organizations, international and local NGOs provide a wide array of services including food delivery, health and mental health care, sanitation, shelter, nutrition, education and training, income generation programs, and social services. In providing the principal staffing at the field level, NGOs offer protection by their very presence. While relief-oriented NGOs are most prevalent in working with forced migrants, development and human rights agencies also are present, mirroring the work of their counterparts in the United Nations. The involvement of development NGOs is particularly seen in dealing with forced migration in the post-conflict period.

The final actors in the humanitarian system are the forced migrants themselves. In thinking about humanitarian issues, there is a tendency to see refugees and other displaced populations as victims, rather than active participants in the humanitarian system. Although the forced migrants may, in fact, have been the subjects of armed attacks, rapes and other violence, and human rights abuses, it is a mistake to underestimate their capacity for self-assistance or the role that they play in determining their own future. Yet, mechanisms to elicit the participation of forced migrants in the decision-making process are generally inadequate. For example, forced migrants tend to be excluded from interagency coordination groups of international organizations, governments, and nongovernment agencies.

Efforts to Coordinate Responses

As this review of mandates indicates, a number of international organizations with differing mandates take part in humanitarian operations. The impetus for recent reforms of the international regime for handling complex migration emergencies stemmed from frustration about the UN's *ad hoc*, slow responses to several crises during the late 1970s and 1980s. Within rapid succession, the United Nations was faced with massive population movements in Southeast Asia, the horn of Africa and Afghanistan. Coordination problems plagued responses in many of these situations.

The UN has put in place somewhat different organizational responses to address coordination problems. They fall into three principal categories: (1) designation of responsible lead agencies or operations; (2) regional coordination approaches; and (3) system-wide coordination efforts. These three approaches are not mutually exclusive. In many crises, all three approaches overlap.

Lead Agency/Operation

The United Nations has designated lead agencies to assist (and sometimes protect) specific categories of forced migrants, often, as discussed below, dividing organizational responsibility for refugees and those remaining within their home country. In some cases, an existing organization was given the lead for those in-country whereas in other cases, new semi-autonomous operations were created to take on the responsibility. More recently, the UN has designated a single lead agency to assist and/or protect all forced migrants in specified geographic locations. The experience with lead agencies has a lengthy history. The brief review that follows focuses on three major emergencies drawn from three different decades: Bangladesh, Cambodia and Bosnia.

Bangladesh

Displacement within and from east Pakistan in the years leading up to the establishment of Bangladesh set the pattern for dual lead agencies, UNHCR for refugees and another designated lead for those remaining within the home country. As movements escalated, in April 1971, the Secretary General designated the UNHCR to be the Focal Point for all UN activities on behalf of refugees from East Pakistan in India, who eventually numbered in excess of nine million persons. UNHCR coordinated with UNICEF, WFP and the World Health Organization and they set up a unified funding appeal. In the near term, emergency operations took precedence, but UNHCR emphasized that it would also seek longer-term solutions to the crisis.

In June 1971, the Secretary General established a counterpart UN East Pakistan Relief Operation (UNEPRO) to coordinate humanitarian assistance to the internally displaced and others requiring international aid. The Secretary

General made clear that the UNHCR and UNEPRO operations were distinct, but he noted that with repatriation, the two would become more intertwined. The terms of reference for UNEPRO were spelled out in a letter from the Secretary General to the government of Pakistan, which agreed to its presence. Interestingly, the Secretary General, using his good offices under the UN Charter, established both the Focal Point and UNEPRO prior to any General Assembly resolution. It was not until December 1971 that the General Assembly adopted Resolution 2790 endorsing the humanitarian operations. By then, conflict had broken out between Pakistan and India, necessitating the withdrawal of most UNEPRO staff. The Secretary General kept a small contingent in Dacca, however, so that the United Nations would be in a position to resume humanitarian operations when conditions permitted.[48]

Fearing the humanitarian consequences of the conflict, the Secretary General also appointed a Special Representative to seek a solution to the growing crisis. The Special Representative shuttled between Delhi, Islamabad and Dacca, focusing in particular on concerns about minorities in the seceding territory and the ability of Bengalis in Pakistan to move to the newly constituted Bangladesh. These activities paved the way for the eventual repatriation of the nine million refugees from India.

Thai-Cambodian Border

Divided responsibilities for refugees and other affected populations persisted in addressing the crisis in Southeast Asia at the end of the decade. In Thailand, UNHCR assumed responsibility for assisting and protecting Vietnamese and Laotian refugees and worked with third countries to guarantee resettlement. With regard to Cambodians, however, more complicated organizational arrangements developed. Thailand permitted about 150,000 Cambodians who arrived in Thailand before January 24, 1980, to enter UNHCR administered camps. The remaining 750,000 Cambodians who massed along the border were consigned to an essential no-man's zone. They did not receive designation as refugees and UNHCR did not request or gain access to them. Rather, UNICEF and ICRC, designated the Joint Mission by the Thai government, assumed responsibility for food distribution, medical care, and other assistance to the border population. At the same time, the Joint Mission was responsible for relief aid inside Cambodia.

At the end of 1981, when about 250,000 Cambodians remained in border encampments, UNICEF turned over its responsibilities to the World Food Program. The UN Border Relief Operation (UNBRO), directed by the UN Resident Representative in Bangkok who also served as the WFP representative, was established to assist the border population. Through the next decade,

UNBRO operated the displaced persons camps, even after a series of Vietnamese attacks prompted the movement of the camps onto what was clearly Thai territory. It was not until the withdrawal of Vietnamese troops and the signing of peace accords that responsibility for the displaced populations was consolidated, with UNHCR taking the lead in assisting the repatriation of the border population to whom it had previously had no access.

The decision to divide responsibility reflected deep-seated political considerations in addition to differences of view as to the best way to manage the emergency. The border camps were highly militarized, closely allied with the resistance forces, including the Khmer Rouge, that were fighting the Vietnamese installed government in Cambodia. The UNHCR early on set out the conditions under which it would assume responsibility for the camps: that the camps be moved away from the border, be demilitarized, and UN access be unrestricted. A senior UNHCR official later said that the agency laid out these conditions because they did not want to assume responsibility for the border population, many of whom were still under the dominance of the Khmer Rouge.[49] Major donor governments shared a reluctance to give UNHCR the responsibility, not only because of an interest in maintaining the Cambodian resistance but also because of concerns about UNHCR's capabilities. The U.S. Ambassador to Thailand wrote:

> UNHCR had a mentality which saw itself as a small agency providing protection against *refoulement*, staffed by people who had been working for thirty years on European problems and were totally unprepared for this new thing . . . handling large emergencies.[50]

By contrast, UNICEF and ICRC initially assumed an activist stance. As the Joint Mission, they pledged to provide assistance in a neutral and impartial manner, both cross border from Thailand to the displaced population along the border and through the Phnom Penh government to Cambodians in the interior.

The operational arrangements had both strengths and weaknesses. The Joint Mission succeeded in getting substantial amounts of food into a starving Cambodia, in part because it was operating on both sides of the border. As one analysis held:

> Had one set of organisations attempted to administer the border program while another set administered the Phnom Penh program, the Vietnamese might have simply closed access to the border completely. The Phnom Penh authorities might have refused to allow a program to begin through Phnom Penh. By coordinating both programs, the Joint Mission kept the negotiation process going.[51]

These same analysts, however, questioned whether both programs "might have been freer to develop more adequate responses to their particular problems if different organizations had run the two channels." They concluded, though, that even in retrospect the actual effects were difficult to deduce.[52]

The longer-term consequences of designating the border Cambodians as displaced persons rather than refugees were significant although it is unclear that UNHCR would have succeeded in enhancing their protection had it had lead responsibility. The major problem was one of security. . . . During the decade of displacement, regardless of which side of the border they were technically based, the border Cambodians remained at significant security risk. The camps themselves were unsafe. Although UNBRO tried to separate civilians and military units, the camps were heavily militarized with arms flowing within them.[53] Rape, robbery, and other crimes of violence were reported every day. Vietnamese troops, as well as rival Cambodian factions, frequently attacked the camps and forced them to relocate. The military factions that controlled the camps prevented the civilian population from leaving the camps to return to their homes or seek asylum elsewhere. At the same time, forced recruitment into the military occurred routinely.

There was little, if any, political will to demilitarize the camps or to move the civilians to a more secure environment. Although some efforts were made to separate civilians from military, and to distribute relief in a manner that would reduce the likelihood it would be diverted to military hands, the essential character of the border camps as resistance centers remained in tact. The only innovation to enhance security was the introduction of private security forces hired by UNBRO to identify ways to reduce crime within the camps. Its report led to various reforms, including replacement of Thai military forces with a civilian security force known as the Displaced Persons Protection Unit, establishment of a Cambodian police force, and education and training programs.

Bosnia

Responding to displacement within and from the former Yugoslavia, the United Nations broke this pattern of divided responsibility. The Secretary General assigned UNHCR lead agency responsibility for refugees and internally displaced persons, recognizing that UNHCR already had a sizeable presence in all of the republics of the former Yugoslavia. Under this mandate, UNHCR was to operate not only in safe countries of refuge but also in the midst of conflict and ethnic cleansing. In keeping with its broad role, the UNHCR proposed the 'Comprehensive Response to the Humanitarian Crisis in the Former Yugoslavia' that was adopted in July 1992. The plan included respect for human rights and humanitarian law, preventive protection, humanitarian access to those in need, measures to meet special humanitarian needs, temporary protection measures, material assistance, and return and rehabilitation.[54]

UNHCR interpreted its lead agency responsibility broadly to include "prime responsibility for logistics/transport, food monitoring, domestic needs, shelter, community services, health, emergency transition activities in agriculture and income generation, protection/legal assistance, and assistance to other agencies in sectors under their responsibility."[55] Coordination responsibilities involved policy-making, the dissemination of information, allocating tasks according to sectoral expertise, coordinating field activities, acting as an interface between the other UN agencies, NGOs, UNPROFOR, the European Commission's Humanitarian Office, NATO, and the military and political representatives of the belligerents.[56] At the height of the crisis, more than 250 international humanitarian organizations operated under UNHCR coordination, with ICRC the only major agency operating independently.

Not surprisingly the agency was criticized for spreading its capacities too thinly and for succumbing to foreseeable conflicts in its mission to protect refugees, on the one hand, and aid those still entrapped in their home country, on the other. By spring 1992 the UNHCR found itself operating, for the first time in a war situation where it had to make heart-wrenching decisions between facilitating people's departure from life-threatening circumstances and being in effect, an accomplice to the invidious war objective of ethnic cleansing. UNHCR eventually took a compromise position:

> During the early stages of the war in 1993, UNHCR was involved in carrying out a mass evacuation of residents from Srebrenica. However, this led to heavy criticism that UNHCR was assisting ethnic cleansing, and as a result, both UNHCR and ICRC adopted policies (also followed by UNPROFOR) of only assisting with mass evacuations in special "emergency" cases.[57]

As the agency increased its efforts regarding internally displaced persons, UNHCR had to change its approach, which was "reactive, exile-oriented and refugee-specific, to one that was proactive, homeland-oriented, and holistic."[58] In the former Yugoslavia this initially took the shape of in-country preventive protection. Although not necessarily a new role for UNHCR, which had a long history of responding to internal displacement,[59] the agency clearly saw itself as moving into new territory.

Commentators who regarded this new emphasis on in-country solutions as an unacceptable politicization of the agency's activities criticized the shift.[60] Concern was evinced that the agency was bowing to the demands of its donor states, which wished to contain any imminent flow of refugees at the expense of potential asylum-seekers. As one author described the response in Bosnia, as well as Iraq, Somalia and Rwanda, "UN-backed interventions regarding displaced civilians were primarily about deterring, sometimes preventing them from escaping places of conflict."[61] This characterization ignores the hundreds of thousands of Bosnians who were accorded temporary protection in Europe, as well as the myriad reasons that people become internally displaced even when borders remain relatively open for escape.

Even more seriously for those who were internally displaced, there were practical problems with attempting to provide protection inside a country at war. Attacks on the safe havens established in Srebrenica and elsewhere were merely the most egregious violations of the safety of those under UNHCR mandate. Compromising its effectiveness, UNHCR became identified with and shared the blame for mishaps by any of the agencies operating under its umbrella as lead agency. As UNHCR itself observed, "The coordination of humanitarian efforts with political and military actions in refugee-producing conflicts is not without its difficulties. . . . It blurs traditionally distinct roles and, if mismanaged, could compromise the strictly neutral character of humanitarian aid, which is the best guarantee of access to people in need."[62]

As the Bosnian operation grew, and negotiating humanitarian access with the warring parties grew in complexity, UNHCR granted licenses and identification cards to an increasingly diverse array of organizations. In some cases, UNHCR gave identification documents to donor government officials representing countries that the Serbs, in particular, saw as biased in favor of the Bosnian Federation. UNHCR itself was perceived as hostile when it openly criticized one side or the other for human rights violations against refugees and internally displaced persons.

The relationship with UNPROFOR was particularly noteworthy, given the peacekeeping operation's responsibility to assist in "creating conditions for the effective delivery of humanitarian aid" and protecting six internationally created safe zones. The relationship was something of a mixed blessing. As one commentator observed:

> Although UNPROFOR did much to improve security for humanitarian personnel, there were times when it did the opposite. The Bosnian Serbs, in particular, were very hostile to UNPROFOR after it called for punitive NATO air strikes against them, and UNHCR's close co-operation with UNPROFOR often had the effect of further jeopardising its attempts to present itself as impartial. On a number of occasions, UNHCR convoy teams complained that the presence of UNPROFOR escorts had the effect of drawing fire onto them, and that they would be safer with no military escort.[63]

The single lead-agency model for refugees and internally displaced, with UNHCR as that agency, presented organizational strengths as well as challenges. The organizational arrangement permitted a more comprehensive policy approach. For example, from an early point, UNHCR sought to ensure that the policies of receiving countries did not contribute to further ethnic cleansing. UNHCR urged States to offer temporary protection to those fleeing Bosnia to send a clear message that the international community expected the refugees to repatriate. Because this policy comported with the European reluctance to offer permanent admission, most European countries readily agreed to this formulation.

Equally important, unlike the situation in many conflict zones, in the former Yugoslavia, the needs of the internally displaced and other war-affected populations received early and appropriate attention by an agency with the experience to carry out the aid program.

> The fact that UNHCR was able to deliver almost a million tonnes of food, medical supplies and other urgently needed items in the midst of an active armed conflict, was in itself a remarkable achievement. Humanitarian organisations did an enormous amount to alleviate human suffering. Many Bosnian civilians who are alive today would not have survived without them.[64]

Although humanitarian assistance was a poor substitute for the political will needed to address the underlying causes of the tragedy in Bosnia, in many parts of the world, neither humanitarian aid nor long term solutions are forthcoming for those still trapped in their home countries.

Regional Approaches

A second approach to enhancing international attention for all forced migrants involves the establishment of regional mechanisms. Looking at an emergency in a regional context, with focus on countries of origin as well as countries of destination, permits a more comprehensive assistance effort. Two types of regional approaches have been used. The first establishes a regional body with operational coordination responsibility, while the second convenes all regional parties concerned with a crisis to work cooperatively in solving it.

Operational Coordination

The Office of Emergency Operations in Africa (OEOA) is perhaps the best example of the first approach. Drought and famine in east Africa, complicated by continuing civil wars in the most affected countries, produced massive movements of people. In response to what the Secretary General referred to as "an extraordinary emergency of catastrophic proportions,"[65] millions moved internally while hundreds of thousands sought refuge outside of their borders, affecting neighboring states also suffering from the drought, and in some cases, conflict: more than thirty-five million people in some twenty African countries were affected by the emergency, and of these almost ten million abandoned their homes and lands in search of food and water.[66]

The OEOA was created in December 1984 in an effort to bring a higher level of political visibility and organizational coherence to UN relief efforts in Africa which had, until this point, taken a more country-by-country approach.[67] In response to the "pitiful lack of coordination" of international humanitarian efforts, the OEOA was organized to function in a rather unconventional way under the leadership of two outstanding personalities. The Secretary General asked Bradford Morse, Director of the UN Development Program, to coordinate the UN relief operation. Maurice Strong, an experienced UN administrator, took on day-to-day responsibility for the new operations.

The central functions of the OEOA were to promote international coordination and Cupertino in the response of the UN system to the emergency in Africa; to facilitate the gathering and dissemination of timely, coherent and comprehensive information on the scope and evolution of the emergency; to promote and support resource mobilization efforts on behalf of the affected countries; and to expedite the delivery of emergency supplies by the international donors, both governmental and nongovernmental.[68]

In order to satisfy its mandate of assisting the Secretary-General "in ensuring effective coordination of the assistance and support of the United Nations for [the] African countries which have been so cruelly and tragically affected by catastrophic drought and famine," the OEOA developed a management and operational structure aimed at maximizing a collaborative, problem-solving capability that became known as the Africa Emergency Response System.

The system functioned on four interrelated levels. The first coordination mechanism convened the executive directors of the UN agencies most active in the relief efforts—UNDP, UNHCR, UNICEF, and WFP—to provide policy guidance in consultation with OEOA's director and executive coordinator.

A small secretariat at UN headquarters in New York served as a second mechanism of coordination. In addition to supporting the work of OEOA's director and executive coordinator, the secretariat administered four operational units: field liaison and operations; monitoring and evaluation; public information and external relations; and liaison with nongovernmental organizations and the private sector.

The third cooperative arrangement was found in the series of emergency operations groups at the field level. Under the chairmanship of the UNDP resident coordinators designated in most African countries to administer OEOA assistance and, in the case of Ethiopia and the Sudan where the magnitude of the disaster was unmatched, the Special Representatives of the Secretary-General appointed to coordinate emergency assistance, field-based emergency operations groups comprised of representatives of the Economic Commission for Africa (ECA), FAO, UNDP, UNDRO, UNHCR, UNICEF, WFP, and WHO met regularly, in consultation with the host Governments, to assess emergency requirements and priorities and to discuss these assessments and other emergency-related problems with local representatives of bilateral programs, nongovernmental organizations, and other concerned parties. Information compiled by emergency operations groups regarding assistance requirements at the field level was forwarded directly to the OEOA secretariat for inclusion in OEOA's monthly status reports and in other statements of emergency need.

The fourth component of Africa Emergency Response System and the key to the effectiveness of the OEOA in performing its coordination functions was the African Emergency Task Force. Although administratively independent of the OEOA, the African Emergency Task Force convened high-level representatives of ECA, FAO, UNDP, UNDRO, UNHCR, UNICEF, WFP, and WHO in a forum in which OEOA policies were discussed, refined, and translated into operation directives, or conversely, where practical problems from field operations could be addressed and resolved.[69]

Assisting the affected African countries to mobilize resources to meet their emergency needs constituted one of OEOA's most important functions. OEOA provided leadership and focus to the multiplicity of resource mobilization efforts, through current needs assessments and constant contact with the African Governments and key donor organizations concerned. The OEOA's openness to providing broad support for mobilizing resources to meet Africa's emergency needs from all possible sources, regardless of which organization was to be responsible subsequently for implementing the related emergency programs and activities, fostered African Governments and donor organizations' acceptance of OEOA leadership.[70] The OEOA's establishment of consolidated appeals administered by the UN further facilitated coherent resource mobilization. Under the leadership of Morse and Strong, who commanded great respect within the international system and had far-reaching connections in the public and private spheres, OEOA was able to generate tremendous fund-raising momentum, raising $4.6 billion in emergency assistance and accelerating multilateral and bilateral relief operations in the region.[71]

The resource mobilization process was not, however, successful in every respect. Donors proved to be far more responsive to needs for food aid and for logistical requirements that could be provided out of existing stocks than to the funding of critical needs for medical and health supplies, drinking water and sanitation facilities, cash for internal transportation requirements, and essential agricultural and pastoral inputs.

Beyond OEOA's coordination framework and resource mobilization efforts, critical factors in the organization's success were its establishment of effective information gathering systems, its maintenance of close, regular contacts with the media, effective in directing attention and stimulating international response to the African emergency, and the organization's recognition of the importance of the private sector and, in particular, nongovernmental organizations and popular movements.[72]

When OEOA's mandate ended in October 1986, good rains had returned to most of the area, the food crisis had eased and relief needs were abating. Serious emergencies continued only in Mozambique, Angola, Ethiopia, and the Sudan, where civil strife rather than the weather was the chief catalyst.

Policy Coordination

In the late 1980s, the second approach to regional coordination was tested in Southeast Asia and Central America and then, in the 1990s, in the former Soviet Union. In each case, an international conference laid the framework for a more comprehensive approach to forced migration that included refugees, displaced persons and returnees.

Southeast Asia　The Comprehensive Plan of Action (CPA) brought the source and asylum countries in Southeast Asia together with the UNHCR and donor governments to spell out a new strategy to address continuing movements within the region. The CPA was comprehensive in several ways. It outlined a comprehensive strategy to deal with all facets of the Indochinese movements, from screening to repatriation. The CPA involved all countries in the region, including the countries of origin and the countries of asylum. And, finally, the CPA dealt with all types of migration, from the *bonafide* refugee to the rejected asylum seeker.

Months of negotiations produced a comprehensive strategy that guaranteed access to asylum screening procedures to determine if new arrivals met refugee criteria, resettlement of long-staying populations and those determined to be refugees in the new procedures, and assisted and monitored repatriation of those whose claims to asylum were rejected. In addition, the CPA aimed to discourage organized clandestine departures from Vietnam and Laos and promoted orderly departure mechanisms as an alternative.[73]

The return provisions generated the most controversy. The signatories agreed that every effort should be made to encourage voluntary return by those denied refugee status but "if, after the passage of reasonable time, it becomes clear that voluntary repatriation is not making sufficient progress toward the desired objective, alternatives recognized as being acceptable under international practice would be examined." Although a large part of the Vietnamese who repatriated volunteered or, at least, acquiesced in their return, countries within the region resorted to forced repatriation for others who resisted return. By 1993, more than 44,000 Vietnamese had returned home and the clandestine outflow from Vietnam had reduced to a trickle.

One of the more innovative aspects of the CPA was the role of UNHCR in the return program. Although the returnees had been determined not to meet the refugee criteria, UNHCR nevertheless assisted and protected them upon repatriation. Recognizing that it had no clear mandate to exercise on behalf of these "non-refugees," the Secretary General designated the High Commissioner to coordinate and monitor the returnees program to Vietnam."[74] Initially, UNHCR provided cash grants to the voluntary returnees, but later had to cut back on this assistance because some returnees reentered countries of asylum to obtain additional cash grants. UNHCR even took steps to encourage return by limiting assistance to the screened-out population in countries of asylum. The agency maintained a presence in Vietnam, however, to monitor the safety of the returnees and to assist local communities in the reintegration process.

Central America   Following the Exquipulas II peace accords to end decades of fighting, the governments of Belize, Costa Rica, El Salvador, Guatemala, Honduras, Mexico, and Nicaragua assembled the Conference on Refugees, Displaced Persons and Returnees in Central America (CIREFCA). CIREFCA had two major purposes: to resolve the situation of hundreds of thousands of uprooted individuals within the region and to seek pledges of funding from outside donors to support the regional initiatives. The principal countries of asylum—Costa Rica, Honduras, and Mexico—assumed that most refugees would return but set out conditions for local settlement of persons who could not repatriate. The principal countries of origin—Nicaragua, El Salvador, and Guatemala—set out plans for reintegration of refugee returnees as well as the thousands of internally displaced persons within their own borders.

UNHCR and the UN Development Program were the principal United Nations agencies in the CIREFCA plan. Donors pledged $420 million for a variety of programs to help a total of 1.9 million people—146,400 refugees, 61,500 returnees, 872,000 persons internally displaced in their own countries, and about 900,000 Central Americans who did not have proper documentation. The Italian government, in addition, provided $115 million to support a related program, the Development Program for Displaced Persons, Refugees and Returnees in Central America (PRODERE).

CIREFCA is generally considered to be an effective instrument for developing and implementing a comprehensive response to the multifaceted forms of migration within the region. UNHCR has itself identified a number of factors that explain its relative success.[75] First, there was considerable political will to make the peace process work and resolution of problems of forced migration was seen as a pivotal element of peace.

Second, CIREFCA strove for broad consensus and intensive dialogue. "The Plan of Action was carefully worked out by the seven countries of the region, together with major donor states, UN agencies, and the non-governmental organizations, including those based in the region. . . . One of CIREFCA's most important achievements was to foster a dialogue amongst the actors involved, providing a neutral forum for discussions between people who had formerly distrusted, opposed and even fought each other."[76]

Third, CIREFCA resulted in substantial contributions toward projects that aimed at the reintegration of uprooted populations. In UNHCR's view, "these resources not only allowed UNHCR and its partners to implement a wide range of practical integration programs, but also provided the governments of the region with a strong incentive to respect the Plan of Action."[77]

Fourth, CIREFCA prompted organizational cooperation between UNHCR and the UN Development Program in support of effective reintegration and rehabilitation of conflict-destroyed communities. The cooperation "underscored the need to support the regional peace process by means of interlocking relief, rehabilitation, and development efforts."[78] CIREFCA spawned a repatriation model, the quick impact project, which served as a bridge between the relief needs of returnees and the longer-term development needs of their communities. As the general focus shifted from relief to development, responsibility initially held by UNHCR was to shift to UNDP. Although handover problems persisted, CIREFCA provided a framework for identification of roles and responsibilities.

CIS Conference   Soon after the break-up of the Soviet Union, it became apparent that mass migration within and between the newly independent states would pose challenges to the emerging democracies. The potential for migration reflected both positive and negative trends. On the positive side, the fall of the Iron Curtain permitted greater freedom of movement. On the negative side, ethnic and religious conflicts proliferated, and, in combination with political and economic instability, caused millions to flee their places of residence.

As early as 1993, UNHCR and IOM, in a paper presented to the Conference on Security and Co-operation in Europe, asserted that a regional approach was needed if these movements were to be addressed effectively. The paper laid out eight issues requiring inter-agency, regional cooperation: effective protection of refugees, effective management of migration, contributing to democratic and economic development, effective action against clandestine migration and exploitation, effective implementation of international standards applicable to all types of migrants as well as stateless persons, effective responses to humanitarian emergencies, effective prevention, and information.[79]

The Regional Conference to address the problems of refugees, displaced persons, other forms of involuntary displacement and returnees in the countries of the Commonwealth of Independent States and relevant neighboring States met in May 1996, pursuant to General Assembly Resolution 50/151. UNHCR initiated the process, in close association with the International Organization for Migration and the Organization for Security and Co-operation in Europe (OSCE)'s Office for Democratic Institutions and Human Rights (ODIHR).

The concluding statement described the objectives of the Conference as threefold:

> to provide a reliable forum for the countries of the region to discuss population displacement and refugee problems in a humanitarian and non-political way; to review the population movements taking place in the CIS countries, clarifying the categories of concern; and to elaborate a non-binding Program of Action for the CIS countries.

The conference adopted a Program of Action, including "measures aimed to establish national migration systems and to develop appropriate policies and operational activities. Preventive measures have been devised to address the causes of possible displacement. Strengthening international cooperation and cooperation with the relevant international organizations and nongovernmental organizations is a necessary complement to measures taken by the CIS countries. The strategy also includes implementation and follow-up activities so as to ensure the sustainability of the Conference process."

The CIS conference made explicit reference to the wide range of forced migrants likely to require attention: refugees, internally displaced persons, illegal migrants, persons in refugeelike situations, repatriates, involuntarily relocating persons, formerly deported peoples, and ecological migrants. Other categories of movements, such as labor migrants, deported persons and returning military personnel were not part of the scope of the Conference. The situation of internally displaced persons received specific attention, with the recognition that the CIS would see significant levels of internal movements that would, in turn, require international assistance:

> International concern for the plight of internally displaced persons stems from the recognition that involuntary displacement increases the vulnerability of affected populations to abuses of human rights. The human rights and fundamen-

tal freedoms of internally displaced persons, as contained in international human rights and humanitarian law instruments, should therefore be fully guaranteed.

Unlike the CPA and CIREFCA processes, which occurred at the end of a decade-long refugee crisis, the CIS conference was convened with the aim of preventing emergencies and, where prevention was not possible, ensuring early and effective responses to mass migration. The conference urged funding of concrete programs toward these ends, recognizing, in particular, the roles to be played by the Office of the Human Commissioner of Human Rights and the Department of Humanitarian Affairs, in addition to the core agencies: UNHCR, IOM, and OSCE.

The results of the CIS Conference process have been mixed. On the positive side, the conference and its follow-up raised the visibility and interconnectedness of migration issues within the CIS. It led to practical steps to develop and implement national laws and practices to improve migration management. The follow-up activities enhanced the sharing of information and statistics. The conference and its aftermath precipitated new roles for nongovernmental organizations in countries that had little in the way of civil societies.

On the negative side, though, progress in dealing with some of the fundamental issues precipitating forced migration has been constrained. In its 1998 meeting, the Steering Committee described a number of the constraints on greater effectiveness:

> lack of high level political support; lack of political solutions of conflicts; tension between democratisation and the priorities of state-building; gaps between legislation and its implementation; lack of adequate co-operation on a regional or bilateral level; global decrease in financial resources; insufficient level of involvement of international financial institutions.[80]

The slow pace of contributions to the CIS activities presents a particular cause for concern. UNHCR requested $44 million to support CIS related activities in 2000. By mid-1999, however, UNHCR had raised less than half of the $32 million requested and projected a $5 million shortfall at the end of the year. Similar funding shortfalls occurred in prior years. Having raised expectations among the CIS countries for international aid to support a comprehensive approach, the absence of continuing donor commitment undermined the effectiveness of the CIS conference process.

System-Wide Coordination

In 1990, the Economic and Social Council requested the Secretary General to "initiate a United Nations systems-wide review to assess the experiences and capacity of various organizations in the coordination of assistance to all refugees, displaced persons and returnees, and the full spectrum of their needs, in supporting the efforts of the affected countries." Based on this review, the Secretary General was to recommend ways of maximizing cooperation and coordination among the various organizations. The Secretary General engaged a consultant, Jacques Cuénod, recently retired from UNHCR after a long and distinguished career, to prepare the study.

The Cuénod report took as its point of departure that the main weakness of the existing system is:

> the difficulty that the United Nations entities have and the time it takes to agree among themselves on an acceptable coordination arrangement to decide on how to assess the situation, to reach a clear division of responsibilities, to work out a unitary plan of action and to get the Secretary-General to launch a joint appeal.[80]

After describing the major institutions with responsibility for humanitarian assistance, the Cuénod report set out four groups of concern in emergencies: refugees, externally displaced persons, internally displaced persons, and returnees. Emergencies requiring aid to internally displaced persons, he noted, offer the greatest challenges to the international system. No one agency within the United Nations system had specific responsibility for this population. The Cuénod report did not, however, propose that the Secretary General designate one entity whose mandate would be extended to provide protection and/or assistance to internally displaced persons. Rather, it argued that "as situations of refugees, displaced persons and returnees vary from each other and as the causes of forced migration within a country differ greatly, the responsibilities of each organization cannot be determined in advance and will have to be agreed upon according to basic coordination arrangements."[82]

The objectives of the coordination arrangements proposed in the Cuénod report were as follows:

> To make the choice of the coordination arrangement, most relevant to a given situation, as automatic as possible while also limiting the choice to a few basic scenarios with the possibility to add the flexibility required by the specificities of each situation;
> To promote a unitary approach by the United Nations humanitarian entities;
> To involve the United Nations development entities from the beginning of an emergency in order to promote a quick transition from relief to rehabilitation, reconstruction, and development.

The Cuénod report recommended establishing a permanent humanitarian coordination mechanism that would operate even in the absence of new emergencies in order to follow current situations and ensure the continuum from emergency response to development.

In keeping with the Cuénod report, the Department of Humanitarian Affairs (DHA) was created pursuant to General Assembly Resolution 46/182 in 1991. Resolution 46/182 mandated the appointment of a high-level official who was to coordinate and facilitate the UN emergency response, manage a central emergency fund, facilitate access by humanitarian organizations to populations in need, process requests for assistance, collect and analyze early disaster-warning information, organize collective interagency needs, make consolidated appeals for funding, prepare an annual report to the Secretary General, and establish a central register of specialized personnel to employ on short notice. This high-level official would combine the functions previously carried out in the coordination of United Nations response by representatives of the Secretary-General for major and complex emergencies, as well as by the United Nations Disaster Relief Operation (UNDRO).

The Resolution also created the Inter-Agency Standing Committee (IASC), composed of the heads of the major UN humanitarian and development agencies, which institutionalizes the cooperation of the humanitarian coordinator with the International Committee of the Red Cross and all other concerned NGOs.

The resolution dealt with field-level coordination as well. It affirmed that the resident coordinator should normally coordinate the humanitarian assistance of the United Nations system at the country level. The resident coordinator would facilitate the preparedness of the United Nations system; assist in a speedy transition from relief to development; promote the use of all locally or regionally available relief capacities; and chair an emergency operations group of field representatives and experts from the system.

DHA's performance did not meet expectations, largely because of confusion between its coordinating role and its more operational roles, and because it did not have resources or clout to require coordination. Cuénod, assessing the new coordination mechanisms fifteen months after their creation, concluded that the office had no natural constituency to support and promote its success. "In the absence of such backing, DHA will have many critics, few friends and become the scapegoat for humanitarian failure whenever it occurs."[83] Cuénod believed DHA could succeed but only with significant reform of its staff (many of whom had no operational emergency experience) and demonstrated leadership to assign responsibilities in the earliest stages of emergencies.

A more scathing commentary came from Thomas Weiss who said that the reforms were a "cosmetic adaptation of UN diplomatic and coordination machinery rather than any serious rethinking or restructuring of humanitarian action."[84] Bureaucratic inefficiencies, lack of centralized authority, insufficient resources, and uncoordinated activities remained barriers to effective UN responses.

In response to criticisms of DHA, the Secretary-General proposed reforms aimed at reinvigorating the institutions created under Resolution 46/182 rather than replacing the DHA system with an untried new structural arrangement. The Secretary General's Program for Reform agreed that DHA took on operational activities without adequate capacities and expertise. The Office for the Coordination of Humanitarian Assistance (OCHA) would focus instead on three core functions: policy development and coordination in support of the Secretary-General, so as to ensure that all humanitarian issues, including those which fall between the gaps in existing mandates of agencies such as protection and assistance for internally displaced persons, are addressed; advocacy of humanitarian issues with political organs, notably the Security Council; and coordination of the UN's humanitarian emergency response, by ensuring that an appropriate response mechanism is established, through IASC consultation, on the ground.

A key role of OCHA is the development of consolidated funding appeals. Under DHA, the UN began to issue consolidated appeals for each emergency, with all of the UN agencies presenting their requests. In a new development, in December 1998, United Nations Consolidated Appeals for Emergencies were jointly launched under the auspices of OCHA. In 2002, the Consolidated Appeals Process (CAP) issued nineteen appeals for individual and regional emergencies. Almost all appeal countries are in the midst of conflict situations or in the immediate post-conflict phase of rehabilitation, reconstruction, and reconciliation, and many of the beneficiaries are uprooted people. By simultaneously requesting funds for the principal emergency situations throughout the world, this approach "seeks to provide an enhanced strategic overview and establish the operational goals and activities of the international humanitarian community."[85] The effectiveness of the CAP is discussed in chapter 4.

Failure of the Collaborative Approach

Even with improvements in humanitarian responses, a fundamental problem still exists in the international system: Lack of consistency in the treatment of forced migrants, particularly differences in treatment of refugees versus internally displaced persons. As described above, a large number of international organizations with differing mandates take part in humanitarian operations that involve displacement. The UN High Commissioner for Refugees has principal responsibility for refugees while the International Committee of the Red Cross (ICRC), the International Organization for Migration (IOM) and various UN agencies and funds provide services and, in the case of ICRC, protection to forced migrants. Moreover, national governments have important responsibilities toward forced migrants, including internally displaced persons. And, nongovernmental organizations and the forced migrants themselves play significant roles in providing assistance and, in a more limited way, protection.

Four principal problems result from this complicated regime:

- Lack of coordination that makes emergency responses slow and inefficient and hampers efforts to solve the underlying causes of forced migration;
- Lack of consistency in the treatment of forced migrants, particularly differences in treatment of refugees versus internally displaced persons;
- Gaps in response when no organization has an explicit mandate to assist or protect a given category of forced migrant, and;
- Overlapping mandates that hinders smooth handover of responsibility as the emergency phase of a crisis ends and longer-term issues require attention.

The absence of clear mandates and the still *ad hoc* mechanism by which UNHCR has been increasingly called upon to provide assistance to a broader range of displaced persons than those defined in its Statute or the 1951 Convention, leads to mixed messages and approaches to forced migrants. The problem has persisted for more than a decade. An evaluation of peacekeeping operations in Rwanda highlights the problem:

> While UNHCR took the lead role in providing assistance to refugees, there was no clear assignment of responsibility vis-à-vis the internally displaced. UNHCR and UNAMIR (the peacekeeping operation) adopted different approaches in their dealings with IDPs. Whereas UNAMIR saw the need to facilitate the early closure of IDP camps and also provided transport to IDPs wishing to return to their home communes, UNHCR gave precedence to conditions of return, as well as counseling and preparing the returnees to go home with materials ready to start a new life. . . . Some humanitarian agency personnel also felt that within the integrated operations centre more emphasis was being placed on operations leading to eventual camp closure, without critically examining the question of who had responsibility to defend IDP rights with the Rwandese Government.[86]

A more recent U.S. government report also found serious gaps, particularly in protection for IDPs:

> Unlike international organizations' efforts to provide assistance (e.g., food aid and health care) to internally displaced persons where there are established

working groups to share information and plan and coordinate action, there are no counterpart coordination mechanisms for protection concerns. For example, in our three case-study countries, we were told that there was little to no discussion among international organizations concerning protection issues. There were no focal points to raise the profile of protection or ensure its place on the agenda of those organizations working in the field. Officials engaged in protection activities in these countries told us that because there are no established mechanisms to share information, there is a lack of (1) basic information on where protection officers are posted, (2) common thinking and approaches to protection, and (3) knowledge about what protection interventions work or do not work.[87]

Our fieldwork in Burundi in 2000 revealed significant gaps in responsibilities for internally displaced persons. The UN significantly pulled back its presence, withdrawing all nonessential international staff following the murder of two UN officials and seven Burundians who were carrying out a humanitarian mission in the southeastern province of Rutana in October 1999. The weakness of the UN presence in Burundi at the time of the site visit was particularly pertinent in relation to IDPs. Most agencies recognized that insufficient assistance and protection was being provided to IDPs but none was willing to step forward to insist that more be done. As one international head of agency reported, "the UN is still floundering" in relation to IDPs. UNHCR appreciated that it would deal with IDP needs in the areas it would be operational in the event of a repatriation and that it would make sense to implement some of its plans, such as peace-building and reconstruction of infrastructure, ahead of a return. But UNHCR also said it would not get involved with IDPs in areas where the agency would not otherwise be operational, namely those regions where there would be few returnees.[88]

This last point raises a fundamental problem. The current arrangements are highly static, not recognizing that forced migrants move from one type of displacement to another. For example, an internally displaced person who is unable to find safety within his or her own country may well cross an international border and become a refugee. Similarly, a refugee who repatriates but cannot return safely to his or her home village might become internally displaced. Treating each of these situations as unique events, with no relationship between policies adopted on one side of the border and those adopted on the other side, fails to address the complexity in forced migration.

These static responses make is particularly difficult to achieve solutions for forced migrants. Despite continued discussions about the need for a smooth transition from relief to development, institutional barriers still impede actual implementation of such approaches. A Roundtable organized by the UNHCR and World Bank in 1999 concluded that "a response to the needs of post-conflict societies organized along two artificially compartmentalized lines, namely the 'emergency/humanitarian' and 'long-term developmental,' did not do justice to the fluidity, uncertainty, and complexity that characterized war-torn societies."[89]

OCHA has attempted to address the gap in protection and assistance for internally displaced persons by establishing a small, dedicated unit. The decision came after a taskforce, headed by Dennis McNamara, the director of the UN's Senior Inter-Agency Network on Internally Displaced Persons, recommended the designation of a specialized, nonoperational office to coordinate UN activities on behalf of IDPs. The network floated the idea of a special emergency fund that would be at the disposal of the office, but this idea was not included in the network's report[90] or in the formation of the unit.

Underlying these developments is a continuing commitment to pursue a collaborative approach to addressing forced migration, with UNHCR having responsibility for refugees and no single agency with responsibility for internally displaced persons. The IDP unit is composed of officials detailed from other United Nations agencies, IOM, and the NGO community. There are arguments for and against continuing with the collaborative approach. In favor is the concern that no one agency within the UN system now has the resources, mandate, or capacity to respond adequately to internal displacement. The research conducted for this project indicates, however, that collaboration has not generally been achieved, particularly at the field level, and that this system perpetuates gaps and inconsistencies in the treatment afforded forced migrants.

A recent evaluation of the Interagency Standing Committee found similar gaps[91]:

> In the one case we examined in a modest degree of detail (that of Iraq), the IDP issue was the most complicated and the least well managed of the overall contingency planning effort . . . characterized as it was by confusion, misinterpretation, inter-agency accusations and last-minute maneuvering for lead roles. Also, in Côte d'Ivoire, an important disagreement between, on the one hand, the Government and the Resident Coordinator and, on the other, much of the humanitarian community about the size of the IDP caseload revealed the still-sharp limits on the system's ability to generate credible information in real time, such as is necessary to shape an adequate response.

A principal weakness in coordination is at the field level. While national governments have the principal responsibility for ensuring effective responses at the field level, the UN plays an important role in ensuring coordination of international efforts, often, but by no means always, in support of national initiatives. In most refugee situations, the host government requests the assistance of the UNHCR in helping to ensure adequate assistance and protection. UNHCR in turn works with implementing partners that include government ministries as well as nongovernmental organizations. UNHCR's ability to operate effectively can be seriously eroded if the national government is uncooperative, is itself hostile to the presence of refugees, or is unwilling or unable to control other actors who disrupt aid operations. UNHCR nevertheless has a clear mandate in such cases to bring the problem to international attention as a barrier to refugee protection and assistance.

In situations of internal displacement, the role of the national government is even more complicated as is the ability of the United Nations to coordinate assistance and protection activities. This is particularly the case when displacement is caused by internal conflict and the national government, as party to the conflict, is at odds with its own civilian population or does not have effective control over territory in which IDPs are living.

In complex humanitarian emergencies, responsibility for coordinating humanitarian assistance and protection for the United Nations generally falls to the UN Humanitarian Coordinator (HC), who is often the UN Resident Representative (RC). UN General Assembly Resolution 44/136 (February 27, 1990) assigns the Coordinator "the function of coordinating assistance to the internally displaced." However, the persons assigned to these offices are responsible for a range of other UN activities and priorities, particularly regarding long-term development, and are not necessarily experienced in complex humanitarian emergencies. Gaining access for operational agencies to forced migrants may not be a high priority, nor does the Humanitarian Coordinator necessarily have the experience and skills to negotiate such access. The recent evaluation of the IASC found clear improvements in the recruitment of HA/RCs, but noted:

> Among the most pertinent problems with the system is that there are still, by common account, a number of RCs in countries experiencing conflict that are less than fully trained or experienced in humanitarian action. Further, many within the IASC are concerned about cases where the RC may be strong within the development arena, but is not addressing vital humanitarian issues, particularly IDPs. This is in part a reflection of discomfort within the wider humanitarian community with UNDP's normal relationship with host governments, seeing in these relationships inadequate distance for humanitarian issues to be raised.[92]

Given the potential for massive loss of life in complex humanitarian emergencies, it is essential that the United Nations assign only those officials who are experienced and committed to assistance and protection for displaced populations to the role of Humanitarian Coordinator. Furthermore, when humanitarian emergencies lead to significant levels of internal displacement, the office of the Humanitarian Coordinator should have a staff person who is designated with responsibility for coordinating assistance and protection activities taken on their behalf.

An evaluation of the IDP Unit in OCHA found that the collaborative approach is still highly flawed. The evaluation concluded:

> To date, the Unit has not had the impact on the UN system that it was intended to achieve. The Unit has not been able to capitalize on its direct link to the ERC, it has failed to get RC/HCs to follow its recommendations, and has not been effective in reporting egregious failures of the system.[93]

A number of factors impeded progress, some related to the unit's own short failings but other more structural and systemic. The evaluation found that the unit was "busy, committed, but scattered" in its activities. It was without a strategic vision or clear objectives. The evaluation also concluded that the United Nations system resisted any changes that the Unit might have accomplished:

> The UN system is not ready for change. The out-going ERC did not effectively use the Unit to fully perform his mandate as the Secretary General's focal point for the internally displaced. UN operational agencies remain more concerned with their organizational interests than with the interests of the internally displaced. They do not display the collegiality necessary for a truly collaborative response to crises of internal displacement.[94]

The evaluation recommended that the Unit be more aggressive in tackling the problems of IDP assistance and protection that it identified. It also urged the Unit to fulfill its responsibilities as the principal advocate for IDPs in the United Nations system: "The Unit should become the premier advocate for the internally displaced within the UN system, advising the ERC on specific breakdowns or weaknesses within the UN's response to internal displacement crises, and making practical recommendations on how to address these problems."[95] The evaluation warned as well that if "after a period of two to three years there is still no progress in the collaborative approach, then the Unit should be shut down—at that point it will have become a veil masking inherent failures of the system."[96]

In keeping with the evaluation's recommendations, the new ERC seems willing to be more aggressive in identifying ways to fill gaps in responses to IDPs. In April 2004, he issued new guidance on procedural steps for developing an IDP response strategy. Stating that "all Country Teams in countries experiencing internal displacement should have in place a comprehensive strategic action plan for meeting the protection and assistance needs of IDPs," the guidance provides a roadmap of steps to be taken to develop such a plan (see table 3.1). Of critical concern for our purposes is what happens if the plan

Table 3.1

1. HC/RC **alerts the ERC, who in turn may alert donors and IASC Principals**, to an evolving or changing crisis of internal displacement.

2. HC/RC ensures **consultations** with the UNCT, other international organizations, the Red Cross movement, NGOs (hereafter "agencies") and organizes, as far as possible, a **joint needs assessment** ensuring inter-agency participation. The assessment should cover all relevant sectors and geographical locations, include consultation with the IDPs themselves and should take into account the capacity and willingness of the government to respond and fulfill its obligations.

3. HC/RC and agencies develop a **Strategic Action Plan to respond to the protection and assistance needs of IDPs**, prioritizing the main activities deemed necessary for responding to the identified needs. The IDP Unit may be requested, if necessary, to assist in the development of a strategic action plan.

4. HC/RC consults with all agencies to **identify which actors have the expertise and capacity in the country to respond** in the ways identified with appropriate activities. The **role of the government** must be supported and complemented wherever possible. The proposals reflect the roles of national and local government authorities, international agencies, and NGOs. Agencies should consult with their respective headquarters on their responsibilities in terms of the Plan.

5. The HC/RC **consult agencies again at the country level** to discuss the strategy and their consultations with headquarters to obtain agreement from agencies on how to fill any gaps. HC/RC reviews the joint response strategy to ensure that priority activities address the assessed needs and that there are no gaps. Both rounds of consultations must be **structured, inclusive, and the results recorded**.

6. If the **response strategy is deemed satisfactory** to all concerned actors at the country level; all major areas of response are adequately addressed; and implementing roles and arrangements are clear, the HC/RC shares the Plan with the ERC.

8. If **response strategy leaves gaps that cannot be solved at the field level**, HC shares the Plan with the ERC, clearly identifying gaps and problems encountered in trying to assign agency responsibilities to fill the gaps. The ERC shares the Plan with the IDP Unit and IASC WG and requests that agencies at the HQ level try and resolve the gaps in response. An *ad hoc* meeting of the IASC-WG may be called if necessary.

7. **ERC shares the Plan with the IASC-WG for information**. (Proceed to step 10)

If some IASC-WG members have **legitimate cause to question either the arrangements or consultation process** carried out at the field level, the ERC requests that the IASC-WG undertake further discussions to resolve differences. (Proceed to step 8)

9. If no progress is made, **ERC draws the attention of the IASC Principals** to the matter and seeks their action **until a plan is agreed upon**.

10. **ERC** then proceeds to **seek political and donor support for agencies** implementing the Plan.

Once the plan is developed and approved, it is the HC/RC's responsibility both during crises and *in protracted situations to monitor and ensure its ongoing* implementation. *The HC/RC should report through regular reporting procedures on the plan's implementation and any problems or changes therein to the ERC.*

leaves gaps in response: "If response strategy leaves gaps that cannot be solved at the field level, HC shares the Plan with the ERC, clearly identifying gaps and problems encountered in trying to assign agency responsibilities to fill the gaps. The ERC shares the Plan with the IDP Unit and IASC WG and requests that agencies at the HQ level try and resolve the gaps in response."[97] Should that process not work, the ERC will then bring the issue to a principals meeting of the IASC, where presumably a plan will be worked out.

While a clear improvement in setting out the steps to be taken, the new plan still does not address a fundamental problem with the collaborative approach. No actor within the UN system has an obligation to respond to the assistance and protection needs of IDPs. The ERC has powers of persuasion that may, in many cases, encourage one or more agencies to offer its help to IDPs, but the ERC has no authority to order compliance. Nor does the ERC have funding to offer to make the decision to respond more appealing. As long as no UN body has the mandate and, hence, obligation to assist and, more important, protect IDPs, gaps are likely to remain.

An *ad hoc* system for assigning responsibility for IDPs also does not address the need for more comprehensive regional responses. Complex humanitarian emergencies generally produce complex patterns of forced migration that affect several countries within a region. Refugees may flee to more than one neighboring country while, of course, IDPs stay within their own country, sometimes in government-controlled areas and sometimes in territory controlled by factions or insurgencies. Needs and responses in one country can profoundly affect needs and responses in another, raising the value of regional coordination mechanisms that ensure greater consistency in programs and cooperation in finding solutions. In the absence, however, of an international presence able, willing, and funded to attend to the full range of assistance and protection needs of forced migrants, comprehensive responses are unlikely to develop.

UN Agency for Forced Migrants

The UN experience with the collaborative approach points to a fundamental flaw in the concept: When everyone is responsible for a particular population or set of activities, no one can be held accountable for failures. The consolidation of assistance and protection responsibilities for all forced migrants into a new organization—the UN High Commissioner for Forced Migrants (HCFM)—would significantly improve responses to forced migration. This agency would replace UNHCR. Its mandate would include refugees covered under the 1951 UN Convention Relating to the Status of Refugees as well as individuals internally and externally displaced because of repression, conflict, natural disasters, environmental degradation, and development-induced displacement. The Refugee Convention and Protocol as well as such regional conventions as the 1969 OAU Convention on the Status of Refugees, would govern its work on behalf of refugees, and its work on behalf of IDPs would be governed by the norms set out in the *Guiding Principles on Internal Displacement*. A primary role of the new organization would be the promotion of these international standards of assistance and protection. A High Commissioner nominated by the Secretary General and appointed by the General Assembly would head the agency.

There are many benefits to be achieved by consolidation. A single agency would ensure more comprehensive and consistent approaches. The High Commissioner for Forced Migrants would be tasked with ensuring that all persons displaced by the same events are afforded comparable treatment, regardless of their location, and that the resolution of the situations causing displacement would take into account all parties that have been displaced. The office would have the mandate to negotiate access and protection of forced migrants with governments and insurgent groups in both home and host countries of forced migrants. It would be responsible for developing a consolidated appeal for funding that would show donors the full range of financial needs in all countries affected by the displacement.

This recommendation differs in a significant way from proposals by then U.S. Ambassador to the United Nations Richard Holbrooke and others to assign responsibility for IDPs to UNHCR. While it recognizes that UNHCR has the greatest competency for assisting and protecting forced migrants, this proposal makes clear that *all* forced migrants would be within this agency's mandate. Asking UNHCR to assume responsibility for IDPs, while its mandate remains primarily as a refugee organization, means that the far larger number of IDPs would be the after-thought in an agency with other priorities. Rather, the new agency should be mandated to treat forced migrants on both sides of borders as equally worthy of its protection and assistance.

Can one agency assist and protect both refugees and IDPs without compromising either group? UNHCR's concern discussed above about the expansion of its own role regarding IDPs—whether it would undermine the principle of first asylum—would need to be addressed forthrightly by States in creating a consolidated agency. In general, fear that States would refuse asylum seekers solely because greater internal protection exists appears overblown. The threat to first asylum stems from other sources, including concerns about security, financial impact, and social and cultural dislocations arising from the admission of large numbers of newcomers. While some governments may use the work of the HCFM as an excuse for its actions, it is likely they would find other reasons to refuse entry of asylum seekers if this excuse were not available. In effect, the "threat to asylum" genie is already out of the bottle and restoring generous asylum systems will require more than keeping UNHCR free of contamination by internally displaced persons. In the meantime, concerns about asylum should not interfere with efforts to improve protection for the far larger numbers who remain within their home countries.

HCFM's mandate would emphasize a dual responsibility to protect forced migrants and find durable solutions for them. As is the case with UNHCR, the organization would be mandated to provide assistance when needed to ensure protection of those under its mandate. Recognizing the national responsibility of States to assist and protect refugees and internally displaced persons, HCFM would work closely with national governments to provide them the means to carry out their obligations under international law. The agency should have clear authority to establish contact in such manner as the High Commissioner may think best with private organizations, including non-state actors that control territory on which forced migrants reside.

HCFM would have a similar governing structure to UNHCR's, with an Executive Committee providing guidance to a High Commissioner appointed by the General Assembly. As with the current situation, HCFM would be funded mostly through voluntary contributions from governments, although it would receive funds for administrative support from the United Nations. HCFM should also have authority to maintain an emergency fund that it can tap to respond quickly to unfolding emergencies involving all types of forced migration. The agency would continue to set out its budgetary requirements within the Consolidated Appeals process, specifying clearly how the assistance and protection of forced migrants fits into the array of other activities (healthcare, food aid, human rights protection, etc.) needed in complex humanitarian emergencies. Similarly, the agency would continue to coordinate with other parts of the United Nations system to ensure that the needs of forced migrants are considered in political negotiations, peacekeeping, and reconstruction and development activities.

Given the difficulties UNHCR has experienced in obtaining adequate funding for its current activities, will the new agency receive adequate resources for this larger mandate? Certainly, without resources, institutional reform is bound to fail and the forced migrants will be no better off. In fact, an argument could be made that the collaborative approach gives donors greater opportunity to provide funding for IDPs because they can choose among a broader range of agencies. While that case may be made for food aid and other specific forms of assistance, the collaborative approach has not led to funding for protection, precisely because no UN agency has stepped forward to take on this responsibility in a comprehensive manner. Furthermore, it may be that some of UNHCR's own funding problems stem from the narrowness of its mandate. With

UNHCR having responsibility for a minority of the world's displaced, donors may well choose to target their funds at agencies, including nongovernmental organizations, which have greater presence in the world's hot spots.

CONCLUSION

The current organizational system for protecting and assisting forced migrants is outmoded, overly fragmented, and in need of significant reform. The current system focuses on a diminishing number of refugees, while response to the increasing number of internally displaced persons and (to a lesser extent) non-Convention refugees remains largely *ad hoc*. In addition, the lack of coordination between today's large numbers of humanitarian actors too frequently results in makeshift and inconsistent responses both within and across forced migrant crises. A system that does not assign specific responsibility for the largest numbers of forced migrants will fail in its protection and assistance efforts, precisely because when everyone within a system can theoretically be responsible for a particular population or set of activities, no one can be held accountable for failures. If comprehensive and coordinated assistance and protection efforts for forced migrants are to evolve, the gaps and inconsistencies in the current system need to be resolved. For these reasons, we recommend the replacement of UNHCR with a UN High Commissioner for Forced Migrants (HCFM), responsible for assistance to and protection of all forced migrants, including not only refugees covered under the 1951 Refugee Convention but also those migrants internally and externally displaced due to repression, conflict, natural disasters, environmental degradation, and development-induced displacement.

The UN High Commissioner for Forced Migrants would use current international law and relevant documents (the 1951 Refugee Convention, its 1967 Protocol, the Geneva Conventions, regional conventions such as the 1969 OAU Convention, and the *Guiding Principles*) to govern its work on behalf of all forced migrants, building upon and guiding the efforts recommended above to enhance legal protections for forced migrants not (sufficiently) protected by current instruments. Similar to UNHCR, HCFM would have a mandate that incorporated assistance, protection, and finding durable solutions, but this responsibility would be clearly stated in founding documents and would extend to all forced migrants. The ability of HCFM to serve as a focal point for all forced migrant issues and to have some financial discretion in the maintenance of an emergency fund would enable HCFM to more effectively address the needs of all forced migrants. Donors might be more willing to contribute funds to an agency that can comprehensively address forced migration issues, while the existence of an agency with specific responsibility for all forced migrants would foster greater coordination between this agency (HCFM) and the other parts of the United Nations system. HCFM would ensure not only more directed and coordinated responses to forced migrant crises but the mainstreaming of consideration of forced migrant needs in political negotiations, peacekeeping, and reconstruction and development activities. A strong agency mandated with the assistance and protection of all forced migrants would be the most effective advocate on behalf of these populations.

NOTES

1. Gil Loescher, *The UNHCR and World Politics—A Perilous Path* (Oxford: Oxford University Press, 2001), 24.

2. Loescher, *The UNHCR*, 24.

3. Gil Loescher, *Beyond Charity: International Cooperation and the Global Refugee Crisis* (New York: Oxford University Press, 1993), 37–38.

4. Loescher, *The UNHCR*. Lack of forethought affected the organizational structure of nearly all the UN organs because most of them were not intended to endure past their initial, limited mandates.

5. Loescher, *The UNHCR*, 25.

6. United Nations High Commission for Refugees (UNHCR), *Partnership: An Operations Management Handbook for UNHCR's Partners* (Geneva: UNHCR, 2003), 3.

7. Loescher, *Beyond Charity,* 25.

8. Loescher, *Beyond Charity*, 25.

9. Loescher, *Beyond Charity*, 43.

10. Loescher, *Beyond Charity*, 43.

11. UNHCR, *Partnership,* 26.

12. Edmund Jan Ozmanczyk and Anthony Mango, eds., *Encyclopedia of the United Nations and International Agreements* (New York: Garland Publishers, 2003), 2479.

13. UNHCR, *Partnership,* 26.

14. UNHCR, *Partnership*, 26.

15. United Nations G.A. Res. 55/72 81st Plenary Mtg. 2000, U.N. Doc. A/Res/55/72.

16. The term "Good Offices" first appeared as a General Assembly resolution attempting to insert UNHCR support in the politically sensitive riff between Hong Kong and Mainland China. See, United Nations G.A. Res. 1167 (XII), 723rd Plenary Mtg. (November 26, 1957), para. 2.

17. Loescher, *Beyond Charity*, 45. Debates in the late 1950s over the concept of "internal refugees" did not result in their inclusion in the Convention—but the United States "offered a significant concession authorizing the High Commissioner to intervene on behalf of other groups of refugees pending consideration by the General Assembly as to whether such groups should be brought under his mandate, thus opening the way for future expansion of the Office."

18. United Nations G.A. Res. 1388 (XIV), 841st Plenary Mtg. 1959, para. 2.

19. UNHCR, *Partnership,* 9. Even today, the UNHCR maintains a dichotomy between Convention Refugees and "Persons of Concern," who the UN General Assembly and Secretary General "have frequently asked UNHCR to take care of . . . on an *ad hoc* basis."

20. UNHCR, *Partnership,* 9.

21. Louise W. Holborn, *Refugees: A Problem of Our Time: The Work of the United Nations High Commissioner for Refugees, 1951–1972* (Metuchen, N. J.: Scarecrow Press, 1975).

22. UNHCR, Division of International Protection, *UNHCR's Operational Experience with Internally Displaced Persons* (Geneva: UNHCR, September 1994), 43.

23. UNHCR, *Internally Displaced Persons: The Role of the United Nations High Commissioner for Refugees* (Geneva: UNHCR, 2000).

24. UNHCR, *Internally Displaced Persons,* 2.

25. UNHCR, *Internally Displaced Persons,* 8.

26. Francis Deng, Statement to the 58th Session of the General Assembly, Third Committee, Item 117, UN Statement (November 11, 2003).

27. UNHCR, *Partnership,* 30.

28. UNHCR, *Partnership,* 30.

29. UNHCR, *Partnership,* 30. Nongovernmental organizations "not only provide substantial aid from their own resources, but frequently carry out specific UNHCR projects."

30. UNHCR, *Partnership,* 28.

31. UNHCR, *Partnership,* 28.

32. Ozmanczyk and Mango, *Encyclopedia,* 2479.

33. Ozmanczyk and Mango, *Encyclopedia,* 2479.

34. UNHCR, *Partnership,* 41.

35. UNHCR, *Partnership,* 41.

36. UNHCR, *Partnership,* 41.

37. UNHCR, *UNHCR Global Appeal 2004* (Geneva: UNHCR, 2003), 21.

38. UNHCR, *UNHCR Global Appeal,* 21.

39. UNHCR, *UNHCR Global Appeal,* 21.

40. UNHCR, *UNHCR Global Appeal,* 21.

41. UNHCR, *UNHCR Global Appeal,* 21.

42. UNHCR, *UNHCR Global Appeal,* 21.

43. UNHCR, *UNHCR Global Appeal,* 21.

44. UNHCR, *UNHCR Global Appeal,* 21.

45. UNHCR, *Partnership,* 41.

46. Marguerite Contat Hickel, "Protection of internally displaced persons affected by armed conflict: concept and challenges," IRRC 83/843, September 2001, 709.

47. For a fuller treatment of regional responses to internal displacement, see Cohen and Deng, *Masses in Flight.*

48. B. G. Ramcharan, *Humanitarian Good Offices in International Law: The Good Offices of the United Nations Secretary-General in the Field of Human Rights* (The Hague: Martinus Nijhoff, 1983), 99.

49. W. Courtland Robinson, *Terms of Refuge: The Indochinese Exodus and the International Response* (London and N.Y.: Zed Books Ltd., 1998).

50. Robinson, *Terms of Refuge*, 73.

51. Linda Mason and Roger Brown, *Rice, Rivalry, and Politics: Managing Cambodian Relief* (Southbend, Ind.: University of Notre Dame Press, 1983), 26.

52. Mason and Brown, *Rice, Rivalry and Politics*.

53. UNHCR faced similar problems in camps in eastern Zaire that were controlled by militant Hutus who had been involved in genocide in Rwanda.

54. Mark Cutts, *The Humanitarian Operation in Bosnia: 1992–1995: the Dilemmas of Negotiating Humanitarian Access, Working Paper No. 8* (Geneva, Switzerland: UNHCR, May 1999).

55. Quoted in S. Alex Cunliffe and Michael Pugh, "The UNHCR as Lead Agency in the Former Yugoslavia," *Journal of Humanitarian Assistance*, www-jha.sps.cam.ac.uk/a/a007.htm (April 1, 1996).

56. Cunliffe and Pugh, "The UNHCR as Lead Agency."

57. Cutts, *Humanitarian Operation in Bosnia*, 17.

58. UNHCR, *The State of the World's Refugees: In Search of Solutions* (Oxford: Oxford University Press, 1995), 43.

59. Erin Mooney, "In-Country Protection: Out of Bounds for the UNHCR?" in F. Nicholson and P. Twomey, eds., *Refugee Rights and Realities: Evolving International Concepts and Regimes*, Cambridge: Cambridge University Press, 1999.

60. See, for example, Cunliffe and Pugh, "The UNHCR as Lead Agency."

61. Cecile Dubernet, *The International Containment of Displaced Persons: Humanitarian Spaces without Exit*, (Aldershot: Ashgate Publishing, 2001).

62. Quoted in Cunliffe and Pugh, "The UNHCR as Lead Agency."

63. Cutts, Humanitarian Operations in Bosnia, 10.

64. Cutts, Humanitarian Operations in Bosnia, 23.

65. United Nations, *Critical Economic Situation in Africa, Report of the Secretary General*, UN Doc. A/41/683 (1986), para. 4.

66. United Nations, *Critical Economic Situation.*

67. Francis M. Deng and L. Minear, *The Challenges of Famine Relief: Emergency Operations in the Sudan* (Washington, D.C.: Brookings Institution, 1992).

68. United Nations, *Critical Economic Situation*; Deng and Minear, *The Challenges of Famine Relief.*

69. Deng and Minear, *The Challenges.*

70. United Nations, *Critical Economic Situation.*

71. United Nations, *Critical Economic Situation.*

72. United Nations, *Critical Economic Situation.*

73. See Courtland Robinson, "The Comprehensive Plan of Action for Indochinese Refugees, 1989–1997: Sharing the Burden and Passing the Buck," Journal of Refugee Studies," Vol 17, No. 3, 2000, 319–333.

74. Robinson, "The Comprehensive Plan of Action."

75. UNHCR, *The State of the World's Refugees—In Search of Solutions* (New York: Oxford University Press, 1995).

76. UNHCR, *The State*, 51.

77. UNHCR, *The State*, 51.

78. UNHCR, *The State*, 51.

79. G. Goodwin-Gill, "Towards a Comprehensive Regional Policy Approach: The Case for Closer Inter-Agency Co-operation," *IOM/UNHCR* (UNHCR:Geneva, 1993); also published in *IJRL* 5/347 (1993).

80. Report of the Steering Group in the follow-up to the Regional Conference to address the Problems of Refugees, Displaced Persons, Other Forms of Involuntary Displacement and Returnees in the Countries of the Commonwealth of Independent States and Relevant Neighboring States, Geneva, June 17–18, 1998.

81. Jacques Cuénod, *Report on Refugees, Displaced Persons and Returnees: Report to the Economic and Social Council*, Economic and Social Council, UN Doc. E/1991/109/Add.1 (June 27, 1991), para. 3.

82. Cuénod, *Report on Refugees*, para. 125.

83. Jacques Cuénod, *Coordinating United Nations Humanitarian Assistance: Some Suggestions for Improving DHA's Performance* (Washington, D.C./Geneva: Refugee Policy Group, 1993).

84. Thomas G. Weiss, "Humanitarian Shell Games: Whither UN Reform?" *Security Dialogue* 29, No. 1 (1998): 10.

85. United Nations Office for the Coordination of Humanitarian Assistance, "Consolidated Appeals Process," *UNOCHA* 2004, http://ochaonline.un.org/webpage.asp?Page=384 (June 27, 2004).

86. United Nations, *Comprehensive Report on Lessons Learned from United Nations Assistance Mission for Rwanda (UNAMIR), October 1993–April 1996*, 1996. Available at www.un.org/Depts/dpko.

87. U.S. General Accounting Office, *Internally Displaced Persons Lack Effective Protection* (Washington, D.C.: General Accounting Office, 2001).

88. Women's Commission for Refugee Women and Children, *Out of Sight, Out of Mind* (New York: Women's Commission, 2000).

89. Brookings Institution, "Roundtable on the Gap between Humanitarian Assistance and Long-Term Development," (Washington D.C.: UNHCR and the World Bank, 1999).

90. United Nations Senior Interagency Network on Internal Displacement, Report from the Special Coordinator on Internal Displacement: Background (N.Y.:UN Office for the Coordination of Humanitarian Affairs, 2001).

91. Bruce Jones and Abby Stoddard, *External Review of the Inter-Agency Standing Committee* (New York: Center on International Cooperation, 2003).

92. Jones and Stoddard, *External Review*, 2003 (Center on International Cooperation 2003).

93. Victor Tanner and Elizabeth Stites, *External Evaluation of OCHA's Internal Displacement Unit* (New York: UN Office for the Coordination of Humanitarian Affairs, 2004).

94. Tanner and Stites, *External Evaluation*, 2004.

95. Tanner and Stites, *External Evaluation*, 2004.

96. Tanner and Stites, *External Evaluation*, 2004.

97. UN Office for the Coordination of Humanitarian Affairs, "Procedural Steps for Developing an IDP Response Strategy," (New York: UNOCHA, 2004).

4

Funding Humanitarian Operations

INTRODUCTION

The expansion in the numbers of humanitarian disasters since the end of the Cold War has been met by neither sufficient levels of funding nor the development and implementation of funding mechanisms and structures adequate to address the complexity of today's humanitarian crises. Inadequate funding resources, inadequate funding mechanisms, and the prevalence of mismatches between donors and programs comprise one of the primary barriers to improving assistance and protection for forced migrants today.

The reasons for inadequate levels of funding and coordination over funding are complex. An increasingly difficult operating environment for humanitarian work and changing donor trends in humanitarian assistance over the past ten years present many challenges. As donors have moved toward providing bilateral aid to nongovernmental organizations (NGOs) and multilateral organizations, donors have become more intimately involved in programming initiatives and the recipients of aid monies have been subjected to stricter control measures. The development of more advanced systems for tracking funds has allowed donors as well as practitioners to question the capacity and performance of humanitarian assistance in terms of cost effectiveness and delivery, and to require a higher level of efficiency and accountability. Higher standards for the use of aid money combined with donor stringency have increased competition among aid agencies for resources and decreased incentives for cooperation. Relatively undeveloped or inefficient coordination structures have been a frequent result. Thus, even in well-funded humanitarian crises, the needs of forced migrants may not be met because of overlaps and gaps in different agency programming. While increasing standards for the use of aid money can and should be a positive development, benefits can only occur when high funding standards are accompanied by comprehensive, thoughtful, and generous funding practices, in what has become referred to as "good humanitarian donorship." Donor investment practices will continue to play an important role in determining the impact of aid programs on humanitarian assistance and protection for forced migrants in a broad range of settings in the coming years.

This chapter will discuss recent changes in the funding environment for humanitarian emergencies as well as the major challenges for and solutions to funding crises for humanitarian emergencies. The chapter begins with efforts by the United Nations to develop more strategic funding plans via the Consolidated Appeals Process, discussing improvements and continuing shortcomings in these plans. It then turns to donor responses, examining the funding strategies of the principal government donors of humanitarian relief as well as initiatives to improve coordination and the overall concept of good humanitarian donorship.

THE CONSOLIDATED APPEALS PROCESS

The Consolidated Appeals Process (CAP) is the primary coordination mechanism, strategic planning document and fundraising tool for UN resource mobilization in complex emergencies. The CAP was established in 1992 and provides a framework for the UN and its partner organizations to develop common humanitarian strategies, advocacy platforms, goals and priorities in a given country or region in response to a complex emergency. The CAP document, which is produced annually and launched globally each November, is often used as a benchmark against which an operation's effectiveness can be monitored and evaluated. However, the CAP does not always function sufficiently as a coordinated planning document, or as a reflection of best practices in joint assessment of needs and capacities. The CAP has been criticized harshly as being more of an agency wish list cut and pasted into a single document, than an actual effort toward coordination.

The CAP is the only coordination mechanism that brings together IASC (United Nations Inter-Agency Standing Committee) members, host governments, NGOs, other bilateral organizations, and donors for shared analysis and discussion of strategies, objectives, and principles for humanitarian assistance. Through the creation of the document itself, and through the planning workshops, agencies share information at the organizational and sectoral levels. The CAP planning process, the CAP document itself, and the CAP mid-year review facilitate information exchange in the field and at headquarters on new programming tools, needs assessments, standards, and common strategies.

The CAP document is structured in two parts. The first part describes the context of the humanitarian situation, its causes and the effect on the vulnerable population. It also outlines possible scenarios and includes a capacities and vulnerabilities analysis. It describes how the agencies in the CAP will complement each other and lists strategic goals for the CAP. The second part includes the Common Humanitarian Action Plan (CHAP), which is a coordinated program of plans and projects based on an agreed strategy designed to achieve shared goals. The CHAP is formed through "common analysis of the political, economic and security constraints in the context of the humanitarian program."[1] It includes an analysis of projected humanitarian needs both in the short and longer term based on sectors and on the competencies and capacities of the humanitarian community. The document aims to identify any potential gaps and includes a statement of goals and objectives (again based on sectors) of the humanitarian community. This statement includes a transition plan for relief to development activities. Generally, the CHAP constitutes the main strategy section of the CAP document, and provides an opportunity to incorporate lessons learned into programming development and to analyze the value-added of the UN system in a particular country. It also links humanitarian interventions to a long-term vision for post-conflict activities.

When fully developed and widely applied, the CHAP should allow humanitarian actors to:

- Improve strategic decision-making through use of a logical framework approach.
- Identify, in a timely way, problems or gaps in the humanitarian response.
- Clarify accountability within the humanitarian system, and between the international system and recipient governments/authorities.
- Ensure that the views of the beneficiaries are represented in the planning process.
- Support resource mobilization.
- Build on existing organizational specific or interorganizational monitoring systems.
- Build consensus and transparency in information collection and analysis.
- Provide the humanitarian community with a basis for monitoring, reviews and evaluations.
- Promote strategic planning and account effectively for resources.

A number of different actors are involved in the CAP process and the creation of the CAP document. The resident in-country humanitarian coordinators (HCs), who report directly to the Emergency Relief Coordinator (ERC) and lead the work, lead the process with the UN country team and other partners. The HCs work with the national government, local authorities, and donor government representatives to establish appropriate policies and programming. Additionally, they may work with academics, think-tanks, and development agencies such as the World Bank to provide input into the CAP.

The CAP is responsible for channeling billions of dollars of donor funds for global humanitarian activities. Over 250 consolidated appeals have been issued through the CAP, with total contributions amounting to over $17 billion. Funding for CAPs peaked in 1994 at $5.7 billion—exceeding 10 percent of total overseas disaster assistance. The 1995 rise was followed by three years of decline, but in 1997 another sharp increase to $4.5 billion was seen.[2] This is characteristic of trends in humanitarian assistance over the past quarter of a century, which has seen a pattern of periodic increases followed by plateaus and subsequent increases.

CAPs funding patterns vary over time, by emergency and by type of project. Even within the overall increase in humanitarian assistance, the proportion of total global humanitarian assistance represented by CAP projects has fallen from an average of 40 percent to an average of 30 percent over the past decade. According to an internal review of the CAP, this lost market share of 10 percent was equivalent to $560 million in 2001.[3] It can be assumed that this 'lost' funding has migrated to the NGO sector. Figures from donors seem to confirm this, with ECHO's NGO funding rising from 30 percent of its total budget in 1990 to 65 percent in 1999.[4]

The UN and other aid agencies are increasingly looking at the efficiency of the donor funding and the impact of funding over the various stages of emergencies. Donors demonstrate both sectoral and geographic preferences in their funding actions. Although donors aim for improved coordination, most state that their funding decisions are only partially impacted by the CAP. Most donors want to see the UN agencies continue to plan and coordinate, but state that the CAP is unlikely to make them fund a project, agency, or sector that they would not fund otherwise.[5] In a survey conducted by a consultant for the WFP in 2001, donor attitudes tended to reflect their funding for the CAP. An illustration of these attitudes is highlighted in figure 4.1.

Donors emphasize the positive effects of the CAP on resource mobilization, yet assert the importance of individual performance for each UN agency. The CAP has increased donor confidence, simplified the decision-making process, served as an education tool, and increased donor coordination. Donors emphasize that the financial tracking mechanisms and the mid-year review are of particular importance for coordination efforts.[6] While taking these factors into consideration, donors also state that "the most important

Fig. 4.1.   Donor Utilization of CAP for Funding Decisions (adapted from WFP)
*Percentages represent the portion of these donors' overall contribution to WFP in 2006.[6]

criteria for determining their response to an appeal is the quantity of funds that they have available for each country, and which sectors they wish to fund. Their decisions will also be strongly influenced by their view of individual agency performance and capacity, at both a global and country-specific level."[7] Donors emphasize that these factors contribute to the discrepancies between funding of different countries and sectors rather than an inherent weakness in the CAP itself.

Yet, donor governments frequently undermine the CAP by making conflicting demands of UN agencies.[8] Government donors also tend to pick and choose what they consider to be priorities with the CAP, which results in some activities being well funded, even to the point of excess, while others are ignored. See below for further discussion of the role of donors in funding humanitarian operations.

The CAP process has not been able to address the problems faced by "forgotten" emergencies, places of protracted and "forgotten" conflict with limited media coverage or funding likelihood. Burundi is a clear example. Burundi is one of the most frequent applicants for funding through the CAP. Individual CAPs were submitted for Burundi in 1993, 1994, 1999, 2000, 2001, 2002, and 2003. The percentage of funding met for Burundi ranges from a low of 27 percent in 2000 to a high of 62 percent in 1994. The average percentage of funds met for Burundi is 46 percent.[9] This is low in comparison to the average of 82.3 percent funds met for the former Yugoslavia, which also submitted CAPs annually from 1993 to 1998. As of May 2003, the donor community had met only 24.5 percent of program funding requests for the most recent Burundi CAP.

Countries where high levels of insecurity make humanitarian access impossible or severely restricted, such as Somalia in the late 1990s, experience limited CAP funding. Difficulties in sustaining or attracting funding also occur in countries with long-running conflicts, in "forgotten emergencies" that lack media coverage, and in conflicts within or involving states not considered to be "good policy" countries, such as the Democratic Republic of Congo. In some cases, the CAP is abandoned when alternative sources of multilateral and bilateral development aid become available, such as occurred in Rwanda in 2000.[10]

One explanation for donor preferences might be the nature of food sector agencies such as WFP. Unlike agencies such as UNICEF, which work in many sectors, WFP's funds go only to food aid and logistics. Programs in areas such as health, education, and agricultural activities often require longer time frames than those allotted by emergency budgets, due to the need to build local capacity. In contrast, food aid may be largely delivered by airdrops with the supervision of international food monitors. This allows food aid to be more easily scaled-up in a short period of time, and allows for quick "proof" of concrete results.

WFP also receives greater funding because its services constitute the only sector in the CAP where the UN is still indisputably dominant in program delivery. Many of the NGOs working in specialized sectors do not even bother to include their projects in the CAP. Funding to NGOs outside of the CAP reflects the dominance of their programs in sectors other than food delivery. For example, Oxfam GB alone spent $35 million in the water and sanitation sectors, almost twice the amount contributed via the CAP. However, the WFP is effective at delivering food in emergency situations and the high amount of financial support may reflect the trust that donors have in WFP's capacity.[11]

REFORMING THE CAP

Since 1992, the CAP has undergone a series of reforms at the initiative of UN staff and IASC members. Many of these changes were undertaken to increase funding for the CAP and to redefine CAP policies and goals. IASC has attempted to take a leadership role in the CAP and has, as a result, undertaken a number of reform and policy initiatives. The leadership structure of the CAP has also changed considerably since the creation of the Office for the Coordination of Humanitarian Affairs (OCHA) in 1997. In addition, different agencies have attempted to reform the CAP process on an individual basis. Recent changes in the process include emphases on staff training, financial tracking, and program documentation. While existing reforms have had a positive impact on the ability of the CAP to generate comprehensive funding for humanitarian emergencies, further reform and refinement are critically needed. This section will first outline the impact of existing reforms before turning to a discussion of the reforms necessary to turn the CAP into a comprehensive, coordinated planning document.

IASC Guidelines and Technical Recommendations

The IASC has written many CAP Policy Guidelines and technical recommendations aimed at standardizing the response to relief, disasters, recovery, rehabilitation, and development. Some of the most important of these documents are the 1994 IASC-endorsed *Guidelines*, IASC working group recommendations, the CHAP technical guidelines, and the 1999 Interagency Training Tool. The 1994 *Guidelines*, in particular, encompassed a "comprehensive set of proposals that ranged from strategy formulation to enhanced responsibility for Humanitarian Coordinators (HCs)."[12] Additionally, annual technical guidelines are disseminated by the IASC to reflect new developments and lessons learned. These guidelines provide a fluid framework for preparing the CAP document and practical guidance to humanitarian coordinators, field offices, and country teams on how to structure and format the document.

The 1994 IASC *Guidelines* were the first major inter-agency attempt to clarify the purpose of the CAP and UN coordination in general. The guidelines remain relevant on a number of important points outlined in a UNICEF report, including:

- "Integrating humanitarian activities to promote cost-effective and efficient relief and recovery activities that eliminate duplication.
- Strengthening the capacities of emergency-affected countries.
- The CAP as a programming process through which regional and international relief systems are able to mobilize and respond to selective major or complex emergencies.
- A definition of major and complex emergencies.
- The leadership role of the ERC in coordinating, facilitating, steering, and sanctioning the CAP process and arbitrating on all matters requiring consensus.
- The crucial strategic role of the country team in assessments, in initiating and preparing the CAP, and in implementing and monitoring programs."[13]

Evaluation and monitoring reforms are also an inter-agency and donor-led priority. The United Nations Economic and Social Council (ECOSOC) resolution 1995/96 requested that agencies develop inter-agency systems for monitoring and evaluating humanitarian assistance. It was believed that strategic monitoring would enable the HC and country team, the ERC and OCHA, and the operational agencies at the headquarters (HQ) level to globally monitor all CHAP elements. Some independent studies such as the "Multi-Donor Evaluation of Humanitarian Assistance," the "Review of Coordination in the Great Lakes Region," and the "Overseas Development Institute (ODI) Study on Coordination" are also relevant to efforts to develop monitoring and evaluation mechanisms.[14]

In 2001, an IASC working group undertook a review of implementation and management issues related to the CAP in order to formulate a new UN policy position. This resulted in a detailed framework for continuing agency commitment, including a Plan of Action with recommendations for increasing senior level involvement, strengthening advocacy, and utilizing the CAP as a strategic planning and coordination tool.[15] Recommendations from the working group included a shift in emphasis from the "appeal" label of the CAP to a strategic planning focus reflecting the changed humanitarian context and the need for increased transparency. Additional recommendations included the placement of the CAP as a standing item on the IASC agenda, with a more central role for those in leadership positions and the increased involvement of senior IASC members and HCs in "events, functions, and missions" in support of the CAP.[16]

Financial reform initiatives have also improved coordination under the CAP. Numerous financial roadblocks that OCHA's predecessor, the Department of Humanitarian Affairs (DHA), encountered in its early years prompted many of the early difficulties of a coordinated process. As one report states, "the DHA was given inadequate resources and was unable to tackle the competitive tendencies of the UN operational agencies, some of which were themselves given coordination responsibilities from time to time. It was also side-tracked by its management of a plethora of small funds for programs that fell outside of other agencies' mandates."[17] One of the major problems of the CAP funding process from the onset was that it often resembled "shopping lists" of agency requirements rather than harmonized and integrated programs and projects.[18] With the increased scope of the CAP, these lists grew, but with little evidence of inter-agency harmonization efforts. This was, in part, due to the early lack of country leadership on the CAP. An IASC review of the CAP states, "While the Resident Coordinators were responsible for the CAP process, they had little authority to prune or eliminate the overlaps and duplications that were frequently evident in the final products. Agencies tended to introduce their pre-determined programs into the CAPs, maintaining that they could not be altered."[19]

The consequence of this open funding process was that the CAP began to include elements of a new relief-development parallelism that was emerging in the international aid community. The CAP was no longer solely about emergency and disaster response, but began to also address development initiatives in emergency settings. However, the HCs and the DHA and then OCHA had little authority to eliminate overlaps and duplication. IASC reports that there were attempts to reconcile these trends by creating yet another instrument, the Expanded Consolidated Interagency Appeal. Despite these efforts, little progress was made and the CAP continues to address both emergency and development needs.

Leadership Structure

In 1997, UN Secretary General Kofi Annan replaced the DHA with the Office for the Coordination of Humanitarian Affairs (OCHA) in order to establish a more centralized leadership structure and a clarification of the responsibilities of the CAP. The office was structured so that an Under-Secretary General for Humanitarian Affairs, who also holds the position of Emergency Relief Coordinator (ERC), would head the office. The ERC was to be responsible for coordinating the various UN humanitarian agencies and held the chairmanship of the Interagency Standing Committee, which brought together all major humanitarian, development, and human rights bodies and promoted initiatives to improve the quality of coordination.[20] The IASC had a sub-working group on the CAP to manage policy issues. The Under-Secretary served as the Secretary General's adviser on humanitarian issues and provided an important interface between the humanitarian community and the intergovernmental organs of the United Nations by working as the Convener of the Executive Committee for Humanitarian Affairs (ECHA), which was created to provide a forum for the humanitarian community and the political and peacekeeping departments to discuss humanitarian crises and issues.

Since this reorganization, OCHA has taken over responsibility for dividing tasks among the various agencies for the CAP and ensuring that humanitarian issues that fall outside existing mandates are sufficiently addressed in coordination, advocacy, and policy development activities. OCHA established its presence on the ground through the deployment of field offices, and by 2002 was present in over thirty-five countries. Since OCHA itself is not operational and does not have to defend its own "turf," it can more effectively mediate disputes among the operating agencies. A key role of OCHA is now the supervision and development of consolidated funding appeals for individual and regional emergencies, and the analysis of specific situations to identify gaps in coverage.[21]

Other Reforms

Additional inter-agency reforms have been made to improve the quality of staff training and technical support. Due to a high turnover rate, there has been a movement to streamline and simplify training tools. Training modules have been developed with a focus on prioritization, scenarios, competencies and capacities, sector objectives, up-to-date examples, projects, monitoring and reporting, and training best practices. Staff members have additionally recommended the development of "CAP in a hurry" training tools for sudden onset emergencies, French language training tools, a summary of policies, and the creation of both a CAP website for trainers and training materials on guidelines such as The SPHERE Standards, the ICRC Code of Conduct and the *Guidelines for Internally Displaced Populations.*[22]

Technical reforms have improved documentation and the production of information related to the CAP. A financial tracking system was launched in 2001 to allow a more flexible and custom-based analysis of funding and donor contributions. CAP documents and mid-year reviews have also been included on the ReliefWeb site to encourage information exchange and to draw attention to issues of under-funding and monitoring.

In addition, a number of agencies have undertaken individual initiatives to improve the CAP process. According to an OCHA review, "UNICEF and WFP have publicly committed to developing a 'corporate approach to CAP' and developed guidelines on participation in the joint planning for field staff."[23] UNHCR has included guidelines on the CAP in the new edition of its manual. WFP and the FAO have also organized workshops on the CAP for staff members, and the FAO is planning to designate focal points in the field for CAP. UNDP is in the process of developing positions and policies on the CAP and resource mobilization in transitional situations as well as in countries transitioning from relief to recovery. Agency heads continue to play increasingly important roles in the global CAP launches and in advocacy to support sectors outside of their own institutional mandates.[24]

Overall, the CAP has undergone extensive reorganization since it was first created as a funding and coordination mechanism for UN agencies. Much of the leadership for these changes has been provided by the IASC and OCHA. Reform initiatives have focused on clarifying the purpose of the CAP and the structure of CAP funding along with the leadership responsibilities of the various agencies and OCHA. Although most of these reforms utilize an inter-agency approach, some agencies have undertaken supplemental internal reform and training activities in order to strengthen their contribution to the CAP process.

Necessary Future Reforms

UN agencies and the donor community have highlighted a number of current reform priorities. First, the role of the CAP needs to be further defined, with the tension between its dual roles, as a fundraising and advocacy instrument on the one hand and as an instrument for inter-agency cooperation on the other hand, resolved or mitigated. Second, the UN is and needs to continue working toward administrative improvements including the prioritization and coordination of aid delivery, improvements in management roles, and an examination of the timing of aid delivery. Third, the CAP needs to take into account more effectively the needs of women and children. Fourth, the UN needs, to clarify the role of outside organizations in the CAP. Finally, mechanisms need to be established for measuring the "value-added" of the CAP and humanitarian aid programs.

Defining the Role of the CAP

Defining the role of the CAP is of central importance. The CAP is used as an advocacy instrument to keep the humanitarian agenda center stage and as a tool for resource mobilization to promote and maintain donor momentum. It is also used to promote strategic planning, prioritization of humanitarian needs and as a monitoring and evaluation tool. This dual role often creates tensions among the various actors involved:

> The issue at the heart of many of the CAP's difficulties is the dual function of the CAP as both a programming process and a fundraising mechanism. The always inherent tension in this dual function has become more visible in recent years . . . significant improvements in joint strategic planning and efforts at greater inclusion of non-UN actors in strategy formulation have been accompanied and to some extent undermined by decreased average percentage contributions to annual appeals.[25]

For instance, many NGOs show an initial strong interest in the CAP, but their engagement slips when they see that their participation does not necessarily result in concrete funding opportunities.

One of the important roles of the CAP is to raise attention to the needs of ongoing humanitarian crises and to serve as an advocacy tool for the UN. The IASC committee recommends further developing CAP themes to increase advocacy on current humanitarian issues. Examples of past themes have been *Women and War* and *Forgotten Emergencies*. The committee also recommends linking the CAP theme to UN events and other ongoing advocacy campaigns. The committee suggests adopting selected emergency countries for mentoring, guidance, resource mobilization, and support by individual Senior IASC members as advocates. It may also be helpful to appoint selected celebrities as Goodwill Ambassadors to raise awareness for the CAP on a year-round basis.[26]

OCHA states that the launch of the CAP may be used as an advocacy and fundraising event. OCHA recommends working with parliamentarians, ministries and departments in the respective donor countries, as well as with media organizations to publicize the CAP launch events. It may be prudent to centralize the launch of the CAP; the WFP found that decentralized CAP launches did not attract adequate media attention. Keeping this in mind, WFP also questioned the "overwhelming" impact of a centralized CAP launch and the fear that the situations be perceived as just one massive problem.[27]

Although the issues of fundraising and strategic planning are often at odds in the CAP, the consensus of most donors and almost all field workers and desk staff involved with the process is that it is not realistic to separate these two functions. The reality of workloads and competing priorities would make it difficult to maintain and elicit involvement of a wide range of participants without the impetus and focus provided by the fundraising element of the appeal. In other words, the institutional support of the CAP is partially prompted because it is a fundraising instrument.[28] For instance, assistance to Georgia in the early 1990s was quickly distributed and adequate enough to meet most needs because of the CAP's strength as a fundraising tool. The UN initiated the first CAP appeal for Georgia in 1993, through which it raised over $20 million in direct assistance that it was unable to attract through prior efforts.

Other UN mechanisms also serve as inter-agency fundraising and financial mechanisms, but these mechanisms have little interaction with the CAP. The Emergency Revolving Fund is used by operational organizations in the early stages of emergencies. The United Nations Development Assistance Framework (UNDAF) also works to build a unified approach toward common development goals. It uses the Common Country Assessment (CCA) instrument to analyze the national development situations and to identify key development issues in countries of operation.[29] It would be beneficial to explore the complementarities of these existing mechanisms with the CAP process.

For these reasons, it is important that the UN system balance the advocacy and fundraising roles of the CAP. While the CAP is an effective fundraising and advocacy tool, it is important that this role complement the organizational basis of the document. Agencies must take caution not to include all requests in the document, but rather prioritize and streamline funding requests. It is also important for the UN to clarify the role of other funding mechanisms and to additionally explore linkages between these mechanisms and the CAP.

System Oversight and Prioritization

The CAP has also been criticized for a lack of system oversight and prioritization. The CAP currently lacks mechanisms for screening projects, setting priorities, improving management, and establishing appropriate timelines and structures for emergency and transition activities. This leaves the CAP as a "toothless instrument for creating coherent, principled and cost-effective programmes."[30] Prioritization is further crippled by the debate over what should constitute priorities in an emergency. While saving lives is important, "humanitarian assistance that saves lives but allows livelihoods to perish is neither strategic nor particularly humanitarian."[31] Projects are often included in the CAP in order to maintain inter-agency working relations, rather than because of their individual value.

Currently there is inadequate time for screening projects and a lack of an organizational structure to undertake the screening process. Prioritization can be improved by delegating the authority for screening projects to committees working at the sectoral level. This model was used in Angola, and resulted in a greater understanding of the proposed project and how it related to the sectoral objectives. Donors also play an important role in prioritization initiatives, since agencies often present projects that they think will be funded rather than on the basis of what is needed. This needs versus resources dilemma highlights a fundamental communication problem between donors and humanitarian agencies operating in the field.

Several administrative recommendations for improving the overall CAP process were outlined in a recent UNICEF report.[32] UNICEF first recommends developing standardized guidelines for joint assessments of priorities and strategic monitoring mechanisms for all actors. UNICEF also recommends the creation of incentives for agencies to comply with the established strategic planning process. In addition, the UN should introduce a reality check on CAP ceilings by encouraging reprioritization and reallocation of resources. Resources should also account separately for food and non-food contributions to eliminate skewing the overall picture of funding. Finally, the UN should develop and present a system for impact analysis to demonstrate the effects of underfunding.

Management changes may also increase the impact of the CAP. On the country level, UNICEF recommends assigning one person the responsibility for the practical preparation of the CAP and for facilitating discussions and support on the country team level. This person could lead in-country IASC meetings.[33] Donors also recommend increasing the participation of senior staff members in the CAP process. Donors recommend giving specific roles to the ERC, Senior IASC and OCHA staff and HCs in CAP to maintain momentum, advocacy for forgotten emergencies, and arbitration on contentious CAP issues. It may be possible to use the annual HC retreat to commit principals and senior staff (HCR, UNICEF, WFP, and OCHA), increase ownership at the high level, and create linkages between staff and certain emergencies in order to promote a stewardship type of system.[34] Donor relations should similarly be delegated to a high-level staff member who sits on subworking groups for the CAP.[35]

An additional problem facing the CAP is that the timing of the CAP cycle does not always match agency internal planning/programming procedures. Although some effort has been made to relate the CAP to other programming mechanisms via UNDAF and CCA, no effective working linkages have been established between these mechanisms. Most major donors do not feel that the CAP cycle in itself stimulates funding, and some donors even feel that it is a hindrance to force emergency cycles into a calendar year. In some countries, due to agricultural cycles and other factors, the CAP might more accurately reflect the situation if it was, in fact, launched at a different time.[36] Another common recommendation is the need to issue emergency CAPs more rapidly to seize the moment and address needs for immediate donor alerts. It is recommended that CAPs be updated on a regular basis and be seen as "ongoing projects" rather than once-a-year reports.[37]

Multiyear CAPs should be explored for chronic emergencies at the same time as efforts are made to ensure that aid provided is consistent with the stage of the emergency. Needs are different at the height of a new emergency than they are in a protracted conflict. And even in protracted conflicts, new displacements and new issues may arise. Transitions such as these, and particularly the transition from relief to development, need significant examination. Donors recommend that an effective transition might be accomplished by: bringing in development actors as early as possible in CHAP formulation; encouraging early donor involvement; identifying appropriate transition mechanisms; promoting coherence from the donors in the various governing boards of UN bodies and international financial institutions in order to advocate for complementary strategic planning; and developing methods (such as special funding mechanisms) to overcome constraints for funding the transitional recovery phase.[38]

The East Timor CAP is a good example of how effective timing and prioritization can positively impact the emergency stage of a conflict. The initial CAP appeal for East Timor, which was jointly submitted with the appeal for West Timor, covered emergency and transitional programs for a nine-month period from October 1999 to June 2000. The East Timor CAP, which was facilitated by OCHA, effectively dealt with prioritization of needs, especially in the early part of the emergency. The programs focused on six common goals during the emergency and transition phases: 1) meet acute needs first; 2) stabilize at-risk populations before their condition becomes acute; 3) reintegrate displaced persons; 4) enhance livelihood strategies; 5) repair essential infrastructure; and 6) help reestablish key institutions essential for economic recovery and good governance. UN agencies and NGOs aimed to define exit strategies early, integrate humanitarian principles, and establish inclusive coordination structures for logistics under the leadership of the WFP.[39]

The rapid response of donors and the international aid community was one of the primary strengths of the East Timor CAP. Overall, the CAP for East Timor generated a significant amount of funding in a short time frame. However, the funding-driven timetable for the response was bound by a nine-month period under the CAP. Despite the fact that the initial appeal was drafted without a lot of background assessment for priority needs, due to security constraints, governments responded with support to the joint military-humanitarian operation.[40] OCHA also successfully coordinated the larger emergency response ahead of time, which enabled a coherent approach even in the early phase of the response.[41] Although NGOs were more involved in the CAP than in the past, slow disbursement of funds did negatively impact many of their projects.

Despite early successes, the transition period in East Timor posed numerous challenges to aid agencies. While the CAP in East Timor met initial needs, with the exception of shelter, it failed to effectively serve as a coordination mechanism for the transition period. The reintegration of refugees, building of government structures, and reconciliation were of central importance. Sufficient food aid had been provided, but there was still a shelter shortage. Humanitarian assistance was scaled down to avoid dependency, and NGOs began to take more of a lead role in health needs. Programs suffered from a lack of communication between NGOs and the newly forming East Timorese civil society. There was also a lack of a long-term transition plan from relief to development and forward planning on issues such as the collection of health data. Overlapping mandates contributed to the transition difficulties, and in retrospect, the CAP projects in East Timor would have benefited from a clearer exit and transition strategy. Other CAP countries such as Georgia have found some success in addressing this problem through incorporating a transition support component into each project to ease the shift from emergency to development assistance.[42]

Overall, as the CAP becomes an increasingly important funding mechanism, the UN finds that it must begin to improve its administration of the process. Standardized guidelines for joint assessments are necessary to prevent underfunding of various sectors and emergencies. Effective management also contributes to successes or lack of successes in the CAP. Other changes, such as the time frame for the CAP and transition plans, are important to effectively meet the differences in financial needs at various stages of an emergency, as is illustrated by the East Timor CAP.

The Role of NGOs and Other Organizations in the CAP

The involvement and participation of NGOs and organizations such as the ICRC in the CAP is a critical issue. One of the goals of the CAP is to support coordination between the UN and other humanitarian actors and to mitigate agencies' self interest. However, NGO coordination with the appeals varies from country to country. NGOs often found themselves on the periphery of the CAP in the past, with their projects included in sectoral sections, but rarely as part of an overall or sector-based strategy. In recent years, there has been a degree of confusion about the extent to which the appeal is a vehicle for projects outside of the UN.

In the past few years, NGOs have increasingly presented their projects through the CAP. Some donors request that NGOs demonstrate program coherence with overall CAP strategy. This indicates that there is a need for set mechanisms and criteria to define and monitor the participation of NGOs and NGO coherence with the CAP strategy. There is also a need to determine how NGO programs should be reflected in CAP appeals when they are not appealing for funds, but are used to illustrate complementarities in programming. Aside from the issue of NGO inclusion, additional problems have also plagued cooperative efforts with NGO actors. Slow disbursement of funds, when distributed, and lack of transparency have further affected operational partnerships between UN agencies and NGOs. While NGOs see the UN as potentially playing a strategic role in negotiating access with the local government or helping them obtain additional resources, NGOs are frustrated when this access and funding opportunities do not come through as promised.

An example of the benefits and problems of NGO participation in an emergency setting is illustrated by the East Timor appeal. This appeal involved substantial cooperation and coordination not only within the UN, but also with international NGO partners. Yet, despite increased NGO participation, the CAP process in East Timor also highlighted the problems of including numerous partners in the CAP appeal; "in East Timor, in 1999, this confusion in the minds of partners in the process as to what extent the CAP was a fundraising document, or an expression of strategic intent brought heightened expectations for many NGOs."[43] Many NGOs complained about the insufficient time given to obtain project information. For those who expected funding under the CAP and did not receive it, frustration was evident. Even those NGOs that did receive funding faced disbursement time frames of up to six months in some cases.[44] Humanitarian agencies, the UN and donors in East Timor overlooked opportunities for greater cooperation with local groups in emergency relief operations. Greater cooperation with local NGOs and church organizations might have provided more complete coverage and effective communication between humanitarian agencies and beneficiaries.

Cases such as East Timor highlight some necessary steps for improving UN-NGO cooperation. Some practitioners feel that Humanitarian Coordinators and OCHA teams should encourage NGO representatives to attend training and planning workshops. Others feel that donors should "request" that NGOs participate in the CAP process by making funding conditional on inclusion of both local and international NGOs into a wider cooperative strategy. For example, ECHO gave preference in this manner to NGOs in North Korea, who included their projects in the CAP. This recommendation requires a great deal of vigilance on the part of the donors, however, to follow through on such requirements, but may eliminate the frustration of the NGOs that occurred in the East Timor case in terms of their expectations for funding.[45]

There are several difficulties, however, with these suggestions. First, it may be problematic to secure the participation of agencies not working in the country of the appeal, which discriminates against those wishing to start up a program in the country. It may be possible to overcome this, by requesting that consortia such as InterAction or ICVA nominate a member agency to represent them. However, many agencies may still remain on the periphery of the planning process. Second, increasing the number of NGO projects may require that UN projects be reduced to accommodate them. This may reduce UN commitment to the CAP process. Third, it is not realistic to expect that all donors will consistently apply pressure on NGOs to participate in the CAP. NGOs also need to be brought into the CAP on a more regular and regulated basis. Although a number of reforms have been completed, there is clearly room for growth and improvements on a number of different fronts.

Improving Coverage for Women and Children

The CAP incorporates and addresses a number of thematic issues, including gender and age. The Capacities and Vulnerabilities Analysis (CVA), first utilized in 2001, bases strategy development and programs on objective assessment of vulnerability in these areas as well as other areas such as staff security and safety. Aid packages in general are often narrowly defined, and gaps can include: education; participation of forced migrants in decision-making; reproductive health care; psychosocial programs; and longer-term shelter. Aid needs to take into account the gender and age of forced migrants in order to appropriately assess specific protection and assistance needs and capabilities. Funding packages also need to ensure that forced migrants do not become a burden on other populations, including residents in the communities to which they relocate. The CVA aims to empower marginalized groups as agents of change by integrating these thematic issues into all training and planning tools used in the CAPs. The CVA gives the IASC Sub-Working Group on the CAP lead responsibility for the synthesis of lessons learned on issues such as gender integration, human rights, IDPs, children's issues, protection for the elderly and disabled, and HIV/AIDS.[46]

Women and children are estimated to account for 80 percent of all victims in situations of armed conflict.[47] Women also have remarkable strength to deal with crises and in many cases are at the center of household and community survival. Because of this, advocates argue that the CAP should have a more detailed focus on gender issues. Projects should support an active role for women in ensuring food, health, education, and shelter for their families. Women should be a part of the planning and decision-making processes for humanitarian assistance.

THE CAP AND FORCED MIGRANTS

The CAP is a potentially important tool for more effectively responding to the global IDP problem, since the majority of the countries covered by the CAP process have a significant number of IDPs. A number of recommendations for making the CAP more sensitive to the needs of IDPs were put forward by Francis Deng, Representative of the United Nations Secretary General on Internally Displaced Persons, who argued that greater attention should be given to IDP protection.[48] Most of the humanitarian crises covered by the appeals occur in countries affected by internal displacement. Deng argued for more attention to a broad spectrum of political, civil, social, economic, and cultural human rights in the CAP in order to better address the holistic needs of IDPs.[49]

Deng suggested several fundamental changes in the CAP to improve and integrate coverage for IDPs.[50] Deng recommended that a brief, but substantive, description of internally displaced populations, their size, condition, primary needs, opportunities, and long-term prognosis be included either in the introduction or the CHAP section of the appeals. He also recommended outlining a viable system for assessing and monitoring the condition of the displaced, or, when system components are not already in place, requesting support for such a system in the Appeal. These changes are necessary because "careful reading of the Consolidated Inter-agency Appeals suggests a disconnect between the frequent references to internally displaced persons as program beneficiaries and the relatively limited program initiatives, beyond traditional humanitarian aid, actually targeted to the displaced." As Deng states:

> appeals documents . . . refer to the displaced generally by noting that they are concentrated in camps, subject to attack, or localized within a region, and descriptions of individual projects (in the health, water, or education sectors, for example) may highlight specific needs. But, most Appeals do not provide a serious, integrated analysis of the political, security, legal, economic, or cultural issues confronting displaced communities. Nor do the Appeals generally describe the process by which international organizations monitor or evaluate these issues in displaced settlements.[51]

These issues are illustrated in an analysis of the 2000 CAP for Burundi. The paper critiques the CAP's lack of substantive information on the specific conditions of the internally displaced population. Although the analysis speculates that this might be for political or security reasons, it points out that this gap makes it difficult for readers to obtain a clear picture of the overall condition of IDPs in Burundi. The CAP does provide a strong program supporting preparation for IDP return, including in the economic, physical infrastructure and protection sectors. However, the analysis of this CAP recommends that the appeal provide a greater focus on the existing challenges of IDPs and the problems IDPs might have in obtaining or reaching services such as those supported by hospitals or clinics proposed within the Appeal.[52]

Serious analysis of long-term solutions for internal displacement, as well as related project proposals appear infrequently in CAP documents. Currently, limited analysis is contained in CAP documents on issues such as whether return is voluntary, if property rights are available upon return, whether safe transport is provided for return, if health and education facilities exist in the area of potential return, whether the return area has been demined, and what conditions for reintegration with local communities are present. Integration of more detailed analysis of refugee return programs in the CAP process may reflect the focused attention of UNHCR to these matters, but needs to be extended to IDP populations. Moreover, implementing development-oriented approaches earlier in displacement situations can empower displaced communities during displacement and move them beyond meeting basic survival needs.

An example of a development-oriented approach to relief funding for IDPs is found in the CAP for Sri Lanka. The CAP, launched in 2002, aimed to shift the focus from the immediate humanitarian crisis to long-term development and human rights challenges. At the same time, substantial budgetary allocations to UNHCR and the WFP highlighted the need for continued attention to humanitarian issues.[53] An ambitious roadmap for reintegration, the CAP has programs in sectors ranging from agriculture, economic recovery and infrastructure, health, mine action, and rule of law programs. However, as of May 2003, only $410,000 of the $24 million proposal has been funded. Initial funds from Norway, Germany, and Switzerland have gone to programs supporting IDPs, food aid, resettlement initiatives by CARITAS and mother-child health programs in the eastern province.

Deng recommended that the Resident/Humanitarian Coordinators (RCs/HCs) and Country Teams examine ways in which environmental building activities, and especially efforts to build local and national protection capacity, could be incorporated into Appeal projects. OCHA staff with responsibility for improving the CAP and IASC Sub-Working group members should note and distill examples of sound environmental building practice that can be disseminated to Country Teams preparing Appeals. Deng states that this could build, in part, on the work undertaken in the IASC-WG publication, *Manual on Field Practice in Internal Displacement: Examples from UN Agencies and Partner Organizations of Field-Based Initiatives Supporting Internally Displaced Persons.* In particularly sensitive political situations, responsibility for IDPs could also be delegated to heads of agencies based outside of the country.[54]

There is some ambivalence among some country teams on how to balance the needs of specified target groups, like internally displaced persons, with the requirement to address problems facing the population at large. In Georgia, for example, the needs of non-IDPs were neglected by most NGOs with the exception of assistance provided by ICRC.[55] In fact, some UN agencies argue against targeted assistance for IDP groups, stating that the CAP documents are not meant to be primary sources of information on IDP-related matters. OCHA asserts that the CAP should not target categories of vulnerable people, but should rather promote awareness that some groups may have "hidden needs." Therefore, one challenge facing the CAP is the need to balance the tension in some Appeals documents between the imperative to focus on special needs groups and the imperative to allocate limited resources among the general population.

Guidance by the IASC to RC/HCs and to Country Teams should clarify that the necessary focus on vulnerable persons is not intended to create a privileged class of individuals, or to create a preemptive entitlement to program benefits. CAP documents should analyze projects necessary to facilitate return or resettlement and reintegration. Documents should also address community and economic development measures beyond the provision of basic services. Moreover, OCHA should examine whether it is possible to compile and make available data on donor funding levels related to important cross-cutting themes and issues like gender and internal displacement, thus allowing donor support to be commensurate with actual need.

THE "VALUE ADDED" OF THE CAP

The development of standardized mechanisms for measuring the "value-added" of humanitarian aid programs is an important step toward increasing donor support for a comprehensive and coordinated CAP process. Currently there are no guidelines for assessments and evaluations of humanitarian aid programs, and therefore disparities exist between countries in terms of prior-itization, monitoring, and strategy-setting activities. Without standardized mechanisms for evaluation, donors have difficulty assessing the field of donor activities, and initiatives such as the CAP cannot function as compre-hensive summaries of needs. Joint assessments of needs led by OCHA do ex-ist, but are not enforced rigorously, while Agency internal controls and mon-itoring practices are often not well developed. Coordinated Agency and inter-Agency guidelines on financial tracking, monitoring, contingency plan-ning, and exit strategies are both necessary and central to the future success of the CAP.

Financial tracking is very important for measuring the impact of the CAP and attracting donor support. Financial tracking provides an analysis of con-tributions and contribution shortfalls, and highlights the positive and negative impacts of funding on programming. Financial tracking systems also allow donors to see current gaps in funding so that they can respond accordingly. These systems require a great deal of agency support. The WFP suggests that a more definite focal point for financial reporting in the various agencies may improve efficiency and will eliminate the current system whereby OCHA needs to request information from each of the field offices.[56]

OCHA provides financial reporting for all of the countries addressed through the CAP process. OCHA collects information for an online database from UN agencies, donor governments, and NGOs for specific appeals. Fi-nancial tables are officially updated once every month on the ReliefWeb site and OCHA reconciles the data against donor reports. Contributions reported by donors are included in the tables after they have been confirmed by the Agencies or relevant organizations. This is necessary since there are often changes in the total amount of contributions between the time of the donor announcement of the pledge and the final agreement between the donor and the Agency.[57]

Despite recent improvements to the mid-term review process, the UN still does not adequately demonstrate the "positive impact on beneficiaries of either projects that are funded or the negative impact on beneficiaries on [sic] projects that are not."[58] Agencies tend to submit mid-term and final reports based on the achievements of their individual projects, rather than the overall sectoral and strategic objectives. Donors would also benefit from a standardized accounting system, which would increase transparency on all levels.

In its current state, the CAP does not operate effectively as a country-monitoring device or as an international indicator of humanitarian assistance. The CAP represents only the UN activities in each country. It also rarely makes comparisons across different sectors or countries, which weakens attempts to make the flow of humanitarian assistance more equitable. In addition, the CAP does not represent the total humanitarian need in a country, but rather a series of UN programs only. This can obscure the fact that programs that did not receive CAP funding may have been alternatively implemented by NGOs with funding outside of the CAP. The comparative advantage of the UN system over NGOs and other players is also not always clarified. Greater attention needs to be given to what the UN system offers compared to the other players in global humanitarian assistance in terms of defining strategic areas and adapting to meet programming gaps. [59]

An OCHA review of the CAP recommends that IASC members carry out at least two field-based evaluations of the CAP each year. It also recommends that individual agencies carrying out reviews or evaluations of the CAP in their own programs ensure that the terms of reference include specific references to the CAP to increase lessons-learned material for the mechanism.[60] The mid-year review should also be treated with as much importance as the launch of the CAP as a benchmark for objectives and programming targets. Donors might facilitate this internal review process by developing country-specific benchmarks.

Additional controls and monitoring practices for the CAP may prompt increased donor support. Financial assessments of CAP projects allow donors to see how their financial contributions impact beneficiaries in the field. Although OCHA updated its financial tracking system, there is room for further improvement. Moreover, there exists a need for international tracking across various emergencies and across various sectors. By focusing on improving initiatives to monitor and evaluate the CAP, the UN may improve programming coverage and equity of funding in emergencies.

HUMANITARIAN DONORSHIP

Reform of the CAP alone will not ensure adequate and thoughtful funding for humanitarian emergencies. Measures can and need to be taken to improve the willingness of donors to fund the response to humanitarian emergencies. Over the course of the 1990s, the concept of good humanitarian donor-ship emerged as a benchmark for donor nations. Donors have recognized that a lack of donor coordination can result in underfunding and overfunding of specific sectors, incomplete response, and inconsistent response to humanitarian emergencies. This section first discusses potential venues for cooperation between donors, the current funding climate, and donor challenges before turning to an examination of existing donor policies and cooperation models. The chapter will conclude with recommendations for how good humanitarian donorship can be promoted to improve the flow and quality of aid to humanitarian emergencies.

The Current Funding Climate

Despite shortcomings in the systems used to track humanitarian aid, it is clear that humanitarian aid is increasing on a global level even if the CAPs are underfunded. From 1990 to 2000 the amount of official humanitarian aid flows doubled in real terms from $2.1 billion to $5.9 billion and as a proportion of official development assistance from 5.83 percent to 10.5 percent.[61] The majority of aid provided for forced migrants is contributed by a small number of bilateral donors including: the United States, (which accounts for one-third of total aid), Canada, Germany, Japan, the Netherlands, Norway, Sweden, Switzerland, and the United Kingdom (UK). The European Community Humanitarian Aid Office (ECHO) is also a major player, contributing 10 percent of humanitarian aid assistance in 2000.[62] If donor funding is to be coordinated, improving the CAP and continuing to explore other, complementary venues for donor coordination will be of critical importance.

In the 1990s and beyond, results-based management, a new public management trend in Western public policy, has influenced donors. The so-called "accountability revolution" in the humanitarian aid sphere led to an increase in and the professionalization of systems to monitor performance.[63] Funding changes were also fueled by new donor concerns regarding the effectiveness of programming and the potential for negative impact. High-profile negative evaluations of humanitarian assistance and the increased presence of the media in conflict areas during the 1990s challenged previously high levels of donor trust: "alongside technical concerns regarding the efficacy of humanitarian aid programs, the devastating idea took shape that, rather than doing good, emergency aid programs were actually doing harm, fueling conflict and, in the case of refugees in Zaire in 1994, feeding killers."[64] Out of this concern emerged a "do no harm" discourse among many donors (see chapter 5 for a further discussion of the "do no harm" concept). Donors and practitioners alike sought to develop an integrated approach to conflict that addressed the root causes of poverty and inequality in the wider context of diplomacy and defense. Donors realized the importance of understanding the role of relief in war economies and the use of relief funding as part of a broader conflict resolution strategy.[65] This realization changed the dynamics of donor funding in a dramatic way, as donors began to question the role and impact of humanitarian aid.

A second recent trend in humanitarian aid is what is now being referred to as the "bilateralization" of aid. Major donors to humanitarian agencies have begun to move away from the traditional aid paradigm, where unearmarked aid was channeled through multilateral institutions, such as the United Nations and the World Bank. All other aid, including earmarked assistance to the UN, NGOs, and the Red Cross Movement, and funds spent by governments themselves is technically 'bilateral' aid. Therefore, the bilateralization of aid describes a movement away from unearmarked and unmonitored grants to multilateral organizations.[66] Bilateralization also indicates the "increased proximity of official donors to humanitarian operations and decision-making."[67] This close proximity of donors has included the development of their own needs analysis and response strategies, disbursement channels, targeting of assistance to priority groups, countries, and issues and adaptation of policy-driven approaches to operations and humanitarian organizations. Donors have become more involved in both the planning and field stages of humanitarian operations.

While bilateralization of aid appears to be part of the new reality for humanitarian organizations, current aid tracking systems may overstate this trend. For example, the Development Assistance Committee (DAC) of the OECD allows members to report as official development assistance (ODA) the money they spend on supporting refugees during their first year of residence. This spending is counted as bilateral, since it stays within each donor country. Thirty-eight percent of the estimated total bilateral humanitarian aid was spent this way in 2000. Although not all countries report their aid this way (the UK, for instance does not), many of the major donors, including the United States, use this formula. Second, with the increasing importance of the Consolidated Appeals Process, which itemizes UN programs, many new contributions to the UN are earmarked and therefore counted as bilateral aid monies.[68] An increase in direct contracting of NGOs and military (and paramilitary) providers by donors has also led to an increase in bilateral aid assistance.

Official estimates of international spending patterns are further complicated by the fact that many organizations both receive and allocate funding. Moreover, many countries are not even included in the list of donor countries. ECHO, for instance, is a recipient of primarily multilateral humanitarian assistance from donor governments, but it is also a donor of primarily ear-marked funding to UN agencies, which are themselves both recipients and donors, and to local and international NGOs. To avoid double counting, hu-manitarian assistance is measured by the allocations from the DAC donor.[69] Using financial figures that only include DAC member states, also excludes regional funding arrangements, funds given by groups of states and funding from groups of states outside of the DAC membership.[70] Some non-DAC aid flows have been substantial. For example, in 1991, Arab countries gave $375 million in aid to Afghanistan and from 1977 to 1981 gave over $100 million annually to Somalia.[71] However, despite such problems in funding analysis, it is clear that the donor mindset has changed and that donor involvement in the projects they fund has significantly increased.

Donor Challenges

While there are positive implications to the increased role of donors in hu-manitarian assistance programming, donors continue to face numerous chal-lenges in the complex post-Cold War world, challenges that help explain both the lack of funding provided for addressing and preventing humanitarian emergencies and the lack of coordination between donors with respect to the funding provided. First and foremost donor governments need to balance the humanitarian imperative with foreign policy, regional peace and security is-sues, and domestic pressures. Second, donors need to rationalize the aid they do provide. To operate responsibly, donors need to establish rational quality-assurance mechanisms for programs they fund, begin funding the essential but often overlooked areas of logistics and training, pay attention to the relief to development gap and aid timing issues, and coordinate with other donors to avoid duplication of effort and ensure a comprehensive response to a hu-manitarian crisis.

Donors are influenced by a number of factors when determining interven-tions and funding strategies. The factors include foreign policy objectives, domestic politics, security concerns, media pressures, humanitarian concerns, and institutional leadership on policy and humanitarian issues. The complex interconnection between these factors can lead to a lack of funding for a hu-manitarian emergency or preventive action when there is either little policy interest in a humanitarian emergency or emerging situation or divisions within a donor government as to whether and how much humanitarian aid should be provided. Humanitarian agencies wishing to acquire more funding for humanitarian emergencies might focus on improving donor understanding of the common "contagion" effect of humanitarian emergencies and the link-ages between sectoral issues (for example, how underfunding health programs might have an impact on education programs), while working from an understanding that donors are motivated by more than humanitarian imperatives.

Foreign policy considerations are central to donors' choice of funding and program planning activities. Most donor nations are more likely to only fund aid programs in countries in which they have an existing political or strategic interest. A lack of foreign policy importance for a country experiencing a humanitarian crisis often leads to "forgotten emergencies" in places such as Liberia, DRC, and Western Algeria, countries of little political, economic or military importance to major donors. Funding is also often frequently higher where major donors have regional foreign policy interests, while interest from major donors in a region can also draw funds from nontraditional donors in that region. Such was the case for China, Pakistan and India to post-9/11 Afghanistan; Malaysia, China, and Singapore to East Timor; and Nigeria, Guinea and Ghana to Sierra Leone.[72] Broad regional peace and security issues can also influence donors and provide a catalyst for funding. For example, good donor coordination and generosity in East Timor in 1999 and 2000 likely had less to do with the emergency itself than with the need for regional stability, secure shipping lanes and access to oil in the Timor Gap: "If humanitarianism had been the primary concern, there would have been considerably more donor action during the previous twenty-five years, during which an estimated 200,000 Timorese died as a result of the brutal Indonesian occupation. In fact, political imperatives rescued East Timor from its forgotten emergency status."[73] Regions such as Africa, of too little political, strategic, or economic importance to many major donors, often suffer from a consequent lack of funding. This is somewhat, but not always, mitigated by historical ties between Britain and Anglophone Africa and France and Francophone Africa, ties that can and often do stimulate funding for humanitarian crises.

More recently, concerns about terrorism have "undercut the relative importance of objective assessments of need. Multi-year programs in lower profile parts of the world have become more difficult to sustain. Particular casualties include natural disaster preparedness and mitigation, which require longer time frames."[74] In Afghanistan, the influx of donor funding post-9/11 also undercut the existing coherence between donors and the coordination framework that had been evolving since 1997. Thus, as one paper states, "while humanitarianism in an age of terrorism may enjoy a higher profile, its new-found visibility is a mixed blessing. Terrorism creates additional humanitarian need and complicates efforts to alleviate it. Likewise, current antiterrorist policies and programs, while ostensibly providing new space to enhance human security broadly understood, themselves heighten the difficulty of humanitarian work."[75]

Despite the growing impact of terrorism on humanitarian action, the needs of humanitarian organizations remain constant: "access to populations in need of humanitarian action, negotiating terms of engagement with non-state actors, extracting from belligerents compliance with international norms, strengthening local institutions, and making the necessary links between relief and development needs."[76] Much in the same way that Cold War humanitarian spending was influenced by political objectives, the new "war on terrorism" has led to the skewing of aid allocations to reflect political priorities. For instance, the UN requested 20 percent of global international assistance in 2002 for Afghanistan. The U.S. administration also made funding the relief effort in Afghanistan a priority, providing at least 70 percent of the emergency assistance.[77] Even with this commitment, U.S. government expenditures for humanitarian assistance and development pale in comparison to expenditures of $1 billion monthly for the war against terrorism in 2002.[78] Under the post-9/11 donor mindset, countries experiencing humanitarian crises in areas that are of little importance to the terrorist fighting agenda of the United States are even less likely to receive funding.

Domestic politics and the lobbies of large Diaspora groups also often influence donor behavior. Food aid is often tied to domestic procurement, because of the impact of domestic agricultural lobbies. Domestic policy pressures also tend to exist for prominent and/or long-term crises such as Afghanistan, Iraq, and Israel/Palestine. Under the George W. Bush administration, the U.S. government has been particularly strong in pushing its domestically generated policy agendas. The government currently requires NGO grantees to certify that their operational partners have no connections with terrorist groups and pressures the UN to do the same. Domestic political agendas, such as the Bush administration's lack of support for family planning activities, have also significantly influenced funding for many programs in the field.

Other factors impacting donor decision-making include the sectoral preferences of certain donors. Although sectoral preference critiques most often focus on the large proportion of funding going to food aid (14 percent of the DAC in 1999), other preferences exist as well. For example, Norway prides itself on its peace and reconciliation programming niche and tends to provide additional support and humanitarian assistance to countries such as Guatemala, Sudan, and Sri Lanka where it is already supporting efforts aimed at peace and reconciliation. In Colombia, donor preferences have similarly significantly affected the scope of programming. Donors have been preoccupied with issues relating to the conflict—or drugs in the U.S. case—resulting in a preference for projects aimed at reconciliation, conflict resolution, and early warning at the expense of institutional strengthening, capacity building, and raising awareness of programs among official organizations and authorities, particularly at the local level.[79]

While donors place a premium on donating to effective agency and programs, quality assurance is an ongoing challenge for donors, particularly in emergency settings. The frequent initial overfunding of high profile emergencies by major donors often leads to a short-term excess of funds, rather than the sustained funding that is needed to comprehensively address humanitarian emergencies. Increased competition among agencies at the onset of high profile emergencies can lead to an excess of agency response to various emergencies, a "battle of logos and T-shirts" by both long-term actors and "briefcase NGOs" which travel from one high profile emergency to another.[80] This constant competition leads to unproductive duplication of effort while hindering coordination and over-arching humanitarian goals as donors become wary about the legitimacy, transparency, cost, capacity, and professionalism of the various agencies facing high competition for funds.

To a great extent, donors encourage competition between NGOs and multilateral organizations to promote quality assurance. One NGO official notes that competition, choice, accreditation, watchdogs, and media coverage are necessary to guarantee service quality in humanitarian operations. Competition may improve the quality of the assistance offered and a market-based approach might allow greater choice for refugees and the recipients of aid programs.[81] While this may be true, competition can also decrease incentives for cooperation among humanitarian agencies and can lead to a proliferation of actors performing overlapping tasks while neglecting others. Donors need to recognize and account for this potential when encouraging competition, and make choices based on rational decisions. Competition among humanitarian agencies that is not matched with coordination of donors will be ineffective at best.

In certain countries, security concerns can cripple the ability of donors to assess humanitarian needs and deliver aid. For example, the security situation outside of Tbilisi, Georgia, has negatively impacted the ability of donors and aid agencies to accurately assess humanitarian needs. The difficulties that donors and aid agencies have in traveling to remote areas frequently cause them to be ignorant of forced migrant conditions and needs. Donors often repeatedly target the same, relatively secure or accessible villages when security concerns do not allow donors and agencies to support more than day-trips to remote areas for fear of robbery, armed hostilities, and kidnappings. This insecurity limits information and makes it difficult to provide assistance to remote areas. Moreover, it has led to a high turnover of personnel resulting in a lack of institutional memory in programs.[82] In such insecure conditions, coordinating aid and working to find opportunities to increase both programming and security are critical.

Donors have traditionally been reluctant to fund logistics and training programs, programs that can allow humanitarian agencies to operate more effectively and efficiently in insecure operating environments: "donor governments generally expect NGOs to bring something to the table . . . usually meaning that NGOs should pay for their own administration and capacity building costs."[83] This reluctance may stem from the fact that logistics and training programs are initiatives for which it is difficult to denote concrete or quick results. Most donors expect these funds to come from private funds and donations. However, support for administrative and training programs may save donors money by allowing agencies to develop more effective and efficient programs: "the provision of adequate administrative overheads should be viewed as an integral part of quality control, rather than a formulaic and unwanted necessity, to be minimized at all cost."[84] Cooperative efforts to train quality aid providers from the country of crisis who are then able to effectively implement programs, similarly saves money for donors when it promotes institutional development of local NGOs and allows for the eventual disengagement of the international donor. Fostering positive competition among aid agencies and generating understanding of the importance of training and logistics programs can greatly increase the efficiency and effectiveness of humanitarian aid donations.

The timing of relief aid is also critical to the success of many programs. NGOs and multilateral organizations struggle with maintaining an even flow of funding for projects over the life of a crisis. Administrative constraints also offer challenges, particularly in time-sensitive interventions. It is difficult for organizations to implement long-term programs and effective relief to development transitions with funding cycles that are most frequently for three to six month time frames.

One of the central issues to timing is the early flow of money to an emergency without sustained assistance for long-term programming needs. Early on in emergencies, donors tend to be less selective in their partners and less demanding of results because of the immediate humanitarian need. Funding becomes more difficult to obtain as an emergency ages. Sometimes NGOs have a comparative advantage over UN agencies in obtaining initial funds because they are able to move faster to mobilize field teams. However, once donors pull the initial emergency funds from the country, NGOs are often not able to complete their projects or to train local staff in long-term programming initiatives needed to support post-conflict activities.

Administrative constraints also influence the timing of funding. Donor financial years affect time-bound appeals, and often create cash flow problems at the end of three or six month funding cycles. Results-based management has severe limitations where time frames are short, and contributes to unrealistic timing expectations by donors of front-line agencies. Many donors struggle with the transition and timing from relief efforts to recovery and reconstruction. Each donor has its own time frame for this process, which causes uncertainty for implementing agencies and unevenness in coordination of relief and development programs. Short-term time frames limit relief to development strategies, the flexibility of NGOs to respond to emerging needs, and the development of sustainable programs.[85]

Since many funding cycles are for three to six month project proposals, it can be difficult for humanitarian organizations to maintain adequate funding levels for their various projects. One report states:

Financial pressures shorten the providers' "operational vision" leading them to plan and budget only for short-term projects and to present the impact of their work in terms of measurable accomplishments such as "lives saved" or "children fed," which may not reflect their actual impact beyond a very limited time frame. Critics assert that crisis-driven funding not only wastes resources but also inhibits long-range planning and undermines the sustainability and effectiveness of programs.[86]

A shift in donors' focus to development aid in many long-term emergencies has led to differences in opinions on how to best assist local populations. Some tensions exist between these development organizations and local NGOs in countries such as Georgia, where local NGOs criticize the international NGOs' focus on development aid and microcredit projects at the expense of humanitarian assistance. A report outlining aid trends in Georgia explains that local groups question the utility of a $500 business loan when the individual is wearing rags, eating scraps, and housed in a human warehouse.[87]

Many NGOs and multilateral organizations urge donors to adopt longer-term proposals with stipulated benchmarks and sufficient flexibility for situational changes that may allow for more cost effective relief in longer-term emergency settings. Some donors are beginning to take the lead on longer-term approaches to recovery. The World Bank, for instance, has a one-year time frame for reconstruction funds. Norway also funded a four-year grant to the IFRC for reconstruction in Bosnia. The Afghan Support Group (ASG), a forum for the major donors in Afghanistan, also recognized the need for more attention to medium and long-term investments. ECHO was the first donor in Afghanistan to adopt a longer-term approach in the early 1990s, but a significant number of other donors such as Sweden, Canada, and Switzerland began moving in this direction by mid-2001 prior to the crisis in September.[88] The move toward a longer time frame for both proposals and benchmarks needs to be encouraged.

Many strategies, incentives, and pressures that go well beyond humanitarian considerations therefore drive donor funding. Donors are particularly influenced by foreign policy objectives and priorities when determining where to grant aid money. Domestic pressures, particularly recently in the United States, can also be of critical importance in determining the flow of aid resources. The profile of a given emergency is highlighted by foreign policy or domestic interest, as well as by media coverage. As donors experience so many demands for funds, and constraints on their ability to fund the response to a wide range of crises and sectoral issues, coordination mechanisms and a greater understanding by donors of the complex needs during humanitarian emergencies are two critical components of the effort to improve response to humanitarian emergencies.

Varying Donor Policies

According to one U.S. government official, the past few years have brought a "widening philosophical gulf" between the United States and Europe on multilateral funding mechanisms and approaches to humanitarian policy.[89] The extent of policy formulation varies from country to country. While countries such as Switzerland, Sweden, the UK, and Australia have outlined donor policies, major donors such as the United States and Canada still have *ad hoc* funding systems. Similarly, the organization of responsibilities for funding humanitarian activities varies between donor governments. In some countries, humanitarian assistance falls under the auspices of an independent development agency, while in others it falls under the control of the foreign ministry. In the United States and other countries with a mixed approach, this responsibility falls under multiple agencies. Some countries also have the ministry of defense involved in these activities. This section outlines some of the differences in the policy approaches of several of the major donor bodies.

ECHO

ECHO was established by the European Commission in 1991 as a temporary agency tasked with the 'coherent administration' and improved efficiency of humanitarian aid, emergency food aid, and disaster prevention and preparedness activities in the European Union (EU). ECHO became a legal entity in June 1996 with the adoption of Council Regulation No. 1257/96, which gave ECHO a more detailed mandate with a budget line in the EU. ECHO quickly became a significant player in the humanitarian aid field; three years after its inception in 1994, it was the world's largest humanitarian aid donor. ECHO is unique in that it both receives donations from the EU member states and allocates aid to other bilateral and multilateral organizations.

Initially, ECHO was expected to gradually build its own capacity for direct action in the field. However, rather than develop an operational capacity, ECHO has instead channeled most of its funding through European NGOs, UN agencies, and the Red Cross organizations.[90] Currently, ECHO spends over half of its budget financing European NGOs and also pledges a significant amount to the UN. In general, ECHO rarely funds local NGOs because of accountability concerns. Only a small proportion of its budget is allocated to non-European NGOs (4 percent in 2000). Although it remains largely a funding organization (with the exception of two direct actions in the Former Yugoslavia and ECHO-flight), some partners express concerns that it could set itself up as a rival organization.[91] ECHO has no overall policy in relation to its coordination role, especially at the field level, and its efforts to coordinate funding are largely *ad hoc* in nature.[92]

Although ECHO has not developed operational capacity many staff members continue to express desire to be 'more than just a bank.' A review of ECHO notes that this is likely a reflection of ECHO's original mandate to create a higher profile for the European Community's humanitarian aid efforts and its international presence generally in the absence of a common foreign policy. As one of the largest humanitarian aid donors in the world, ECHO staff members also feel that ECHO should play a more prominent role in the field, with many desiring a more active role in determining how projects are designed and implemented.[93]

The past leadership of Emma Bonino, who led ECHO from 1995 to 2000, supported these attitudes. Under Bonino, ECHO established a planning, strategy, and policy analysis unit to facilitate information sharing and the dissemination of best practices, and commissioned NGO networks to organize meetings. In November 1999, ECHO also began to take an interest in mainstreaming human rights issues into humanitarian action. It produced a discussion paper entitled "Towards a Human Rights Approach to European Commission Humanitarian Aid?" This paper endorsed increased cooperation and coordination with NGO partners to enable work on human rights issues without compromising impartiality.[94]

This endorsement met with mixed reactions from ECHO's NGO partners, many of who felt ECHO should not have a role in monitoring human rights. It was subsequently difficult for ECHO to include mention of human rights in its revised Framework Partnership Agreement (FPA), the document governing ECHO's relationship with implementing organizations, because of a lack of consensus on this issue by its implementing partners. The Article 20 evaluation of ECHO also contributed to a movement away from this approach, stating that an emphasis on human rights could lead to contradictions with ECHO's priority of saving lives.

The shift within ECHO toward greater professionalism and a more limited role in aid interventions was further supported by the 2000 appointment of Poul Nielson. Under Nielson's leadership, ECHO has refocused its mandate on the provision of emergency assistance, but still maintains an interest in the humanitarian and human rights issues promoted by Bonino. Under Nielson ECHO has drawn away from the 'grey zone' between emergency and development activities, while increasing movement toward specialization in emergency interventions and the recommendations put forward in the Article 20 evaluation. These recommendations included: a return to a stricter definition of emergency aid; the development of a twin-track approach within ECHO itself; and the creation of a long-term planning structure within the Commission but outside ECHO responsible for actions in the 'grey zone.'

For instance, in Colombia, ECHO has limited its activities to short-term relief projects for IDPs, most of which are in regions where government response is weak. According to a report by the Institute for International Studies, many ECHO partners "have grown more frustrated with the inadequacies of assistance limited to emergency relief and have sought support for more durable efforts aimed at income generation."[95] Recently, ECHO has established a funding line for medium- and longer-term projects targeting IDPs in an attempt to shift to more development-oriented activities. Most of these funds are channeled through UNHCR and NGOs for institutional capacity building and income generation projects. Unfortunately, ECHO lacks coherence and direction in its policies regarding IDPs. Although ECHO does not have any guidelines preventing its working with IDP populations or funding programs in countries with oppressive governments, there is no IDPs policy profile within the agency. ECHO states that this is due to their "context driven" approach. In reality, according to a report on EU policy toward IDPs, many officials believe that it is "desirable not to provoke too visible a debate nor elaborate too prominent a policy toward IDPs as such as this would raise the profile of the issue and could set in train a series of actions (resolutions from the European Parliament, additional demands of scrutiny, new budget lines) which they believe could actually constrain or distort the delivery of humanitarian assistance which currently takes place."[96]

As ECHO defines and redefines its role, it also has to address the wish of the European Commission that ECHO be politically neutral. The European Parliament has a strong position on this issue, having requested that the Commission "take appropriate steps to stop the increased politicization of humanitarian aid, because it should essentially address the effects of a crisis, not its causes."[97] While keeping this recommendation in mind, the Council appears to have adopted in practice a more pragmatic approach, noting that the "while maintaining the independence of humanitarian aid, ECHO needs to 'bear in mind' the complementary responsibilities relating to conflict prevention and crisis management assumed by the EU."[98]

Following the international trend toward the adaptation of results-based management systems, and the financial scandals of 1999, ECHO is increasingly making greater use of objectives, performance indicators of NGO partners, and logframes, which "should give partners more flexibility to adapt to changes in the field because they can change activities and even sectors as long as these are within the overall objectives."[99]

Even with this shift, ECHO continues to utilize its system of global plans, introduced in 1994, as funding strategies for long-term crises. Initially, global plans were launched to allow the implementation of twelve-month long country or region-wide strategies. Since 1996, global plans have also been used in nonemergency countries where ECHO has programs of over ten million euros. Currently, approximately 17 percent of ECHO's total aid is provided through global plans. Previous plans often serve as starting points for renewal plans and ECHO has a pattern of funding existing partners and activities for subsequent plans. "If the plan is the first for an area, the choice of partners and activities to be funded by ECHO is usually based on what ECHO is already funding. There does not appear to be a standardized decision-making procedure for deciding how much funding to allocate to a Global Plan and ECHO's choice of partners."[100] While global plans allow ECHO to take a proactive approach, the plans face difficulties including a lack of field consultation and complaints of exclusion by NGOs and the UN. ECHO's concern for a balance of NGOs from different member states has also been exploited by entrepreneurial NGOs, who rely on ECHO's pattern of continued funding for NGOs initially allocated funding for a particular sector.

ECHO has also been increasing the amount of its funding allocated to the NGO sector. In 2000, NGOs received 65 percent of ECHO's funding. However, with Nielson this trend may be shifting. The significant drop in UN funding during 1998 and 1999 may be due to the fact that UN agencies had not yet agreed to ECHO's revised Framework Policy Agreement introduced in January 1999. UN agencies also argue that ECHO's focus on projects does not fit with their programs approach and that this leads to the development of 'artificial' projects. Other possible reasons for the low-level of ECHO funding to UN agencies include inadequate reporting by UN entities on implementation, negative perceptions of ECHO staff on the UN's performance, a lack of visibility of EC financing of operations, and the high personnel costs of the UN.[101] Some staff members at ECHO argue that NGOs offer a better value, particularly since UN agencies often implement programs through NGOs. This bias is partially explained by the fact that many of ECHO's desk and field officers formerly worked for NGOs and the fact that many ECHO staff also perceive NGOs as more efficient and accountable and easier to monitor and control. In response, the UN points out that they have value added in coordination that NGOs do not have.

Nielson has refocused ECHO financing to the UN system. In the spring of 2001 the Commission issued a report entitled "Communication from the Commission to the Council and the European Parliament: Building an Effective Partnership with the United Nations in the Fields of Development and Humanitarian Affairs," aimed at building a more transparent, financially predictable and easily monitored partnership and strengthening the involvement of the EC in policy dialogue with the UN. Despite Neilson's belief that it is important to work with UN agencies in order to promote their global mandates, ECHO desk and field officers continue to prefer the provision of funding to NGOs.

In summary, ECHO's policies have changed significantly since its establishment in 1991. Although ECHO is not operational, it has increased its presence in the field and has developed a more hands-on approach to monitoring programming and developing program strategies. While ECHO staff members continue to give preference to NGO partnerships, the donor agency has recently been increasing its funding to the UN and other multilateral bodies albeit with more involved monitoring structures and requirements in place.

Scandinavian Donors: Danida and NORAD

The Scandinavian donor countries are known for a strong multilateral orientation. Danida and NORAD's activities provide two examples of the donor funding patterns of Scandinavian countries. In recent years, both Danida and NORAD have been implementing more accountability requirements and measurements of programmatic impact. This is, in part, due to the limited monitoring capacities of their small staffs. In addition to their support for the UN and other international organizations, Danida and NORAD also provide the bulk of funding to Scandinavian NGOs.

In the past few years, Danida has increasingly emphasized downward accountability of its operating partners and encouraged the UN to implement internal accountability mechanisms to improve measurements of impact.[102] The Danish Parliament has oversight of the funding initiatives, but Danish NGOs also play a central role in shaping humanitarian policies. Danida has limited operational capacity and a small staff. Its emphasis is on development-oriented humanitarian interventions implemented through Danish NGOs and the UN. Its average annual contribution to UN agencies between 1997 and 2000 was $281 million; its average annual contribution to other agencies was approximately $128 million during the same period. On an annual basis,

Danida provided approximately $6.66 billion of aid, with the rest going to the EU, the World Bank group, and Regional Development Institutions.

Danida focuses on promoting sustainable development through poverty-oriented economic growth. Danida contributes primarily to multilateral organizations, Danish NGOs, and bilateral assistance programs to counties primarily in Africa and Asia. Through these programs, Danida focuses on building local and national strategies and ownership of projects, and promoting the role of the private sector and trade in development activities. It also aims to link Denmark's development policies with Denmark's refugee policy. According to Danida's policy statement, "countries receiving Danish assistance must live up to their international obligation to readmit their own citizens whose applications for asylum in Denmark have been rejected. On the international level, the Government will work to strengthen assistance in neighboring countries to countries undergoing conflicts or civil war."[103] Danida's policies also focus on environmental assistance to developing countries. In all sectors, Danida has an increased focus on efficiency in programming and bases its funding decisions on its partners' demonstration of their organizational efficiency.[104]

The administration of Norwegian development is divided between the Ministry of Foreign Affairs and NORAD. NORAD is responsible for bilateral and long-term projects, while the Ministry is responsible for the administration of aid through international organizations and for emergency relief and humanitarian aid programs. The Ministry of Foreign Affairs also formulates development policy and adopts strategies for cooperation with individual countries. Overseeing the Ministry and NORAD, the Norwegian Parliament determines the objectives of development cooperation, priority regions and countries, and the amount of total funds. The government proposes development guidelines and draws up proposals for the annual development budget.

NORAD focuses its activities on several program areas, including: social development, economic development, environmental and natural resource management programs, peace, democracy and human rights activities, humanitarian assistance programs, and women and gender equality programs. The bulk of NORAD's funding goes toward programs in Africa, with a second largest area of Asia and the Middle East. Like Danida, almost all of NORAD's NGO partners are based in Norway or other Scandinavian countries.

Norway is also a major donor to IDP programming. NORAD supports targeted assistance to IDP populations. It also supports academic research on the needs of IDPs and believes that a specific policy needs to be articulated for the protection of IDPs. Furthermore, NORAD commissions independent academic research, sponsors the Global IDP Data Base maintained by the Norwegian Refugee Council in Geneva, supports the mandate of the Representative of the

Secretary General on Internally Displaced Persons and conducts diplomatic interventions on behalf of IDPs at the UN. NORAD adopts a similar approach to the UK in that it "seeks to root its policy in the wider analysis of crises of war and peace, poverty and good governance. This is on the assumption that it is not possible to aid vulnerable groups if the structural reasons for the conflict are ignored."[105]

In summary, although the Scandinavian donors maintain a strong multilateral orientation, they are increasingly requiring the UN and other partners to demonstrate the impact, efficiency, and outputs of their programs. Both Danida and NORAD demonstrate preference for Scandinavian NGO partners to implement their visions of economic and social development and humanitarian assistance.

DFID

In the UK, humanitarian aid and foreign policy are officially separated. This shift was prompted by the elevation of the International Development Minister to cabinet rank and the creation of DFID as a separate government department in 1997. The International Development Act of 2002 specifies that the Secretary of State for International Development and the head of the Department for International Development (DFID) may "provide any person or body with assistance for the purpose of alleviating the effects of a natural or man-made disaster or other emergency on the population of one or more countries outside the United Kingdom."[106] However, this assistance is not defined, or limited to humanitarian assistance alone.

In practice, humanitarian aid in the UK is aligned with foreign and security policies. A 1997 White Paper states that the UK's "responses to conflict, political instability, poverty and humanitarian assistance would involve the deployment of diplomatic and military instruments as well as aid."[107] Foreign Secretary Jack Straw reaffirmed this position in 2002, stating:

> Where intervention is required, it has to be early and it has to be coordinated. Diplomacy is not enough by itself. Humanitarian and development aid by itself is not enough. Military action by itself is most certainly not enough. But bring those three together, within a clear overarching strategy, and we can far better secure and sustain the peace of the global community."[108]

Under the leadership of Claire Short from 1997 to 2003, DFID adopted a more 'politically astute' approach to the disbursement of humanitarian aid. As one study of donor accountability in the UK states, "DFID has resisted committing itself to a rigid policy or accountability framework that might limit its strategic control and flexibility over the use and disbursement of emergency aid funds."[109] DFID outlines this strategic approach in its 1997 White Paper on International Development, 1998 Ten Principles for a New Humanitarianism and in a policy statement published in 2000 entitled 'Conflict Reduction and Humanitarian Assistance.' However, "the linking of humanitarian assistance with conflict reduction and prevention has made it more difficult for DFID to rebuff charges that its humanitarian assistance might at times be subordinated to broader foreign and security policies."[110]

The central focus of DFID policies is a commitment to the internationally agreed target to halve the proportion of people living in extreme poverty by 2015, together with the associated target programs for basic health care provision and universal access to primary education. To achieve these goals, DFID has focused on providing assistance to the poorest countries in Asia and sub-Saharan Africa. DFID further supports transition and middle income countries elsewhere. It has outlined its donor policies toward specific UN agencies and international organizations in a number of recent partnership plans published between 1999 and 2003.[111]

The partnership plans focus on how DFID will work together with each agency to best achieve its policies, while working toward objectives specific to each partner organization. For instance, its plan for the IFRC/RC outlines a regional capacity building plan that promotes local management strengthening activities, regional disaster preparedness and response, and advocacy work in disaster response, public health, and in the humanitarian impact of various program activities. Its partnership plan with UNICEF aims to improve the impact of UNICEF's core mandate areas and to improve its program design process, conflict response activities and involvement in sectorwide approaches. The plan recognizes the importance of mainstreaming UNICEF's rights based approach. As illustrated by these examples, each partnership plan focuses on funding targeted measures to improve the work of each particular partner agency. The partnership plans between DFID and its partners are for three or four-year programs. The plans require joint working groups, mid-year progress reports, annual work plans and reviews, site visits and external—but participatory—evaluations.

Although DFID's multilateral assistance has remained stable, its bilateral aid has increased significantly in recent years. Most of DFID's bilateral aid is in the form of earmarked funds to UN agencies and assistance to NGOs and Red Cross organizations. Since its aid is earmarked, it is counted as bilateral aid under the DAC system. DFID's focus on the effectiveness of humanitarian aid has also led to its expanded direct operational involvement in humanitarian emergencies, primarily through its rapid response unit CHAD. CHAD's main responsibility is to provide logistics support, assessment, and analysis of conditions, contingency planning, project management, monitoring, and training. CHAD manages DFID's rapid-onset assistance programs and supports its own operations team, which is supplied by a private firm contracted by DFID.[112]

DFID adopts a "needs driven" approach to IDP assistance, so that IDPs do not receive special treatment over other members of vulnerable populations. DFID states that it is often difficult to discern who is an IDP to the extent that targeted assistance may create tensions between host communities and IDPs and in some cases distinction may add to the insecurity of those assisted.[113] There is currently no special structure or expert on IDP issues in the UK administration. De facto responsibility goes instead to the Director of the Conflict and the Humanitarian Affairs Department (CHAD) of the Department for International Development (DFID). Even though it is concerned about the negative impact of targeting assistance to IDPs, DFID remains active in IDP initiatives and meetings and asserts in public statements the importance of the IDP issue and the value of the *Guiding Principles*. Although DFID believes that the UN should play a central role in IDP protection issues, it argues against a lead agency approach since IDPs are not a homogeneous group. Furthermore, DFID argues that the ability of the UN to provide assistance to IDPs differs from country to country depending on operational experience, field presence, and relationships with relevant authorities and local communities.

DFID's de facto alignment of humanitarian aid with foreign and security policies is couched by the government in terms of achieving a more "effective response." DFID is in line with other donor agencies in terms of its trend toward funding more bilateral programs that support foreign policy objectives. It will be important for DFID in the future to further clarify the linkages between its policies concerning humanitarian aid, development assistance, and military action in complex emergencies.

The United States

The United States is currently the largest donor for humanitarian assistance. The United States has developed a more project-based funding approach than many European government donors. Its funds are dispersed through two primary bodies, the Bureau of Population, Refugees and Migration (BPRM) at the Department of State, and the Office of Foreign Disaster Assistance (OFDA) at the U.S. Agency for International Development (USAID).

BPRM is constrained by a narrow mandate to support multilateral assistance to refugees. Traditionally, BPRM has contributed 20–25 percent of UNHCR's total budget. In 2000, $125 million of its $700 million budget was allocated to admitting and resettling refugees in the United States, $60 million was allocated to assisting Jews emigrating to Israel from developing or hardship countries and the rest was allocated for humanitarian assistance to international refugees. The baseline $700 million was additionally augmented by a $100 million account for emergency assistance to urgent and unforeseen events. Although most of these funds go to UNHCR, IOM, and ICRC, BPRM also contributes significant amounts to OCHA, UNICEF, WHO, and NGO partners.

Since BPRM contributes such large amounts to UNHCR, it asserts a strong leadership position on the ExCom, often calling for greater transparency and accountability in the organization. According to one report, BPRM "takes the position that it is not merely a donor, but also a member of the organization." For example, BPRM has recently earmarked many funds to Africa, after determining that UNHCR was underfunding the region. BPRM currently funds 30 percent of UNHCR's Africa programs.[114] Because of such actions, BPRM is often viewed by UNHCR as being a micromanager.

While BPRM has traditionally tended to fund multilateral organizations such as UNHCR, IOM, and ICRC, under the leadership of Julia Taft from 1997 to 2001, BPRM began vocally supporting greater bilateral funding of NGOs. Taft, who previously served as president of the NGO consortium InterAction, argued that NGOs' flexibility and specificity compensated for the deficiencies of multilateral organizations. Like its counterpart agency at USAID, BPRM tends to prefer NGOs with an established regional presence and proven track record. However, more recently under the leadership of Eugene Dewey, BPRM has returned to its traditional role as the funding body for multilateral organizations and some select NGOs.

USAID/OFDA is, historically, the arm of the USG that funds bilateral programs with NGOs for humanitarian operations through grants, contracts, and cooperative agreements. Grants are the primary vehicle for implementing NGO, UN, and international agency partnerships. Contracts are intended primarily for private sector or highly specialized technical actors in the procurement of specific goods and services. USAID prefers using cooperative agreements, a grant with substancial input and control from the donor end. In recent years, the trend has been toward the increased use of contractors and cooperative agreements to implement USAID projects. OFDA's overall funding fluctuates with the occurrence of new emergencies, for which Congress allocates supplemental funding. In the 1990s, OFDA received an average of $153 million per year, excluding 1999, when it received $250 million in response to the Kosovo emergency. It has an unearmarked fund for international disasters (the International Disaster Account) and this is subsequently the most flexible funding of any U.S. foreign aid body.

The percentage of OFDA funds going through NGOs has increased from 60 percent in the 1980s to 70–80 percent in the 1990s. Currently, the major NGO actors in international humanitarian assistance derive between 40–60 percent of funding from the United States. Out of over 400 U.S. organizations, five organizations—CARE, Catholic Relief Services (CRS), the International Rescue Committee (IRC), Save the Children, and World Vision—account for around 30 percent of the government's total annual support (USAID and other government agencies combined) to NGOs.[115] Despite this high level of support, USAID and Congress do place limitations on how much funding NGOs can receive from the U.S. government. Nongovernment cash must make up a minimum of 20 percent of an NGO's budget, with many smaller NGOs struggling to meet this requirement.

In 2000–2001, USAID/OFDA spent the majority of its funds on activities in Africa. In FY 2000, Africa expenditures amounted to 69 percent of total OFDA funds and in FY 2001, expenditures were 66 percent of total OFDA funds. The highest funded emergency for FY 2000 and FY 2001 was Sudan. In both years, Europe and the Near East was the second highest area in terms of total funding, with the majority of these funds going to projects in Serbia and Montenegro in FY 2000 and to Afghanistan in FY 2001.

Results-based management has impacted the way that USAID allocates its funds to NGO partners. One study states, "While U.S. funding to international humanitarian organizations has not declined in real terms, the proportion going to multilateral programs has done so, with an increasingly greater share going to NGOs for specific locations and tasks."[116] This is due to the launch of the results-based management (RBM) initiative during the Clinton administration and the subsequent change in donor-recipient relations within the U.S. government. Recently, the Administrator for USAID, Andrew Natsios called for increased results from aid recipients as well as increased recognition, on the part of these agencies, for the funding received from USAID. He states, "The NGOs do some very good work in communities, and the people think that the NGOs raise the money, do the work, and they have no relationship to the U.S. government and to the central ministry. And so when we go to a village and say we're helping you rebuild, they say, 'No, you're not, you know. The Americans, they've abandoned us.' "[117] Moreover, Natsios suggests that agencies not willing to give credit to the U.S. government or comply with RBM principles and guidelines may lose funding.

As defined by the U.S. government, RBM aims for control over the accountability, transparency, and performance of humanitarian aid in broader U.S. policy. It seeks to achieve substantive managerial oversight through setting specific objectives, performance targets, indicators, monitoring, and evaluation systems according to the Government Performance and Results

Act of 1993. USAID was put into a more direct management position vis-à-vis the grantee and the project, and NGOs were required to provide more quantifiable results under the revamped system.

The creation of USAID Disaster Assistance and Response Teams (DART) in 1985 also had a significant impact on NGO funding patterns. DART teams, which were first fielded in response to an earthquake in Mexico City, have dramatically increased the ground presence of OFDA and its direct involvement in programming. The teams are designed to improve information and communications systems between the U.S. government and its grantees and to speed up project reviews and approvals. An increase in communication and project design initiatives in the field have caused many projects to reflect more of the donor's agenda and priorities with DART teams, often approaching NGOs to undertake specific projects that they have a greater capacity to implement. NGOs have both positive and negative reactions to the DART phenomenon. Some NGOs see positive impacts from the improved communication, review and shorter intervals between approvals and fund disbursement, yet others are concerned that they are forfeiting independence of NGO project development to the agenda of the DART teams and USAID.[118]

Currently in the United States, a portion of the combined budgets for BPRM, OFDA, Food for Peace (FFP), and the Office of Transition Initiatives (OTI) are allocated to IDPs. In countries like Sudan, where the majority of relief programs target IDPs, it is likely that the majority of the U.S. assistance goes to IDPs. However, countries such as Georgia and Peru (which do not receive any disaster funding) are allocated inadequate funds by the United States. Other countries, such as Turkey and Burma, restrict cooperation with international organizations, which limits the effectiveness of U.S. donations to the ICRC and the UN.[119]

In a 1999 study analyzing U.S. assistance to IDPs, it was found that even when programs funded by the U.S. government do reach internally displaced persons, the bulk of the funding goes toward food and other material assistance rather than protection activities such as "essential protection from physical attack or threat, sexual assaults, conscription or forced labor, forced migration, deprivation of identity documents, removal from life-sustaining employment, or other threats to which displaced populations are especially vulnerable."[120] Donors should focus on targeting women and children, who make up the majority of displaced groups, through reproductive health services, micro-credit programs, programs for women victims of violence, psychosocial programs for children, and educational training opportunities.[121] While BPRM states that OFDA should have the lead on internal displacement issues, OFDA does not take a proactive approach to the funding of protection programs that address many of the most immediate needs of IDPs, stating in their Field Operations Guide that, "OFDA Assessment teams and Disaster Assistance Response Teams (DARTs) should support the efforts of the ICRC, UNHCR, and OCHA. However, Assessment teams and DARTs should not assume any responsibility for the protection of DPs (Displaced Persons)."[122]

In conclusion, the U.S. government, like other donors, has placed emphasis on results-based management in recent years. The United States is unique in its division of donor responsibility between BPRM and USAID. Most multilateral funding comes through BPRM, while USAID/OFDA provides the majority of its funding to U.S. NGOs. The creation of DART teams has led to the increased involvement of USAID in program development. While this has many positive aspects, NGOs also feel that the DART teams, in combination with the new management systems, are compromising their autonomy. Because of this, many U.S. NGOs are seeking to find alternative funding sources to decrease their current dependence on U.S. government grants and funding.

CIDA

The Canadian International Development Agency (CIDA) manages Canada's international humanitarian assistance program. CIDA, which has no operational capacity in the field, administers most of its assistance through UN agencies, the Red Cross Movement, and Canadian NGOs and their local partners. The terms for Canada's fluid, response-based assistance are set out in a CIDA/International Humanitarian Assistance (IHA) framework document. CIDA relies on its partners to assess needs and prioritize their requests for relief funds.

CIDA established an emergency response unit in 2000 to manage a stockpile of emergency supplies left over from Canada's Y2K disaster preparedness. It has since gained more responsibilities in emergency settings. This unit has been a point of conflict between CIDA and Canadian NGOs involved in international humanitarian assistance. Many NGOs see CIDA's maintenance and direct dispersal of the stockpile as a movement toward government-led humanitarian assistance teams. This, they feel, compromises the perceived neutrality of Canadian NGOs working in conflict situations. However, "CIDA does not consider the establishment of the emergency response unit and the maintenance of the stockpile of supplies to be indicative of a trend toward the 'bilateralization' of Canadian humanitarian aid. It sees its activities as complementary to NGO efforts and has no plans to become involved in the direct delivery of emergency relief."[123] CIDA adds that it does not plan to increase the size of the stockpile, which currently amounts to thirty tons of supplies worth $200,000; enough for two planeloads. It states that the deployment of emergency relief supplies from Canada can "have a positive humanitarian impact if they are delivered quickly, and if these stocks are not available locally to relief agencies."[124] Furthermore, the visibility of the Canadian response may increase support of the Canadian public, which in turn benefits the Canadian NGO effort.

CIDA's official policy is that a well-functioning multilateral system most effectively addresses global humanitarian needs. About 70 percent of Canadian assistance goes to UN agencies, although this fluctuates from year to year. This does not mean that CIDA gives blindly to the UN. In fact, it has played a strong role in advocating UN reform to more effectively and efficiently deliver aid. Funding the Red Cross has also increased slightly, currently accounting for over 20 percent of CIDA's budget.

Although CIDA has shown constant support for multilateral organizations, it has also consistently increased NGO funding over the past decade. CIDA guidelines support activities that apply the principles of International Humanitarian Law. In 1990–1991, CIDA allocated 7.3 percent of its funds to NGO partners. In 2000–2001, this amount reached a high of 22.3 percent, and in 2001–2002 it was at 14 percent,[125] and, "In contrast to Canadian long-term development assistance, which is heavily tied to the procurement of Canadian goods and services, Canadian humanitarian assistance is fully untied."[126]

Canada, like many donor governments has been increasingly cautious in disbursing untied funds to multilateral organizations. In general, donors have been demanding greater results from both NGOs and multilateral organizations due to both policy shifts and the increasing global popularity of results-based management systems. Moreover, the formation of emergency rapid-response teams by large donors such as ECHO, DFID, USAID/OFDA, and CIDA has led to an increased donor presence in the field, which in turn has prompted donors to become more involved in strategic planning and monitoring activities in the field and in headquarters.

While the largest donors of humanitarian assistance have some characteristics in common (such as an emphasis on results-based management), there are clear and important differences between the ways these donors conceptualize and approve humanitarian assistance. And while levels of donor interaction are increasing, a significant problem in donor coordination is the "widening philosophical gulf" between the United States and Europe on multilateral funding mechanisms and approaches to humanitarian policy.[127] This "philosophical gulf" as well as internal differences on aid allocation processes can make coordination, and even discussions on coordination, challenging. Differences in policy formulation from country to country can pose serious problems. While countries such as Switzerland, Sweden, the UK, and Australia have outlined donor policies, major donors such as the United States and Canada still have *ad hoc* funding systems. Similarly, the organization of responsibilities for funding humanitarian activities varies between donor governments. In some countries, humanitarian assistance falls under the auspices of an independent development agency, while in others it falls under the control of the foreign ministry. In the United States and other countries with a mixed approach, this responsibility falls under multiple agencies. Some countries also have the ministry of defense involved in these activities. Differences between donors are of critical and often divisive importance when coordination mechanisms are established.

TOWARD "GOOD HUMANITARIAN DONORSHIP"

The capacity to respond quickly and effectively in an emergency may stem the damage and the longer-term costs of emergency operations, ease start-up costs, and deter accelerated deterioration of the situation on the ground. Therefore, it is prudent for donors to increase investment in coordination mechanisms to promote cost-effective relief programming. Coordination ranges from the formal and informal efforts in East Timor to donor driven groups in Afghanistan and Sri Lanka. In other crises, such as Colombia and Georgia, the local governments are taking an increasingly active role in coordinating international groups and activities, with some support from Thematic Groups led by the UN. The UN takes the lead in other situations, such as the consortium of humanitarian agencies that has been operating in Sri Lanka since 1996.[128] In other cases, coordination efforts take place on a regional level.

A study from the Center on International Cooperation examined aid flow to post-conflict situations and identifies seven central challenges facing donors in coordinating aid policies. The study calls for closer collaboration in: (1) designing aid intervention; (2) mobilizing resources; (3) deepening institutional reform; (4) harmonizing aid conditions; (5) coordinating assistance locally; (6) enhancing recipient capacities; and (7) ensuring accountability in aid delivery and implementation.[129]

Donors should establish joint frameworks for situations in advance to lay the basis for timely collaborative action. These frameworks might outline general aid principles, goals, and strategies to enable joint assessment of needs. Common sets of tasks in situations should be established in advance to ensure coverage of important sectors.[130] An entrance strategy document that could be used as a common format for assessing needs and responsibilities of donors in emergency situations could also be formulated.[131]

Aid pledging conferences are one important forum for cooperative initiatives introduced by donors themselves. These conferences provide donors with opportunities to formulate, implement, and mediate collective activities.

These conferences increase the prospects for equitable burden sharing and re-inforce the notion of a donor community with a common purpose. It is also often easier for many donors to gain support at home when they work through a larger cooperative effort. At the same time, some donors use these confer-ences to gain publicity by "dressing up" modest pledges, while letting others shoulder the bulk of the aid effort.[132] In a report from a donor retreat, it was found that decentralized CAP launches were a useful improvement.[133] How-ever, donors aimed to foster stronger linkages between the CAP and other mechanisms within the UN system, including UNDAF, PRSP, DPA, and DPKO. Substantive analysis is necessary to better understand questions such as: why are appeals underfunded, how do donors fund the CAPs, what are the total humanitarian resources spent in a specific CAP country, what are the performances and competencies of agencies, what is the impact of under-funding in the field, and what ways are there for the UN to improve informa-tion sharing.[134]

Donors continue to face many challenges in establishing donor forums to coordinate their efforts, while initiatives to coordinate UN and NGO work within different countries or regions are often hampered by a lack of funding and by competition between different agencies (not least for funds). Some donor forums, such as the Afghan Support Group (described below), provide an encouraging example for how donors can work together to improve re-sponses and increase substantive attention to a crisis. Donors need to continue to allocate great importance not only to donor forums but also to funding and emphasizing thoughtful coordination between humanitarian agencies operat-ing within specific crises.

The formation of policies for funding, along with coordinated evaluation mechanisms is central to the success of donor programming. Donor policies should rest on three core principles: commitment to international law and principles, commitment to needs-based programming, and predictable and adequate funding.[135]

Despite many donors' "results" orientation, most donor funding does not appear to be particularly merit based, and lacks a commonly agreed upon set of objectives, indicators, targets and measurement tools.[136] Even agreed upon standards such as Sphere are unachievable if funding is inadequate. Some practitioners recommend using "friends of" groups as donor coordination mechanisms. In other cases, the establishment of a donor policy may also aid in coordination efforts.

Donors also need to work with financial tracking and reporting systems to improve coverage and standardization of humanitarian assistance reporting. These groups include the OECD, DAC, and the FTS of ReliefWeb. Donors should also explore the possibility of standardizing reporting and management requirements.[137] Donors can draw on relevant elements of the Rome Declaration on Harmonization (February 2003) to undertake the formulation of harmonized reporting requirements. It was recommended at a recent meeting on good donor-ship that this be explored with a pilot case.[138]

In recent years, there have been a growing number of initiatives to enhance the quality of humanitarian assistance and evaluations. These initiatives and guidelines include: the IASC guidelines, *Guiding Principles of Internal Displacement*, the Active Learning Network for Accountability and Performance in Humanitarian Action (ALNAP), the Humanitarianism and War Project, the Humanitarian Policy Group at the Overseas Development Institute (HPG/ODI), Sphere, the Red Cross Red Crescent *Code of Conduct*, and the Humanitarian Accountability Project.

The most prominent of these processes addressing the role of donors in improving humanitarian assistance is the Good Humanitarian Donorship (GHD) Implementation group. The GHD Implementation Group met in Stockholm in June 2003 to establish principles and good practices for humanitarian donorship, as well as an implementation plan to ensure these principles and practices are adhered to. The GHD Implementation Plan comprises five main initiatives, each chaired by a major donor nation: 1) Mainstreaming peer review of humanitarian assistance; 2) Establishing pilot CAP programs in Burundi in 2004 and the DRC in 2005; 3) Standardizing statistics and definitions, particularly between the DCA and FDS; 4) Harmonizing aid requirements, focusing particularly on the ICRC, OCHA, and UNHCR; and 5) Conducting an internal review of donors' policies and discussing how to implement GHD.[139] The GHD Implementation Group has the "aim of enhancing humanitarian response through strengthened co-ordination, effectiveness and accountability."[140] The principles and practices are similarly comprehensive, covering issues such as: respect and promotion of IHL; involvement of beneficiaries whenever possible in assistance programs; commitment to 'do no harm' principles; support and promotion of the UN; attempts to ensure more predictable funding and not to abandon 'old' crises for newer ones; reduction of earmarking of funds and making longer-term donations; 'affirming the primary position of civilian organizations in implementing humanitarian action'; and 'ensuring a high degree of accuracy, timeliness, and transparency in donor reporting.'[141]

The GHD process is still in the initial stages. Some promise has been seen in the CAP Pilot program in Burundi, where an assessment reported that UNOCHA demonstrated a "clear commitment" to the GHD process.[142] However, the report also found that "both the CAP/CHAP and the GHD lack a clear marketing strategy for all stakeholders and there are still different perceptions and understanding amongst stakeholders in Burundi. . . . In Burundi there is no joint planning amongst donors, a common humanitarian strategy or a common position on humanitarian aid."[143] The goal of the DRC CAP Pilot is to overcome with experience some of these barriers. A coordination plan also needs to address the still-current lack of substantive coordination efforts on policy and organizational levels. Different donor structures are of importance here. The UK, although a major donor, has no stated policy on humanitarian coordination, even though there is a mandate for it as outlined in the 1997 White Paper on Development. Moreover, even though the United States is a major player in relief assistance, the U.S.'s bifurcated structure for humanitarian funding of USAID/OFDA and BPRM dilutes each agency's capacity to influence decision-making among other donors. Because many smaller agencies such as Denmark's Danida look to the major donors for leadership on coordination issues, the United States, DFID and other major donors will play particularly important roles in promoting donor coordination and cooperation on an international level. It is therefore important that they clarify their positions and streamline their own administrative structures to promote coordination efforts. Tangible commitment to the GHD by such donors is of critical importance.

Besides the GHD initiative, other donor coordination mechanisms have been suggested and at times used successfully. One such mechanism is the "friends of" groups. These groups currently serve as *ad hoc* mechanisms through which the United States and other donors have represented key donor interests to multilateral organizations. These groups also establish new forms of regularized interaction among donors to a particular organization. Organizations that have these groups include: OCHA, UNICEF, UNHCR, and ICRC.

These groups have resulted in increased information to donor organizations and enhanced engagement of donors in the workings of these organizations. Yet, challenges remain, including the need to define a more specific purpose for the groups, rules of conduct, composition, and mechanisms of accountability. It may be beneficial for the groups to also address problems of UN inter-agency relations.[144]

The Afghanistan Support Group (ASG) is another example of positive donor coordination. The ASG is a donor-led coordination structure that provides a forum for dialogue on Afghanistan with an emphasis on the overall direction of the assistance effort. ASG, which has been in operation since June 1998, holds periodic meetings in Islamabad and an annual meeting to which representatives of UN agencies, the World Bank, and NGOs are invited. The ASG operates under a management "troika" comprising the current, former, and future chairs of ASG, to provide overall direction for the group, identify issues to be addressed at the annual meeting, and to form subgroups to deal with specific issues. In addition to the regular cycle of consultations, special meetings of this group have been convened to address emergency situations. In addition to these more formal mechanisms and structures, *ad hoc* coordination structures have also been created by operational agencies in the field and inter-agency groups to address emergency needs. Such groups have had occasional donor participation.

In Colombia, donors have worked cooperatively with a broad range of international organizations, international NGOs and local NGO networks, and the government of Colombia and donors to provide programs aimed primarily at the internally displaced population. The Network of Social Solidarity (RSS) was created by the Colombian government in 1994 to provide services for displaced persons in Colombia. This agency was given responsibility for coordinating the National Plan for Integral Attention to the Population Displaced by Violence, launched by the government of Andres Pastrana in 1999. Under the national plan, the RSS was tasked with upholding the government's basic law on displacement, Law 387, and the subsequent *Guiding Principles on Displacement*. This system operates on the state, departmental, and local levels to meet the challenges of displacement in all its phases. The responsibilities of the Colombian government to IDPs outlined under this Law include: prevention, emergency humanitarian assistance, stabilization activities, social services, and support for return to places of origin.[145]

Although the RSS system in Colombia has one of the most comprehensive structures in the world for IDPs, it faces a number of challenges including underfunding, understaffing, a lack of clearly defined responsibilities for RSS officials, and accountability issues. The programs supported by RSS also face problems of inadequate time frames. For instance, one program to provide emergency assistance for IDPs has a three-month time limit, which is widely recognized as inadequate.[146] Income generation projects are similarly short-term in nature and generally not sustainable.[147] Although RSS is mandated to coordinate programs and projects on behalf of IDPs, it has no authority to create its own programs and projects. Therefore, it can channel funds only if project requests have been submitted.[148] Clearly donor coordination models need improvement and expansion.

Numerous obstacles exist to developing systems of donor accountability. One obstacle is the range of political and policy environments that aid departments operate in and the wide variety of actors involved in the process. Another obstacle is the rapidly changing objectives of official humanitarian assistance ranging from security and protection to development and conflict reduction. Donors also face the challenge of not interacting with the beneficiaries of the aid itself, while attempting to develop effective programming to meet those people's needs.

Donor accountability can be improved on many levels. First, accountability comes at the political, strategic, and legal level. Donors must decide where and how to provide assistance in accordance with foreign policy objectives and within legal limits. Accountability also comes at the managerial level. Donors must focus on outputs, outcomes, and impacts. Few evaluations currently focus on donors' humanitarian assistance programs, with most looking at the role of the implementing agency. External evaluations of DFID, for instance, commissioned by the Conflict and Humanitarian Affairs Department are primarily concerned with assessing the performance of partner organizations.[149]

Donors might use Danida's commissioned evaluation of humanitarian assistance in 1999 to provide a model for this type of evaluation process. This evaluation was based on six case studies and two institutional studies reviewing the capacity and performance of Danida's implementing partners (Danish NGOs, UN agencies, and the Red Cross). The evaluation teams also focused on the performance of Danida's policies and programming of humanitarian assistance, thereby holding the agency itself accountable. A number of significant areas of weaknesses and strengths were highlighted and recommendations were put forward. The report was also released to the general public and, encouraged by attention from public officials, a number of key recommendations have been implemented.[150]

Donors must also work to improve financial accountability and aid flows across the humanitarian system. The variety of channels available for donor funding makes it difficult to track donors' spending across different emergencies/forms of assistance and do not reflect contributions by non-aid actors such as the military to assistance initiatives.

There are currently no international mechanisms to evaluate the system and its financial spending patterns as a coherent whole. The Development Assistance Committee of the OECD sets standards and monitors through periodic peer reviews and through its Working Party on Aid Evaluation; however, there exists no accepted standards of donor behavior or unified reporting standards. The GHD Implementation Group has identified the OECD DAC as a potentially useful source of information and a peer review mechanism that donors could utilize to improve their coverage of humanitarian action.[151] Donors must examine the timing and allocation of their aid monies across various emergencies.

Some suggestions include the establishment of parliamentary and congressional oversight mechanisms. Current oversight mechanisms rarely realize their potential even in countries like Denmark and Canada, which have committees responsible for examining overseas assistance programs; and in the UK where the International Development Committee (IDC) conducts frequent inquiries and offers nonbinding recommendations.

Current donor audits investigate financial and managerial performance, but are not concerned with ways that programs and policies are implemented. Donor-led examinations of programs and policies might be introduced as a way to improve accountability within the humanitarian system as a whole.

Donors must address a variety of concerns in upcoming years in order to improve and streamline assistance. Issues of paramount importance include: policy coordination, the creation of viable evaluations and measurement systems, and increased coordination of donor standards and procedures. Donors must also strive for increased accountability on political, strategic, and legal levels both on a national and international basis. The GHD Implementation Group has begun some of this work.

CONCLUSION

Donor funding patterns are changing the face of global humanitarian assistance. It is difficult to accurately track the actual spending patterns of donors without standardized systems to assess and measure aid flows to humanitarian activities and programming. Yet it is apparent that bilateralization and earmarking of aid funds have increased with the results-based management revolution of the 1990s. Donors are becoming increasingly involved in monitoring and evaluating programs.

As the relationships of donors and their partner organizations grow more intertwined, donors are facing new challenges. Donors must choose between NGOs and governmental and military partners in emergency settings. Donors are increasingly undertaking efforts to streamline their activities and money flows with other donors through participation in and facilitation of coordination bodies. As the media and the general public question the equity of aid flows, donors must take a number of different factors into consideration while providing funding. As the humanitarian communities understanding of assistance programs evolves, donors must also consider the impact of factors such as timing on their programming choices. It is also becoming increasingly important for donors to focus on central issues such as programming for IDPs, and the preventative role of human rights, advocacy, and protection activities.

As demonstrated above, donors address these challenges in a number of different ways. It is clear that the formulation of common means of evaluation, measurements, standards, and procedures in emergencies, along with accountability mechanisms, will support a more inclusive and efficient global humanitarian assistance regime. Understanding and working to improve donor response to future and ongoing crises will be a central part of improving programming for forced migrants and for humanitarian assistance in general. In particular, improving the ability of the CAP to function as a comprehensive, coordinated planning document instead of a disorganized agency wish list is critical.

While the CAP has become an important catalyst for inter-agency UN funding and cooperation initiatives over the past eleven years, significant problems remain. Such problems need to be resolved if donors are to prioritize coordination, relief to development transitions, and improved coverage for vulnerable groups such as women and IDPs. Even though CAP has substantial room for improvement, it is an evolving fundraising and advocacy mechanism that will continue to play a central role in coordinating programming and meeting the needs of persons in emergency settings in the years to come. Its improvement is essential.

The lack and mismatch of financial resources provided to address humanitarian emergencies have significantly constrained effective assistance and protection of forced migrants. Two major areas have been the subject of efforts to reform the system by which funds are requested and granted. First, the concept of good humanitarian donorship has emerged as a way for donors to take ownership of their role in addressing the gaps and inconsistencies created by disorganized funding patterns. Second, the United Nations Consolidated Appeals Process (CAP) has undergone significant reforms in an attempt to make it function as a tool to coordinate the financial response to humanitarian emergencies. Concepts of good humanitarian donorship need to be further explored and defined, with all major donor governments participating in this process. Instead of individual agency "wish lists" combined under one rubric, the CAP needs to become a respected, comprehensive planning document that identifies priorities for humanitarian assistance and protection and then assigns responsibilities to UN (or other) agencies to respond to these needs. Such a reform of the CAP is critical not only for a more coordinated and comprehensive agency response to humanitarian emergencies, but also for donors to consider the CAP a framework under which they can respond effectively to humanitarian emergencies.

The CAP is theoretically a tool that allows the United Nations to develop common humanitarian strategies, advocacy platforms, goals and priorities in given countries and regions in response to a complex emergency. In order for the CAP to reach these goals, five future reforms are essential. First, the role of the CAP needs greater clarification, with the tension between its advocacy, funding, and programming roles resolved and its relationship to other UN funding mechanisms explored and then explicated. Second, the CAP needs to establish an oversight and program prioritization system to screen projects, set priorities, and establish timelines and structures for emergency and transition activities. These responsibilities might be delegated to committees operating at the sectoral level, as worked in Angola, with significant participation by senior level staff. Third, given the large presence of NGOs in humanitarian emergency response, the greater involvement and participation of NGOs in the CAP, and their growing investment in the process, is essential to make the CAP function as a more cohesive document. Disbursement processes and cooperation structures need to be ironed out. Fourth, greater attention to the needs of vulnerable populations is needed to ensure the requirements of these populations are addressed within the overall assistance and protection context. Finally, developing standardized mechanisms for measuring the impact and "value-added" of CAP programs and humanitarian aid may facilitate greater donor support. Thus, inter-agency guidelines on financial tracking, monitoring, contingency planning, and exit strategies should be created. These measures will not only increase the scope and coverage of CAP programs in emergency settings, but also make the CAP more efficient, directed, and coordinated.

Donors also bear significant responsibility to make the funding of humanitarian emergency response more comprehensive and effective. Reforming the CAP so that it is truly a document that represents the wide range of needs present in given emergencies is a critical first step. Donors need to build upon this reform by providing good humanitarian donorship. First, given a good CAP, donors should use the opportunity to inform themselves about sectors other than those they tend to fund, and to provide funding where it is needed as well as where it is traditionally provided. Second, donor aid pledging conferences are an important part of the process of avoiding gaps and overlaps. At such conferences donors can formulate, implement, and mediate collective activities, increasing the potential for equitable burden sharing and reinforcing the notion of a donor community with a common purpose. Third, donors need to understand relief to development transitions and their financial needs, avoiding the early flow of money to an emergency without sustained assistance for long-term programming needs. Finally, donors need to stop fostering negative competition between humanitarian agencies as an easy way to ensure quality assurance. Rather, donors should establish rational quality assurance mechanisms for programs they fund as a more positive way to ensure quality.

Donors have many pressures. They need to balance the humanitarian imperative with considerations such as foreign policy, regional peace and security issues, and domestic pressures. The number of humanitarian agencies requesting funding from donors is certainly daunting. However, by increasing their involvement in efforts such as the CAP process, rationalizing the aid that they do provide, and developing a greater understanding of major issues such as the importance of logistics and training, the relief to development gap, and the needs of different phases of emergencies, donors should be able to develop more comprehensive and thoughtful responses to humanitarian crises.

NOTES

1. World Health Organization (WHO), "The Consolidated Appeals Process," World Health Organization, www.who.int/disasters/repo/7396.html (November 22, 2004).

2. United Nations Inter-Agency Steering Committee (IASC), "IASC Review of the CAP and Plan of Action for Strengthening the CAP (April 8, 2002)," IASC, www.reliefweb.int/cap/policy/CAP_PolicyDoc.html (November 22, 2004).

3. Toby Porter, *An External Review of the CAP*: Commissioned by OCHA's Evaluation and Studies Unit, (Geneva: OCHA, April 18, 2002), 2.

4. Porter, *An External Review of the CAP,* 28.

5. Porter, *An External Review of the CAP.*

6. WFP, "Review of Resource Mobilization," adapted from WFP.

7. Porter, *An External Review of the CAP,* 30.

8. Joanna Macrae, et al. "Uncertain Power: the Changing Role of Official Donors in Humanitarian Action," *Humanitarian Policy Group (HPG) Reports*, No. 12 (December 2002).

9. Reflects an average of funds met in 1993, 1994, 1999, 2000, 2001, and 2002.

10. Porter, *An External Review of the CAP.*

11. Porter, *An External Review of the CAP.*

12. IASC, "IASC Review of the CAP," 4.

13. David S. Bassiouni, "A Review of the Consolidated Appeal Process (CAP): Being an Interim Report Prepared for Consideration by the Directors of Emergency," Confidential Report (Geneva: September 3, 2001, on file with authors), 6.

14. Bassiouni, "A Review of the CAP," 11.

15. IASC, "Consolidated Appeals Process Workshop Report: CAP Best Practices and Lessons Learned" (document produced at the third annual CAP Best Practices and Lessons Learned Workshop, Versoix, Switzerland, February 13–15, 2002), www.reliefweb.int/ocha_ol/CAP/CAPWorkshopRpt_Feb02_final.pdf, 32–36 (November 22, 2004).

16. IASC, "Consolidated Appeals Process Workshop Report."

17. Macrae, "Uncertain Power."

18. Author Interview with OCHA, New York (2001).

19. IASC, "IASC Review of the CAP."

20. Interview with UNICEF (September 27, 2001).

21. Interviews with OCHA and UNHCR staff members, Geneva (2001).

22. United Nations Consolidated Inter-Agency Appeal Process, "Retreat Report." (Document from CAP Trainers Retreat: Field Debriefing, Tools Improvement, and Policy Development, February 20–23, 2001, in Morges, Switzerland).

23. Porter, *An External Review of the CAP,* 11.

24. For example, "the executive director of WFP recently led a long-running and high profile advocacy campaign to increase funding to non-food sectors during the recent drought in the Horn of Africa." Porter, *An External Review of the CAP*.

25. Porter, *An External Review of the CAP*, 13.

26. IASC Sub Working Group on CAP, "Plan of Action: Recommendations for a New Agenda for Strengthening the Consolidated Appeals Process" (Geneva: United Nations, March 4, 2002).

27. World Food Programme, "Review of Resource Mobilization," 13.

28. Porter, *An External Review of the CAP*.

29. United Nations Office of the High Representative for the Least Developed Countries, Landlocked Developing Countries and Small Island Developing States (OHRLLS), "CCA/UNDAF/PRSP," www.un.org/special-rep/ohrlls/cca_undaf_prsp .htm (July 21, 2003).

30. Porter, *An External Review of the CAP*, 23.

31. Porter, *An External Review of the CAP*, 24.

32. Bassiouni, "Review of the CAP."

33. Author Interview with UNICEF (September 27, 2001).

34. Author Interview with UNICEF (September 27, 2001).

35. Bassiouni, "Review of the CAP."

36. WFP, "Review of Resource Mobilization."

37. United Nations Consolidated Inter-Agency Appeal Process, "Retreat Report."

38. United Nations Consolidated Inter-Agency Appeal Process, "Retreat Report."

39. OCHA, "UN Consolidated Inter-Agency Appeal for East Timor Crisis" (Geneva: OCHA, October 27, 1999).

40. This assessment was conducted with aerial surveys and interviews with local experts.

41. IASC, "East Timor Consolidated Appeal Process (CAP) Review: Phase 3, External Review" (Dili, East Timor: Consolidated Inter-Agency Appeal Process Steering Committee, May 2000).

42. UN Department of Humanitarian Affairs, "Mid-Term Review of the UN Consolidated Inter-Agency Appeal for the Caucasus" (Geneva: UN Department of Humanitarian Affairs, November 30, 1996).

43. Porter, *An External Review of the CAP*, 13.

44. IASC, "East Timor Consolidated Appeal Process (CAP) Review: Phase 3, External Review."

45. Porter, *An External Review of the CAP*.

46. United Nations Consolidated Inter-Agency Appeal Process, "Retreat Report."

47. Notes from the 2001 CAP Launch, *Women and War* (November 29, 2000).

48. Global Launch of the UN Inter-Agency Consolidated Appeals for 2001, Oslo, Norway (November 29, 2000).

49. Francis Deng, "Reaching the Vulnerable: Statement by Representative of the Secretary General on Internally Displaced Persons, Dr. Francis M. Deng" (presented at the Global Launch of the 2002 Inter-Agency Appeals, Helsinki, Finland, November 2001).

50. Francis M. Deng, "The Consolidated Appeals and IDPs: The Degree to which UN Consolidated Inter-Agency Appeals for the Year 2000 Support Internally Displaced Populations" (Washington: Brookings Institution, August 2000).

51. Deng, "The Consolidated Appeals and IDPs," 5.

52. Jim Kunder, "Analysis of Whether Consolidated Appeals Documents Support Internally Displaced Populations" (October 24, 2000, on file with authors).

53. Van Hear and Darini Rajasingham-Senanayake, "Displacement and the humanitarian regime in Sri Lanka," for the collaborative project *Complex forced migration: towards a new humanitarian regime*, Copenhagen and Colombo, July 2002.

54. Author Interview with UNICEF (September 27, 2001).

55. Matthew Karanian, "Georgia's Forced Migrants" (Washington, D.C.: Institute for the Study of International Migration, 2001).

56. WFP, "A Review of Resource Mobilization."

57. Relief Web, "Financial Tracking System Information," www.reliefweb.int (May 13, 2003).

58. Porter, *An External Review of the CAP*, 25.

59. Porter, *An External Review of the CAP*.

60. Porter, *An External Review of the CAP*.

61. Buchanan-Smith, Margie, and Judith Randel, *Financing International Humanitarian Action: A Review of Key Trends*, Humanitarian Policy Group (HPG) No. 4 (London, Overseas Development Institute (ODI), 2002), 1.

62. Joanna Macrae, "The changing role of official donors in humanitarian action: a review of trends and issues," HPG Briefing No. 5 (London: ODI, December 2002).

63. Chris Johnson and Jolyon Leslie, "Coordinating Structures in Afghanistan," HPG Background Paper (London: ODI, December 2002), 9.

64. Joanna Macrae, "The 'bilateralisation' of humanitarian response: trends in the financial, contractual and managerial environment of official aid," A Background Paper for UNHCR (London: ODI, October 2002).

65. Macrae, "The 'bilateralisation' of humanitarian response."

66. Macrae, "The changing role of official donors in humanitarian action."

67. Macrae, "The 'bilateralization' of humanitarian response."

68. Although contributions to CAPs represent only about 30 percent of total global humanitarian assistance, high levels of earmarking (up to 85 percent in the case of WFP and UNHCR) within the CAP has contributed to this phenomenon.

69. Judith Randel and Tony German, "Trends in the financing of humanitarian assistance," in *The New Humanitarianisms: A Review of Trends in Global Humanitarian Action*, ed. Joanna Macrae (London: ODI, April 2002).

70. DAC members are: Australia, Austria, Belgium, Canada, Denmark, Finland, France, Germany, Greece, Ireland, Italy, Japan, Luxembourg, the Netherlands, New Zealand, Norway, Portugal, Spain, Sweden, Switzerland, the UK, the U.S., and the Commission of the European Union.

71. Randel and German, "Trends," 19.

72. Ian Smilie and Larry Minear, "The Quality of Money: Donor Behavior in Humanitarian Financing," Humanitarianism and War Project, The Feinstein International Famine Center (Somerville, Mass.: Tufts University, April 2003).

73. Smillie and Minear, "The Quality of Money," 8.

74. Smillie and Minear, "The Quality of Money," 9.

75. Larry Minear, "Humanitarian action in an age of terrorism," Working Paper No. 63 (Medford, Mass.: Humanitarianism and War Project, Feinstein International Famine Center, Tufts University, August 2002), 1.

76. Minear, "Humanitarian action," 2.

77. Minear, "Humanitarian action," 15.

78. Minear, "Humanitarian action," 16.

79. Patricia Weiss Fagen et al., "Internal Displacement in Colombia: National and International Responses," IIS Working Paper (Copenhagen: Institute for International Studies, June 2003).

80. Shepard Forman and Rita Parhad, "Paying for Essentials: Resources for Humanitarian Assistance" (New York: Center on International Cooperation, New York University, September 1997).

81. Interview with Reynold Levy, Executive Director, International Rescue Committee, July 2001.

82. Karanian, "Georgia's Forced Migrants."

83. Smillie and Minear, "The Quality of Money," 29.

84. Smillie and Minear, "The Quality of Money," 31.

85. ISIM Interview, Levy, IRC.

86. Shepard Forman and Rita Parhad, "Paying for Essentials," 4.

87. Karanian, "Georgia's Forced Migrants," 76.

88. Chris Johnson and Leslie Jolyon write, "Switzerland started spending development funds, which had reportedly not been done in Afghanistan for 20 years. Canada set up mechanisms for longer-term funding, and Sweden shifted to two-year funding, with a provision for three-year cycles in the future," in "Coordinating Structures in Afghanistan," *Humanitarian Policy Group (HPG) Background Paper*, December 2002.

89. William Garvelink, quoted in Abby Stoddard, "The U.S. and the 'bilateralisation' of humanitarian response," HPG Background Paper (London: ODI, 2002), 8.

90. Tasneem Mowjee and Joanna Macrae, "Accountability and influence in the European Community Humanitarian Aid Office," HPG Background Paper (London: ODI, December 2002).

91. Mowjee and Macrae, "Accountability."

92. Nicola Reindorp and Anna Schmidt, "Coordinating humanitarian action: the changing role of official donors," HPG Briefing No. 7 (London: ODI, December 2002).

93. Mowjee and Macrae, "Accountability."

94. Mowjee and Macrae, "Accountability."

95. Fagen et al., "Internal Displacement in Colombia," 46.

96. Philip Rudge, "The Need for a More Focused Response: European Donor Policies Toward Internally Displaced Persons (IDPs)" (Washington: Brookings-CUNY

Project on Internal Displacement, Norwegian Refugee Council, and the U.S. Committee for Refugees, January 2002), 7.

97. Mowjee and Macrae, "Accountability," 8.

98. Council of the European Union, quoted in Mowjee and Macrae, "Accountability," 8.

99. Mowjee and Macrae, "Accountability," 10.

100. Mowjee and Macrae, "Accountability," 11.

101. European Parliament cited in Mowjee and Macrae, "Accountability."

102. Margie Buchanan-Smith and Ulrik Sørensen Rohde, "Danida's international humanitarian assistance programme: a case study of accountability mechanisms," HPG Background Paper (London: ODI, December 2002).

103. Danida website, www.um.dk/English/dp/ddp.asp (September 12, 2003).

104. Danida, "Multilateral Development Assistance Framework," www.um.dk/English/dp/mda.asp (September 12, 2003).

105. Philip Rudge, "The Need for a More Focused Response," 31.

106. Sarah Collinson, "Donor Accountability in the UK," HPG Background Paper (London: ODI, December 2002), 5.

107. DFID (1997), quoted in Collinson, "Donor Accountability," 5.

108. Cited in Collinson, "Donor Accountability," 5.

109. Collinson, "Donor Accountability," 6.

110. Collinson, "Donor Accountability," 6.

111. DFID partnership plans for UNHCR, UNHCHR, OCHA, UNDP, UNICEF, IFRCRC, and ICRC.

112. Collinson, "Donor Accountability."

113. Rudge, "The Need for a More Focused Response."

114. Abby Stoddard, "The U.S. and the 'bilateralization' of humanitarian response," HPG Background Paper, Background research for HPG Report 12, December 2002.

115. Joanna Macrae, ed., "The New Humanitarianism: A Review of Trends in Global Humanitarian Action," HPG Report 11 (London: ODI, April 2002), 15.

116. Abby Stoddard, "The U.S. and the 'bilateralization' of humanitarian response," 1–3.

117. Andrew Natsios (remarks made at the Interaction Forum, May 23, 2003).

118. Abby Stoddard, "The U.S. and the 'bilateralisation' of humanitarian response," and Abby Stoddard, "Trends in US humanitarian policy," in "The New Humanitarianisms: A Review of Trends in Global Humanitarian Action," HPG Report 11, ed. Joanna Macrae (London: ODI, April 2002).

119. James Kunder, "The U.S. Government and Internally Displaced Persons: Present, But Not Accounted For" (Washington: Brookings Institution and the U.S. Committee for Refugees, November 1999).

120. Kunder, "The U.S. Government," 12.

121. Susan Martin and Trish Hiddleston, "Burundi: A Case of Humanitarian Neglect," in Van Hear and McDowell, eds., *Catching Fire*, Lanham, Md.: Lexington Books (forthcoming 2005).

122. USAID/OFDA, *Field Operations Guide*, quoted in Kunder, "The U.S. Government," 12.

123. Margie Buchanan-Smith and Natalie Folster, "Canada's international humanitarian assistance programme: policy oversight mechanisms," HPG Background Paper (London: ODI, December 2002), 2.

124. Buchanan-Smith and Folster, "Canada's international humanitarian assistance," 2.

125. Buchanan-Smith and Folster, "Canada's international humanitarian assistance," 2.

126. Buchanan-Smith and Folster, "Canada's international humanitarian assistance," 3.

127. William Garvelink, quoted in Abby Stoddard, "The U.S. and the 'bilateralisation' of humanitarian response," 8.

128. Van Hear and Rajasingham-Senanayake, "Displacement and the humanitarian regime."

129. Shepard Forman, Stewart Patrick, and Dirk Salomons, "Recovering from Conflict: Strategy for an International Response," Paying for Essentials Policy Paper Series (New York: Center for International Cooperation, 2000).

130. For instance, in post-conflict situations, Forman and Patrick identify these sectors as: repatriation and resettlement, demobilization and reintegration, restoration of public safety and security, rehabilitation of basic infrastructure, revival of agriculture and assurance of food security, provision of basic social services such as health and education, reestablishment of governance structures, and preparation for elections and rule of law programs. See Forman, Shepard, Stewart Patrick, and Dirk Salomons, "Recovering from Conflict."

131. Forman, Patrick, and Salomons, "Recovering from Conflict."

132. Forman, Patrick, and Salomons, "Recovering from Conflict," 40–41.

133. Montreux IV, "Donors Retreat on the CAP and Coordination in Humanitarian Emergencies," conference held March 1–2, 2001 in Montreux, Switzerland.

134. Montreux IV, "Donors Retreat on the CAP and Coordination in Humanitarian Emergencies."

135. Macrae, "The changing role of official donors."

136. Smillie and Minear, "The Quality of Money."

137. Debriefing on the outcome of the International Meeting on Good Humanitarian Donorship, June 16–17, 2003, in Sweden, outlined in notes from the IASC Weekly Meeting, June 25, 2003.

138. Good Humanitarian Donorship Implementation Group, "Implementation Plan for Good Humanitarian Donorship," elaborated in Stockholm, June 17, 2003, www.odi.org.uk/hpg/papers/Implementationpercent20Plan.pdf (November 29, 2004).

139. Good Humanitarian Donorship Implementation Group, "Good Humanitarian Donorship-Current Status of Implementation Work," Informal presentation for 69th HAC meeting, Brussels, June 24, 2004, http://www.reliefweb.int/ghd/ (July 29, 2004).

140. Good Humanitarian Donorship Implementation Group, "Implementation Plan for Good Humanitarian Donorship."

141. Good Humanitarian Practice Implementation Group, "International Meeting on Good Humanitarian Donorship-Stockholm June 16–17, 2003, Principles and Good Practice of Humanitarian Donorship," www.reliefweb.int/ghd/ (November 29, 2004).

142. Salvator Bijojote and Christian Bugnion, "External Baseline Evaluation of the Burundi Good Humanitarian Donorship Pilot," Reliefweb 2004 www.reliefweb.int/ghd/Brundi%20GHD%20Pilot%20external%20baseline%20evaluation%2014%20June.pdf (June 22, 2004), 5.

143. Bijojote and Bugnion, "External Baseline Evaluation," 7.

144. Nicole Reindorp and Anna Schmidt, "Coordinating Humanitarian Action.

145. Patricia Weiss Fagen, et. al, "Internal Displacement in Colombia."

146. This opinion was expressed by members of the research team and officials of RSS, cited in Fagen et al., "Internal Displacement in Colombia," 25.

147. Fagen et al., "Internal Displacement in Colombia."

148. Fagen et al., "Internal Displacement in Colombia."

149. Sarah Collinson, "International humanitarian action and the accountability of official donors," HPG Briefing No. 6 (London: ODI, December 2002).

150. Buchanan-Smith and Rohde, "Danida's international humanitarian assistance."

151. Good Humanitarian Donorship Implementation Group, "Implementation Plan for Good Humanitarian Donorship."

5

Providing Security to Forced Migrants and Humanitarian Operations

INTRODUCTION

Security for forced migrants and humanitarian aid workers is a significant problem in the post-Cold War era. The end of the Cold War in 1989 was followed by a proliferation of intrastate conflicts in which civilians faced considerable dangers and became seen by combatants as legitimate targets of war. As armed conflict forced many civilians to migrate, the international political climate allowed for the greater involvement of international actors in national peace and security crises. Humanitarian aid workers and international peacekeepers began to deploy into countries characterized by instability, violence, a proliferation of non-state actors, and large numbers of civilians both fleeing from and targeted by violence. As civilians began to be killed and drawn into war in record numbers, the relatively straightforward and restrictive definition of refugee in the 1950s changed into the complex and encompassing post-1990s idea of the forced migrant. At the same time, insecure environments for civilians and insecure environments for humanitarian work emerged as perhaps the most significant barrier to effective assistance and protection of forced migrants.[1]

National governments, the United Nations, humanitarian aid organizations, and regional organizations can all take steps to ensure increased security for forced migrants and humanitarian aid workers. National governments are the actors most able to prevent or resolve armed conflict in other countries or their own. National governments are also responsible for upholding standards of international humanitarian law and international human rights when a humanitarian crisis or war occurs in or affects their territory (see chapter 2). When national governments cannot or will not adhere to these responsibili-

188

ties, the United Nations, other international organizations, and/or regional organizations can and have come forward to assist and protect populations in danger. Such assistance and protection has taken predominantly two forms: (1) providing humanitarian aid and (2) dispatching peacekeepers and/or civilian police. While there has been much public criticism about, and some praise for, the levels of humanitarian aid and the performance of international peacekeepers, the international political community has lagged most significantly behind in the development and utilization of both conflict prevention measures and credible deterrents to or sanctions for attacks on forced migrants and aid workers. Conflict prevention measures are specifically discussed in chapter 6 of this volume. This chapter will first examine the nature of forced migration, conflict, and insecurity in the world today before turning to a discussion of what national governments, international agencies, regional organizations, and nongovernmental organizations can do, and in some cases have done, to successfully address insecurity during a "hot" conflict. Creating political will to follow through on these recommendations is of vital importance.

THE CHANGING FACE OF CONFLICT, MIGRATION, AND HUMANITARIAN RESPONSE

As discussed in chapter 1, conflict is a principle cause of both refugee movements and internal displacement. The rise in intrastate conflict since 1989 has had serious repercussions for civilians, including forced migrants. The majority of conflicts since the end of World War II has been intrastate and has occurred in the developing world.[2] Intrastate conflict in the 1990s and beyond has been characterized by attacks on civilians, erosion in law and public order, a proliferation of non-state actors bearing small arms, and a breakdown of state structures.[3] In such a climate, social services are lost, daily life becomes challenging and dangerous, development work becomes difficult if not impossible, and many civilians are forced to flee their homes. And as fighting centers within a country, civilians become "political and military objectives"[4] in struggles where polarized sides often identify with race, religion, or ethnic divisions.[5] For civilians, the world has become a more dangerous place.

As the number of armed conflicts and civilians adversely affected by these conflicts increased, humanitarian agencies multiplied and began to send their staff into increasingly dangerous operating environments where conflict was often ongoing.[6] At the same time the definition of international peacekeeping underwent a revolution, and peacekeepers became tasked with complex and comprehensive mandates in peace enforcement situations. Military actors became tasked with humanitarian response, and civilian and military actors began to both be present in complicated uncertain environments.[7] International military and police action began to extend beyond UN action to coalitions of the willing and to private military companies (PMCs). The combination of armed conflict, multiple armed factions, a lack of law and order, and frequent population displacements created chaotic situations where humanitarian agencies and international peacekeepers not only operated within an uncertain environment but also became seen as participants in conflict and were directly and indirectly impacted by the lack of protection for civilians in armed conflict.[8] Aid agencies also experienced difficulties adequately distinguishing themselves from non-UN military coalitions such as the American-led coalition in Iraq in 2003–2004.[9] The landscape within which humanitarian response to forced migrant crises occurs became increasingly complicated.

Humanitarian aid workers and civilians in general, have been at significant risk during armed conflict in the 1990s and beyond. In contrast to the First World War, where 1 percent of the casualties of armed conflict were civilians, it is estimated that up to 90 percent of the casualties of armed conflict in the 1990s and beyond are civilians.[10] The internally displaced have been particularly difficult to assist and protect. In the intrastate conflicts of the 1990s and beyond, this protection was frequently not present. While the United Nations and regional organizations have responded quickly to the need to increase international legal protections for civilians during armed conflict, this has not always translated into actual protection in the field.

The dangers facing humanitarian workers have also changed significantly since 1989. A study of 382 humanitarian aid worker deaths from 1985 to 1998 noted that deaths of humanitarian aid workers were on the rise for NGOs, tended to occur as a result of intentional violence (68 percent of deaths)[11], and that almost a third occurred within ninety days of deployment regardless of previous deployment history.[12] In particular, 77 percent of ICRC staff deaths were as a result of intentional violence.[13] After an analysis of humanitarian aid worker deaths from 1997 to 2001, a second study found that "more civilian humanitarian aid workers are killed by acts of violence than in accidents," and that most intentional deaths were as a result of ambushes on vehicles or convoys (47 percent), and affected local staff (74 percent of intentional casualties) versus expatriate staff (26 percent of intentional casualties), and NGOs (59 percent of intentional casualties) versus UN workers (41 percent of intentional casualties).[14] NGO, UN, and ICRC staff, and increasingly international contractors today face significant dangers that are no longer limited to banditry and by-products of the conflict environment (collateral damage, traffic accidents) but now include the high risk of intentional attack. This conclusion is supported by the individual statistics of the International Committee of the Red Cross (ICRC). From 1989 to 1998, ICRC records demonstrated a significant increase in physical threats, increased banditry, and particularly deliberate targeting of staff.[15] Such direct targeting of aid workers is likely to continue in conflicts such as Iraq, where there is a proliferation of non-UN military actors, significant international ambivalence about the presence of these non-UN military actors, the desire among radical elements to remove both the military forces and humanitarian aid workers from the country and an inability of the humanitarian aid organizations to adequately distinguish themselves from the U.S.-led coalition.[16]

In the dangerous operating environments of the 1990s and beyond, insecurity plays a critical role in determining what types of humanitarian intervention is both required and possible, as well as determining the severity of a forced migrant crisis. Insecurity often prevents humanitarian assistance from reaching migrants in significant need. As an ICRC staff member stated in 1998: "Today we are torn between the necessity to pursue an indispensable humanitarian mission and conditions in the field so unsafe that they make that mission, in places like Burundi and Chechnya, quite simply unfeasible."[17]

Addressing Insecurity During Conflict

In such a context, what can governments and humanitarian agencies do? In the context of insecurity and intrastate conflicts, national governments are the most empowered to act. Not only are they commonly understood to have the responsibility of providing for public security within their borders,[18] but in the international context it is governments who have the political, economic, and social power to address armed conflicts in the conflict prevention, conflict management, and conflict resolution stages. The international human rights movement and the emergence of the idea of sovereignty as responsibility at the end of the Cold War have removed some of the barriers to governments intervening in the affairs of other nations.[19] However, governments are not the only actors who can address insecurity for civilians and humanitarian aid workers during armed conflict. And since governments often do not intervene in humanitarian emergencies or use financial support as a substitute for substantive political involvement,[20] the role of humanitarian NGOs and the United Nations is increasingly important. Humanitarian agencies can take and have taken a wide range of measures to ensure migrants and humanitarian staff are protected from a variety of physical and sexual threats and have worked to adhere to the "do no harm" principle. Most recently NGOs, the ICRC, and the UN have begun to address insecurity directly with the creation of security programs, civilian security offices, and security coordination. As humanitarian agencies work to increase security for the populations they protect and for their workers, national governments need to design and implement diplomatic interventions as well as robust and effective peace operations when they are necessary, and to provide the United Nations and regional organizations with the resources and political support needed to comprehensively address and resolve insecurity.

THE ROLE OF NATIONAL GOVERNMENTS AND INTERNATIONAL AND REGIONAL ORGANIZATIONS

Governments frequently have significant but underutilized political, economic, and social capital when it comes to managing and resolving conflict. First, governments have a range of diplomatic options available to address potential or existing armed conflict. Such efforts are at times undertaken in tandem with conflict prevention, conflict management, and/or conflict resolution agencies such as the United States Institute for Peace (USIP) or The Carter Center. Second, the end of the Cold War and the increased ability of international actors to intervene in political and security crises led to a dramatic increase in the ability of governments to mount international UN peace operations.

During the 1990s, international civilian police and military personnel were dispatched to crises such as Mozambique and Cambodia. When failures of UN peacekeeping in the early 1990s led to a reluctance to approve and dispatch UN peace operations to places such as Rwanda and (initially) Sierra Leone, UN peace operations were replaced by a third governmental option to address conflict: regional peace forces such as ECOWAS (Economic Community of West African States) and NATO (North Atlantic Treaty Organization). Governments also began to use private contractors and "coalitions of the willing" to resolve conflict and/or provide security during armed conflicts with humanitarian crisis dimensions.

While international and/or regional intervention in intrastate conflicts can bring assistance and protection to civilians in need, interventions are too often ill thought out, ill-funded, ill-supported, and inadequate or inappropriate responses to humanitarian crises that might have been avoided with preventive action.[21] Governments need to learn to identify and seize opportunities for crisis prevention, management, and resolution. Governmental use of conflict prevention measures can avoid the need for costly and inappropriate military and/or police interventions (see chapter 6 for more on conflict prevention). Until conflict prevention is more widespread, other diplomatic, police, and military interventions are likely to continue occurring in humanitarian crises, and therefore how to make such interventions sufficiently credible, legitimate, and appropriate is of critical importance.

Civilian Police

Achieving public security is a crucial component of international intervention to address humanitarian crises.[22] In the early 1990s, UN missions began dispatching international civilian police (CIVPOL) alongside UN peacekeeping or peace enforcement troops. CIVPOL components of peace operations gradually increased in size and stature over the 1990s. While the movement toward including CIVPOL in multifaceted peace operations is a positive development, two major problems remain. First, finding and equipping international civilian police is difficult. Second, the understanding that public security needs to be addressed has not always been accompanied by an understanding that only those trained and equipped to handle public security should do so. Many military actors have been delegated responsibility for public security tasks for which they have been ill-trained, and political decision makers have not always understood the differences between military and police capacities. The grave complications this can pose and the importance of separating out and properly delegating military and police responsibilities have been seen in crises such as Bosnia and Iraq.

Civilian policing options to protect forced migrants, humanitarian aid, and humanitarian aid workers in intrastate conflicts are needed not only because of the insecurity and instability for civilians of such conflicts but also because of the failures of local governments to address public safety. Attacks on refugees/IDPs and aid workers, banditry, diversion of aid resources, and lawlessness are all the responsibility of states to address.[23] In many intrastate conflicts today, governments have shown themselves to be unable or unwilling to address these issues.[24] During periods of intrastate conflict, the police are often neither trusted, seen as civilian, nor able to fill the security void left by the lack of a political-military or political-police divide.[25] In countries hosting refugee populations, the perceived link between refugees and physical, economic, and environmental insecurity can engender hostility from local populations and can create conditions where the national police are indifferent or outwardly hostile to refugee populations.[26] When peace is declared and the difficult process of refugee and IDP return begins, national police often have the responsibility of ensuring safety for returning populations, but cannot or will not do so unless they are organized as a professional and neutral force and have a rule of law to uphold that recognizes human rights. The creation of such a police force requires significant amounts of training, resources, and time. In the 1990s, UN international civilian police became seen as the actors with the best qualifications to assist in this process. The idea of addressing many security issues through the use of civilian police (national, international, hired directly by NGOs and other humanitarian agencies) increased in popularity, particularly as the likelihood and perceived desirability of military peacekeepers decreased.

Over the course of the 1990s, UN CIVPOL responsibilities in peace operations quickly expanded from a pure monitoring role in Namibia in 1989 to a police training and reform role in Haiti, Cambodia, Somalia, and Bosnia. Over the 1990s, a new concept of CIVPOL in UN peace operations evolved: police became involved in monitoring, training, and mentoring of local police forces, investigated human rights abuses and reformed and/or established local police forces.[27] In Bosnia, Haiti, Mozambique, and Cambodia CIVPOL were drawn into additional responsibilities for the protection of UN staff, while in Bosnia, Kosovo, Cambodia, and Mozambique CIVPOL assisted in refugee return. Until East Timor and Kosovo, CIVPOL performed these responsibilities as unarmed independent advisors, monitors and teachers. Because CIVPOL are traditionally unarmed they rely on the force of example (impartiality, professionalism) to gain the respect of local communities, governments, and armed forces.[28]

The use of CIVPOL by the United Nations to monitor law and order in a humanitarian crisis is a positive development for humanitarian actors working to assist and protect forced migrants, as CIVPOL can alleviate some of the security threats—banditry, unlawful taxing of humanitarian convoys, crimes against migrants (rapes, murders, assaults, forced conscription)—faced by humanitarian actors and forced migrants without creating some of the complications of military actors. CIVPOL can greatly assist in the reconciliation process by contributing to a stable climate of law and order, while their presence as a neutral force that works intensively with the local communities can help reestablish the idea of a social contract without resorting to the idea of military solutions.[29] As CIVPOL often have a mandate to monitor and train local police, they will work side by side with national police to monitor their behavior, and thus theoretically decrease violations of human rights and international humanitarian law, as they provide training to turn local police forces into professional, neutral, and respected upholders of law and order; such a CIVPOL mission will, if successful, greatly increase security for forced migrants, humanitarian aid workers, and humanitarian aid operations.[30] However, in a situation where "baseline law and order" needs to be established in a post-conflict setting, CIVPOL need to allow the military to perform this duty before they are able to continue with their tasks.[31]

CIVPOL actors face significant challenges. As unarmed officers present in often violent situations, they rely on moral force, communication, and their example to protect themselves, aid workers, and forced migrants.[32] Their presence can often be threatening to local authorities and a blurring of CIVPOL and military responsibilities during peace operations or a compromised position for CIVPOL as a result of identification with specific political objectives can be particularly dangerous as it can draw unarmed CIVPOL into military situations.[33]

Because CIVPOL operations depend on the willingness of UN member states to contribute personnel to a mission, UN CIVPOL face many drawbacks shared by UN military operations.[34] Thus, in crises such as Burundi that are experiencing severe public security deficits, CIVPOL operations are often not approved. When missions are approved, CIVPOL personnel contributed to operations are often ill equipped, ill trained, and enter conflict with a limited understanding of local realities.[35]

As multinational coalitions, CIVPOL units can also experience cohesion problems.[36] International policing standards—such as the "Basic Principles on the Use of Force and Firearms by Law Enforcement Officials"—refer to relatively vague terms such as the use of "appropriate force." Interpretations of "appropriate force" can differ greatly based on background experience even as the actions of a few CIVPOL can negatively impact an entire deployment.[37] A lack of transparency about the role of CIVPOL in a crisis can lead to too high expectations (and quick disillusionment) among local populations.[38] As international actors can often experience difficulties distinguishing themselves from other components of international intervention during humanitarian crises, failures of CIVPOL can negatively impact both the security and the credibility of humanitarian aid operations.

The UN has attempted to address many of the drawbacks of the current CIVPOL system in order to better utilize the many benefits a CIVPOL operation can bring. CIVPOL need to be trained in international humanitarian and human rights law and provided with clear, robust, and enforceable mandates as well as sufficient resources and personnel.[39] CIVPOL are neither trained nor able to stop military conflict.[40] When given duties outside possible mandates (such as that given to UNMIK police in Kosovo to ensure the security of returnees), the failure of CIVPOL to achieve its mandate will decrease respect for CIVPOL in the local community and decrease their ability to provide public security for humanitarian aid operations, humanitarian aid workers, and forced migrants. All actors involved in dispatching CIVPOL missions need to understand the use, limits, and requirements of CIVPOL if their considerable benefits are to be realized.

The drawbacks of the current CIVPOL system and concurrent demand for CIVPOL actors in crises around the world have led to an upsurge in the movement to create a standing UN police force. A standing UN police force would allow for the dispatching of professional, trained, and cohesive CIVPOL units to humanitarian crises around the world, while avoiding the problems of co-ordination, legitimacy, and coherence that UN CIVPOL have frequently faced. Two members of the United States Congress have recently introduced a bill, commonly referred to as the McGovern-Houghton The International Rule of Law and Anti-Terrorism Act of 2003 (HR 1414), that would help cre-ate a standing UN Civilian Police Corps (UNCPC) to "maintain the rule of law and promote peace and stability in post-conflict situations."[41] Forces would be under UN command and would be considered UN employees,[42] thus alleviating command problems such as those experienced under current UN operations. A UNCPC would also assist in a thorough security transition from military to police forces following a military peace operation and allow military actors not to perform police activities for which they are untrained.[43] The bill is supported by a coalition of forty-seven NGOs led by the Campaign for UN Reform and Refugees International. The creation of a standing UNCPC needs to be significantly prioritized by the United States and other governments. Not only could a UNCPC be of great assistance in a crisis such as Iraq in 2004,[44] but "public security is absolutely critical to the successful execution of humanitarian relief and development efforts."[45] Civilian police are the actors best equipped to address public security.

International Military Options

The 1990s witnessed unprecedented military action by the United Nations to address international peace and security crises around the world. The concur-rent greater involvement of humanitarian agencies in such crises led to in-creased and often uneasy interaction between military and humanitarian ac-tors, as the military became tasked with the protection of humanitarian aid and humanitarian aid staff, and humanitarian agencies began to operate within war zones. While military and civilian actors have worked to develop models for cooperation in the security realm, collaboration remains difficult, military and civilian actors often struggle over authority issues, and many hu-manitarian actors resist any association with military forces.[46] Because of the complicated record of UN peacekeeping through the 1990s and the political nature of military deployments, UN peacekeepers are not guaranteed partici-pants in future humanitarian crises. Instead, an evolving international inter-vention model is emerging where threats to international peace and security, when addressed internationally, are being addressed not only by the United Nations but also by coalitions of the willing (generally sanctioned by the UN), regional organizations and mercenaries/private military companies. This proliferation of military actors has created complications for humanitarian agencies[47] even as intrastate conflicts have proved extraordinarily difficult to "solve" through military solutions.[48] However, when conflict reaches a critical level of violence, all tactics of humanitarian actors,[49] CIVPOL,[50] and diplomatic interventions will be in the first and second case insufficient to stop conflict, and in the third case likely to take time. Given little political action to stop potential or low-level conflict, military actors will likely remain important in the conflict management and conflict resolution fields.

The authority and legitimacy of UN peace operations is derived from the UN Charter, in which the United Nations, and specifically the UN Security Council, is vested with the power to address threats to international peace and security. The UN Charter has been interpreted to give the UN Security Council the ability to address threats to international peace and security through either Chapter VI (peacekeeping) or Chapter VII (peace enforcement) operations. During the Cold War, peacekeeping operations were limited to what is now termed "traditional peacekeeping," where UN military forces were used to physically separate combatants, provide an acceptable way for involved parties to back down, and prevent conflicts from erupting into conflagrations with potentially dangerous global implications.[51] These traditional peacekeeping operations were entered into with the consent and cooperation of local parties, with the understanding that UN forces operated only in self-defense and under the command of the UN Secretary-General and with no troop participation from the Security Council's five permanent members.

The immediate end of the Cold War period saw a tremendous rise in UN peacekeeping operations and a great confidence in the ability of the UN to address challenges to international peace and security. Boutros Boutros Ghali's "Agenda for Peace" and the 1991 Persian Gulf War witnessed the emergence and acceptance of the idea of sovereignty as responsibility, the idea that respect for sovereignty would not trump respect for human rights.[52] In the insecure operating environments of intrastate conflicts in the 1990s, peacekeepers became tasked with an increased number of activities, including the introduction of good governance, demobilization and disarmament, the creation of neutral national military forces, and the protection of humanitarian operations and/or civilians.[53] Peacekeepers began to be sent to places where there was no official "peace" to uphold, where there was a proliferation of armed groups and where they were not specifically requested by both sides of (or multiple sides to) a conflict.[54] Thus, even as "peacekeeping became more possible, more necessary, and more desired. . . . It also became much harder to do successfully."[55] There were new challenges that needed to be met with a different form of peacekeeping. The United Nations has met this challenge with a mixed record.

UNHCR's work with the United Nations Protection Force (UNPROFOR) in Bosnia in the early 1990s illustrates the significant security difficulties created by new levels of interaction between the military and humanitarian agencies in a crisis with political, military, and humanitarian dimensions. In the absence of political commitment to stop ethnic cleansing in the former Yugoslavia, UNPROFOR was given a mandate to protect humanitarian assistance delivery to Sarajevo and surrounding areas, and to ensure UNHCR access throughout Bosnia-Herzegovina in 1992.[56] The firm linking of UNHCR with UNPROFOR in a climate of great hostility toward UNPROFOR led to direct as well as indiscriminate attacks on UNHCR, and a heated debate rose within the international assistance community as to whether association with the military actor UNPROFOR negatively impacted the neutrality of assistance.[57] Even as UNHCR was able to provide greater amounts of humanitarian assistance than would have been possible without military protection, UNPROFOR's inability and unwillingness to address genocide led to a serious loss of credibility with both local communities and the humanitarian assistance community.[58] In a situation where humanitarian assistance became seen as a participant in conflict, humanitarian action was promoted as a substitute for political action, and UNPROFOR was given a confusing peacekeeping and peace enforcement mandate, many UNPROFOR and UNHCR workers lost their lives, the UN sustained a serious loss of credibility, humanitarian assistance was diverted to support combat, and UNHCR's evacuation of civilians at risk was widely criticized as assisting ethnic cleansing.[59] Similar criticisms have been raised about countries such as Sudan, where Operational Lifeline Sudan was considered to have compromised humanitarian principles for access purposes.[60]

Peace operations in Somalia, Rwanda, and Sierra Leone were no more successful in protecting humanitarian aid, humanitarian aid workers, and forced migrants/civilians. In a climate where international military actors are often not clearly distinguished by local military forces, and are associated with the same political goals, the existence of enforcement actions can place peacekeeping actors in great physical danger. Resentment against seemingly partisan enforcement interventions led to a highly insecure operating environment for humanitarian agencies that were not clearly distinguished from international military actors who possessed humanitarian mandates.[61] Such was the situation in Somalia, where UNITAF's pursuit of General Aidid compromised not only UN humanitarian agencies but also relations between the United Nations and NGOs in Somalia.[62] In Somalia, aid agencies were also present in large enough numbers, and made sufficient compromises with local forces, that they demonstrated vividly how humanitarian agencies could fail to do no harm: it has been estimated that up to two-thirds of food shipments intended for refugees were stolen in some areas, while the large amounts of food entering the area destroyed local markets, facilitated continued conflict, and enriched black market profiteers.[63] In Rwanda, Somalia, and Sierra Leone, the UN dispatching of ill-equipped, ill-prepared, and ill-supported troops who lacked a deep understanding of the political situation and were not backed by political conflict resolution efforts, led to the failure of the UN to achieve its mandate and to serious losses of credibility and life.[64] The UN failures negatively impacted security conditions for aid work, decreasing the ability of humanitarian agencies to operate or protect their staff and forced migrants.

In August 2000, the United Nations released a "Report of the Panel on United Nations Peace Operations" (commonly referred to as the "Brahimi Report") to begin the process of understanding and overcoming the peacekeeping failures of the 1990s. Sustained political commitment, sufficient financial backing, and "significant [UN] institutional change" were isolated as essential for the UN to carry out future peace operations.[65] It was recognized that the UN member states needed to commit to supporting peace operations through the donation of sufficient resources and troops, and that clear, robust, and achievable mandates needed to be given to UN peace operations. In addition, well-trained and well-equipped forces needed to be *rapidly* deployed to deal with a conflict situation, and the United Nations operational definition of neutrality needed to mean not impartiality between sides to a conflict regardless of their actions, but "adherence to the principles of the [UN] Charter."[66] Achieving such change has not been and will not be easy in an environment where nations with well-trained and well-equipped troops are reluctant to dispatch them for peacekeeping missions, the UN is experiencing a funding crisis and the creation of a standing UN peacekeeping force appears extremely unlikely. The U.S.-led war on terror has also diverted many of the best trained and equipped troops to crises such as Afghanistan and Iraq at the expense of crises such as Congo and Burundi. Reform of the United Nations system of peacekeeping is important for humanitarian agencies as UN peace operations may continue to be deployed to ensure secure operating environments for humanitarian agencies.

Along with the essential reforms of the UN peacekeeping system detailed above, military and humanitarian actors need to together take explicit steps to improve the security of forced migrants, humanitarian aid, and humanitarian aid workers. Working within intrastate conflicts in the 1990s demanded a complex mandate for peacekeepers that often conflicted with traditional military training.[67] Peace operations force military personnel to work extensively with civilians and within an environment that stresses negotiation rather than the use of force to obtain mission goals, tasks for which many are untrained.[68] Military actors experience great frustration when dealing with civilians that they consider scattered and disorganized.[69] At the same time, there is a corresponding lack of understanding of the military culture among civilian decision makers at the United Nations (who misunderstand the level of force and resources required to achieve certain mandates) and humanitarian aid staff in the field.[70] Humanitarian actors often have a great reluctance to become associated with military forces on the ground, while the military is often frustrated by the need to provide security for uncooperative civilians and fearful that these responsibilities will lead to mission creep.[71] The civilian-military disconnect is important to understand and overcome if civilians and the military are to cooperate—or at least not clash—in a time of conflict. Greater understanding among peacekeepers of human rights and international humanitarian law and a greater willingness to become involved to assist populations at risk will increase the profile of military actors among humanitarian agencies, but needs to be accompanied by appropriate mandates and resources.[72] In the post-conflict phase, military actors also need to be removed from public security tasks that they are ill-trained to perform, because their attempts to address public safety may only lead to heightened violence and tension within a society, violence and tensions that create dangers for humanitarian agencies.[73] On the flip side, basic security training for and a greater understanding of security issues among humanitarian staff will improve military opinions of humanitarian agencies.[74] And as in Bosnia, Somalia, and Timor, civilian and military actors can establish a forum for discussion. While there is no imperative for humanitarian agencies and the military to coordinate on (all aspects of) work in the field (and great resistance to this notion makes it unlikely to occur), a higher level of understanding and cooperation—as well as the removal of the military from policing tasks—will improve disconnects and lead to greater protection for forced migrants, humanitarian agencies, and humanitarian aid work.[75] Most fundamentally, military actors need to understand the dangers they create for humanitarian actors when they ally themselves too strongly with humanitarian efforts in a "hearts and minds" campaign.[76]

The experience of the UNTAET in Timor does demonstrate how a United Nations force can work with other actors to successfully provide security and protection for forced migrants. UNTAET was present in Timor from October 1999 to May 2002, and provided an executive and legislative authority during East Timor's transition to independent government. UNTAET is commonly regarded as a success by the United Nations and independent evaluators because of the close collaboration between the UN and other actors responding to the crisis, and the establishment of an independent government.[77] While the executive model may be difficult to apply to larger countries, and difficult to fund, the Timor example demonstrates the vast potential accomplishments of UN, military, and humanitarian actors in assisting and protecting forced migrants.[78]

When international military intervention is required to end a crisis, United Nations troops unquestionably possess the most legitimacy and highest degree of international participation and accountability. However, the record of United Nations peace operations and the current method of their organization and deployment pose great difficulties. Deployment of a UN mission with an insufficiently robust mandate or insufficient troops is likely to only worsen a crisis. International politics are also inherently a part of United Nations decision-making. The unwillingness of many nations to be under the command and control of the United Nations has been a significant barrier to effective performance of United Nations troops. The unwillingness of those with the best trained troops to deploy to politically "unimportant" crises has also hampered the record of UN peace operations, and has led to increased emphasis on regional peace operations. Command and control struggles have led to the development of a "coalition of the willing" model, whereby a UN-sanctioned operation is dispatched to a crisis under the command and control of a lead nation. The United States action in Afghanistan was one such operation. The United States operation in Iraq is a more troubling and complicated example of a nation leading an effort with limited international support, and conducting operations that have arguably directly worsened local conditions. And French operations in the Ivory Coast, now undertaken in conjunction with United Nations troops, point to another new model: where one nation's forces work alongside United Nations forces. As military operations become more complicated, the intersection between military and humanitarian actors, and the negative impacts military operations can have on the security and safety of forced migrants and humanitarian aid workers, only increase. The United Nations needs to find and refine its leadership role in the field of peace operations, at the same time as it places more importance on conflict prevention.

Regional Military Options

As the burden of global peacekeeping rose after the end of the Cold War amidst a proliferation of "hot" conflicts, and failures of UN peacekeeping in the early 1990s led to reluctance among developed nations to contribute troops for peace operations, the idea of regional organizations playing an active role in security issues gained credence.[79] Regional organizations are granted a potential role in maintaining international peace and security under Chapter VIII of the UN Charter, and some, particularly in Africa and Europe, have begun to participate in peace operations and to work to develop regional capacity.[80] Proponents of regional peacekeeping stress the theoretical advantages regional organizations possess when addressing security issues in their region: greater knowledge of the actors and terrain, more appropriate mechanisms and military technology, and greater investment and political acceptance in the area.[81] The example of ECOWAS in West Africa, SADC in Southern Africa, and NATO in Europe demonstrate that regional organizations may also be able to mobilize more quickly than the UN.[82] However, regional organizations can be hampered in peace operations by their lack of a clear international security mandate, their potential to be politically involved in the region (as opposed to the "impartiality" of the UN) and often limited resources.[83] Many regional organizations in areas of conflict do not have the well-developed structures, strong resources, enforcement mechanisms, and sufficient political will essential to succeed in a peace mission and to ensure the credibility, legitimacy, and accountability of such operations. Despite the often significant drawbacks of regional organizations, the reluctance of the UN Security Council to approve UN peace operations—particularly in situations requiring a Chapter VII mandate—has led to greater involvement of and international investment in regional peace operations. The development of regional peace forces with sufficient capacity and legitimacy is of particular importance in Africa, a region of the world experiencing both a high level of intrastate conflict and often limited extraregional commitment to stopping them.

Regional organizations in Africa have been among the most proactive in addressing intrastate conflict. The AU/OAU (African Union, formerly Organization of African Unity), ECOWAS, and SADC have taken different approaches to peace operations, with the AU/OAU focusing first on preventive diplomacy and observer missions, and ECOWAS and to a lesser extent SADC on mounting military peace operations. While the AU's pan-African membership confers greater legitimacy, the AU struggles between its founding principle of nonintervention in domestic matters of other states and intervention, a position that has negatively impacted its credibility internationally.[84] As the AU/OAU has sometimes absented itself from military action, other African organizations have assumed a regional peacekeeping role. The AU remains important as a possible peacekeeper and a proponent of conflict prevention and resolution measures, whose mediation efforts have played a role in ensuring stability and security on the continent.

ECOWAS is Africa's most active participant in the field of peace operations. While ECOWAS was established in 1975 to promote the economic integration and development of West Africa, ECOWAS intervened militarily in Liberia in 1990 and Sierra Leone in 1997 under the leadership of Nigeria. ECOWAS's deployment of a military unit entitled ECOMOG (ECOWAS Monitoring Group) in the early to mid-1990s and its *relative* success led to the *de facto* acceptance in the international community that ECOWAS could pursue a security agenda in light of Western and UN noninvolvement or disinterest.[85] While UN-ECOMOG cooperation in Liberia in 1994 opened a new chapter in Africa-UN relations, neither the Liberia nor the Sierra Leone ECOWAS missions made significant contributions to security for forced migrants, humanitarian aid, or humanitarian aid actors. ECOMOG operations in Liberia were seen as contributing to conflict in Sierra Leone, and ECOMOG demonstrated some serious drawbacks to regional interventions.[86]

In Liberia and Sierra Leone, ECOMOG revealed itself to possess none of the theoretical attributes of regional organizations in quantities sufficient to make it an effective peacekeeping force.[87] ECOMOG's pursuit of concurrent peacekeeping and peace enforcement in Liberia resulted in serious confusion over goals and mandates.[88] This confusion, and the questionable actions of individual soldiers and units, led to ECOMOG being seen as a participant in conflict.[89] In both Liberia and Sierra Leone, ECOMOG was accused of human rights abuses and participation in resource wars. ECOMOG demonstrated limited knowledge of the terrain and actors (particularly in Liberia), lack of capacity, resources, and political will and a Franco-Anglo divide centering on the hegemonic role of Nigeria.[90] While at times more successful than the other international actors in Liberia and Sierra Leone, ECOMOG failed to create lasting conditions of security for local populations, aid workers, and the delivery of aid. While ECOWAS has attempted to address many of its operational difficulties through the creation of a new security mechanism (Mechanism for Conflict Prevention, Management, Resolution, Peacekeeping, and Security) in December 1999 and the development of a standby force with the capacity for humanitarian intervention and peacekeeping, ECOWAS still lacks the experience, political will, and resources to extensively assist in humanitarian and peace operations.[91] Training given to ECOWAS troops in the Ivory Coast may assist in alleviating some of these drawbacks.

In the mid to late-1990s, the United States, France, and the UK established bilateral efforts to address Africa's lack of military capacity to promote security and address intrastate conflicts. The United States created the ACRI in 1997, the UK established the British-Africa Peacekeeping Initiative in 1995, and France initiated the RECAMP (Reinforcing of African Capacity to Maintain Peace) program in 1997. Under American President George W. Bush, the ACRI was renamed the African Contingency Operations Training and Assistance (ACOTA). These initiatives have thus largely been aimed at training African militaries to perform humanitarian support tasks such as the protection of refugees and humanitarian convoys, in a system where interoperability is assured. The ACRI has worked with humanitarian agencies such as UNHCR, ICRC, WFP, USAID, and Refugees International to develop its programs, and has provided African militaries with training on human rights and international humanitarian law.[92] These initiatives have been undertaken in coordination with each other and have made a concerted effort not to develop a standing military force or military capacity on the continent that could be used for other than peacekeeping efforts.[93] Such initiatives need continued funding and investment from international donors, as the likelihood of African peacekeepers solving African problems remains high. Recent G-8 meetings in June 2004 have highlighted the importance of developing local capacity to address conflicts. ACOTA, RECAMP, and the British-Africa Peacekeeping Initiative do remove perhaps the largest barrier to regional peace operations (interoperability), and do promote greater understanding of human rights. However, realistically many African conflicts will require the deployment of peace enforcement and not peacekeeping troops in order for "hot" crises to be adequately addressed. Until Western nations are comfortable training local troops for tasks beyond peacekeeping, it is likely that the regional peace operations model in developing nations will continue to depend on unilateral military actions by countries such as France and Britain to stabilize conflict situations and prepare the ground for United Nations or regional forces.

While NATO possesses many of the advantages that ECOWAS lacks (highly evolved security structure, resources, well-equipped and trained member nation troops), NATO operations have been hampered by confusing or inappropriate mandates in both Bosnia and Kosovo. In particular, it has been commonly noted in Bosnia that NATO successfully addressed and accomplished the military objectives to "solve" conflict after the failure of the UN UNPROFOR mission, but has been unable to accomplish the same results with the "civilian" goals (return of refugees, integration efforts, democracy). NATO recently took an unprecedented step when it assumed control of the International Security Assistance Force (ISAF) in Afghanistan in August 2003, involving itself in an extra-regional conflict. Particularly interesting is that under NATO the ISAF has finally extended its reach beyond Kabul, a move long called for by humanitarian agencies as essential to provide security across Afghanistan. It remains to be seen whether NATO can measurably increase security for humanitarian agencies across Afghanistan. The example of NATO demonstrates that interoperability and capacity do not ensure success; political will, appropriate and full mandates, and appropriate, early responses to crises are better predictors of success.

Mercenaries or Private Military Companies

A final military option for restoring security during an intrastate conflict is the use of what have become referred to as private military companies (PMCs), or alternately Private Military Firms (PMFs), MSPs (Military Service Providers), or mercenaries. PMCs gained fame and some credibility in the 1990s as an alternative for governments who were experiencing intrastate conflict and lacked either the professional militaries qualified to end conflict or any international interest likely to lead to UN (or regional) involvement. While governments or non-state actors have not used PMCs to provide security specifically for forced migrants, PMCs have protected humanitarian aid workers and humanitarian aid while also directly affecting the security of forced migrants and humanitarian aid workers by providing (even temporary) security in a crisis situation. As more governments, and at times UN agencies and NGOs, turn to PMCs to provide security and training, the legitimacy and accountability of PMCs is important for those attempting to provide security for humanitarian assistance, humanitarian workers, and forced migrants.

The debate on PMCs has changed significantly since 1994 when then UN Under Secretary-General for Peacekeeping Kofi Annan considered the use of PMCs in Rwanda before concluding that "the world may not be ready to privatize peace."[94] Now many governments depend on PMCs for logistics and what is referred to as 'force multiplier' roles. The United States also depends on PMCs to recruit its personnel for CIVPOL missions. In a world where many governments are unwilling to approve or to contribute to large UN peace operations, PMCs provide the potential for action. The relatively lower cost of PMCs as compared to UN peace operations is an added attraction: while Kofi Annan estimated a $418 million price for a 5,600 soldier mission to Burundi, the cost of a PMC operation to Sudan might be as low as $30 million.[95]

While the impressive successes of PMCs such as Executive Outcomes in providing relatively inexpensive, rapid, and effective intervention to resolve security crises is tantalizing, the use of PMCs entails many problems of accountability and legitimacy. These problems appear to be the major reason the United Nations has refused to consider the use of PMCs on a large scale.[96] Since governments have used PMCs in conflicts as different as Afghanistan, Liberia, Sierra Leone, Yugoslavia, the DRC, and Angola,[97] the British government argued in 2002 that PMCs are indisputably part of the new post-Cold War security environment, and that regulating PMCs is the best option to ensure their legitimacy and accountability.[98] Both proponents and opponents of PMCs tend to agree that the accountability issue can be somewhat resolved by the establishment of a licensing system.[99] The IPOA (the International Peace Operations Association), an independent association of PMCs, has gone a step toward accountability in creating a code of conduct for its members and advocating for transparency by PMCs.[100] Regulation is arguable also built into local systems of accountability in countries such as the United States and United Kingdom, where many PMCs are based.

Some PMCs are also moving toward a model that understands their role in the humanitarian response process as limited to baseline security. As the

IPOA motto reads, "Security is 90 percent of the problem, but [only] 10 percent of the solution." PMC advocates such as the IPOA argue that PMCs provide necessary security in areas where national militaries are unwilling or unable to venture, and that in such crises humanitarian needs are too pressing to wait for an international regulation system when regulations in countries such as the United States and the UK already provide sufficient oversight to inspire confidence.[101] As more humanitarian agencies and the United Nations turn, context by context, to private companies to provide security for their operations,[102] PMC use is hotly contested within the UN and particularly the NGO community. The participation of U.S.-hired CACI employees in the Abu Ghraib prisoner-abuse scandal attests to the accountability problem of PMCs and their employees.[103] The use of PMCs in humanitarian crises—by governments, by the United Nations, and by humanitarian agencies—is evidently not a clear-cut issue, nor one that is going to disappear. However, the new position of the ICRC—that humanitarian agencies such as ICRC can accept armed escorts for humanitarian convoys when the neutrality and impartiality of the ICRC is under threat[104]—is the best indicator of the many compromises humanitarian agencies are making to ensure security for their operations. In a world where the neutrality and impartiality of humanitarian operations is under daily siege, having another option to provide security could be of vital importance. Governments and NGOs should work together to ensure a strong regulation system is in place to resolve problems of PMC accountability and legitimacy, whether it be a full international regulation system or, temporarily, a preliminary system of guidelines or cooperation with a few known agencies where accountability is built into the contracts.

European Constabulary Forces

Finally, as the merits of civilian police versus military actors in providing post-conflict security are debated, Refugees International has suggested a third military/police actor that can respond to humanitarian emergencies: European Constabulary Police. Constabulary police receive both military and police training, and might thus be best equipped to address the most common public security problems in post-conflict environments today: "widespread looting and violence, major civil disturbances, and organized crime and extremist activity."[105] In environments where unarmed or even armed civilian police might be overwhelmed by the sheer level of violence, but where military force is excessive and counter-productive, constabulary police might possess the exact skills and training required to address environments such as Iraq in 2003–2004, where rioting, organized crime, and extremists present many of the dangers.[106] Constabulary police have successfully been used in

Kosovo, another environment where the required initial response fell in "between traditional policing and military combat."[107] Constabulary forces could therefore serve well in the initial transfer process between military and police forces, or during the initial phases of a peace operation, working in conjunction with UN Civilian Police (CIVPOL).

Constabulary forces do have a few significant drawbacks. First, not many countries have well-trained and professional constabulary forces. Second, many of the constabulary forces outside Europe are a relict of colonialism, and many previous colonies associate constabulary forces with colonialism. Overcoming the significant prejudices against constabulary forces in many parts of the world experiencing humanitarian crises might pose large difficulties. And moving to a system under which the potential participation is small is by definition limiting. However, increasing the involvement of European Constabulary forces in peace operations, and their training with a standing United Nations Police Force, might increase the ability of the United Nations to succeed in difficult post-conflict environments. More study is needed.

THE ROLE OF HUMANITARIAN AGENCIES

In the 1990s and beyond, operational environments for humanitarian agencies assisting and protecting forced migrants have been notoriously complex. At the same time, donor, media, and organizational pressures for a rapid response to a developing humanitarian crisis, and a concurrent limited allocation of money to overhead costs such as staff training or security coordination, have resulted in the rapid deployment of insufficiently trained and prepared staff to complex humanitarian emergencies.[108] The tragic results have been seen in places as diverse as Guinea, Colombia, Afghanistan, and Iraq. While humanitarian agencies do not bear specific responsibilities for establishing and maintaining a secure environment for aid work or forced migrants, humanitarian agencies can and should assume responsibility for operating in ways that increase security. First, humanitarian agencies need to establish effective and appropriate aid programs that are designed with a comprehensive understanding of the political, economic, social, and security environments in which forced migrants are located and of the specific vulnerabilities of the forced migrant population.[109] Second, humanitarian agencies need to incorporate both security procedures and plans and oversight mechanisms into staff training and aid programming.[110] And, third, humanitarian agencies need to utilize innovative civilian security and private security models if conditions are appropriate. These requirements need to be properly communicated to the donor community.

Security of Forced Migrants

The protection of forced migrants during and after a humanitarian crisis is a topic of growing concern for the international community. As the vast majority of forced migrants (approximately 80 percent) are women and children, and violent targeting of forced migrants has increased dramatically during recent intrastate conflicts, most attention has focused on the specific vulnerabilities of women and children during periods of forced migration. Part of the problem is financial.[111] In seeking to meet the protection needs of forced migrants, humanitarian agencies are hampered by a traditional lack of funding for certain protracted refugee/IDP crises, and by UNHCR's often criticized practice of "low balling" funding requests to ensure politically palatability.[112] These funding characteristics have perpetuated an environment where there is insufficient attention to and funding for protection issues and there are insufficient resources to meet assistance needs.[113] Thus, even when women and children overcome the significant dangers of travel and reach a refugee or IDP camp assisted by the international community, refugee/IDP women and children remain vulnerable to sexual exploitation, physical and sexual violence, and forced recruitment into armed forces. Returnees often face the same dangers. This volume contends that more attention in the field and at the headquarters planning level needs to be taken to reduce these risks.

The proliferation of armed groups, breakdown in public order and traditional social structures, and lack of respect for human rights and/or international humanitarian law during intrastate conflicts have made women and children significantly vulnerable to sexual and physical violence both on their routes of escape and within refugee/IDP camps or settlements.[114] While humanitarian aid agencies can often do little to directly protect forced migrants on the immediate path of flight (other than deploying protection monitors along paths of flight as per UNHCR Guidelines),[115] there is much that can be accomplished in the camp or settlement setting. Camps for forced migrants tend to be established under "emergency" conditions, where expediency and cost can prevail at the expense of security issues.[116] The layout of a camp can fail to adequately protect women and children.[117] The use of a shared building for male and female bathing can provide opportunities for assault, as can the location of latrines (for sanitary purposes) in an isolated area of the camp. Most camps and settlements also lack security patrols, or patrols may be self-conducted by those not always interested in protecting women and children from sexual violence.[118] Crowded conditions, shared accommodations, and a lack of participation by refugees/IDPs (and thus a lack of investment) in the camp structures that have replaced traditional social structures create a systematic process of dehumanization, breeding violence and fear—"Inhuman surroundings can beget inhumane actions."[119]

Humanitarian agencies can take a variety of steps to reduce the vulnerabilities of forced migrant women and children to sexual and physical assault. In the refugee/IDP camp setting, agencies can ensure that their structures are not leaving women and children vulnerable, following the *Guidelines on the Protection of Refugee Women* (1991) and *Guidelines for the Prevention and Response to Sexual and Gender-Based Violence Against Refugees, Returnees and Internally Displaced Persons* (2003). Aid agencies can decrease the "acceptability" of assaults by educating migrants, local populations and local police and military forces about human rights and international humanitarian law, with particular respect to sexual assault.[120] Humanitarian agencies can deter assaults by ensuring that attackers are prosecuted or sanctioned and by establishing security patrols and strategies based on protection needs discussions that involve the participation of forced migrant women.[121] Aid agencies can also deploy female protection officers and work to increase the involvement of forced migrants in the new social structures represented by a camp or settlement.[122] In the returnee context, aid agencies can additionally ensure that returnees are vulnerable neither because of too little nor of too visible resources. Providing resources in a way that benefits the entire communities to which returnees are returning, and not just the returnees themselves, can decrease the likelihood of returnees experiencing physical and/or sexual violence. Highlighting and disseminating international principles, ensuring forced migrants have access to acceptable living conditions, and coordinating efforts with local governments are important measures to increase the protection and assistance of forced migrants.[123] All these measures require education of and commitment by aid agency staff to be successful, as well as a significant allocation of time and resources. Aid agencies will need to work to balance the funding of such initiatives with the funding of assistance programming.

A related problem for forced migrant women and children is that of vulnerability to sexual exploitation, an issue prominently and distressingly highlighted in February 2002 with the release of a draft report commissioned by UNHCR and Save the Children/United Kingdom on the exploitation of women and children in West Africa. While the UNHCR/Save the Children/United Kingdom report could not be completely verified, a follow-up UNOIOS (UN Office of Internal Oversight Services) report concluded that increased attention needed to be paid to issues of security for refugee/IDP populations, listed the qualities of current protection practices that could place forced migrants at risk, and suggested potential remedies.[124] The UNOIOS report isolated insufficient assistance to forced migrant families, general poverty, and a lack of economic opportunities as the three critical factors contributing to the sexual exploitation of children.[125] Exploitation is additionally facilitated by the lack of high-level oversight in camps, and an absence of clear hiring guidelines for staff, making it difficult to establish codes of conduct or follow-up for violations.[126] In crises such as those in West Africa where aid and other resources are scarce, in high demand, and often require money, a lack of oversight can lead to individual discretion in distributing relief supplies, and thus create opportunities for sexual exploitation.[127] Those with responsibility (aid workers, teachers, peacekeepers, food distributors) in a refugee/IDP environment are in positions of significant power and can use this power to sexually exploit women and children when their actions are not properly overseen.

The UNOIOS report states measures that can be taken to reduce the vulnerabilities of women and children to sexual exploitation. Aid agencies need to create clear terms of employment and codes of conduct for their workers, as well as establish coordinated interagency systems to identify, investigate, and address potential violations and protect victims of violations from retaliation.[128] In addition, agencies can accomplish a great deal by educating both forced migrants and aid staff on the right of forced migrants to assistance and on the issues of exploitation.[129] Similarly, close monitoring of systems for providing food and other assistance, the involvement of women in distribution services, and the practice of hiring women as well as men for temporary jobs taken by forced migrants will decrease opportunities for exploitation and increase economic opportunities available to women.[130] Women also need access to employment and micro-credit opportunities. Finally, a greater presence in camps by high-level agency staff can also assist in protecting forced migrants.[131] As with sexual/physical violence, the challenge for the international community is to allocate increased importance to security issues, while the challenge for the international donor community is to assign importance to funding security measures.

Beyond basic and critical physical security issues, aid agencies also need to ensure that their programs and actions are contributing neither to continued conflict nor to the creation or perpetuation of long-term vulnerabilities among the forced migrant population. The concept that humanitarian agencies should attempt to "do no harm" arose after experiences in the early 1990s demonstrated that humanitarian aid, though provided with the goals of neutrality and impartiality, could instead be diverted by combatants to serve the purposes of continued conflict, distort local economies, and create an unintended culture of dependence.[132] Such effects undermine the humanitarian mission while placing both forced migrants and aid workers at risk. As defined by Mary Anderson, the "'do no harm' principle requires humanitarian agencies to ensure that they provide humanitarian assistance and protection in a way that enables communities to progress toward addressing sources of conflict and creating peace."[133] Doing no harm is thus deeply consistent with the ideology of the humanitarian mission, but is difficult to implement when an emergency or crisis mentality within a humanitarian agency leads to the quick formation of programs without sufficient analysis of local conditions.

Forced migrants by definition are vulnerable. Refugees and IDPs have been forced (often under violent conditions) to leave their homes, are separated from traditional forms of economic life and governance and have been placed in a context of uncertainty and often insecurity. Returnees also face living conditions different from those they were used to, and frequently return to homes that no longer exist, in an environment that is often far from stable. In a protracted crisis, it is easy for forced migrants to become dependent on international assistance at the expense of maintaining or re-creating local capacities, and to see the conflict environment as normal.[134] This process is facilitated when aid agencies enter a conflict or post-conflict environment with outside resources, and fail to identify or use local resources and skills.[135] Aid agencies can avoid creating dependence by actively seeking ways to positively incorporate local capacities into aid programming and by promoting "connectors" in a society.[136] UNICEF "Days of Tranquility" and "Corridors of Peace" such as those conducted in Afghanistan are examples of such connectors, as is the reinforcement of local markets. Aid agencies can also establish programs to promote the capacities of forced migrants, address the emotional burdens of warfare, and facilitate dialogue and interactions between civilian sides of a conflict.[137] While this process of establishing appropriate programming which utilizes local skills and responds to local needs is complicated and requires significant investment of time, the promotion of local capacity will decrease short- and long-term dependence at the same time as promoting peace will establish a more secure environment.

As a final note, small arms proliferation and the large numbers of combatants in today's intrastate conflicts are significant impediments to security.[138] Humanitarian agencies have been strong proponents of, and have often forced, government and UN actions to created international regulation of the small arms trade and to disarm, demobilize, and reintegrate ex-combatants.[139] Some DDR successes have occurred, as in Sierra Leone, but DDR programs often remain underfunded, and when incomplete pose serious problems.[140] Governments need to fund initiatives to regulate the small arms trade, stop illegal arms sales, and support critical DDR initiatives if the security dilemma that permitted conflict is to be resolved.

Security of Aid Workers and Humanitarian Aid

Along with forced migrants, humanitarian aid workers have become increasingly vulnerable in recent intrastate conflicts. Humanitarian aid workers have also recently faced significant risks in Iraq. In order to protect their staff, humanitarian agencies need to establish a serious commitment to security plans and procedures that are comprehensive, flexible, and understood by staff, and that operate in coordination with the security plans of other agencies in the region.[141] In an environment where there are serious violations of international humanitarian law, humanitarian agencies also need to look outside the box and consider designating specific personnel as security officers or hiring outside protection. Agencies need to find the "balance between operational and security imperatives . . . without compromising staff security."[142]

The International Committee of the Red Cross (ICRC) is the international, UN-affiliated organization delegated with the responsibility of protecting civilians during times of conflict, a category that extends to humanitarian aid workers as long as they do not physically take up arms during a conflict. The ICRC has developed a complex strategy for action within armed conflicts, based on the three tenets of impartiality, neutrality, and independence.[143] Because of its importance in the field of humanitarian response, the ICRC is often a highly visible participant in forced migrant crises. As such, it has been an increasingly frequent target for deliberate attack.[144] In response, the ICRC has developed an elaborated model for security in its field operations, based largely on continued dialogue, insistence on remaining neutral in conflict, and a new willingness to make ICRC operations "more mobile and less visible."[145] In 2000, Koenraad Van Brabant identified what may make the ICRC approach more dangerous in today's conflicts, stating that engagement approaches can be highly effective but tend to break down when those committing violence see themselves as outside social structures.[146] The new ICRC approach stressing increased engagement and flexibility may succeed in reducing the dangers of its historic security approach.

There is no one security strategy that is appropriate for all agencies in all circumstances. Security approaches need to be guided by the mandate and character of a humanitarian agency as well as by the threats and vulnerabilities of the operating environment.[147] Aid agencies need to choose a security plan, be flexible, and mainstream the plans within their organization.[148] Security management strategies tend to fall into three general categories: seeking local acceptance; decreasing vulnerability through self-protection measures; and deterring threats with counter threats.[149] All have their advantages and disadvantages, many of which are context specific.

Humanitarian agencies need to spend time and resources to develop and maintain context-specific security strategies using a guidebook such as Koenraad Van Brabant's "Operational Security in Violent Environments." Involving staff in the determination and evolution of a security strategy and ensuring that all staff possesses a security mindset are critical steps toward increasing the protection of humanitarian aid workers and the humanitarian assistance that they provide.[150] All staff of aid agencies need to be aware of the impact humanitarian assistance can have on local structures.[151] The presence of aid in a region can allow military factions to use their resources to continue conflict, or inspire attacks on aid workers with the purposes of removing aid from the region or diverting resources for the purposes of continued conflict.[152] Aid agencies need to understand security risks and respond to them through a variety of initiatives such as increasing the transparency of aid operations, hiding or displaying their affiliation, and delivering aid on unpredictable schedules.[153] Plans need to be frequently reevaluated.[154] Security coordination and the development of civilian security options should also be explored.

While aid agencies need to devote individual resources to creating agency security plans and to educating staff on security matters, cooperation and coordination with other agencies is equally critical for two major reasons. First, aid actors (with the potential exception of the ICRC) tend not to be distinguished from each other in the minds of local populations and armed forces, and thus actions taken by one agency either to counter security threats or in the process of their programming can negatively impact other agencies.[155] The decision by one agency to pay bribes at checkpoints can lead to an expectation that all agencies will do the same, even as the decision by one agency not to worry about displaying its wealth can lead to an expectation that all agencies may have goods worth stealing. And the decision by one agency to be associated with any military force may lead to an automatic assumption that all agencies have the same association, thus potentially placing the unarmed or unescorted aid agencies at significant risk of attack.

Second, reliable security assessments depend on having the most current information available on security incidents and developments.[156] Knowledge of local conditions, expectations, and traditions is essential to security. Security threats may vary significantly from one part of a country to another. In Burundi, for example, one NGO determined that a decal on its vehicles when in the capitol risked attack but its logo increased its security in the countryside. The solution was to use a flag with its logo while driving outside of the city and to lower it in the capitol. If there is no structured attempt by aid agencies to share information and/or coordinate its collection and dissemination, agencies will establish individual security plans and procedures without full information.

Coordination on the development and implementation of security procedures —encompassing both what to do in a security crisis and how to avoid creating one— is extremely important.

The United Nations recently developed the most comprehensive security coordination mechanism among humanitarian agencies today. As of August

2002, a full-time UN Security Coordinator (UNSECOORD) at the Assistant Secretary General level establishes policy for UN security in the field, coordinating with UN agency representatives at the headquarters level and also in the field through a DO (designated official) and security management team.[157] The DO, the security management team, and UNSECOORD field security officers (FSOs) create security plans, manage security threats, and coordinate the UN response to security conditions in the field.[158] Under this system, UN agencies operate under five phases designed to regularize the UN response to security threats, on a continuum of responses from cautious engagement to staff removal.[159] UN security phases and requirements under the UNSECOORD system also apply to the personnel of organizations who have signed MOUs (memorandum of understanding) with the UN. And as of January 2003, UN agencies are required to operate under (or be in the process of establishing compliance with) Minimum Operating Security Standards (MOSS) for staff security training, security planning, security equipment and communication systems.[160]

While UNSECOORD is a significant step toward increasing coordinated security for UN and associated aid workers in the field, UNSECOORD is still significantly understaffed, inadequate resources exist for "mandatory" staff security training, and the requirement that UN and associated agencies individually pay for UNSECOORD services and MOSS compliance[161] may complicate agencies' abilities to fully implement new procedures. UNSECOORD also only addresses the UN system and associated personnel, despite the fact that UN, NGO, and other agency staff face similar threats in the field, and the decisions of each can impact the other. While UNSECOORD is currently working under a framework for UN-NGO security coordination in the field (the "UN-NGO Security Collaboration"), and has reported considerable compliance with security guidelines and resource collaboration initiatives,[162] the system is still new and will likely be complicated by traditional NGO desires for independence. The UNSECOORD system does, however, highlight a principle that can greatly assist in increasing the security of all humanitarian personnel: staff security training is essential to help avoid security incidents. Having all staff aware of the existence and importance of coordinated security procedures can do a great deal to reduce vulnerability, while coordinating security in crises such as Afghanistan and Iraq is of critical importance. UNSECOORD is a critical first step in the development of civilian capacity to provide security.

The UNSECOORD system utilizes a concept that is gaining credence among humanitarian agencies: in intrastate conflicts where public safety issues create many of the dangers faced by forced migrants, humanitarian aid workers, and humanitarian assistance, civilian methods may successfully increase the security of forced migrants, aid operations, and aid workers. The most direct way to follow this precept is to deploy staff into the field with a specific security mandate. This is the principle behind the UNSECOORD FSO (Field Security Officer) system.[163] Under UNSECOORD, FSOs are deployed to areas of conflict to manage security issues for UN field operations and staff, to respond to and work to prevent security incidents and to prepare crisis readiness plans and structures.[164] FSOs work directly for the UNSECOORD designated official (DO) but cooperate with all UN agencies present in a humanitarian crisis to ensure security coordination. FSOs also liaise with local police forces, and have responsibilities to: identify security threats; maintain communications equipment; conduct security drills; brief staff and dependents on security conditions and their requirements; prepare evacuation plans; report crimes and continually evaluate security conditions in areas of aid operations and staff habitation.[165]

In May 2002, UNHCR proposed its own version of the FSO system: the creation of a pool of Humanitarian Security Officers who would be experts in law enforcement and public security. These Humanitarian Security Officers would deploy with UNHCR in insecure humanitarian crises and have additional responsibilities to liaise with and develop the capacity of national law enforcement personnel.[166] While this idea has not received much funding, or commitment by states, to develop a standby capacity, it does point to the need for agencies to continually develop strategies to increase the security of aid operations, aid staff, and forced migrants. Civilian options to provide security for humanitarian operations, humanitarian aid workers, and forced migrants have great potential that needs to be further explored. As many of the threats of an intrastate conflict environment can be classified as public safety issues, civilian security officers with appropriate training are best equipped to design and implement security plans. Because they are unarmed, civilian security officers are less threatening than military officials, and are less likely to upset the balance of power in an area.[167] Aid agencies with civilian security capacity should be better able to understand and respond to security conditions and are thus less likely to leave a country of operation because of direct attacks or to experience significant levels of banditry that would prevent aid from reaching its intended recipients. However, the civilian security option is still in the beginning stages. In order to function effectively, civilian security officers will need to be well trained, professional, capable of leading by example, and able to work well with the local community to decrease security risks. Failing to meet these requirements can only decrease security, and does not take advantage of the enormous potential positives of civilian security methods.

Also needed are mechanisms to hold accountable those who attack humanitarian aid operations and the beneficiaries of their assistance. The Rome

Statute of the International Criminal Court (ICC) defines deliberate attacks against civilians and humanitarian aid workers as war crimes. Specifically, the Court lists the following under war crimes:

> Other serious violations of the laws and customs applicable in international armed conflict, within the established framework of international law, namely, any of the following acts:
> (i) Intentionally directing attacks against the civilian population as such or against individual civilians not taking direct part in hostilities;
> (ii) Intentionally directing attacks against civilian objects, that is, objects which are not military objectives;
> (iii) Intentionally directing attacks against personnel, installations, material, units, or vehicles involved in a humanitarian assistance or peacekeeping mission in accordance with the Charter of the United Nations, as long as they are entitled to the protection given to civilians or civilian objects under the international law of armed conflict.[168]

International and national action to sanction those responsible for such war crimes has largely been restricted to public statements condemning the attacks and calling for prosecution of those committing the crimes. The United Nations has been able to pass several resolutions/conventions aimed at increasing safety for civilians and humanitarian aid workers during conflict, and has issued several in-depth reports.[169] However, the establishment of the Court itself remains the largest step taken to prevent attacks on civilians and humanitarian aid workers.

Attacks against civilians and aid workers will continue as long as there are no credible deterrents to these war crimes. The International Criminal Court has an enormous potential deterrent role in "putting would-be violators on notice that impunity is not assured."[170] Unfortunately opposition from the United States has limited the ability and reach of the ICC. If attacks against civilians and humanitarian aid workers are to be deterred, all governments need to participate in action to give the ICC "the resources, capacities, information and support it needs to investigate, prosecute and bring to trial those who bear the greatest responsibility for war crimes, crimes against humanity and genocide, in situations where national authorities are unable or unwilling to do so."[171]

CONCLUSION

The end of the Cold War and the ensuing proliferation of intrastate conflicts have led to great insecurity for the larger numbers of forced migrants at the same time as the decision by humanitarian agencies to deploy into security environments characterized by multiple actors, general instability and at times state collapse has led to greater insecurity for humanitarian aid workers. Both issues are of increasing concern to the international community, not least because a lack of security is often the most stubborn barrier to the effective delivery of humanitarian assistance to populations in need. Insecure conditions impede access to vulnerable populations for delivery of aid, create protection problems for forced migrants and aid workers, and make it impossible to monitor and evaluate the effectiveness of aid operations. Efforts to address insecurity are too often haphazard, with insecure humanitarian emergencies often ignored until a very severe security crisis exists. Because of insecurity-induced access issues, forced migrants are therefore too often "out of sight and out of mind" of the very humanitarian system that is designed to assist and protect them. National governments, either on their own or through international and regional organizations, and humanitarian aid organizations both can and need to take measures to improve security conditions for forced migrants and humanitarian aid workers from the onset of a humanitarian emergency. We have therefore made different but complementary recommendations for each of these actors.

Governments frequently possess significant but underutilized political, economic, and social capital in the prevention, management, and resolution of conflicts. Beyond using more of the conflict prevention tools at their disposal, governments need to seriously evaluate their use of international and/or regional military interventions. First and foremost, governments need to recognize that early attention to a crisis can avert the need for more costly and involved interventions. More attention needs to be paid to conflict prevention, conflict resolution, and conflict management strategies. Second, governments need to provide all support possible to ensure that the ICC has the resources and capacity to prosecute war crimes. Third, governments need to understand that many of the security problems present during humanitarian emergencies (banditry, unlawful taxation, physical and/or sexual assaults) are public security concerns, and thus appropriate for police and not military intervention. It is for this reason that our major recommendation to improve the security of forced migrants and humanitarian actors during humanitarian emergencies is the creation of a professional, well-trained, standing UN police force with the capacity to deploy rapidly and cohesively into emergency situations. We also recommend that the use of European Constabulary Police in association with such a police force be considered. Fourth, when situations arise where military interventions are necessary, appropriate forces need to be dispatched. International or regional peacekeepers need to possess robust, achievable, and appropriate mandates, including, when necessary, a clear mandate to protect civilian populations and humanitarian relief operations. Peacekeepers also need a stronger understanding of international humanitarian law and the distinctions between humanitarian and military actors. As UN peacekeepers are often politically difficult to deploy into a conflict, programs such as ACOTA and RECAMP that develop regional peacekeeping capacity need to be supported. And finally, the proliferation of private military companies (PMCs) and their use across many conflict situations calls for greater attention to regulation and transparency.

Humanitarian aid agencies need to individually and collectively take greater responsibility for their own security. First, at the start of each complex humanitarian emergency, a professional security assessment should be undertaken and a security plan implemented. The assessment should cover the vulnerabilities of both forced migrants and aid workers, and reassessments should occur on a regular basis to ensure that security issues are comprehensively understood and that security plans and oversight mechanisms are well-integrated into staff training and aid programming. Second, humanitarian agencies need to ensure that their programs have been developed with a comprehensive understanding of the political, economic, social, and security environments in which forced migrants are located, and that they are effective and appropriate responses to the specific vulnerabilities of the forced migration population. Specific measures need to be taken to prevent and address sexual or physical assault or murder of forced migrants and aid workers. Greater oversight, sanctioning of perpetrators, and wider dissemination of humanitarian principles will be essential. Humanitarian agencies also need to avoid creating dependence among local populations; this can be accomplished by strict adherence to the "do no harm" principle. Finally, civilian capabilities to protect forced migrants need to be further developed. While UN-SECOORD is a significant step toward increasing coordinated security for UN and associated aid workers in the field, security needs to be coordinated over a wider number of actors with adequate resources provided for staff training and MOSS compliance. If humanitarian aid is to reach larger numbers of populations in need, governments and humanitarian agencies need to act responsibly and reach out to new ideas that proactively address security.

NOTES

1. Nicholas Van Hear and Christopher McDowell, eds., *Catching Fire: Containing Complex Displacement in a Volatile World* (Lanham, Md.: Lexington Books, 2005, forthcoming).

2. Mohammed Ayoob, "State Making, State Breaking, and State Failure," in *Turbulent Peace: The Challenges of Managing International Conflict*, Chester Crocker, Fen Osler Hampson, and Pamela Aall, eds. (Washington: USIP, 2001).

3. Chester A. Crocker, Fen Osler Hampson, and Pamela Aall, "Introduction," in *Turbulent Peace: The Challenges of Managing International Conflict*, Chester Crocker, Fen Osler Hampson, and Pamela Aall, eds. (Washington: USIP, 2001); UNHCR, "Introduction," in *The State of the World's Refugees: Fifty Years of Humanitarian Action*, (New York: Oxford University Press, 2000); Herbert Howe, *Ambiguous Order: Military Forces in African States* (Boulder, Co.: Lynne Rienner Publishers, 2001); Dennis C. Jett, *Why Peacekeeping Fails* (New York: Palgrave, 1999).

4. Paul Grossrieder, "Protecting the Protectors" (Official Statement—New York: Fifteenth Annual Seminar for Diplomats on International Humanitarian Law, January 28, 1998), 2.

5. Crocker et al., "Introduction," UNHCR, *The State*.

6. Pamela Aall, "NGOs and Conflict: Responses to International Conflict: Highlights from the Managing Chaos conference," (Washington: USIP, 1996); UNHCR, *The State*; Alex Morrison and Stephanie A. Blair, "Transnational Networks of Peacekeepers," in *International Security Management and the United Nations*, Muthiah Alagappa and Takashi Inoguchi, eds. (Tokyo: United Nations University Press, 1999).

7. Diane Paul, "Protection in Practice: Field-Level Strategies for Protecting Civilians from Deliberate Harm," *Relief and Rehabilitation Network* (London: Overseas Development Institute, July 1999); Jane Barry and Anna Jefferys, "A bridge too far: aid agencies and the military in humanitarian response," *Humanitarian Practice Network* (London: Overseas Development Institute, January 2002); see UNHCR, *The State*.

8. UNHCR, *The State*; VENRO, "Minimum Standards Regarding Staff Security in Humanitarian Aid" (Bonn: VENRO, 2003).

9. Nicolas de Torrente, "Humanitarian Action Under Attack: Reflections on the Iraq War," *Harvard Human Rights Journal* 17 (Spring 2004): entire.

10. Grossrieder, "Protecting the Protectors."

11. Mani Sheikh, Maria Isabel Gutierrez, Paul Bolton, et al., "Deaths among humanitarian workers," *British Medical Journal 321* (July 15, 2000): 166–168.

12. Sheikh et al., "Deaths among humanitarian workers."

13. Sheikh et al., "Deaths among humanitarian workers."

14. Dennis King, "Paying the Ultimate Price: Analysis of the deaths of humanitarian aid workers (1997–2001)," (New York: UN Office for Coordination of Humanitarian Affairs, 2002), 2.

15. Grossrieder, "Protecting the Protectors."

16. De Torrente, "Humanitarian Action Under Attack."

17. Grossrieder, "Protecting the Protectors," 2.

18. John McFarlane and William Maley, *Civilian Police in United Nations Peace Operations: Working Paper No. 64* (Sydney: Australian Defense Studies Centre, 2001); Paul, "Protection in Practice."

19. Herbert Howe, *Ambiguous Order*.

20. Paul, "Protection in Practice."

21. Michael E. Brown and Chantal de Jong Oudraat, "Internal Conflict and International Action," in *Nationalism and Ethnic Conflict: Revised Edition*, Michael E. Brown, Owen R. Cote, Jr., Sean M. Lynn-Jones, and Steven E. Miller, eds. (Cambridge, Mass.: The MIT Press, 2001), 163–192.

22. Robert Schoenhaus, *Training for Peace and Humanitarian Relief Operations: Advancing Best Practices* (Washington, D.C.: United States Institute of Peace, 2002).

23. United Nations Security Council, "Report of the Secretary-General to the Security Council on the Protection of Civilians in Armed Conflict,"S/2001/311 (2001).

24. United Nations Security Council, "Report of the Secretary-General to the Security Council on protection for humanitarian assistance to refugees and others in conflict situations," UN Document S/1998/883 (1998).

25. McFarlane and Maley, *Civilian Police*.

26. United States Committee for Refugees (USCR), "In the Name of Security: Erosion of Refugee Rights in East Africa" (Washington: USCR, June 2002), www .refugees.org/world/articles/wrs00_eafrica.htm (July 21, 2004).

27. Schoenhaus, *Training for Peace*.

28. McFarlane and Maley, *Civilian Police*.

29. McFarlane and Maley, *Civilian Police*.

30. William Lewis, Edward Marks, and Robert Perito, *Enhancing International Civilian Police in Peace Operations* (Washington: United States Institute of Peace, 2002).

31. USIP, *US Civilian Police in UN Peace Missions: Lessons Learned and Ideas for the Future—Report 71* (Washington, D.C.: USIP, July 6, 2001).

32. McFarlane and Maley, *Civilian Police*.

33. USIP, *US Civilian Police*.

34. Lewis et al., *Enhancing International Civilian Police*; McFarlane and Maley, *Civilian Police*; Schoenhaus, *Training for Peace*.

35. Lewis et al., *Enhancing International Civilian Police*; Refugees International, "47 Organizations call on Congress to support UN civilian police capacity improvements" (Washington, D.C.: Refugees International, 2003), www.refugeesinternational .org/content/article/detail/1008/ (November 22, 2004).

36. Schoenhaus, *Training for Peace*.

37. Refugees International, "47 Organizations."

38. USIP, *US Civilian Police*.

39. Schoenhaus, *Training for Peace*.

40. McFarlane and Maley, *Civilian Police*, USIP, *US Civilian Police*.

41. United States Congress, "HR1414: UN Civilian Police Corps for International Peacekeeping, 108th Congress, 1st Session" (Washington: U.S. Congress, 2003), 1, www.theorator.com/bills108/hr1414.html (November 21, 2004).

42. United States Congress, "HR 1414."

43. United States Congress, "HR 1414."

44. Campaign to End Genocide, "UN Peace Operations Reform," www.endgenocide .org/ceg-rrf/index.htm (November 26, 2004).

45. Schoenhaus, *Training for Peace*, 32.

46. Roland Koch, "The Relations of UN Agencies and Non-Governmental Organizations in Cross-Border Humanitarian Assistance," in *International Security Management and the United Nations,"* Muthiah Alagappa and Takashi Inoguchi, eds. (Tokyo: United Nations University Press, 1999); Michael C. Williams, *Civil-Military Relations and Peacekeeping—Adelphi Paper 321* (New York: Oxford University Press, 1998).

47. Aall, "NGOs and Conflict"; ICRC, *Report on the use of armed protection for humanitarian assistance* (Geneva: International Committee of the Red Cross, 1995); De Torrente, "Humanitarian Action Under Attack."

48. Howe, *Ambiguous Order*.

49. Paul, "Protecting the Protectors."

50. USIP, *US Civilian Police*.

51. Brown and Oudraat, *Internal Conflict*, 3; Barry and Jefferys, "A bridge too far."

52. Koch, "Relations of UN Agencies"; Howe, *Ambiguous Order*.

53. Jett, *Why Peacekeeping Fails*; Barry and Jefferys, "A bridge too far"; Morrison and Blair, "Transnational Networks of Peacekeepers."

54. Jett, *Why Peacekeeping Fails*.

55. Jett, *Why Peacekeeping Fails*, 11.

56. UNHCR, *The State*.

57. UNHCR, *The State*.

58. UNHCR, *The State*.

59. UNHCR, *The State*.

60. Van Hear and McDowell, *Catching Fire*.

61. UNHCR, *The State*.

62. Koch, "The Relations of UN Agencies."

63. David D. Laitin, "Somalia: Civil War and International Intervention," in *Civil Wars, Insecurity, and Intervention*, Barbara Walter and Jack Snyder, eds. (New York: Columbia University Press, 1999).

64. Adekeye Adebanjo, *Building Peace in West Africa: Liberia, Sierra Leone, and Guinea-Bissau* (Boulder, Co.: Lynne Rienner Publishers, 2002).

65. Panel on United Nations Peace Operations, *Executive Summary Report of the Panel on United Nations Peace Operations (United Nations Brahimi Report)*, UN Document A/55/305-S/2000/809 (2000), 1.

66. Panel on United Nations Peace Operations, *Executive Summary*, 2.

67. Williams, *Civil-Military Relations*.

68. Williams, *Civil-Military Relations*.

69. Williams, *Civil-Military Relations*.

70. Williams, *Civil-Military Relations*.

71. Koch, "The Relations of UN Agencies"; Williams, *Civil-Military Relations*.

72. Williams, *Civil-Military Relations*.

73. Campaign to End Genocide, "UN Peace Operations Reform."

74. Williams, *Civil-Military Relations*.

75. Williams, *Civil-Military Relations*.

76. De Torrente, "Humanitarian Action Under Attack."

77. Van Hear and McDowell, *Catching Fire*.

78. See chapter 6 for more about Timor.

79. Muthiah Alagappa, "Introduction," in *International Security Management and the United Nations*, Muthiah Alagappa and Takashi Inoguchi, eds. (Tokyo: United Nations University Press, 1999), 269–278.

80. Margaret A. Vogt, "Regional Arrangements, the United Nations, and Security in Africa," in *International Security Management and the United Nations*, Muthiah

Alagappa and Takashi Inogushi, eds. (Tokyo: United Nations University Press, 1999).

81. Howe, *Ambiguous Order*; Alagappa, "Introduction."

82. Howe, *Ambiguous Order*, on ECOWAS.

83. Alagappa, "Introduction"; Howe, *Ambiguous Order*.

84. Alagappa, "Introduction."

85. Vogt, "Regional Arrangements."

86. Howe, *Ambiguous Order*.

87. Howe, *Ambiguous Order*.

88. Herbert Howe, "Lessons of Liberia: ECOMOG and Regional Peacekeeping," in *Nationalism and Ethnic Conflict: Revised Edition*, Michael E. Brown, Owen R. Cote, Jr., Sean M. Lynn-Jones, and Steven E. Miller, eds. (Cambridge, Mass.: The MIT Press, 2001), 267–298.

89. Howe, *Ambiguous Order*.

90. Howe, *Ambiguous Order*.

91. Howe, *Ambiguous Order*.

92. United States Department of State (DOS)/IIP, *Summary of the African Crisis Response Initiative*, usinfo.state.gov/regional/af/acri/acrisummary.htm (June 21, 2004).

93. USDOS/IIP, *Summary*; United States Department of State (DOS)/IIP. *African Crisis Response Initiative,* usinfo.state.gov/regional/af/acri (November 21, 2004).

94. Refugees International, "Firms seek to sell UN on privatized peacekeeping," Washington: Refugees International, 2004, www.refugeesinternational.org/content/article/detail/1092 (November 21, 2004), 2.

95. Refugees International, "Firms."

96. Refugees International, "Firms."

97. United Kingdom House of Commons, *Private Military Companies: Options for Regulation—Return to an Address of the Honorable the House of Commons* (London: The Stationary Office, 2002).

98. United Kingdom House of Commons, *Private Military Companies*.

99. United Kingdom House of Commons, *Private Military Companies*; Peter H. Gantz, "The Private Sector's Role in Peacekeeping and Peace Enforcement" (Washington, D.C.: Refugees International, 2003).

100. Refugees International, "Firms."

101. Personal interview, Douglas Brooks, June 9, 2004.

102. United Kingdom House of Commons, *Private Military Companies*.

103. Refugees International, "Firms."

104. ICRC, *Report on the use of armed protection for humanitarian assistance*.

105. Refugees International, "European Constabulary Police Needed to Improve UN Peace Operations," May 2004, www.refugeesinternational.org/content/article/detail/966/ (November 22, 2004), 1.

106. Refugees International, "European Constabulary Police."

107. Refugees International, "European Constabulary Police," 2.

108. UNHCR, *The State*; Schoenhaus, *Training for Peace*; VENRO, "Minimum Standards."

109. Mary Anderson, *Do No Harm: How Aid Can Support Peace—Or War* (Boulder: Lynne Rienner Publishers, 1999).

110. Koenraad Van Brabant, *Operational Security Management in Violent Environments: A Field Manual for Aid Agencies*, Good Practice Review 8 (London: Overseas Development Institute, 2000).

111. See chapter 4 for greater discussion.

112. United States Committee for Refugees (USCR), "Blame All Around: Sexual Exploitation of West African Refugee Children," USCR Background Analysis, 2002, www.refugees.org/news/press_releases/2002/022802.cfm (November 21, 2004).

113. USCR, "Blame All Around."

114. USCR, "In the Name of Security."

115. Paul, "Protection in Practice," 20.

116. UNGA, "Report of the Secretary-General on the activities of the Office of Internal Oversight Services: Investigation into sexual exploitation of refugees by aid workers in West Africa," October 11, 2002, UN Document A/57/465.

117. Susan F. Martin, *Refugee Women* (Lanham, Md.: Lexington Books, 2004).

118. UNGA, "Report of the Secretary-General on the activities of the OIOS"; Martin, *Refugee Women*.

119. Martin, *Refugee Women*, 49.

120. Paul, "Protection in Practice," 20.

121. Paul, "Protection in Practice."

122. Paul, "Protection in Practice," 20.

123. UNGA, "Report of the Secretary-General on the activities of the OIOS"; Van Hear and McDowell, *Catching Fire*.

124. UNGA, "Report of the Secretary-General on the activities of the OIOS."

125. UNGA, "Report of the Secretary-General on the activities of the OIOS."

126. UNGA, "Report of the Secretary-General on the activities of the OIOS."

127. UNGA, "Report of the Secretary-General on the activities of the OIOS."

128. UNGA, "Report of the Secretary-General on the activities of the OIOS."

129. UNGA, "Report of the Secretary-General on the activities of the OIOS."

130. UNGA, "Report of the Secretary-General on the activities of the OIOS."

131. UNGA, "Report of the Secretary-General on the activities of the OIOS."

132. Aall, "NGOs and Conflict"; Laitin, "Somalia."

133. Anderson, *Do No Harm*, 37–38.

134. Anderson, *Do No Harm*.

135. Anderson, *Do No Harm*.

136. Anderson, *Do No Harm*; VENRO, "Minimum Standards."

137. Anderson, *Do No Harm*.

138. ICRC, *Report on the use of armed protection for humanitarian assistance*.

139. See HRW and AI advocacy, especially: Human Rights Watch (HRW), "Arsenals on the Cheap: NATO Expansion and the Arms Cascade," www.hrw.org/reports/1999/nato/ (1999), and Amnesty International (AI), "No Arms for Atrocities: G8's Uncontrolled Trade in Arms and Military Aid Undermines Fundamental Human Rights and Sustainable Development," *Terror Trade Times* No. 3, www.web.amnesty.org/web/web.nsf/pages/ttt3_arms (June 2002).

140. United Nations Security Council, "Report of the UNSG on Ways to Combat Subregional and Cross-Border Problems in West Africa," UN Document S/2004/200 (March 12, 2004).

141. VENRO; Van Brabant, *Operational Security Management*; UNEC, "United Nations Executive Committee of the High Commissioner's Programme. *Safety and Security Issues,* United Nations High Commission for Refugees, EC/52/SC/CRP.11, 2002."

142. UNHCR, "Safety and Security Issues," Executive Committee of the High Commissioner's Programme, Standing Committee 24th Meeting (May 30, 2002), UN Document CE/52/SC/CRP.11, 1.

143. ICRC, "Who is bound by the Geneva Conventions?" Extract from "International humanitarian law: answers to your questions," International Committee of the Red Cross, 2004, www.icrc.org/Web/Eng/siteeng0.nsf/iwpList104/3D0F7A4F95BB755FC1256CF5004B6181 (November 22, 2004).

144. Grossrieder, "Protecting the Protectors."

145. Philippe Dind, *Security in ICRC Field Operations* (Helsinki: Finnish Red Cross, 2002); ICRC, "Humanitarian action: Today's new security environment has forced us back to basics," Speech by ICRC Director General Angelo Gnaedinger (Geneva: ICRC, 2004), 1.

146. Van Brabant, *Operational Security Management.*

147. Van Brabant, *Operational Security Management.*

148. VENRO, "Minimum Standards."

149. Van Brabant, *Operational Security Management*; VENRO.

150. Van Brabant, *Operational Security Management.*

151. Anderson, *Do No Harm.*

152. VENRO, "Minimum Standards."

153. VENRO, "Minimum Standards."

154. VENRO, "Minimum Standards."

155. Van Brabant, *Operational Security Management*, 13; VENRO, 16–17.

156. Van Brabant, *Operational Security Management*, 48.

157. UNHCR, "Safety and Security Issues."

158. UNHCR, "Safety and Security Issues."

159. UNGA, "Safety and Security of United Nations personnel: Report of the Secretary-General," UN Document A/55/494 (2000).

160. UNHCR, "Safety and Security Issues."

161. UNHCR, "Safety and Security Issues."

162. UNHCR, "Safety and Security Issues."

163. UNHCR, "Safety and Security Issues."

164. United Nations General Assembly (UNGA), "Prevention of Armed Conflict: Report of the Secretary-General," UN Document A/55/985-S/2001/574, 2001.

165. UNGA, "Prevention of Armed Conflict."

166. UNHCR, "Safety and Security Issues."

167. McFarlane and Maley, *Civilian Police.*

168. International Criminal Court/Cour Pénal Internationale, "Rome Statute of the International Criminal Court, www.icc-cpi.int/library/about/officialjournal/Rome_Statute_120704-EN.pdf (November 21, 2004), 11.

169. See particularly the following United Nations documents: "Convention on the Safety of United Nations and Associated personnel" for 1994 (UN Document A/49/49); "Report of the Secretary-General to the Security Council on protection for humanitarian assistance to refugees and others in conflict situations" for 1998 (UN Document S/1998/883); "Report of the Secretary-General to the Security Council on the protection of civilians in armed conflict" for 1999 (UN Document S/1999/957), 2001 (UN Document S/2001/331), and 2002 (UN Document S/2002/1300); "Safety and Security of United Nations personnel: Report of the Secretary-General" in 2000 (UN Document A/55/494); "Inter-organizational security measures: implementation of section II of General Assembly resolution 55/238 of 23 December entitled 'Safety and security of United Nations personnel: Report of the Secretary-General" in 2001 (UN Document A/56/469); "Prevention of Armed Conflict: Report of the Secretary-General" for 2001 (UN Document A/55/985-S/2001/574); United Nations Security Counci, "Resolution 1502 (2003)," UN Document S/RES/1502 (2003), (August 26, 2003); and "Report of the UNSG on Ways to Combat Subregional and Cross-Border Problems in West Africa," UN Document S/2004/200 (March 12, 2004).

170. United Nations Security Council, "The rule of law and transitional justice in conflict and post-conflict societies: Report of the Secretary-General," United Nations Document S/2004/616 (August 23, 2004), 16.

171. United Nations Security Council, "The rule of law and transitional justice," 16.

6

Challenge of Finding Solutions for a Growing Population of Forced Migrants

INTRODUCTION

Perhaps at no time in a humanitarian crisis do the distinctions between different categories of forced migrant become more blurred than at the point of solutions. For purposes of this study, the term "solutions" refers to durable solutions, that is, forms of integration that entitle forced migrants to the same legal, political, and economic rights and responsibilities as other citizens, as well as the ability to sustain themselves. As we have seen in previous chapters, the forced migrants in question are people who have been obliged to leave their regions or countries of origin due to an event or situation not of their own making and who seek acceptable options for restarting their lives. Invariably, forced migrants require assistance. In the short run, they may depend for survival on availability of protection from immediate threats, as well as shelter and/or economic assistance for those without personal resources. If migrants cross borders, they must acquire legal status. If their displacement or exile lasts for months or years, they will need to have access to health care, education, and other services. These services are necessary pending return or integration elsewhere, but they do not constitute durable solutions.

This first part of this chapter reviews the evolution of the existing solutions for resolving the consequences of forced migration, and elaborates the impediments to effective action. These include the fragmentation of categories of migrants and financial arrangements, the obstacles rooted in political agendas, and the narrow approaches that aim to alleviate without solving underlying problems. It also describes the progress made in understanding needs, providing support, and designing more effective programs. The second part of the chapter turns to the efforts on the part of the international community to combine resources toward more comprehensive and durable solutions that include political and economic support for prevention and for long-term integration strategies

DURABLE SOLUTIONS FOR FORCED MIGRANTS

As the chapters in this book elaborate, the only categories of forced migrants for which there are formal internationally recognized legal mechanisms in place are refugees and successful refugee applicants. For other categories, there are normative forms of alleviation but not obligatory solutions. Nor are the categories always fixed. As other chapters have described, people forced to move are more than likely to change from one to another status as they seek to resolve their situations. Although there are many useful projects and programs to alleviate the plight of forced migrants of different kinds—including refugee applicants whose claims are not recognized, internally displaced persons, environmental and development induced migrants—the international community has rejected any notion of binding responsibility on their behalf. As we will show, even the solutions intended to resolve the situation of refugees have broken down to one degree or another and, because of this, large numbers of refugees are likely to remain in protracted situations with no solution in sight or, at some point, to fall into another category of forced migrant. Because forced migration is a massive phenomenon, we will argue, the solutions require short- as well as long-term efforts to establish viable governments and economies, rule of law, and respect for human rights.

The Limited Success of Solutions for Refugees

There are three internationally recognized "durable solutions" for refugees through which they can attain integration and citizenship: firm resettlement offered by a third country; local integration that occurs when the first refugee haven permits the new arrivals to remain as legal residents and potential citizens; and repatriation "in safety and dignity," when the conditions that cause flight presumably have changed. Political asylum is a fourth durable solution that falls between resettlement and local integration. Because access to durable solutions exists only for refugees, many people claim to warrant this status, although their claims to meet refugee criteria are dubious. Among those not meeting refugee criteria, the needs are often compelling. As will be shown below, the refugee solutions to which so many aspire are themselves at risk of deteriorating.

Firm resettlement allows refugees who are temporarily in one country to be relocated for permanent residence to another, upon selection by the government in the latter.[1] Resettlement benefits a minority, identified by the resettlement country as persons who have ties to that country, are at special risk where they are, or, most often, who besides being refugees, are seen as desirable immigrants. UNHCR refers some refugees for resettlement when they are at risk and in need of protection.[2] Otherwise, resettlement country officials select refugees for resettlement from among persons that UNHCR or the destination country has designated as Convention refugees, choosing categories identified within the resettlement countries to be of interest. The system discriminates against refugees lacking ties to any destination country, and impedes onward movement by refugees accepted by a resettlement country, even when there are family or professional ties in a different country.

Political asylum in Europe, Australia, and North America is a highly desirable durable option for individuals who seek refugee status after having arrived in or at the borders of the countries where they hope to settle. While these individuals collectively constitute a small portion of the total at risk population, they have generated considerable anxiety and controversy in the more developed countries. Asylum review procedures have improved in some countries, especially the United States, but obtaining political asylum has become increasingly difficult everywhere. This is due largely to the greater obstacles in the way of access to asylum procedures and assessment of individual claims.[3] There have been successful asylum seekers from all the country cases discussed in this volume.

The option of *local integration*, in different forms, was once the most common option for politically motivated migrants. In Africa and Latin America, regional agreements and custom supported the practice of welcoming such migrants. In the latter, during the nineteenth and twentieth centuries, numerous political exiles settled for as long as necessary in neighboring countries. In the former, large groups forced to flee their countries were considered refugees. They were either allowed to settle where they chose or, more often, settled in camps where there was sufficient land to farm and establish a fair measure of self-sufficiency. Local integration options, however, have lost ground due to several factors. In the past two decades the frequency and size of mass refugee flights, the protracted nature of refugee emergencies, security concerns, and the decline in international resources to help sustain the refugees in the country have discouraged governments from welcoming refugees generously.

Whereas once countries as diverse as Tanzania and Costa Rica offered land and opportunities for refugees to live and work in urban and rural settings, and opened the way to eventual citizenship, these and other countries pulled the welcome mat some time ago. Costa Rica absorbed thousands of refugees from the Central American conflicts of the 1970s and 1980s, and a sizable population of Nicaraguans remained in the country. Nicaraguans continue to arrive in Costa Rica as a labor migration and encounter highly restrictive policies. Colombians who claim to be refugees are reviewed on an individual rather than a group basis.

Tanzania was one of the last countries to adhere to an open door for refugees during, and for a time after, the Nyerere government, from 1964 to 1985. As independent Tanzania's first president, Nyerere welcomed refugees for ideological reasons, rooted in traditions of African hospitality, as well as his belief in African unity and in his country's obligation to support the anti-colonial struggle in Africa by aiding those who were fighting for this end. Nyerere and those surrounding him also believed, first, that the country had sufficient land and resources to share and, second, that the refugees either would return quickly to their countries of origin or would settle as loyal Tanzanian citizens. Instead, Tanzanians complained that massive influxes of impoverished refugees were damaging the country economically and ecologically.[4] In 1996, the government acquiesced to a problematic repatriation of Rwandans. In 1998, a restrictive Tanzanian Refugee Act was passed, and at a still fragile moment in the peace process, the political leadership promoted the repatriation of Burundians, a group Tanzania has sheltered since the early 1960s.

In the poorer nations that have been countries of first asylum for most mass refugee flights from conflict, small numbers of better-educated urban refugees and vulnerable groups have access to national or international status determinations. Obtaining refugee status and living in urban centers rarely includes the right to most forms of employment. The majority of war-induced migrants are recognized collectively to be *ad hoc* or *prima facie* refugees. Many are sent to remote areas. Their refugee credentials are not reviewed individually unless they are selected for possible resettlement, nor are they given the right to settle locally. They remain in a refugeelike status that precludes integration, housed in camps or temporary settlements. Because employment opportunities are few and their movements outside of their assigned areas are restricted, they depend on international assistance. In wealthier countries, war refugees may be granted temporary permission to reside and to work, but are not on a path toward citizenship. In both cases temporary status can be and, on occasion, has been withdrawn.

Whether in refugee camps and settlements in poor countries, or with time-bound permission to remain in developed countries, *prima facie* refugees are being sheltered on the assumption that they will return to their countries of origin when peace has been restored. There are international legal obligations on host countries to protect refugees but not to assimilate them. Consequently, when wars persist for decades, when refugees remain fearful of return, and when governments in the countries of origin will not allow return, refugees and their children find themselves with no firm place of residence. In Africa, at least three million refugees are in protracted refugee situations, often having spent more than a decade in refugee camps.[5]

Repatriation is the durable solution most likely to be available to refugees today in large part because it is the only solution available. This means that refugees often return to places lacking in physical and economic security. Sometimes they return voluntarily, wishing to reestablish themselves at home or recognizing there are no alternatives. At times, return appears coerced, with host governments reducing the level of assistance and protection available in camps. Advocates of refugee rights rightly criticize those governments who expel forced migrants (recognized as refugees or not) to difficult and dangerous conditions and/or who mount repatriation programs before countries of origin are ready to absorb the returnees. They argue for continued refugee support until conditions warrant, even if this means that the refugees must remain camp-bound. Advocates of better international responses to war induced migration emphasize the vital importance of well-funded, long-range programs in countries of origin so that integration proceeds along with support for post-conflict rebuilding, restoration of rule of law, and economic revitalization. These positions are not contradictory.

UNHCR assists large scale movements to countries of origin as well as individuals who decide to repatriate. When individuals still have lingering fears, do not possess adequate documentation, or want financial assistance for the move, UNHCR will obtain government assurances of safety and restoration of status and rights, and will usually extend needed financial help. The large scale refugee movements normally occur following either a cessation of conflict or a change of government.[6] Such returns require prior negotiations, which may be quite protracted depending on relations between and among the governments involved and on the refugees' demands and needs upon arrival. The terms are established in a memorandum of understanding between refugee host country and country of origin governments. Before refugees return *en masse*, UNHCR officials inform the refugees of the conditions they are likely to face in their home countries, and what assistance will be made available to them. The fundamental principle in UNHCR regarding repatriation is that it should be voluntary, with each and every refugee agreeing to it. The extent to which refugee returns in recent times have been fully voluntary is a matter of debate.

Discussions about how to return people to their countries of origin should not focus solely on recognized refugees. In this regard, countries in the European Union, as well as the United States and Canada, are formulating return programs for other forced migrants from conflicts that include training, seed money for productive enterprises, or other potential forms of economic integration.[7] During the 1990s, UNHCR invested in reintegration projects and reconstruction in several post-conflict countries receiving repatriates, and made programs available to other war uprooted people in the same area. The efforts met with mixed success, and were cut back significantly due to declining donor support and criticism about mandate creep. In the current decade, UNHCR is increasingly partnering with other agencies and NGOs whose mandates are more appropriate for assisting in war-to-peace transitions, including reintegration of war uprooted populations. In the early years of the current century, as major conflicts in Africa are finally ending, governments and agencies will be well advised to make serious financial and political commitments to supporting the integrative aspects of war-to-peace transitions over several years, while, at the same time, avoiding pushing for premature repatriation.[8]

Limited Options for IDPs

The number of refugees has declined but the numbers of internally displaced persons have increased, for reasons described elsewhere in this volume. The number of IDPs is now believed to be twice that of refugees. Yet, as has also been described, not only are the motives of flight for IDPs and refugees apt to be very much the same, but the same people may be both refugees and IDPs at different times. Premature and ill-prepared repatriations are a major source of internal displacement. In several of our case studies, refugee returnees have been unable or unwilling to return to their home communities after repatriation because of continued insecurity from conflict, banditry, and landmines. Lack of economic opportunities in hometowns and villages also impede return, as do disputes over property rights. In fact, both refugees and IDPs may find other war-affected populations living in homes they abandoned when they left the country.

Thanks to the *Guiding Principles on Internal Displacement*, IDPs have received more attention, and governments have been under pressure either to improve conditions or to grant access to international agencies. Therefore, it is more likely that international assistance will be available to persons who have been uprooted inside their own countries. Such assistance rarely extends beyond the provision of relief, delivery of needed services, and advocacy. Longer-term development and integration programs are hardly ever put in place for IDPs because both governments and international relief agencies perceive being displaced to be a temporary problem, eventually to be resolved once an emergency ends or peace has been established.[9] There is considerable evidence from virtually every war-torn country that people who have lost their land and homes due to conflict, more often than not, settle in other places and struggle to start anew.

There is an important discussion underway concerning the "end of displacement," i.e., what should be the criteria used to determine that people no longer are displaced, hence no longer in need of international assistance or the same degree of assistance.[10] Establishing criteria that determine the "end" to displacement presumably would mean that international agencies and governments could better target assistance and gauge the extent of need. Presently there are vast differences in the estimated numbers of displaced persons in nearly every country where they are numerous. The troubling aspect of the question is the implied implication that people are in one category or the other; that is either displaced or not displaced. In fact, displacement may be resolved by a return to the abandoned home, or it may gradually become more or less resolved by decisions and opportunities that lead to other options. Whatever the case, IDPs do not cease to need support. Rather the nature of the support needed changes and evolves.

Environmental, development induced, and economic "refugees"[11] and displaced persons are recent terms. The association of these adjectives with the concept of "refugee" represents growing recognition that national governments and development agencies carry some blame for creating migrants in these categories, and should consider migration consequences in economic projects. The World Bank has taken important steps toward recognizing the displacement consequences of development projects it supports by insisting that recipient governments submit budgets and planning documents that include measures to resettle those displaced by these projects. For now, however, such enlightened approaches are all too infrequent.

Accelerated rural-urban flight in poor countries is rooted in modernization and globalization. Peasant farmers lose out to commercial interests. Having lost their land, they lack means of survival and move to cities and towns. There, they may find IDPs who have been driven from their homes by conflict. The same relief agencies may assist them all, having found them mixed in makeshift transient communities. People who leave their homes due to environmental degradation or have been pushed out by economic interests and development projects perceive their situation to be similar to that of refugees. Indeed many have, in fact, been targeted for economic reprisals because of ethnic, religious, or nationalist reasons that are difficult to prove. Large numbers have crossed borders and entered the political asylum stream, claiming to be refugees, albeit rarely with success.

Important as it is to respect the distinct characteristics of refugees in need of protection, failing to take into account the interconnections between different types of forced migrants undermines the quest for effective solutions. The same countries that produce refugees also produce other forced migrants who have compelling conflict-induced, environmental, developmental, and other economically rooted reasons for leaving and possibly returning. Just as politically motivated, recognized refugees ultimately need economic opportunities, health care, and employment as well as safe haven and protection, so too do the people forced to relocate internally because of conflict, repression, development, and environmental disruption. They are all, in effect, seeking durable solutions.

RESPONSES V. SOLUTIONS

International Mechanisms

Only the most fortunate among forced migrants have been able to find safe, long-term refuge. In the twenty-first century, refugee-receiving governments are increasingly determined to return the people they have agreed temporarily to protect, whether or not conditions in the country of origin are adequate for their protection. This is the case both in wealthy and poor receiving countries (e.g., Bosnians in Germany, Burundians in Tanzania, Somalis in Ethiopia, Myanmar Karen in Thailand). On the other side, refugees and IDPs who want to return often are unable, or do so at great risk, because neither national nor international mechanisms are in place for security, land mine removal, or economic revitalization (e.g., Afghans, Kosovar Serbs, Angolans, Sierra Leonians). Finally, in some instances, insurgent rivals have maintained control over the civilian population within their territorial jurisdictions in order to further their national political strength or to use as a captive population to parley greater international recognition and assistance (Tamil Tigers, Georgian/Abkhasia/Ossetian rivals).

National governments and international organisms need to reinforce their political capacities and will to design and implement comprehensive solutions for these many groups of forced migrants. Humanitarian agencies, hitherto funded and equipped to render only short term, superficial relief and a few basic services, need resources, mandates, and partnerships to effect comprehensive, multifaceted strategies that permit millions of forced migrants to remake their lives and contribute to their new or established societies.

The following pages outline the major flaws in the present humanitarian regime that impede international efforts to achieve durable solutions.

First, the mechanisms that supposedly differentiate refugees from other groups, so that those most in need will receive protection, are inconsistently and ungenerously applied. More relevant to the subject at hand, the old assumption that solutions are mandatory and available for refugees must be reassessed today in light of the fact that durable solutions like resettlement and asylum are mandatory only for individuals fleeing persecution, as contemplated in the

1951 Refugee Convention and 1967 Protocol. Most of the world's approximately twelve plus million recognized refugees are *prime facie*, meaning they face life-threatening situations but cannot establish that they are individually targeted victims. They receive protection and assistance, but usually not residence status or resettlement.

Second, the humanitarian regime now in place is responding more effectively to emergencies, but still very inadequately to protracted crises involving massive displacement. To meet the challenges of what we now call "complex humanitarian emergencies," state and organizational actors launch appeals, dispatch tons of relief, and assemble multifaceted teams. These teams are prepared to act immediately but not to stay beyond a period of months or a very few years. They are prepared to distribute what is needed but not to build the institutions and capacities required for productive and strong societies. While the concept of "emergency," helpfully, spurs a rapid response, a "rapid response" is not and cannot be sufficiently comprehensive, sustained, or coordinated to help people restart their disrupted lives. Although aid experts in the United States and Europe understand the need for comprehensive approaches and attention to transition periods, the budgets for such transitions are pitifully small and, too often, dependent on demonstrating measurable short-term results.

Third, internationally managed humanitarian assistance regimes, especially among NGOs, tend to be formulated independently of national efforts. Unquestionably, when government policies and institutions exacerbate tensions and produce forced displacement, international assistance must bypass government structures to provide urgently needed means of survival. At a different stage or in other circumstances, however, where there are serious intentions within government to address displacement, international assistance that bypasses official structures may be doing long-term harm even if it continues to serve short-term relief needs. Sustainable solutions must be expanded beyond the communities where the humanitarian and relief teams are working, and this can only take place through national structures with political backing.

On the development and financial side, it is indeed problematic when development actors support the long-term agendas of governments that are unresponsive to humanitarian needs. Few of the efforts to tie aid, trade, and assistance to stronger national commitments to poverty alleviation, human rights, and reconciliation have as yet been effective, and a better understanding of how to establish such links is very much needed. Moreover, the institutional gaps between relief, development, human rights, peacekeeping, and peacemaking operations, alluded to in chapter 3, impede efforts toward comprehensive and sustainable solutions.

Progress and Setbacks in Resolving Displacement: Case Examples

The trajectory of learning has been slow and uneven. The positive news is that there is at present ample international knowledge as to how to work in emergency and post-emergency situations. The unfortunate reality is that all too often the so-called "best practices" are ignored, are underfunded, or are politically impossible to realize. The brief descriptions below elaborate progress over the past ten to fifteen years in international support for promoting durable solutions for forced migrants in such areas as:

- "Comprehensive Plan of Action" (burden sharing)
- Settlement in place (facilitating benefits to hosts)
- Reintegration in the context of a regional plan for peace and reconstruction (comprehensive approach)
- Repatriation and return incentives (creating migration-development links)
- Adoption of international principles for internally displaced persons (international norms applied to treatment of citizens)
- Nation building after war

The examples, while flawed, demonstrate that there are good practices as well as costly failures. Each of the initiatives has been positive in intent and has produced positive results, at least in part. All have encountered obstacles rooted in national political agendas and surviving hostilities, diminishing political will, funding gaps and short-term commitments on the part of those promoting the initiatives, and weak capacities of new national governments. These obstacles have not been overcome and may fairly be described as leading to ever-worsening situations in several parts of the world.

Comprehensive Plan of Action: Indochina

Between 1975 and 1979, over 500,000 Indochinese fled war and Communist domination.[12] They arrived at the borders of neighboring countries or traveled by boat to nearby ports, and sought refuge. In the face of the nearly universal unwillingness of the governments in the South East Asian region to permit refugees to settle, governments in Europe, Australia, and especially North America agreed to resettle them. To this end, the UN organized an international conference on Indochinese refugees in July 1979 for multilateral commitments to Indochinese resettlement. The resettlement process was organized among the states as a form of burden sharing, to remove the refugees from the regional countries, among which only the Philippines was a party to the Refugee Convention. The countries of Southeast Asia agreed to keep open their borders, and Vietnam agreed to establish an orderly departure process that would enable applicants to apply for resettlement without seeking asylum outside of the country.

This approach was highly successful in maintaining first asylum for refugees, but it had certain unfortunate consequences. Because of limits on eligibility for the orderly departure program, and the high probability of finding a resettlement opportunity in one of the first asylum countries, many Vietnamese continued to risk departure on small, leaky boats amid threats of piracy in the South China Sea. Resettlement itself became a magnet for departures, even among persons with little need of international protection.

By the end of the 1980s, the Cold War was winding down and resettlement country authorities had adopted a more skeptical view of the refugee credentials of resettlement applicants. A second conference on Indochinese refugees in 1989 produced a Comprehensive Plan of Action that encompassed continuing resettlement as well as repatriation for persons who did not qualify as refugees. The regional governments in countries of first asylum remained adamant in their refusal to integrate more than a handful of the refugees arriving at their shores. Therefore, the large number of first asylum refugees who were not "screened in" for resettlement, using the more stringent status determination procedures, had no option but repatriation. Faced with considerable criticism for this unprecedented action, UNHCR introduced systematic follow-up monitoring of human rights and initiated integration projects inside Vietnam and Laos.[13]

Since this time, UNHCR has based protection and assistance staff in all major repatriation countries that are prone to conflict, have problematic human rights records, or are too poor to integrate returnees without international assistance. In nearly all cases of returns after conflict, such international presence is essential to help returnees recover their rights and properties and to make national governments more accountable for upholding these rights. While resettlement continues as a durable solution, governments and UNHCR try to avoid the 'magnet' effect that the large-scale admission of Vietnamese caused by targeting resettlement on a narrower range of persons who require protection from *refoulement* or endangerment or who would otherwise benefit from permanent admission in a third country.

Local Integration: Africa, Central America

Policies favoring local integration of refugees and other forced migrants range from small-scale community projects in refugee receiving areas to opportunities for refugees to benefit from citizenship and full legal rights in the host country. Refugee advocates have frequently argued in favor of local integration as a far more humane solution than the camps that keep refugees isolated and dependent on outside assistance. These advocates contend that camps do not even facilitate protection, as evidenced by the numerous forms of violence, and social insecurity one finds in nearly all camp situations.[14] Until the latter part of the last decade, a number of countries in Africa and Latin America encouraged projects that brought together refugees and local populations. These initiatives, in many ways, brought benefits to the host countries. In 1984, when African governments called for international support to a refugee and development approach,[15] the international response was not encouraging. But, in another theater, refugee assistance and political affinities briefly worked to the advantage of refugees and hosts. The Sandinista government in Nicaragua incorporated Salvadoran refugees into peasant cooperatives, and the international assistance they received benefited all cooperative members. (Later, civil war undermined the cooperatives and the subsequent government broke them up.) Namibians received a wide range of rights in Angola prior to repatriation in 1989, and Tutsis refugees in Rwanda—Paul Kagame, its present ruler being a case in point—rose to high levels in the Ugandan military and society.

There are still examples of partial local integration that allow refugees to earn their livelihoods as opposed to depending fully on relief, but there no longer are open doors to local settlement for large refugee groups. With larger numbers of refugees remaining longer periods and receiving less and less international support, African hospitality receded decisively, as already described in the case of Tanzania.

Reintegration, Peace, and Reconstruction: Central America

For well over a decade, internal conflicts raged in Guatemala, El Salvador, and Nicaragua. During the 1980s, these became proxy wars rooted in east-west ideological competition, and defied efforts on the part of regional leaders to achieve peaceful resolution of the conflicts. Only at the close of the decade and the end of the Cold War was it finally possible to achieve both regional and international consensus in support of a peace process in this ideologically divided area (see chapter 3). The governments in the region collectively sought and obtained international agreement for tying their compliance with peace arrangements to assurances of outside humanitarian aid and development assistance. The result was a comprehensive plan for regional reconstruction, the CIREFCA[16] Plan of Action of 1989. The CIREFCA Plan was specifically intended to find "permanent solutions to the problems of uprootedness within the framework of national development and as an integral part of efforts toward peace and democracy." To this end it targeted 1.9 million uprooted people throughout the region.[17] All the governments in the region participated in CIREFCA and benefited from projects whether or not the wars had been fought on their territories, because the displacement and violence generated by the fighting had affected them all.

The creation of the CIREFCA process encouraged donors to channel funds for reintegration and community development. Through CIREFCA, the major donors in North America, Europe, and Japan worked with several UN agencies, the governments of the six CIREFCA member countries, and nongovernmental organizations in each country to channel humanitarian assistance funds to the diverse populations uprooted by war. The Secretariat was jointly operated by the UNHCR and UNDP. The partnership, unique at that time, allowed both organizations to design programs and projects that benefited refugees, former refugees, internally displaced persons, and other categories of vulnerable people—especially targeting women. Beyond serving as a channel for humanitarian assistance, CIREFCA was designed as a forum of reconciliation and cooperation among national leaders, between and among opposing groups, between former refugees and governments, and between governments and nongovernment organizations.[18]

To bring about durable solutions, the process aimed to link the relief projects needed for immediate survival with longer-term economic revitalization, capacity building, and rebuilding. The signature assistance mode of CIREFCA was the "quick impact project" QIP. QIPs are short term, one time, donor infusions to enable local groups to collectively select and implement needed economic and social infrastructure projects or productive enterprises. Donors in Central America found QIPs to be very attractive since they seemed to promote community development without requiring long-term donor involvement. The results of thousands of these small-scale projects, however, were mixed and often disappointing.[19] Within the CIREFCA framework, an Italian-funded project under the UNDP, PRODERE,[20] also executed projects promoting regional cooperation and inter-agency collaboration in former conflict areas.

While these initiatives did serve to promote dialogue, reconciliation, and short-term economic improvements throughout the region, they did not often link with or lead to wider development efforts. Hence, once the actions were completed—if they were completed—there was no assured follow-on, and they were rarely sustainable.[21] The CIREFCA model provided a framework for addressing displacement comprehensively. However, CIREFCA neither solved nor significantly alleviated the pervasive poverty and inequality in Central America, nor did it resolve serious flaws in governance in the affected countries. The long-term benefits of the process lay in contributing meaningfully to lasting peace in the region and promoting a broadly-based, enduring, and serious discussion about social and economic change in the region.[22]

Incentives to Return Following Temporary Protection: Former Yugoslavia

Much can be learned, both positive and negative, from international actions in Bosnia and Herzegovina. On the positive side, international intervention in the former Yugoslavia pulled the region back (albeit belatedly) from a hugely destructive war and produced a durable, if troubled, peace. The war had killed or displaced approximately half its original population of 4.4 million.[23] The General Framework for Peace in Bosnia and Herzegovina (the Dayton Peace agreement) at the end of 1995 gave the international community significant powers to impose reform and enforce the measures that had been agreed upon.

Donors and international agencies invested heavily in rebuilding and reconciliation, and were particularly interested in funding programs that encouraged minority return and reintegration. This could have been an important precedent for other return programs. During the conflict the international community had responded generously to the need for safe haven for Bosnians (and later for Kosovars). Having done so, however, host country governments were eager to dispatch those they were temporarily protecting back to their places of origin. Host country governments falsely assumed that repatriation and minority returns could be made viable in the face of inadequate physical and economic security. Therefore, and unfortunately, much funding in Bosnia was wasted.

The efforts to encourage and provide for minority returns, for the most part, were unsuccessful because they were badly flawed in timing and sequence. Support for minority returns was strongest immediately following the war, in 1997–1998, while the refugee receiving countries sought to compel people to go back. The donors and international agencies seemed to believe that if they designed and funded attractive return programs, people would take advantage of them—even if conditions for absorption and integration did not exist. They particularly underestimated the extent to which the local and national officials who should have overseen the returnees' integration process were determined to undermine it. Bosnians originally from the area that became Republika Srpska (RS) lost their safe haven status in Europe between 1996 and 1998. Yet, these refugees were at such high risk of both physical and economic insecurity in the RS that they could not and would not try to recover their homes there. Instead, they returned to Bosnia and Herzegovina but lived as internally displaced persons in the Federation area. There, they joined the ethnic majority, but were usually entirely dependent on international assistance.

Not until 1999–2000 did the NATO forces take the necessary steps to improve security, enforce property rights, and exercise authority over the nationalist opponents to the Dayton Peace Accord. These steps were the essential prerequisites for any serious return movement and should have been taken early in the process. After 2000, with security conditions somewhat improved, growing numbers among the internally displaced in the Federation manifested interest in returning to their original homes. Many did so, despite the still present hostility of local officials, police, courts, etc. More would have done so had it not been for the dismal state of the economy in the RS.[24] The movement might have been far larger, had it not been, first, that by 2000 the ample humanitarian assistance initially available for returnees no longer existed and, second, that the international community punished the RS for its noncompliance with the peace goals by denying investment and general assistance.

On the humanitarian side, international donors cut back dramatically on funding for housing reconstruction and relief by 2000, concluding that after four years, such costs should be assumed by local governments. In this instance, even if local authorities had been willing to assist returnees—which they rarely were—they did not have the means to do so. Therefore, neither international nor national funding could be mobilized to assist those contemplating return. Policy remained strongly in favor of minority return, but donors no longer were interested in funding the actions needed for it to occur.

Since 2000 donors sought to fund longer term development-oriented projects and to encourage investment throughout Bosnia and Herzegovina, but the RS has received much less international investment or development assistance than the Federation and is poorer by far. This is in large part because donors do not wish to reward their nationalist Serb leaders who have consistently flaunted the Dayton Accords. The irony here is that poverty and lack of employment in the region further discourage return and settlement. As is so often the case with political sanctions, punishment has not produced better behavior, but has made residents both bitter and more amenable to the nationalist message.

Some lessons were learned and have been applied to Kosovo,[25] but again international action has been stymied by the failure to resolve the larger issues. As in Bosnia, returns generally and minority returns in particular were and remain an international priority. In Kosovo, contrary to Bosnia and Herzegovina, international action with regard to security was decisive at the outset. Approximately 850,000 ethnic Albanians fled Kosovo in the wake of fighting during 1998 and 1999 and harsh Serb retaliation against the majority Albanian ethnic population. After the 1999 intervention of NATO forces against the former Yugoslavia, the majority of the displaced Albanians were able to return fairly quickly. In Kosovo a massive return was viable because international force had changed realities on the ground. With the return of the Albanian population, there was a displacement of minorities.

Though Kosovo like Bosnia and Herzegovina was meant to be a multi-ethnic entity, the present context is not promising. The Albanians initially from predominantly Serb areas went to other areas. Between 230,000 to 280,000 ethnic Serbians in Kosovo left and few have returned, despite both international urging to do so. The Kosovar Serbs have not been well received in Serbia proper or Montenegro where they are concentrated, partly because their departure is seen to strengthen Kosovo's claim to a separate status and partly because, ethnicity notwithstanding, they are considered outsiders. Another 22,000 to 23,000 Serbs left their communities but stayed within Kosovo, along with another 100,000 non-Serb minority residents.[26] Although the presence of international peacekeepers has reduced violence, there have been serious outbreaks of conflict, most notably in 2004.

At this writing, four years after the end of the fighting, Kosovo is still far from secure, ethnic hostilities continue to explode, and criminal activities dominate the economy. To some extent, patience and a continued UN presence has been rewarded with a slow progress in the civilian leadership's ability to assume responsibilities of governance.[27] The UN Mission in Kosovo UNMIK has initiated actions aimed at promoting rule of law and reducing ethnic discrimination. For example, international judges and prosecutors have been used to strengthening protection of minorities in the judicial sector and to providing a counter weight to the strong ethnic biases in the courts.[28] Nevertheless, although the UN mission declared its priorities to build capacities in governance and rule of law, there is little evidence of institutional strengthening or significantly increased local management capacities.

International officials and donors cite corruption, crime, and ethnic violence as reasons for moving slowly. They still proclaim their goal to be ethnic pluralism or, at least, ethnic peace that permits both Serbs and the majority Albanian population to coexist. However, there is a growing consensus, shared by many in the international community, that pursuing the goal of ethnic pluralism under current conditions is unrealistic and exacerbates—not solves—ethnic tensions. In this view, international actions in Kosovo will be largely counterproductive until it is possible to resolve the issue of Kosovo itself. Kosovo is still an entity officially attached to Serbia, which belies the legitimacy of its separate government and institutions and creates confusion regarding its government responsibilities. Without doubt the most important objective of the Kosovar leadership is to find a formula for independence. It is urgent to begin a process aimed at resolving the status of Kosovo, its frontiers, and the rights of its minority populations, Serbs in particular. Doing so is a prerequisite to producing a government that is more accountable and better able to enforce minority rights. Unfortunately, since 1999, the lack of international will to resolve the status of Kosovo has been allowed to undermine peacekeeping and humanitarian efforts.

INTERNATIONAL PRINCIPLES FOR INTERNALLY DISPLACED, BUT STILL NO SOLUTIONS: COLOMBIA

If national legislation, jurisprudence, and organization were the measures of adequate response to forced displacement, the internally displaced population in Colombia would be the best attended in the world. As already noted, Colombia passed a comprehensive law in 1997 regarding internally displaced persons that replicated the international *Guiding Principles on Internal Displacement*. A nationwide Network of Social Solidarity is charged to oversee IDP assistance and promote prevention and integration. Colombian courts provide recourse for those whose rights are denied. Unfortunately, the IDPs in Colombia are not well attended because programs for attention to displaced persons—though improving—still encompass too few people, are unevenly implemented for too short a period of time, and are underfunded. The mechanisms for integration, resettlement, prevention, and return are especially ineffective.

The government of President Alvaro Uribe has declared IDP return to be the best solution, and has made it a strong priority. But, the government remains incapable of assuring adequate physical or economic security for returnees while the conflict continues. In a 2000 report, the Representative of the UN Secretary General on Internally Displaced persons recommended greater international and government presence to monitor returnee conditions. In view of the ongoing conflict, however, the report expressed skepticism regarding safety and durability of return movements;[29] the conflict has not abated in the interim. Indeed, because of the insecurity associated with returns, few international agencies are eager to support them meaningfully with the economic assistance needed for sustaining livelihoods. In the UN Humanitarian Action Plan for Colombia 2003, international agencies in Colombia prioritized longer-term reintegration and institutional strengthening, but international agencies have neither the funding nor national backing to make significant impacts in these areas. Colombians at national and local levels continue to tailor policies to the assumption that displacement is temporary and can be reversed.

Much more needs to be done to enable and encourage municipalities receiving IDPs fleeing from the conflictive rural areas to integrate them. Virtually all cities in the country have been receiving tens of thousands of displaced families and have been neither able nor willing to provide new arrivals with more than minimal public education and health care, much less employment. Not only is political will lacking to accept the IDPs as permanent residents, but national institutional and budgetary structures impede flexible municipal responses.[30]

Thus, as the number of IDPs climbs toward three million and refugee flight also increases, government and international assistance remain the overwhelming responses. The flawed assumption that IDPs and refugees can and will return to their places of origin not only is misleading but also has reinforced the tendency to bypass opportunities for supporting integration. This observation is not meant to underestimate the importance of advocating the right to return and the need to support return movements. Rather, it is intended to advocate support for multiple solutions, in both rural and urban settings, designed to absorb and integrate IDPs in the places where they are and/or to help them to find alternative places to live and work. Even if they may eventually return to their places of origin, their lives in the interim should not remain in limbo, in an unhappy holding pattern with few if any options.

Nation Building after War and Recurring Displacement: Afghanistan[31]

Afghans constituted the largest single group of refugees in the world during the 1980s. About six million Afghans resided in Pakistan and Iran, with large numbers in several countries of Europe, North America, and Australia as well. Both Pakistani and Iranian governments facilitated Afghan refugee settlement during the years of Soviet domination, but stopped short of offering the rights to permanent residence and citizenship. (In practice, many among the early Afghan arrivals in both countries did achieve permanent status.) Physical integration within the local population was more widespread in Iran because that country received very little international assistance, and Afghans were permitted to settle in cities and towns where they could earn a living. In Pakistan, there was ample international support for the refugee population. Afghans there lived more often in internationally supported camps and settlements until assistance was cut back in the late 1990s, whereupon they too found it necessary to reside in urban settings.

After the collapse of the Soviet Union in 1991, international support largely shifted from refugee assistance to repatriation and rebuilding in Afghanistan. Over a million refugees repatriated from Pakistan in the first years of that decade, and a few hundred thousand left Iran. The returnees received relief and relatively small sums of money. Within Afghanistan international agencies and NGOs were reconstructing war-damaged parts of the country and restoring local agriculture. The approach to the repatriation and reintegration process might have proved a model for other major return movements[32] had not the large scale returns been undercut by internal forces that undermined security and local survival. A number of factors precluded Afghanistan's prospects for future peace and development: murderous domestic conflict among rival powers, the subsequent Taliban repression and retaliations and, finally, regional conflict and widespread drought. Instead of continuing repatriation, these factors generated new waves of internal and external flight during the rest of the decade.

Fearing just such new influxes during the 1990s, both Pakistani and Iranian governments increased restrictions on the refugee population, harassed them, tried to prevent further entries, and took stronger actions to resist Afghan integration. The international donors already had cut back significantly on Afghan refugee assistance in Pakistan; food aid ended in 1995. UNHCR and some NGOs maintained only health, educational, and a few additional services, and low levels of protection. The loss of international humanitarian revenue, in turn, intensified Pakistani reluctance to accept new entries.

The United States-led intervention in 2001 that brought down the Taliban government intensified these tendencies. The fall of the Taliban, the creation of a new Afghan government, and promises from donors to contribute generously to rebuilding the country led Pakistan and Iran, as well as governments throughout Europe and India, and the UNHCR to vigorously promote the repatriation option. The U.S. resettlement program ground almost to a halt. With conditions worsening and other options disappearing, the refugees had little choice but to try their luck in their own country. About two million have returned at this writing, far more than had been anticipated. All concerned has hailed the number as a testament to Afghans' strong ties to their places of origin but, as can be seen, there were strong "push" factors at work as well.

Afghanistan is a country that exemplifies the problem of the state not having enough capacity to control its territory or foster the institutions necessary to protect its citizens.[33] Donors such as the U.S. government are impatient with this reality, complaining that billions of dollars have been spent to reconstruct Afghanistan with few tangible results. Even priority issues like education for girls have been stymied by insecurity and local resistance. President Hamid Karzai himself recognizes that Afghanistan today is "a nation without a state."[34]

Significantly fewer Afghans returned during 2003[35] than had returned in the previous year, but the numbers began again to rise in 2004. Afghanistan is still poorly prepared to absorb the incoming returnees. Political consolidation is fragile and slowly taking place. On the international side the UN has played a less central role in rebuilding than it did during the first repatriation.

This is due, in large part, to pervasive insecurity. UNDP and the World Bank, to a large extent in partnership with UNHCR, however, have launched important programs in institutional capacity-building and reintegration. Although international NGOs poured into Afghanistan after 2001, all but a few lacked relevant past experience in the country. Neither UN agencies nor NGOs have operated from a common premise or plan. The Afghan government suffers from its inability to rule effectively beyond the capital city. This being the case, NGOs, donors, and UN agencies—understandably—have accepted the legitimacy of local sources of power, thereby strengthening the latter at the expense of the central government.

The presence of a large number of agencies has not translated into widespread assistance, service, and reconstruction in Afghanistan. Parts of the country, especially in the south, are too dangerous for foreigners and foreign agencies to mount projects; throughout the country, high levels of criminal activity, extortion, and generally weak security discourage sustained programs. The returning refugees may be able to rebuild houses and clean plots of land, but they cannot perform the major reconstruction required to make the rural areas economically viable. Increasingly, returnee families or some members of these families have found it necessary to move from rural areas to larger cities and/or try to reenter Pakistan and Iran in order to earn a livelihood.[36]

Nation Building After War: Timor Leste 1999–2002

Among the groups in the review, East Timor, now Timor Leste is the most dramatic example of a durable solution following a tragic series of events. As will be shown, its success has been marred by two factors, first by the inability of the UNHCR or UN peace keepers to protect Timorese from the militias that caused their flight; second by the premature reduction of humanitarian assistance for returnees and the war-affected population generally.

Having voted for independence from Indonesia in 1999, the entire population came under attack by irregular Indonesian and pro-Indonesian forces. The already poor territory was devastated and an estimated two thirds (more than 500,000 people) of the 750,000 population were driven from their homes. About half the people (approximately 240,000) who fled from the violence of 1999 crossed into West Timor as refugees. They were divided between those escaping life-threatening reprisals and destruction, and others who, it is likely, had facilitated the violence in some way. The latter fled when the Australian-led UN force defeated the anti-independence militia forces and, to a large extent, they dominated genuine refugee groups in West Timor. Not only was the UNHCR unable to protect the refugees there, but when two of its own staff members were murdered the expatriate staff left altogether.

When Timor Leste achieved independence and the UN mission oversaw the creation of a new state in May 2002, the refugees along with those who had fled to remote internal locations were able to return as full citizens of their own country. Nearly all the refugees returned. Nevertheless, once again the weak protection regime put them at risk. First, the presence and power of the militia groups in West Timor first prevented refugees from returning for a considerable period, then proved decisive in facilitating; second, the militia members not only were able to return with the refugees, but negotiated an amnesty from prosecution for war crimes they may have permitted. Consequently, at the present time, former militia groups are effectively controlling many villages. Other members of the militias have remained in West Timor with their families and they are unlikely either to return or to face sanctions of any kind.[37]

Not since the UN Transitional Authority in Cambodia, 1992–1993, has the United Nations assumed such far-reaching responsibility for nation building. The UN Transitional Administration for Timor Leste, UNTAET oversaw both the rebuilding of the country and the creation of what would be the national institutions of government between October 1999 and May 2002. Contrary to the Cambodian example,[38] the UN approach in Timor Leste was to move gradually toward handing over administrative responsibilities to national and local authorities. Elections were scheduled late in the process and, in the interim, efforts were made to enhance local capacities in all areas of governance. Not least of the challenges facing UNTAET and the government was to receive and reintegrate the more than 500,000 people displaced directly or indirectly by the assaults of Indonesian militia following the Timorese referendum vote.

In sum, under UN oversight and presently with its own government, Timor Leste has made admirable progress politically and economically. But, it will long remain a war-torn country with a fragile economy in need of assistance. In a process reminiscent of Bosnia and Herzegovina, international peacekeepers did not eliminate the power of the former militias over Timorese returnees. Critics of the UN process—which all agree was fundamentally well-conceived and executed—also have called attention to an overly accelerated movement from humanitarian relief to development assistance. Rather than a planned transition that maintained assistance for basic needs (shelter, help for vulnerable sectors, health care) as required—for example, as people gradually returned from West Timor—the donors and UNTAET replaced emergency aid in favor of efforts to prepare the country for self-government. As of March 2001, the emergency funding that had been obtained from the Consolidated Appeal Process, (CAP) was exhausted. The initial CAP had successfully mobilized generous amounts of emergency funding, but with short time frames for execution. Given the dire conditions in Timor Leste and the continuing returns of people to their homes, there remained serious need for international relief in various forms thereafter.[39]

This pattern of ample but short-term emergency aid that prematurely ends is all too common in post-conflict rebuilding. As was noted above, the premature abandonment of relief assistance had a similarly negative impact on the ability of families wishing to return to their homes in the RS in Bosnia. What makes the repetition of the pattern particularly troublesome in the case of Timor Leste is that in so many ways, the rebuilding process was exemplary in its adoption of lessons gleaned from other experiences.

The handover from UN supervision to a new Timor Leste government in May 2002 was a satisfying conclusion to a long struggle against the 1975 forced annexation of the territory. But the newly independent nation's future prospects are still tenuous due the previous neglect under Indonesian rule, the scars of the destruction produced by the Indonesian militia in 1999 and the inexperience of much of the new leadership. As affirmed by Christopher Mc-Dowell, in his 2003 case study of Timor Leste, the country will require the security provided by an international military presence, as well as financial aid for some years to preserve the gains achieved and permit it to progress.[40] In January 2004, five months before the end of the UNTAET two-year mandate in Timor, a UN inspection team strongly recommended its renewal.[41]

THINKING COMPREHENSIVELY ABOUT LONG-TERM SOLUTIONS

The major reason for inadequate international resources and commitments seems to be that when emergencies occur, donor governments neither anticipate nor plan for long-term multifaceted forms of involvement. International funding alone is insufficient to induce meaningful political, economic, and social reforms or to ensure that people who have been uprooted can remake their lives safely and productively. Likewise, aid professionals know that a large and longstanding international presence is almost sure to stifle local initiative. Nevertheless, there are all too many indications that governments will continue to opt for too little funding and will continue to insist on time frames too short to fulfill stated objectives.

Post-Conflict Reintegration, Traditional Expectations V. Realities

The assumption that the majority of forced migrants can and will return to their original homes after conflict has often proved more myth than reality. If the conflict has been long term, demographic realities will have changed in the conflict zones. Those who have left homes behind are likely to find them to have been destroyed, or with other people living in them. In war-torn regions, where deadly land mines dot the landscape, and the destruction of roads and basic communication links isolate productive areas from markets, returnees encounter serious obstacles to recovering their former livelihoods. In many societies, property ownership is not formally documented and land is difficult to recover. Returning large numbers of people to these situations requires legal mechanisms to adjudicate land conflicts as well as funding to compensate those who have lost land and material goods; conflict resolution mechanisms to reestablish the bases of community life; programs to rebuild economic and social infrastructure; economic support systems such as credits, micro finance, and productive inputs; and local officials that do not discriminate on ethnic, religious, or other grounds. For these reasons, IDP and refugee advocates have been (or should be) paying greater attention to broad post-conflict rebuilding and governance. Successful return movements depend on long-term international support for post-emergency rebuilding.

It is difficult to document, but anecdotal evidence indicates that persons who have been displaced for long periods frequently choose not to return to their initial homes even if the option is available. Solutions focusing on urban areas are especially important and, in the present context, all too rare. Local integration implies measures to provide uprooted people with access to schools, health care, job opportunities, and titles to property—such as the makeshift homes and bits of land they may have acquired. Additionally, when large numbers of difficult to assimilate people arrive, it is important to design measures to overcome local hostility and to support initiatives intended to incorporate IDP families into the social fabric.

Supporting Self-Help and Building Capacities

International responses to emergencies operate at early stages and often without taking into account the self-help and survival mechanisms already in place among internally and externally displaced groups.[42] To be sure, humanitarian and development entities have supported microfinance and income generation projects among refugees and other displaced populations, and these have been important to survival in many instances, especially for women-headed households. Such projects are inadequate for large-scale job creation, however. More than anything else, the groups described in this volume want and need the ability to support themselves and their families, if not in their countries of origin then outside of it. One small step, for example, would be incentives for national governments to grant work permits to refugees, especially those in urban areas, which would permit self-sufficiency in this otherwise highly dependent sector.

Because the important source of survival for the families that have lost their former means of livelihood is the ability of some members to find paid employment, forced migration in almost every instance generates labor migration. Because labor opportunities are few in the regions where displacement occurs, workers seize opportunities to migrate. Recent research has shown that millions of poor families, including families uprooted by war, chaos, famine, environmental degradation, and unfavorable economic developments, live on remittances from relatives living in other countries, often illegally. Remittances are receiving much international attention at the present time,[43] and the agencies that underwrite microfinancing, income generation, and community development are slowly beginning to experiment with ways to increase the value of remittances by using some funding for these purposes. International financial institutions, government aid agencies, and development experts applaud the positive development impacts of remittances (which are sent at great sacrifice to the wage earners). This continued "success story," however, depends on continued access to employment. To the extent that countries where labor opportunities are plentiful take more stringent measures to curtail unwanted unauthorized migration, the ability of so many working age people to earn and remit will diminish.

National Governments as Factors in Achieving Solutions

National governments have the primary responsibility for preventing and resolving the political and economic conditions that may bring about forced migration, but international programs and assistance are essential. Perhaps the greatest obstacle to international efforts to improve economic conditions overall in poor countries is the all too frequent phenomenon of government partners that fail to build responsive institutions, uphold rule of law, or address poverty. This is especially common among fragile post-conflict states and states in transition from dictatorship. In attempting to reward or punish governments, international agencies and donors have increased or decreased the amount of assistance they make available. Or, they have decided to bypass altogether those governments that lack capacity, accountability, commitments, acceptance by civil society, etc., and to channel funds through nongovernmental agencies instead. In Haiti, for example, the U.S. government refused to support any programs operated by the government of Jean Bertrand Aristide, but sent relief and social funding through private agencies. A logical and more productive approach is to devote greater resources to capacity building for both public and private sector entities, and to reward improved accountability and anticorruption measures. Incentives and sustained capacity building serve both to enhance professional skills and as an antidote to corruption.

Because the positive effects of capacity-building efforts become evident only in the long rather than short term, donors historically have not been as forthcoming with resources for this purpose as for quick-yield projects. But attitudes internationally appear to be changing with greater recognition that security and sustainable development depend on well-functioning transparent government structures. In the World Bank and regional financial institutions, and in the United Nations, good governance support and training are being systematically incorporated into much program support. The World Bank Institute has an Anti Corruption Unit that incorporates capacity building and good governance training. The United Nations Development Program portrays its Capacity Development Program as a process that "entails the sustainable creation, utilization and retention of . . . capacity, in order to reduce poverty, enhance self-reliance, and improve people's lives."[44] Civil society groups in several countries have made fighting corruption a major priority. Candidates who made commitments to transparency and accountability won recent elections in Kenya, Zambia, Nicaragua, and Guatemala. As for incentives, the potential is demonstrated by the greater attention to good governance and anticorruption programs in countries whose governments wish to benefit from the Millennium Challenge Account. This U.S. government initiative will make significant aid available only to countries meeting criteria of governance and open economies.[45] In arguing for this kind of approach, the Administrator of USAID linked effective development assistance with the existence good policies and institutions.

> Put simply, economic development assistance in poor countries works best when you are pursuing good policies that are conducive to growth. We know that good governance, policies and institutions are key; real country ownership is also essential.[46]

Results on the ground are less heartening. International expectations about improving governance performance in a few years are probably unrealistic in the fragile and conflictive countries that generate much of the displacement and out migration. Moreover, despite the welcome donor support for institution building, accountability, and human rights, there are scant resources and little training to help meet these goals at departmental and local levels. Poor local economies, corrupt local administration, and lack of security are prominent factors inducing migration and impeding effective reintegration.

Conflict Prevention

The most obvious, but thus far elusive solution for forced displacement is to reduce its occurrence. Conflict is the primary cause of displacement, and conflict prevention is on the agenda of governments and aid agencies alike. The root causes of conflict are much debated and, while it is not the purpose of this essay to review the various arguments, it is fair to say that both national and international actions are involved. On the solution side, measures such as preventive diplomacy, preventive deployment, early warning systems, arms control, norms creation, and the establishment of credible deterrents can be effective conflict-prevention tools. The end of the Cold War has created a larger space for governments and international agencies to use their power and influence to these ends.

Conflict prevention not only will save lives but avoid forced migrant crises. UNHCR has become a strong advocate of using prevention tools for averting refugee flows. It has promoted the concept of "soft intervention" approaches that emphasize diplomatic initiatives and development projects.[47] For this approach to succeed, however, governments must take the lead. Governments, for their part, have found abundant justifications for failing to expend the resources and diplomatic capital needed for these approaches to succeed.

Yet, prevention, as is very often repeated, is far less costly than conflict management or conflict resolution. A 2001 study actually quantified the cost differences between preventive action and action taken after the onset of armed conflict.[48] This study estimated that the cost of preventive action in Bosnia might have been $33.3 billion as opposed to the estimated $53.7 billion actually spent. For Haiti, the preventive costs might have been $2.3 billion versus the $5 billion spent, and for Somalia the preventive costs might have been $1.5 billion instead of $7.3 billion. The study does not calculate the multiple costs of conflict-induced displacement. Choosing to intervene early can dramatically reduce humanitarian loss; here, one need only contemplate the violence, suffering, and displacement that might have been avoided in Rwanda, Bosnia-Herzegovina, Afghanistan, and so many other places.

Failures in the 1990s, to predict the onset and severity of conflicts or to easily and comprehensively address conflicts, led to a multitude of early warning centers and early warning systems designed to alert international actors to potential or low-level conflicts. Early warning centers analyze statistics on indicators such as forced displacement, political instability, human development, and human rights from a variety of sources in order to assist conflict prevention efforts.[49] Early warning, as Rwandans learned bitterly, does not necessarily bring early response. The former demands expertise and judgment, but the latter, additionally, requires political will and the capacity to mobilize action.

Small arms are the single largest nonproliferation issue with respect to intrastate conflict and insecure environments for forced migrants and humanitarian aid workers. According to the United Nations Development Program (UNDP), small arms were the weapon of choice in forty-seven of the forty-nine major conflicts since 1990.[50] The importance of small arms in fueling and perpetuating intrastate conflict cannot be exaggerated: the proliferation of small arms across conflict zones allows for greater damage during conflict, longer conflicts, blurs lines between civilians and combatants, and makes conflict harder to resolve.[51] The international community has responded minimally to the threats posed by small arms. To be sure, it has imposed arms embargoes against countries involved in conflicts with significant human rights dimensions. From 1990 to 2000, eleven arms embargoes were imposed on countries ranging from the former Yugoslav republics in 1991 to Sierra Leone in 1997.[52] Unfortunately, embargoes suffer from serious implementation and effectiveness problems, and are effective only when all parties, including those selling the arms, uphold the embargo.[53]

Trade agreements, financial restructuring, and pressures to reduce public spending are rightly regarded as tools for creating stronger economies over time. However, in country after country, when these policies have been put in place, the short and medium term effects have been detrimental to wide swaths of poor and middle class citizens. Inequalities have increased markedly in recent years in Latin America, Africa, and Asia. People of productive age who are able to move search elsewhere for the jobs they no longer can find at home. Newcomers, migrants, refugees, or returnees who try to find a place for themselves in regions or countries unable to employ, much less support, their own populations are unlikely to find a warm welcome.[54]

BUILDING PEACE MEANS PREPARING DURABLE SOLUTIONS

Logic, as well as history, indicates that war-to-peace transitions are bound to be long and troubled, facts that international assumptions regarding state obligations must take into account. Building basic state structures and legislative bodies are a *sine qua non* for protecting vulnerable persons. Improving local and national infrastructure and communications are fundamental to enable humanitarian and development agendas to move forward. Additionally, reintegrating refugees, IDPs, and former combatants in the framework of a difficult transition calls for new roles and responsibilities on the part of both citizens and the state. Although international assistance cannot and should not manage war-to-peace transitions, external involvement is essential at every stage to move the process forward. Land mine identification and removal, infrastructure restoration, communication access are the *sine qua non* for development. International oversight, assistance, and training devoted to demobilizing, disarming, and professionalizing armed parties and police, not only establish conditions favorable to security and safety, but lay the groundwork for future civilian control over these armies and militias. Financial resources, technical expertise, and the cumulative effects of capacity building and institution building efforts can buttress those governmental and nongovernmental sectors committed to a peace agenda.

At this writing in 2004, Angola and Liberia are experiencing peace for the first time in decades. Refugees and internally displaced persons are repopulating a number of towns and villages, sometimes despite the continued presence of land mines or armed factions. The international support for bringing people back to Angola has been fairly generous, although donors are understandably reluctant to underwrite the reconstruction process in view of the disappointing response on the part of the oil rich Angolan government to the enormous needs of its people.[55] International donors at a pledging conference in February 2004 finally demonstrated significant humanitarian support for Liberia, having pledged $520 million over two years for recovery and reconstruction. The conference, sponsored by the United States, the UN, and the World Bank, raised more funds than expected. The entire region, however, is likely to remain unstable and subject to armed violence for some time. Early indications are that international operations in both countries will reflect important lessons learned about planning and coordination in post-conflict rebuilding. Close behind Angola and Liberia, Sri Lanka is on the verge of peace after decades of war. Many of the internally displaced have been able to reclaim land and villages once fully controlled by the rebel Tamil Tigers. And, if peace agreements materialize in Burundi, Sudan, and the Democratic Republic of Congo, there will be new challenges for reintegrating millions of people who have spent decades either as refugees in squalid and unproductive camps, or have been in nearly perpetual flight.

The past decade has produced positive organizational changes within the major UN agencies and international financial institutions, involving: emergency response units, joint planning missions, technical support expertise, communications between headquarters and field operations, and staff deployment. Nongovernment agencies have become less compartmentalized, somewhat more cooperative, and more often allied with local agencies. Special representatives, and sometime special humanitarian coordinators now operate in a number of crises countries to organize, coordinate, and plan comprehensive UN operations. These steps, and a greater sensitivity within agencies to vulnerabilities and social dynamics, have contributed to an improved understanding of what is needed in humanitarian emergencies. In theory if not in practice, there is also a strong understanding of the need for longer-term and more comprehensively planned commitments.

Unfortunately, virtually all long-range programs that could link humanitarian and development assistance are underfunded. Although there have been initiatives within governments and the financial institutions to facilitate technical assistance and funding for post-emergency countries still in transition, the programs are still too small to have meaningful impacts. Donors were not receptive in 2000 to a promising proposal from UNHCR, World Bank, and UNDP for commonly formulated and agreed operational responses to span relief to development transitions. The proposal was largely abandoned. Subsequently, UNHCR has established a framework for Durable Solutions that brings together issues related to development assistance to refugees, a "4 Rs" approach to repatriation/reintegration/rehabilitation, and reconstruction, and development through local integration. A September 2003 document explaining the framework[56] underscores the need for comprehensive planning with partners representing development agencies. The "4 Rs" is an integrated approach with other international organizations and agencies for joint implementation and resource mobilization strategies. In this model, UNHCR would focus on its traditional strengths, but would engage with a range of humanitarian and development partners and donors from the outset to strengthen burden sharing, development, and capacity building components for refugees and other similarly affected populations.

This is a positive and sensible approach, which at this writing is beginning to be implemented. The long term international resources needed to support it may or may not be forthcoming. The major reason for inadequate international resources and commitments seems to be that when emergencies occur, donor governments neither anticipate nor plan for long-term multifaceted forms of involvement. It is well understood that international funding alone is insufficient to induce meaningful political, economic, and social reforms or to assure that people who have been uprooted can remake their lives safely and productively. Likewise, aid professionals know that a large and longstanding international presence is almost sure to stifle local initiative. Nevertheless, there are all too many indications that governments will opt for too *little* funding and will continue to insist on time frames too short to fulfill stated objectives. Progress inevitably occurs more slowly in some sectors than in others. The argument for multi-agency integrated planning and transition strategies and for "staying the course" is that realities on the ground—not prefabricated projects and previously established time frames—should determine the nature of international interventions and the funding needed for these interventions.

Migrants who already have been forcibly displaced—as has been repeated throughout this work—need assistance that leads toward integration, whether in the place of refuge, places of origin, or elsewhere. The political components of integration are legal status, formal equality under the law, and the right to work. For the formula to achieve success, however, it is also essential that national governments correct serious deficiencies: corruption, cultural, and religious obstacles undermine theoretically positive programs. Equally important for integration to be feasible—and here national governments do not control the full deck of cards—economic development must be strong enough to sustain the local population, settlers, and/or returnees.

NOTES

1. See Joanne Van Selm, *Study of Feasibility of Setting up Resettlement Schemes in EU Member States or at EU Level* (Washington, D.C.: Migration Policy Institute, 2003).

2. UNHCR has asked for resettlement for 78,642 cases in 2004. This does not represent the actual need for resettlement services but rather the number of cases UNHCR can reasonably process given its limited resources, according to Van Selm, *Study of Feasibility*, 17.

3. See Stephen Castles, "The International Politics of Forced Migration," *Development* 46, No. 3 (September 2003): 11–20.

4. See Khoti C. Kamanga, "Durable Solutions: the Option of Local Integration," Working Paper (on file with authors).

5. Jeff Crisp, "No Solution in Sight: The Problem of Protracted Refugee Situations in Africa," Center for Comparative Immigration Studies, Working Paper No. 68 (December 2002), www.repositories.cdlib.org/cgi/viewcontent.cgi?article=1010andcontext=ccis (November 22, 2004). The most recent figures are from the end of 2001, www.unhcr.ch.

6. At some point following a peace agreement and/or change of government, UNHCR may invoke a cessation clause that removes refugee protection on grounds that the refugees are under the protection of their own national governments or, more problematically, because the circumstances that caused them to be refugees have ceased.

7. Commission of the European Communities, *Green Paper on a Community Return Policy on Illegal Residents* (Brussels: Commission of the European Communities, October 2002). See also Khalid Koser, "Return, Readmission and Reintegration: Changing Agendas, Policy Frameworks and Operational Programmes," in *Return Migration, Journey of Hope or Despair?* Bimal Ghosh, ed. (Geneva: United Nations and International Organization for Migration, 2000).

8. Two of these countries, Angola and Liberia, failed to maintain peace arrangements in the past, and critics lay partial blame for this on international neglect.

9. Patricia Weiss Fagen, "Looking Beyond Emergency Response," *Forced Migration Review*, No. 17 (May 2003): 19–21.

10. See the special edition of *Forced Migration Review*, No. 17 (May 2003), and especially the essay by Erin Mooney on this theme.

11. See Richard Black, *Refugees, Environment and Development* (London: Long-man, 1998); and, Christopher McDowell, ed., *Understanding Impoverishment: The Consequences of Development-Induced Displacement* (Providence, R.I.: Berghahn Press, 1996).

12. UNHCR, *The State of the World's Refugees* (New York: Oxford University Press, 2000), chapter 4.

13. UNHCR, *The State*, 88–91, 97–102. The massive repatriation to Cambodia, which is not discussed here, took place in 1992–1993, in the framework of international operations under the Paris Peace Plan.

14. Barbara Harrell Bond is among the most outspoken critics of camp life in favor of integration and development that, she contends, benefit refugees and host countries.

15. At the Second International Conference on Assistance to Refugees in Africa (ICARA II).

16. The name, Conference on Refugees of Central America derived from the conference where the plan was determined, in 1989.

17. UNHCR, "International Conference on Central American Refugees, CIREFCA: Report of the Secretary General, 3 October 1989," UN Document A/44/527; *Review of the CIREFCA Process*, Evaluation Report (Geneva: UNHCR, May 1, 1994).

18. See Patricia Weiss Fagen, "Peace in Central America: Transition for the Uprooted," in *World Refugee Survey* (Washington: U.S. Committee for Refugees, 1993), 30–39. Recommended strategies for QIPs in and beyond CIREFCA are outlined in UNHCR, EC/1995/SC2/CRP.4, "Assistance Policies and Strategies for the Promotion of Durable Solutions: Achieving Sustainable Reintegration," 8.

19. QIPs are critically discussed in Ian Smillie, "Relief and Development: The Struggle for Synergy," Occasional Paper #33 (Providence, R.I.: Thomas J. Watson, Jr. Institute for International Studies, 1998), chapter 1.

20. Development Program for Refugees, Displaced Persons and Repatriates.

21. Jeff Crisp cites UNHCR acknowledgement to this effect in "Mind the Gap! UNHCR, Humanitarian Assistance and the Development Process," The Journal of Humanitarian Assistance Working Paper No. 43 (November 2001), www.jha.ac/articles/u043.htm (November 21, 2004).

22. An early critical assessment of CIREFCA is in Aldolfo Aguilar Zinser, *CIREFCA: The Promises and Reality of the International Conferences on Central American Refugees* (Washington: Georgetown University Hemispheric Migration Project, 1991).

23. On displacement and programs for return and reintegration, see Patricia Weiss Fagen, "Post-Conflict Reintegration and Reconstruction: Doing it Right Takes a While," in *Problems of Protection: The UNHCR, Refugees, and Human Rights*, Niklaus Steiner, Mark Gibney, and Gil Loescher, eds. (New York: Routledge, 2003), 197–224; Jose H. Fischel de Andrade and Nicole Barbara Delaney, "Minority Return to South-Eastern Bosnia and Herzegovina: A Review of the 2000 Return Season," *Journal of Refugee Studies*, Vol 14. No. 3, 2001; Nicola Dahrendorf and Hrair Balian, "Case Study: Bosnia and Herzegovina, Workshop on the Limits and Scope for the Use of Development Co-operative Incentives and Disincentives for Influencing Conflict

Situations" (Paris: OECD/DAC Task Force on Conflict, Peace, and Development, June 1999); Reports of UNHCR/RTTF (Reconstruction and Return Task Force of the Office of the High Representative.)

24. See Patricia Weiss Fagen, "The Long-term Challenges of Reconstruction and Reintegration: Case Studies of Haiti and Bosnia-Herzegovina," in *Refugees and Forced Displacement*, Edward Newman and Joanne Van Selm, eds. (Tokyo: United Nations Press, 2003), 233–234. The UNHCR figures show minority returns since the Dayton Accord to total 430,426, as of the close of 2003. The largest movements were between 2000–2002, and declined somewhat in 2003, www.unhcr.ba./press/2003pr.091/htm.

25. This section is drawn primarily from the International Crisis Group (ICG), "Return to Uncertainty: Kosovo's Internally Displaced and the Return Process," Balkans Report No. 139 (Brussels: ICG, December 2002), which offers a comprehensive summary of the events and issues.

26. ICG, "Return to Uncertainty."

27. ICG, "Two to Tango: An Agenda for the New Kosovo SSRG" (Pristina/Brussels: ICG, September 2003); ICG, "Return to Uncertainty."

28. Michael E. Hartmann, *International Judges and Prosecutors in Kosovo: A New Model for Post-Conflict Peacekeeping*, Special Report (Washington: US Institute for Peace, October 2003).

29. Francis M. Deng, *Profiles in Displacement: Follow Up Mission to Colombia*, UN Doc. E/CN/4/2000/83/Add.1 (Geneva: UN Commission on Human Rights, January 11, 2000), 3–31.

30. See Patricia Weiss Fagen, Amelia Fernandez Juan, Finn Stepputat and Roberta Vidal Lopez, "Internal Displacement in Colombia: National and International Responses," in *Catching Fire: Containing Complex Emergencies in a Volatile World*, Nicholas Van Hear and Christopher McDowell, eds. (Lanham, Md.: Lexington, 2005, forthcoming).

31. Much of the information in this section comes from Peter Marsden, "Afghanistan," in Van Hear and McDowell, eds., *Catching Fire* (2005, forthcoming). Sarah Petrin has also contributed to the writing of this section, and to parts of the conclusion.

32. The program is described in Alan Kreczko, "The Afghan Experiment: The Afghan Support Group, Principled Common Programming and the Strategic Framework," *Disasters* 27, issue 3 (September 2003): 239–258. Hiram Ruiz gives a more pessimistic account of donor priorities in Afghanistan in "Repatriation: Tackling Protection and Assistance Concerns," in *World Refugee Survey* (Washington: U.S. Committee for Refugees, 1993), 27.

33. An assumption exists that due to the large-scale return of refugees to Afghanistan, and in some areas the return of IDPs to their communities of origin, that internal and external flight has ceased to occur. However, clashes in the northern and western provinces continue to push Pashtun communities south, and numerous returnees in the South have again sought refuge in Pakistan due to an upsurge in Taliban activity since early 2003. A particularly interesting phenomenon is that many families who returned to the South together now send their female relatives back to

Pakistan with one male relative (a *muharram*) to serve as their protector. This exemplifies the fact that the national government is not yet able to protect its people.

34. President Hamid Karzai, "The Story of Afghanistan" (lecture at Oxford University, June 2003).

35. UNHCR, *Refugees* 4, No. 133 (2003): 5.

36. In her article, "The Role of Protection in Ending Displacement," Roberta Cohen reports an estimate of some 40 percent among the two million returnees having moved from outlying areas into Kabul, Herat, and other cities, *Forced Migration Review* 17 (May 2003): 21–23.

37. Christopher McDowell, "Displacement, Return and Justice in the Creation of Timor Leste," in *Catching Fire,* forthcoming.

38. Cambodia's UNTAC organized elections for a year after its arrival, and left almost immediately after these elections had taken place.

39. Christopher McDowell, "Displacement, Return and Justice in the Creation of Timor Leste," in *Catching Fire*, 2005, forthcoming.

40. McDowell, "Displacement, Return and Justice."

41. See www.unwire.org (January 15, 2004).

42. See the case studies in Marc Vincent and Birgitte Refslund Sorensen, eds., *Caught Between Borders: Response Strategies of the Internally Displaced*, and especially the "Conclusion" by the editors (London: Pluto Press/Norwegian Refugee Council, 2001).

43. See Inter American Development Bank, *Beyond Small Change: Making Migrants' Remittances Count*, Steven Wilson, ed., 2004; Inter-American Dialogue, *All in the Family, Latin America's Most Important Financial Flow* (Washington: Task Force on Remittances, Inter-American Dialogue, January 2004); DIFID, World Bank, and International Migration Policy Programme, "Report and Conclusions of the International Conference on Migration and Remittances" (October 9–10, 2003).

44. UNDP, "Capacity Development," www.capacity.undp.org/ (November 22, 2004).

45. In March 2002 at a UN Summit, President Bush announced his intention to create a new account that would rise over three years to $5 billion annually, over current aid levels.

46. Address by Andrew Natsios to the Foreign Operations Subcommittee, Committee on Appropriations U.S. House of Representatives (May 21, 2003).

47. Sadako Ogata, "International Security and Refugee Problems after the Cold War: Assuring the Security of People: the Humanitarian Challenge of the 21st Century," (Olof Palme Memorial Lecture, presented at Berwald Concert Hall, Stockholm, Sweden June 14, 1995).

48. Bruce W. Jentleson, "Preventive Diplomacy: A Conceptual and Analytic Framework," in *Opportunities Missed, Opportunities Seized: Preventive Diplomacy in the Post-Cold War World*, ed. Bruce W. Jentleson (Lanham, Md.: Rowman & Littlefield, 2000).

49. Michael Nobleza, "Generating the Means to an End: Planning Integrated Responses to Early Warning," The International Development Resource Center 2000, web.idrc.ca/en/ev-41507-201-1-DO_TOPIC.html (July 22, 2004).

50. United Nations Development Program (UNDP), "Small Arms and Light Weapons," *UNDP* 2002, www.undp.org/bcpr/smallarms/docs/essentials.pdf (April 19, 2005).

51. United Nations Security Council (UNSC), *Small Arms: Report of the Secretary-General*, September 20, 2002, UN Document S/2002/1053.

52. Chantal de Jonge Oudraat, "UN Sanction Regimes and Violent Conflict," in *Turbulent Peace: The Challenges of Managing International Conflict*, Chester Crocker, Fen Osler Hampson, and Pamela Aall, eds. (Washington D.C.: United States Institute of Peace, 2001).

53. Joost Hiltermann and Loretta Bondi, "State Responsibility in the Arms Trade and the Protection of Human Rights," *Human Rights Watch* 1999, hrw.org/land-mines/Geneva-0299.htm (March 22, 2004); Oudraat "UN Sanctions Regimes," and UNSC *Small Arms*.

54. For an example related to the disadvantages experienced by urban refugees, see Deborah Mulumba, *Refugee Economy and Livelihood in East Africa: Urban Refugees in Kampala and Their Survival Mechanisms* (Kampala: Makerere University, February 2003).

55. The Angolan government has promised to use financial resources to rebuild and reintegrate, but instead, on the one hand, has sought further international assistance while, on the other, refused to account for billions of dollars taken by the state in oil revenues.

56. UNHCR Standing Committee, "Framework for Durable Solutions for Refugees and Persons of Concern," UN Doc. EC/53/SC/INF.3 (September 16, 2003).

Bibliography

Aall, Pamela R. *NGOs and Conflict: Responses to International Conflict: Highlights from the Managing Chaos Conference.* United States Institute of Peace. Washington: USIP, 1996.

———. "What Do NGOs Bring to Peacemaking?" Pp. 365–383 in *Turbulent Peace: The Challenges of Managing International Conflict,* edited by Chester Crocker, Fen Osler Hampson, and Pamela Aall. Washington: USIP, 2001.

Adebanjo, Adekeye. *Building Peace in West Africa: Liberia, Sierra Leone, and Guinea-Bissau.* Boulder, Co.: Lynne Rienner Publishers, 2002.

Alagappa, Muthiah. "Introduction." Pp. 269–294 in *International Security Management and the United Nations,* edited by Muthiah Alagappa and Takashi Inoguchi. Tokyo: United Nations University Press, 1999.

Amnesty International (AI). "No Arms for Atrocities: G8's Uncontrolled Trade in Arms and Military Aid Undermines Fundamental Human Rights and Sustainable Development." *Terror Trade Times* No. 3, 2002. web.amnesty.org/web/web.nsf/pages/ttt3_arms (July 20, 2004).

Anderson, Mary. *Do No Harm: How Aid Can Support Peace-Or War.* Boulder, Co.: Lynne Rienner Publishers, 1999.

Annan, Kofi. "Preface." Pp. xix–xxii in Roberta Cohen and Francis Deng, *Masses in Flight—The Global Crisis of Internal Displacement.* Washington: The Brookings Institution, 1998.

"Arusha Peace and Reconciliation Agreement for Burundi, Arusha, August 28, 2000." www.usip.org/library/pa/burundi/pa_burundi_08282000_toc.html (November 29, 2004).

Asian-African Legal Consultative Organization. *Asian-African Legal Consultative Organization Resolution 40/3.* (New Delhi: Asian-African Legal Consultative Organization, 2001).

Ayoob, Mohammed. "State Making, State Breaking, and State Failure." Pp. 127–142 in *Turbulent Peace: The Challenges of Managing International Conflict*, edited by Chester Crocker, Fen Osler Hampson, and Pamela Aall. Washington: USIP, 2001.

Barry, Jane, and Anna Jefferys. *A bridge too far: aid agencies and the military in humanitarian response.* Humanitarian Practice Network Paper 37. (London: Overseas Development Institute (ODI), 2002).

Bassiouni, David S. "A Review of the Consolidated Appeal Process," Confidential Report. (September 3, 2001; on file with the authors).

Beyer, Gregg A. "Establishing the United States Asylum Officer Corps: A First Report." *International Journal of Refugee Law* 4, No. 4 (July 1992): 455–486.

———. "Reforming Affirmative Asylum Processing in the United States: Challenges and Opportunities." *American University Journal of International Law* 9, No. 4 (November 1994): 43–78.

Bijojote, Salvator, and Christian Bugnion, "External Baseline Evaluation of the Burundi Good Humanitarian Donorship Pilot," Reliefweb 2004 www.reliefweb.int/ghd/Brundi%20GHD%20Pilot%20external%20baseline%20evaluation%2014%20June.pdf (June 22, 2004), 5.

Black, Richard. *Refugees, Environment and Development.* London: Longman, 1998.

Brookings Institution. *Roundtable on the Gap Between Humanitarian Assistance and Long-Term Development.* (Washington, D.C.: UNHCR and the World Bank, 1999).

———. "Toward a strengthened partnership for Angolan recovery and development." Brookings Institution Press Release, 2003. www.reliefweb.int/w/rwb.nsf/0/31d527ec2f881a9749256dd4001e02a4?OpenDocument (November 28, 2004).

Brookings Institution-SAIS Project on Internal Displacement. "Conference on Internal Displacement in the IGAD Sub-Region: Report of the Experts Meeting, Khartoum, Sudan: August 30–September 2, 2003." Brooking Institution. www.brookings.edu/dybdocroot/fp/projects/idp/conferences/IGAD/20030903.pdf (November 28, 2004).

Brookings Institution-SAIS Project on Internal Displacement, The Representative of the United Nations Secretary-General on Internally Displaced Persons, and The United Nations Children's Fund. *Seminar on Internal Displacement in Southern Sudan, Rumbek, Sudan: November 25, 2002.* Brookings Institution. (Washington: Brookings Institution, 2002).

Brooks, Douglas. Personal Interview. June 9, 2004.

Brown, Michael E., and Chantal de Jong Oudraat. "Internal Conflict and International Action." Pp. 163–192 in *Nationalism and Ethnic Conflict: Revised Edition*, Michael E. Brown, Owen R. Cote, Jr., Sean M. Lynn-Jones, and Steven E. Miller, eds. Cambridge, Mass.: The MIT Press, 2001.

Bryne, Rosemary, and Andrew Shacknove. "The Safe Country Notion in European Asylum Law." *Harvard Human Rights Journal* 9 (Spring 1996): 185–228.

Buchanan-Smith, Margie, and Sarah Collinson. *International humanitarian action and the accountability of official donors.* Humanitarian Policy Group Briefing No. 6. (London: Overseas Development Institute (ODI), 2002).

Buchanan-Smith, Margie, and Natalie Folster. *Canada's international humanitarian assistance programme: policy oversight mechanisms.* Humanitarian Policy Group Background Paper. (London: Overseas Development Institute (ODI), 2002).

Buchanan-Smith, Margie, and Judith Randel. *Financing international humanitarian action: a review of key trends.* Humanitarian Policy Group Briefing No. 4. (London: Overseas Development Institute (ODI), 2002).

Buchanan-Smith, Margie, and Ulrik Sørensen Rohde. *Danida's international humanitarian assistance programme: a case study of accountability mechanisms.* Humanitarian Policy Group Background Paper. (London: Overseas Development Institute (ODI), 2002).

Campaign to End Genocide, "UN Peace Operations Reform." Campaign to End Genocide. www.endgenocide.org/ceg-rrf/index.htm (November 26, 2004).

CARE. "CARE International applauds successful conclusion of Loya Jirga—However, Afghanistan's journey towards peace is far from over." CARE. www .reliefweb.int/w/rwb.nsf/s/A289D409886332D8C1256E150045636D (May 27,2003).

Castles, Stephen. "The International Politics of Forced Migration." *Development* 46, No. 3 (September 2003): 11–20.

Cohen, Roberta. "Nowhere to Run, No Place to Hide." *Bulletin of the Atomic Scientists* 58, No. 6 (November 2002): 37–45.

———. "The Role of Protection in Ending Displacement." *Forced Migration Review* 17 (May 2003): 21–23.

Cohen, Roberta, and Jacques Cuénod. *Improving Institutional Arrangements for the Internally Displaced.* Washington: Refugee Policy Group, 1995.

Cohen, Roberta, and Francis M. Deng. *The Forsaken People: Case Studies of the Internally Displaced.* Washington: Brookings Institution, 1998.

———. *Masses in Flight—The Global Crisis of Internal Displacement.* Washington, D.C.: The Brookings Institution, 1998.

Cohen, Roberta, Walter Kalin, and Erin Mooney, eds. *The Guiding Principles on Internal Displacement and the Law of the South Caucasus.* Washington: The American Society of International Law and the Brookings Institution-SAIS Project on Internal Displacement, 2003.

Collier, Paul. "Economic Causes of Civil Conflict and Their Implications for Policy." Pp. 143–162 in *Turbulent Peace: The Challenges of Managing International Conflict*, edited by Chester Crocker, Fen Osler Hampson, and Pamela Aall. Washington, D.C.: USIP, 2001.

Collinson, Sarah. *Donor Accountability in the UK.* Humanitarian Policy Group Background Paper. (London: Overseas Development Institute (ODI), 2002).

———. *International humanitarian action and the accountability of official donors.* HPG Briefing No. 6 (London: ODI, December 2002).

Commission of the European Communities. "Scoreboard to Review Progress on the Creation of an Area of 'Freedom, Security and Justice' in the European Union." Commission of the European Communities. 2000. europa.eu.int/eurlex/en/com/pdf/2000/com2000_0167en02.pdf. (November 21, 2004).

———. "Proposal for a Council Directive on minimum standards for the qualifications and status of third country nationals and stateless persons as refugees or as persons who otherwise need international protection." Commission of the European Communities. (Brussels: Commission of the European Communities, September 12, 2001). europa.eu.int/eur-lex/en/com/pdf/2001/com2001_0510en01.pdf (November 22, 2004).

———. *Green Paper on a Community Return Policy on Illegal Residents.* Commission of the European Communities. (Brussels: Commission of the European Communities, October 2002). europa.eu.int/eur-lex/en/com/gpr/2002/com2002_0175en01.pdf (November 22, 2004).

Consortium of Humanitarian Agencies (CHA). *Guiding Principles on Internal Displacement:* A Toolkit for Dissemination, Advocacy and Analysis—What You Can Do. CHA. (Colombo, Sri Lanka: CHA, 2001).

Consortium of Humanitarian Agencies and The Brookings-SAIS Project on Internal Displacement. *Practitioner's Kit for Return, Resettlement, Rehabilitation and Development.* CHA. (Colombo, Sri Lanka: Consortium of Humanitarian Agencies (CHA), March 2004).

Contat Hickel, Marguerite. "Protection of internally displaced persons affected by armed conflict: concept and challenges," *IRRC* 83/843 (September 2001): 699–711.

Council of the European Union. "Joint Position of 25 October 1996 on pre-frontier assistance and training assignments." *Official Journal of the European Communities* No. L 281 (October 31, 1996):1.

———. "Council Directive 2001/55/EC of 20 July 2001 on minimum standards for giving temporary protection in the event of a mass influx of displaced persons and measures promoting a balance of efforts between Member states in receiving such persons and bearing the consequences thereof." *Official Journal of the European Communities.* No. L 212 (August 7, 2001): 12–23.

———. "Council Directive 2004/83/EC of 29 April 2004 on minimum standards for the qualification and status of third country nationals or stateless persons as refugees or as persons who otherwise need international protection and the content of the protection granted." *Offical Journal of the European Union*, L 304 (April 2004): 12–23.

Crisp, Jeff. "Mind the Gap! UNHCR, Humanitarian Assistance and the Development Process." *The Journal of Humanitarian Assistance* Working Paper No. 43 (November 2001). www.jha.ac/articles/u043.htm (November 21, 2004).

———. "No Solution in Sight: The Problem of Protracted Refugee Situations in Africa." Center for Comparative Immigration Studies, Working Paper No. 68 (December 2002). repositories.cdlib.org/cgi/viewcontent.cgi?article=1010&context=ccis (November 22, 2004).

Crisp, Jeff, and Karen Jacobsen. "Refugee Camps Reconsidered." *Forced Migration Review* 3, (December 1998): 27–31.

Crocker, Chester A. "Intervention: Towards Best Practices and a Holistic View." Pp. 229–248 in *Turbulent Peace: The Challenges of Managing International Conflict,* edited by Chester Crocker, Fen Osler Hampson, and Pamela Aall. Washington: USIP, 2001.

Crocker, Chester A., Fen Osler Hampson, and Pamela Aall. "Introduction." Pp. xv–xxix in *Turbulent Peace: The Challenges of Managing International Conflict,* edited by Chester Crocker, Fen Osler Hampson, and Pamela Aall. Washington: USIP, 2001.

Cuénod, Jacques. "Report on Refugees, Displaced Persons and Returnees, Report to Economic and Social Council." United Nations Economic and Social Council Document E/1991/109/Add.1 (June 27, 1991).

——. Coordinating United Nations Humanitarian Assistance: Some Suggestions for Improving DHA's Performance. Washington/Geneva: Refugee Policy Group, 1993.

Cunliffe, S. Alex, and Michael Pugh. "The UNHCR as Lead Agency in the Former Yugoslavia." *Journal of Humanitarian Assistance.* www.jha.ac/articles/a008.htm (November 21, 2004).

Cutts, Mark. *The Humanitarian Operation in Bosnia: 1992–1995: The Dilemmas of Negotiating Humanitarian Access.* Working Paper No. 8 (Geneva, Switzerland: UNHCR, May 1999).

Dahrendorf, Nicola, and Hrair Balian. *Case Study: Bosnia and Herzegovina, Workshop on the Limits and Scope for the Use of Development Co-operative Incentives and Disincentives for Influencing Conflict Situations* (Paris: OECD/DAC Task Force on Conflict, Peace, and Development, 1999).

Danida. "Multilateral Development Assistance Framework." DANIDA. www.um.dk/English/dp/mda.asp (September 12, 2003).

Deng, Francis M. "Internally Displaced Persons." Report of the Representative of the Secretary-General, Mr. Francis M. Deng, Submitted Pursuant to Commission on Human Rights Resolution 1993/95. Fifty-First Session of the Commission on Human Rights (January 30, 1995).

——. "Flocks without Shepherds: The International Dilemma of Internal Displacement." Pp. 1–13 in *Rights Have No Borders: Worldwide Internal Displacement.* Oslo: Norwegian Refugee Council, 1998.

——. "Internally Displaced Persons." Report of the Representative of the Secretary-General, Dr. Francis Deng, Submitted Pursuant to Commission on Human Rights Resolution 1998/50. Fifty-Fifth Session of the Commission on Human Rights (January 25, 1999).

——. "Profiles in Displacement: Follow Up Mission to Colombia." United Nations Doc. E/CN/4/2000/83/Add.1. Geneva: United Nations Commission on Human Rights, January 11, 2000.

——. *The Consolidated Appeals and IDPs: The Degree to which UN Consolidated Inter-Agency Appeals for the Year 2000 Support Internally Displaced Populations.* (Washington: Brookings Institution, August 2000).

——. "Reaching the Vulnerable: Statement by Representative of the Secretary General on Internally Displaced Persons, Dr. Francis M. Deng." Presented at the Global Launch of the 2002 Inter-Agency Appeals, Helsinki, Finland, November 2001. www.brook.edu/fp/projects/idp/articles/CAP2002FDstatement.htm (November 21, 2004).

——. "Statement to the 58th Session of the General Assembly, Third Committee, Item 117." United Nations Statement (November 11, 2003).

Deng, Francis M., and Larry Minear. *The Challenges of Famine Relief: Emergency Operations in the Sudan.* (Washington, D.C.: Brookings Institution, 1992).

de Torrente, Nicolas. "Humanitarian Action Under Attack: Reflections on the Iraq War." *Harvard Human Rights Journal* 17 (Spring 2004): entire.

DFID, World Bank, and International Migration Policy Programme. "Report and Conclusions of the International Conference on Migration and Remittances" (October 9–10, 2003).

Dind, Philippe. *Security in ICRC Field Operations*. (Helsinki: Finnish Red Cross, 2002).

Donini, Antonio. *UN Co-ordination in Complex Emergencies: Lessons from Afghanistan, Mozambique and Rwanda*. Occasional Paper No. 22. (Providence, R.I.: Watson Institute, 1996).

Dubernet, Cecile. *The International Containment of Displaced Persons: Humanitarian Spaces without Exit* (Aldershot: Ashgate Publishing, 2001).

European Council on Refugees and Exiles. *Guidelines on Fair and Efficient Procedures for Determining Refugee Status*. (Brussels: European Council on Refugees and Exiles, 1999).

——. *The Promise of Protection: Progress towards a European Asylum Policy since the Tampere Summit*. (Brussels: European Council on Refugees and Exiles, 2001).

——. "ECRE Information Note on the Council Directive 2004/83/EC of 29 April 2004 on minimum standards for the qualification and status of third country nationals or stateless persons as refugees or as persons who otherwise need international protection and the content of the protection granted." ECRE, IN1/10/2004/ext/CN.

Fagen, Patricia Weiss. "Peace in Central America: Transition for the Uprooted." Pp. 30–39, in *World Refugee Survey*. Washington: U.S. Committee for Refugees, 1993.

——. "Looking Beyond Emergency Response." *Forced Migration Review*, No. 17 (May 2003): 19–21.

——. "The Long-Term Challenges of Reconstruction and Reintegration: Case Studies of Haiti and Bosnia-Herzegovina." Pp. 221–249 in *Refugees and Forced Displacement*, edited by Edward Newman and Joanne Van Selm. Tokyo: United Nations Press, 2003.

——. "Post-Conflict Reintegration and Reconstruction: Doing it Right Takes a While." Pp. 197–224, in *Problems of Protection: The UNHCR, Refugees, and Human Rights*, edited by Niklaus Steiner, Mark Gibney, and Gil Loescher. New York: Routledge, 2003.

Fagen, Patricia Weiss, et al. *Internal Displacement in Colombia: National and International Responses*. Institute for International Studies Working Paper. (Copenhagen: Institute for International Studies, 2003).

Fagen, Patricia Weiss, Amelia Fernandez Juan, Finn Stepputat, and Roberta Vidal Lopez. "Internal Displacement in Colombia: National and International Responses," in *Catching Fire: Containing Complex Emergencies in a Volatile World*, edited by Nicholas Van Hear and Christopher McDowell. Lanham, Md.: Lexington, 2004.

Faite, Alexandre. *Legal considerations relating to the protection of humanitarian workers in the field*. (Helsinki: Finnish Red Cross, 2002).

Fischel, Jose H., et al. "Minority Return to South-Eastern Bosnia and Herzegovina: A Review of the 2000 Return Season." *Journal of Refugee Studies*, Vol. 14. No. 3 (September 2001): 315–330.

Forman, Shepard, and Rita Parhad. *Paying for Essentials: Resources for Humanitarian Assistance* (New York: Center on International Cooperation, New York University, 1997).

Forman, Shepard, Stewart Patrick, and Dirk Salomons. *Recovering from Conflict: Strategy for an International Response*. Paying for Essentials Policy Paper Series (New York: Center for International Cooperation, 2000).

Forster, Jacques. "Rome Statute of the ICC: Implementation at the national level." Opening remarks made by Mr. Jacques Forster, International Committee of the Red Cross (ICRC), at conference entitled "The Rome Statute of the International Criminal Court: implementation at the national level," Moscow, Russian Federation, February 4–5, 2004.

Frushone, Joel. "Unevenly Applied, More Often Denied: Refugee Rights in Africa." Pp. 74–81 in *World Refugee Survey 2004*. Washington: U.S. Committee for Refugees, 2004.

Fullerton, Maryellen. "Failing the Test: Germany Leads Europe in Dismantling Refugee Protection." *Texas International Law Journal* 36, No. 2 (2001): 231–275.

Gantz, Peter H. "The Private Sector's Role in Peacekeeping and Peace Enforcement." Refugees International. www.refugeesinternational.org/content/article/detail/918 (November 22, 2004).

George, Alexander, and Jane E. Holl. "The Warning-Response Problem and Missed Opportunities in Preventive Diplomacy." Pp. 21–36 in *Opportunities Missed, Opportunities Seized: Preventive Diplomacy in the Post-Cold War World*, edited by Bruce W. Jentleson. Lanham, Md.: Rowman & Littlefield, 2000.

Ghali, Boutros Boutros. *An Agenda for Peace: Preventive Diplomacy, Peacemaking, and Peacekeeping*. New York: United Nations, 1992.

Global IDP Project. www.idpproject.org/.

——. *Workshop on the UN Guiding Principles on Internal Displacement: Borjomi, Georgia: 13–15 November 2000*. (Geneva: Global IDP Project, 2000). www.idpproject.org/training/reports/Borjomi_workshop_2000.pdf (November 22, 2004).

——. *Workshop on the UN Guiding Principles on Internal Displacement and the National IDP Legislation in Colombia: Santa Fe de Antioquia, Colombia 15–17 May 2001*." (Geneva: Global IDP Project, 2001). www.idpproject.org/training/reports/Colombia_2001November 2004.pdf. (November 22, 2004).

Global Policy Forum. *Small Arms and Light Weapons*. www.globalpolicy.org/security/smallarms/salwindx.htm. (November 21, 2004).

Gnaedinger, Angelo. "Humanitarian Action: Today's new security environment has forced us back to basics." Speech by ICRC Director General Angelo Gnaedinger to the Donor Retreat on the Consolidated Appeals Process and Coordination in Humanitarian Emergencies, Montreux, Switzerland, February 26–27, 2004.

Good Humanitarian Donorship Implementation Group. "Implementation Plan for Good Humanitarian Donorship," Elaborated in Stockholm, June 17, 2003.www.odi.org.uk/hpg/papers/Implementation%20Plan.pdf (November 29, 2004).

——. "International Meeting on Good Humanitarian Donorship-Stockholm June 16–17, 2003, Principles and Good Practice of Humanitarian Donorship." www.reliefweb.int/ghd/ (November 29, 2004).

———. "Good Humanitarian Donorship—Current Status of Implementation Work." Informal presentation for 69th HAC meeting, Brussels, June 24, 2004. www .reliefweb.int/ghd/ (July 29, 2004).

Goodwin-Gill, Guy S. "Towards a Comprehensive Regional Policy Approach: The Case for Closer Inter-Agency Cooperation." *IOM/UNHCR*. Geneva: UNHCR, 1993; also published in IJRL 5/347 (1993).

———. *The Refugee in International Law*, 2nd ed. Oxford: Clarendon Press, 1998.

Grossrieder, Paul. "Protecting the Protectors—Official Statement." www.icrc.org/ Web/Eng/siteeng0.nsf/iwpList308/422EF21F7FEAD7E6C1256B66005B63DF (November 22, 2004).

Guardian Unlimited. "A history of war in west Africa." www.guardian.co.uk/ westafrica (March 10, 2003).

Hamilton, Lee H. "Foreward." Pp. xi–xiii in *Opportunities Missed, Opportunities Seized: Preventive Diplomacy in the Post-Cold War World*, edited by Bruce W. Jentleson. Lanham, Md.: Rowman & Littlefield, 2000.

Hara, Fabienne, and Comfort Ero. "Ivory Coast on the brink." *Observer Online— Worldview Extra: Unseen Wars* (2002). www.crisisweb.org/home/index.cfm?id= 2195&l=1 (November 22, 2004).

Hartmann, Michael E. *International Judges and Prosecutors in Kosovo: A New Model for Post-Conflict Peacekeeping*. United States Institute of Peace Special Report. (Washington: USIP, 2003).

Hathaway, James. *The Law of Refugee Status*. Toronto: Butterworths, 1991.

Headquarters Asylum Division, Office of Refugee, Asylum, and International Operations, United States Citizenship and Immigration Services, Department of Homeland Security. *Credible Fear Statistics, FY 2000–2003* (on file with the authors).

Helton, Arthur C. *The Price of Indifference: Refugees and Humanitarian Action in the New Century*. Oxford: Oxford University Press, 2002.

Hiltermann, Joost, and Loretta Bondi. "State Responsibility in the Arms Trade and the Protection of Human Rights." Paper prepared for the Workshop on Small Arms, organized by the Government of Switzerland, Geneva, February 18–20, 1999.

Holborn, Louise W. *Refugees: A Problem of Our Time: The Work of the United Nations High Commissioner for Refugees, 1951–1972*. Metuchen, N.J.: Scarecrow Press, 1975.

Holtzman, Steven. *Rethinking 'Relief' and 'Development' in Transitions from Conflict*. The Brookings Institution Occasional Paper. (Washington D.C., The Brookings Institution, 1999).

Howe, Herbert. *Ambiguous Order: Military Forces in African States*. Boulder, Co.: Lynne Rienner Publishers, 2001.

———. "Lessons of Liberia: ECOMOG and Regional Peacekeeping." Pp. 267–298 in *Nationalism and Ethnic Conflict: Revised Edition*, edited by Michael E. Brown, Owen R. Cote, Jr., Sean M. Lynn-Jones, and Steven E. Miller. Cambridge, Mass.: The MIT Press, 2001.

Human Rights First. "New Regulations Threaten to Turn Board of Immigration Appeals into Rubber Stamp." Human Rights First Media Alert. 2002. www .humanrightsfirst.org/media/2002_alerts/0828.htm (November 21, 2004).

Human Rights Watch (HRW). Arsenals on the Cheap: NATO Expansion and the Arms Cascade. Human Rights Watch. 1999. www.hrw.org/reports/1999/nato/ (April 22, 2004).

———. "Tanzania: In the Name of Security—Forced Round-Ups of Refugees in Tanzania." Human Rights Watch 11, No. 4 (July 1999). www.hrw.org/reports/1999/tanzania/index.htm#TopOfPage (April 22, 2004).

Ingram, James. "The Future Architecture for International Humanitarian Assistance." Pp. 170–194 in *Humanitarianism Across Borders: Sustaining Civilians in Times of War*, edited by Thomas G. Weiss & Larry Minear. Boulder, Co.: Lynne Rienner, 1993.

Inter-American Dialogue Task Force on Remittances. *All in the Family, Latin America's Most Important Financial Flow: Report of the Inter-American Dialogue Task Force on Remittances*. (Washington: Inter-American Dialogue Task Force on Remittances, 2004). www.oas.org/udse/ingles2004/interamerican04.pdf (November 21, 2004).

International Committee of the Red Cross (ICRC). *Basic rules of the Geneva Conventions and their Additional Protocols*. ICRC. 1988. www.icrc.org/Web/Eng/siteeng0.nsf/iwpList74/03500E5921864FF2C1256C550042A893 (November 22, 2003).

———. "The ICRC and Internally Displaced Persons." *International Review of the Red Cross*, No. 305 (1995): 181–191.

———. *Report on the use of armed protection for humanitarian assistance: Extract from Working Paper, Council of delegates, 1995*. (Geneva: ICRC, 1995). www.icrc.org/Web/Eng/siteeng0.nsf/iwpList308/209B1D50B7089A49C1256B66005A58D3 (November 21, 2004).

———. *Who is bound by the Geneva Conventions?: Extract from "International humanitarian law: answers to your questions."* International Committee of the Red Cross, 2004. www.icrc.org/Web/Eng/siteeng0.nsf/iwpList104/3D0F7A4F95BB755FC1256CF5004B6181. (November 22, 2004).

International Criminal Court/Cour Pénal Internationale. "Overview." International Criminal Court. 2004. www.icc-cpi.int/library/about/officialjournal/Rome_Statute_120704-EN.pdf (August 17, 2004).

———. *Rome Statute of the International Criminal Court*. UN Doc. A/CONF.183/9. www.un.org/law/icc/statute/romefra.htm (November 22, 2004).

International Crisis Group (ICG). *Return to Uncertainty: Kosovo's Internally Displaced and the Return Process*. Balkans Report No. 139. (Brussels: ICG, 2002).

———. *Two to Tango: An Agenda for the New Kosovo SSRG*. International Crisis Group (Pristina/Brussels: ICG, 2003).

International Organization for Migration. *International Comparative Study of Migration Legislation and Practice*. Dublin: Stationary Office, April 2002.

Jentleson, Bruce W. "Preventive Diplomacy: A Conceptual and Analytic Framework." Pp. 3–20 in *Opportunities Missed, Opportunities Seized: Preventive Diplomacy in the Post-Cold War World*, edited by Bruce W. Jentleson. Lanham, Md.: Rowman & Littlefield, 2000.

———. "Preventive Statecraft: A Realist Strategy for the Post-Cold War Era." Pp. 249–264 in *Turbulent Peace: The Challenges of Managing International*

Conflict, edited by Chester Crocker, Fen Osler Hampson, and Pamela Aall. Washington, D.C.: USIP, 2001.

Jett, Dennis C. *Why Peacekeeping Fails*. New York: Palgrave, 1999.

Johnson, Chris, and Jolyon Leslie. *Coordinating Structures in Afghanistan*. Humanitarian Policy Group Background Paper (London: Overseas Development Institute (ODI), 2002).

Jones, Bruce D. "Military Intervention in Rwanda's 'Two Wars': Partisanship and Indifference." Pp. 116–145 in *Civil Wars, Insecurity, and Intervention*, edited by Barbara Walter and Jack Snyder. New York: Columbia University Press, 1999.

Jones, Bruce, and Abby Stoddard. *External Review of the Inter-Agency Standing Committee* (New York: Center on International Cooperation, 2003).

Kalin, Walter. "Temporary Protection in the EC: Refugee Law, Human Rights and the Temptations of Pragmatism." *German Yearbook of International Law* 44 (2001): 202–236.

Kamanga, Khoti C. *Durable Solutions: the Option of Local Integration*. Working paper (on file with the authors).

Karanian, Matthew. *Georgia's Forced Migrants*. Institute for the Study of International Migration Working Paper. (Washington, D.C.: Institute for the Study of International Migration, 2001).

Karzai, Hamid, President of Afghanistan. "The Story of Afghanistan." Lecture at Oxford University, June 2003.

King, Dennis. *Paying the Ultimate Price: Analysis of the deaths of humanitarian aid workers (1997–2001)* (New York: UN Office for Coordination of Humanitarian Affairs, 2002).

Koch, Roland. "The Relations of UN Agencies and Non-Governmental Organizations in Cross-Border Humanitarian Assistance." Pp. 210–242 in *International Security Management and the United Nations*, edited by Muthiah Alagappa and Takashi Inoguchi. Tokyo: United Nations University Press, 1999.

Koser, Khalid. "Return, Readmission and Reintegration: Changing Agendas, Policy Frameworks and Operational Programmes." Pp. 57–99 in *Return Migration, Journey of Hope or Despair?*, edited by Bimal Ghosh. Geneva: United Nations and International Organization for Migration, 2000.

Kreczko, Alan. "The Afghan Experiment: The Afghan Support Group, Principled Common Programming and the Strategic Framework." *Disasters* 27, No. 3 (September 2003): 239–258.

Kunder, James. "Analysis of Whether Consolidated Appeals Documents Support Internally Displaced Populations" (October 24, 2000, on file with authors).

——. *The U.S. Government and Internally Displaced Persons: Present, But Not Accounted For.* Brookings Institution and the US Committee for Refugees (Washington: Brookings Institution and the U.S. Committee for Refugees, 1999).

Laitin, David D. "Somalia: Civil War and International Intervention." Pp. 146–180 in *Civil Wars, Insecurity, and Intervention*, edited by Barbara Walter and Jack Snyder. New York: Columbia University Press, 1999.

Lari, Andrea. *Returning home to a normal life? The plight of Angola's internally displaced*. African Security Analysis Programme Occasional Paper 85 (Pretoria: Institute for Security Studies, 2004).

Lee, K. "Finding a Better Way for Humanitarian Action—Creating a Global Institutional Framework: A Rejoinder." *Security Dialogue* 29, No. 2 (1998): 151–55.

Legomsky, Stephen H. "An Asylum Seeker's Bill of Rights in a Non-Utopian World." *Georgetown Immigration Law Journal* 14, No. 3 (2000): 619–641.

Lewis, William, Edward Marks, and Robert Perito. *Enhancing International Civilian Police in Peace Operations*. United States Institute of Peace Special Report 85. (Washington, D.C.: United States Institute of Peace (USIP, 2002).www.usip.org/pubs/specialreports/sr85.html (November 19, 2004).

Loescher, Gil. *Beyond Charity: International Co-operation and the Global Refugee Crisis*. New York: Oxford University Press, 1993.

——. *Beyond Charity: International Cooperation and the Global Refugee Crisis*. Oxford: Oxford University Press, 1996.

——. *The UNHCR and World Politics: A Perilous Path*. Oxford: Oxford University Press, 2001.

Macrae, Joanna. *The 'bilateralisation' of humanitarian response: trends in the financial, contractual and managerial environment of official aid*. Background Paper for UNHCR (London: Overseas Development Institute (ODI), 2002).

——. *The changing role of official donors in humanitarian action: a review of trends and issues*. Humanitarian Policy Group Briefing No. 5 (London: Overseas Development Institute (ODI), 2002).

Macrae, Joanna, ed. *The New Humanitarianisms: A Review of Trends in Global Humanitarian Action*. Humanitarian Policy Group Report 11 (London: Overseas Development Institute (ODI), 2002).

Macrae, Joanna, et al. *Uncertain Power: the changing role of official donors in humanitarian action*. Humanitarian Policy Group Report 12 (London: Overseas Development Institute (ODI), 2002).

Malone, David. "The Security Council in the post-Cold War Era." Pp. 394–408 in *International Security Management and the United Nations*, edited by Muthiah Alagappa and Takashi Inogushi. Tokyo: United Nations University Press, 1999.

Mann-Bondat, Lydia. *Humanitarian Action in Post-September 11 Afghanistan*. Institute for the Study of International Migration Working Paper (Washington, D.C.: Institute for the Study of International Migration, 2001).

Marsden, Peter. "Afghanistan." Pp. in *Catching Fire: Containing Complex Emergencies in a Volatile World*, edited by Nicholas Van Hear and Christopher McDowell. Lanham, Md.: Lexington, 2005.

Martin, Susan F. "Development and Politically Generated Migration." in *Determinants of Emigration from Mexico, Central America, and the Caribbean*, edited by Sergio Diaz-Briquets and Sidney Weintraub. Boulder: Westview Press, 1991.

——. "Global migration trends and asylum." UNHCR Working Paper No. 41. *Journal of Humanitarian Assistance* (2001). www.jha.ac/articles/u041.htm (November 23, 2004).

——. *Refugee Women*. Lanham, Md.: Lexington Books, 2004.

Martin, Susan, and Trish Hiddleston, "Burundi: A Case of Humanitarian Neglect," in *Containing Complex Emergencies in a Volatile World*, edited by Nicholas Van Hear and Christopher McDowell. Lanham, Md.: Lexington, 2005.

Martin, Susan, and Andrew I. Schoenholtz. "Temporary Protection: U.S. and European Responses to Mass Migration." In *Immigration Control and Human Rights*, edited by Kay Hailbronner and Eckart Klein. Heidelberg: C.F. Muller Verlag, 1999.

———. "Asylum in Practice: Successes, Failures, and the Challenges Ahead." *Georgetown Immigration Law Journal* 14, No. 1 (2000): 589–617.

Martin, Susan, Andrew I. Schoenholtz, and Deborah Waller Meyers. "Temporary Protection: Towards a New Regional and Domestic Framework." *Georgetown Immigration Law Journal* 12, No. 4 (Summer 1998).

Mason, Linda, and Roger Brown, *Rice, Rivalry, and Politics: Managing Cambodian Relief*. Southbend, Ind.: University of Notre Dame Press, 1983.

McAdam, Jane. *The European Union proposal on subsidiary protection: an analysis and assessment*. UNHCR Working Paper No. 74 (Geneva: UNHCR, 2002).

McDowell, Christopher, ed. *Understanding Impoverishment: The Consequences of Development-Induced Displacement*. Providence, R.I.: Berghahn Press, 1996.

McFarlane, John, and William Maley. *Civilian Police in United Nations Peace Operations*. Australian Defense Studies Centre Working Paper No. 64 (Sydney: Australian Defense Studies Centre, 2001).

Minear, Larry. *Humanitarian action in an age of terrorism*. Working Paper No. 63 (Medford, Mass.: Humanitarianism and War Project, Feinstein International Famine Center, Tufts University, August 2002).

Mooney, Erin D. "In-Country Protection: Out of Bounds for UNHCR?" Pp. 200–219 in *Refugee Rights and Realities: Evolving International Concepts and Regimes*, edited by Frances Nicholson and Patrick Twomey. Cambridge: Cambridge University Press, 1999.

Morrison, Alex, and Stephanie A. Blair. "Transnational Networks of Peacekeepers." Pp. 243–265 in *International Security Management and the United Nations*, edited by Muthiah Alagappa and Takashi Inoguchi. Tokyo: United Nations University Press, 1999.

Morrison, John, and Beth Crosland. *The trafficking and smuggling of refugees: the end game in European asylum policy?* UNHCR Working Paper No. 30 (Geneva: UNHCR, April 2001).

Mottino, Felinda. "Moving Forward: The Role of Legal Counsel in Immigration Court." New York: Vera Institute of Justice, 2000 (on file with authors).

Mowjee, Tasneem, and Joanna Macrae. *Accountability and influence in the European Community Humanitarian Aid Office*. Humanitarian Policy Group Background Paper (London: Overseas Development Institute (ODI), 2002).

Mulumba, Deborah. *Refugee Economy and Livelihood in East frica: Urban Refugees in Kampala and Their Survival Mechanisms* (Kampala: Makerere University, February 2003).

National Framework for Relief, Rehabilitation and Reconciliation in Sri Lanka (June 2002). www.erd.gov.lk/publicweb/ERDDOCS.html (November 29, 2004).

Natsios, Andrew. Remarks made at the Interaction Forum. Washington (May 23, 2003).

———. Testimony of Andrew Natsios, Administrator, U.S. Agency for International Development (USAID) on the Millenium Challenge Account Before the House Financial Services Subcommittee on Domestic and International Monetary Policy, Trade and Technology, Wednesday June 11, 2003, Washington, D.C. financialservices.house.gov/media/pdf/061103an.pdf (July 29, 2004).

Newland, Kathleen. "The Soul of a New Regime: Progress and Regress in the Evolution of Humanitarian Response." Paper prepared for the Conference on the Evolution of International Humanitarian Response in the 1990s, White Oak Plantation, Yulee, Florida, April 23–26, 1998.

Nobleza, Michael, "Generating the Means to an End: Planning Integrated Responses to Early Warning," The International Development Resource Center 2000, web.idrc.ca/en/ev-41507-201-1-DO_TOPIC.html (July 22, 2004).

Norwegian Information Services. "The Norwegian Government has announced that as of 2 October it will require visas from Bosnian refugees entering Norway, as the last country in northern Europe to do so." *Norwaves* No. 31 (October 5, 1993). www .norwaves.com/norwaves/Volume1_1993/v1nw31.html (November 29, 2004).

Notes from the 2001 CAP Launch. *Women and War*. Rome (November 29, 2000, on file with authors).

Ogata, Sadako, "International Security and Refugee Problems after the Cold War: Assuring the Security of People: the Humanitarian Challenge of the 21st Century," (Olof Palme Memorial Lecture, presented at Berwald Concert Hall, Stockholm, Sweden June 14, 1995).

O'Hanlon, Michael. "Help Africa Help Itself Militarily." *Baltimore Sun*, March 18, 2002.

Olsen, Howard, and John Davis. *Training U.S. Army Officers for Peace Operations: Lessons from Bosnia*. United States Institute of Peace (USIP) Special Report 56 (Washington: United States Institute of Peace (USIP), 1999).

Organization for African Unity (OAU). *Convention Governing the Specific Aspects of Refugee Problems in Africa*. UNTS No. 14, Vol. 691 (1969).

Oudraat, Chantal de Jonge. "UN Sanction Regimes and Violent Conflict." Pp. 323–351 in *Turbulent Peace: The Challenges of Managing International Conflict*, edited by Chester Crocker, Fen Osler Hampson, and Pamela Aall. Washington: USIP, 2001.

Ozmanczyk, Edmund Jan, and Anthony Mango, eds. *Encyclopedia of the United Nations and International Agreements* New York: Garland Publishers, 2003.

Panel on United Nations Peace Operations. *Executive Summary—Report of the Panel on United Nations Peace Operations (United Nations Brahimi Report)*. UN Document A/55/305-S/2000/809. 2000.

Paul, Diane. *Protection in Practice: Field-Level Strategies for Protecting Civilians from Deliberate Harm*. Relief and Rehabilitation Network Paper No. 30 (London: Relief and Rehabilitation Network, 1999).

Philippine National Disaster Coordinating Council. *Policy Guidelines on the Delivery of Basic Services to Displaced Children in Disaster Situations*. NDCC Circular No. 14 (2002). www.ocd.gov.ph/POLGUIDE.pdf (November 29, 2004).

Porter, Toby. *An External Review of the CAP: Commissioned by OCHA's Evaluation and Studies Unit*. Office for the Coordination of Humanitarian Assistance (OCHA). 2002 (Geneva: OCHA, 2002).

Presidencia de la República, Red de Solidaridad Social (RSS). 2002. *PrensaRED,* *13.02.02.*

Ram Charan, B. G. *Humanitarian Good Offices in International Law: The Good Offices of the United Nations Secretary-General in the Field of Human Rights.* The Hague: Martinus Nijhoff, 1983.

Randel, Judith, and Tony German. "Trends in the financing of humanitarian assistance." Pp. 19–28 in *The New Humanitarianisms: A Review of Trends in Global Humanitarian Action,* edited by Joanna Macrae. London: Overseas Development Institute (ODI), April 2002.

Refugees International. "47 Organizations call on Congress to support UN civilian police capacity improvements." Refugees International, 2003. www .refugeesinternational.org/content/article/detail/1008/ (November 22, 2004).

———. "The Private Sector's Role in Peacekeeping and Peace Enforcement." Refugees International. 2003. www.refugeesinternational.org/cgibin/ri/bulletin? bc=00681 (November 22, 2004).

———. "European Constabulary Police Needed to Improve UN Peace Operations." Refugees International. 2004. www.refugeesinternational.org/content/article/detail/ 966 (November 22, 2004).

———. "Firms seek to sell U.N. on privatized peacekeeping." Washington, D.C.: Refugees International. 2004. www.refugeesinternational.org/content/article/detail/ 1092/ (November 21, 2004).

Reindorp, Nicola, and Anna Schmidt. *Coordinating humanitarian action: the changing role of official donors.* Humanitarian Policy Group Briefing No. 7 (London: Overseas Development Institute (ODI), 2002).

ReliefWeb. "Financial Tracking System Information." www.reliefweb.int> (May 13, 2003).

———. "Early Warning." ReliefWeb. 2004. www.reliefweb.int/resources/ewarn.html (January 5, 2004).

Representative of the Secretary General for Internally Displaced Persons. *Guiding Principles on Internal Displacement.* Geneva: UN Office for the Coordination of Humanitarian Affairs, 1999.

Republic of Liberia. "Republic of Liberia Declaration of the Rights and Protection of Liberian Internally Displaced Persons (IDPs)." Declaration by Minister of Justice and Attorney General Lvely Kobbi Johnson, September 26, 2002.

Robinson, Nehemiah. *Convention Relating to the Status of Refugees: Its History, Contents and Interpretation.* New York: Institute of Jewish Affairs, 1953.

Robinson, W. Courtland. *Double Vision : A History of Cambodian Refugees in Thailand.* Bangkok: Asian Research Center for Migration, Institute of Asian Studies, Chulalongkorn University, 1996.

———. "The Comprehensive Plan of Action for Indochinese Refugees, 1989–1997: Sharing the Burden and Passing the Buck," *Journal of Refugee Studies* 17, No. 3 (2000): 314–33.

Rudge, Philip. *The Need for a more Focused Response: European Donor Policies Toward Internally Displaced Persons (IDPs)* (Washington: Brookings-CUNY Project on Internal Displacement, Norwegian Refugee Council, and the U.S. Committee for Refugees, 2002).

Ruiz, Hiram. "Repatriation: Tackling Protection and Assistance Concerns." Pp. 20–29 in *World Refugee Survey 2003*. Washington: U.S. Committee for Refugees, 1993.

Schoenhaus, Robert. *Training for Peace and Humanitarian Relief Operations: Advancing Best Practices*. United States Institute of Peace (USIP) *Peaceworks* 43 (Washington, D.C.: United States Institute of Peace (USIP), 2002).

Schoenholtz, Andrew I., and Jonathan Jacobs. "The State of Asylum Representation: Ideas for Change." *Georgetown Immigration Law Journal* 16, No. 4 (2002): 739–772.

Sheikh, Mani, Maria Isabel Gutierrez, Paul Bolton, et al. "Deaths among humanitarian workers." *British Medical Journal 321* (July 15, 2000):166–68.

Smillie, Ian. *Relief and Development: The Struggle for Synergy*. Watson Institute Occasional Paper No. 33. (Providence, R.I.: Thomas J. Watson, Jr. Institute for International Studies, 1998).

Smillie, Ian, and Larry Minnear, *The Quality of Money: Donor Behavior in Humanitarian Financing* (April 2003), Humanitarianism and War Project, Tufts University. 2003. hwproject.tufts.edu/new/pdf/donor_behav.pdf (November 29, 2004).

Smith, Merrill. "Warehousing Refugees: A Denial of Rights, a Waste of Humanity." Pp. 38–56 in *World Refugee Survey 2004*. Washington: U.S. Committee for Refugees, 2004.

Stoddard, Abby. *The U.S. and the 'bilateralisation' of humanitarian response*. Humanitarian Policy Group Background Paper (London: Overseas Development Institute (ODI), 2002).

——. "Trends in US humanitarian policy." Pp. 39–50 in *The New Humanitarianisms: A Review of Trends in Global Humanitarian Action*, edited by Joanna Macrae. London: Overseas Development Institute (ODI), April 2002.

Sullivan, Eileen, Felinda Moltino, Ajay Khashu, and Moira O'Neill. *Testing Community Supervision for the INS: An Evaluation of the Appearance Assistance Program: Volume 1*. Vera Institute of Justice. 2002 (New York: Vera Institute of Justice, 2002).

Tanner, Victor, and Elizabeth Stites, *External Evaluation of OCHA's Internal Displacement Unit* (New York: UN Office for the Coordination of Humanitarian Affairs, 2004).

United Kingdom Home Department. *Secure Borders, Safe Haven: Integration with Diversity in Modern Britain*. CM 5387 (February 2002).

United Kingdom House of Commons. *Private Military Companies: Options for Regulation—Return to an Address of the Honorable the House of Commons*. London: The Stationary Office, 2002.

United Nations. *UN Convention relating to the Status of Refugees* (July 28, 1951).

——. *Critical Economic Situation in Africa, Report of the Secretary General*. UN Doc. A/41/683 (1986).

——. "Comprehensive Report On Lessons Learned From United Nations Assistance Mission For Rwanda (UNAMIR), October 1993–April 1996." www.un.org/Depts/dpko (November 21, 2004).

——. *Renewing the United Nations: A Program for Reform, Report of the Secretary General*. UN Document. A/51/950 (1997).

——. *Report of the Panel on United Nations Peace Operations*. UN Document A/55/305-S/2000/809. 2000.

United Nations Consolidated Inter-Agency Appeal Process. "Retreat Report." Document from CAP Trainers Retreat: Field Debriefing, Tools Improvement, and Policy Development. Morges, Switzerland: February 20–23, 2001.

United Nations Department of Humanitarian Affairs. *Mid-Term Review of the UN Consolidated Inter-Agency Appeal for the Caucasus* (Geneva: UN Department of Humanitarian Affairs, 1996).

United Nations Development Program (UNDP), "Small Arms and Light Weapons," *UNDP* 2002, www.undp.org/bcpr/smallarms/docs/essentials.pdf (April 19, 2005).

United Nations Economic and Social Council (ECOSOC). "Specific Groups and Individuals Mass Exoduses and Displaced Persons." Report of the Representative of the Secretary-General on Internally Displaced Persons, Francis M. Deng, UN Commission on Human Rights, 59th Session (January 21, 2003). UN Document E/CN.4/2003/86.

——. "Specific Groups and Individuals Mass Exoduses and Displaced Persons." Report of the Representative of the Secretary-General on Internally Displaced Persons, Francis M. Deng, UN Commission on Human Rights, 60th Session (March 4, 2004). UN Document E/CN.4/2004/77.

United Nations General Assembly. *UNGA Res. 428(V), Annex to the Statute of the Office of the United Nations High Commissioner for Refugees*. December 14, 1950.

——. *UNGA Res. 1006 (ES-II)*, November 9, 1956.

——. *UNGA Res. 1167 (XII)*, November 26, 1957.

——. *UNGA Res. 1286 (XIII)*, December 5, 1958.

——. *UNGA Res. 1388 (XIV)* 841st Plenary Mtg. (1959).

——. *UNGA Res. 1389 (XVI)*, November 20, 1959.

——. *UNGA Res. 1500 (XV)*, December 5, 1960.

——. *UNGA Res. 1671 (XVI)*, December 10, 1961.

——. *UNGA Res. 1672 (XVI)*, December 18, 1961.

——. "Convention on the Safety of United Nations and Associated Personnel, G.A. res. 49/59, 49 UN GAOR Supp. (No. 49) at 299." UN Document A/49/49. 1994.

——. "Report of the Secretary-General to the Security Council on protection for humanitarian assistance to refugees and others in conflict situations." UN Document S/1998/883. 1998.

——. "Report of the Secretary-General to the Security Council on the protection of civilians in armed conflict." UN Document S/1999/957. 1999.

——. "Report of the Secretary-General on the implementation of the report of the Panel on United Nations peace operations." UN Document A/55/502. 2000.

——. UNGA Res. 55/72 81st Plenary Mtg. 2000. UN Document A/Res/55/72.

——. "Safety and Security of United Nations personnel: Report of the Secretary-General." UN Document A/55/494. 2000.

——. "Implementation of the recommendations of the Special Committee on Peacekeeping Operations and the Panel on United Nations Peace Operations: Report of the Secretary-General." UN Document A/55/977. 2001.

——. "Implementation of the recommendations of the Special Committee on Peacekeeping Operations and the Panel on United Nations Peace Operations: Report of the Secretary-General." UN Document A/56/732. 2001.

———. "Inter-organizational security measures: implementation of section II of General Assembly resolution 55/238 of 23 December entitled 'Safety and security of United Nations personnel: Report of the Secretary-General'" UN Document A/56/469. 2001.

———. "Prevention of Armed Conflict: Report of the Secretary-General." UN Document A/55/985-S/2001/574. 2001.

———. "Report of the Secretary-General to the Security Council on the protection of civilians in armed conflict." UN Document S/2001/331. 2001.

———. "Report of the Secretary-General on the activities of the Office of Internal Oversight Services." UN Document A/57/465. 2002.

———. "Report of the Secretary-General to the Security Council on the protection of civilians in armed conflict." UN Document S/2002/1300. 2002.

United Nations Inter-Agency Steering Committee (IASC). "East Timor Consolidated Appeal Process (CAP) Review: Phase 3, External Review" (Dili, East Timor: Consolidated Inter-Agency Appeal Process Steering Committee, May 2000).

———. "IASC Review of the CAP and Plan of Action for Strengthening the CAP (April 8, 2002)." IASC, www.reliefweb.int/cap/policy/CAP_PolicyDoc.html (November 22, 2004).

———. "Consolidated Appeals Process Workshop Report: CAP Best Practices and Lessons Learned," (document produced at the third annual CAP Best Practices and Lessons Learned Workshop, Versoix, Switzerland, February 13–15, 2002). www .reliefweb.int/ocha_ol/CAP/CAPWorkshopRpt_Feb02_final.pdf. 32–36 (November 22, 2004).

United Nations Inter-Agency Steering Committee, Sub Working Group on CAP. "Plan of Action: Recommendations for a New Agenda for Strengthening the Consolidated Appeals Process" (Geneva: United Nations, March 4, 2002).

United Nations Office for the Coordination of Humanitarian Affairs (OCHA). "UN Consolidated Inter-Agency Appeal for East Timor Crisis." UN-OCHA, October 27, 1999. www.reliefweb.int/w/rwb.nsf/0/bbd22ecaad05abd5c1256817002d9f18? OpenDocument (November 29, 2004).

———. *Procedural Steps for Developing an IDP Response Strategy*. New York: UNOCHA, 2004.

———. "Consolidated Appeals Process." *UNOCHA* 2004. ochaonline.un.org/ webpage.asp?Page=384 (June 27, 2004).

United Nations Office for the High Commissioner for Human Rights. *Basic Principles on the Use of Force and Firearms by Law Enforcement Officials*. Geneva: United Nations, 1990.

United Nations Office for the High Commissioner for Refugees. *International Conference on Central American Refugees, CIREFCA: Report of the Secretary General, 3 October 1989*. United Nations Document A/44/527.

———. *Handbook on Procedures and Criteria for Determining Refugee Status Under the 1951 Convention and the 1967 Protocol relating to the Status of Refugees*. Geneva: UNHCR, January 1992.

———. Speech by High Commissioner Sadako Ogata, June 26, 1992.

———. "Note on International Protection." UN Document A/AC.96/815 (1993).

——. *Review of the CIREFCA Process*, Evaluation Report. Geneva: UNHCR, May 1, 1994.

——. "Assistance Policies and Strategies for the Promotion of Durable Solutions: Achieving Sustainable Reintegration." UNHCR Document EC/1995/SC2/CRP.4.8 (Geneva: UNHCR, 1995).

——. "Internally Displaced Persons: UNHCR's Perspective." Symposium on Internally Displaced Persons. Chavannes-de-Bogis, Geneva, October 23–25, 1995.

——. *The State of the World's Refugees—In Search of Solutions*. New York: Oxford University Press, 1995.

——. *The State of the World's Refugees 1997–1998—A Humanitarian Agenda*. New York: Oxford University Press, 1998.

——. *Internally Displaced Persons: The Role of the United Nations High Commissioner for Refugees*. Geneva: UNHCR, 2000.

——. *The Kosovo refugee crisis: an independent evaluation of UNHCR's emergency preparedness and response*. Geneva: UNHCR, 2000.

——. *The State of the World's Refugees 2000: Fifty Years of Humanitarian Action*. New York: Oxford University Press, 2000.

——. *Improving the Security and Safety of Staff-UNSECOORD*. UNHCR 2002 Global Appeal (Addendum), 2002.

——. *Note for Implementing and Operational Partners by UNHCR and Save the Children-UK on Sexual Violence and Exploitation*. London: UNHCR, 2002.

——. *Asylum Applications Lodged in Industrialized Countries: Levels and Trends, 2000–2002*. Geneva: UNHCR, Population Data Unit, 2003.

——. *Partnership: An Operations Management Handbook for UNHCR's Partners* (Geneva: UNHCR, 2003).

——. *Refugees* 4, No. 133 (2003): 5.

——. *UNHCR Global Report 2002—Zambia* (Geneva: UNHCR, 2003).

——. "States Parties to the 1951 Convention relating to the Status of Refugees and the 1967 Protocol," as of February 1, 2004. www.unhcr.ch (November 21, 2004).

——. *UNHCR Briefing Notes: Caucasus, Colombia, Afghanistan/Pakistan, Burundi 13 October 2000*. www.pcpafg.org/news/afghan_news/year2000/2000_10_16 (November 21, 2004).

——. *UNHCR Global Appeal 2004* (Geneva: UNHCR, 2003).

United Nations Office for the High Commissioner for Refugees, Division of International Protection. *UNHCR's Operational Experience With Internally Displaced Persons*. Geneva: UNHCR, September 1994.

UNHCR Executive Committee (UNEC). *Safety and Security Issues*. UNHCR Document EC/52/SC/CRP.11 (Geneva: UNHCR, 2002).

UNHCR, Population Data Unit, Population and Geographic Data Section. *Asylum Applications in Industrialized Countries: 1980–1999*. Geneva: UNHCR, November 2001.

UNHCR Standing Committee. "Framework for Durable Solutions for Refugees and Persons of Concern." UN Document EC/53/SC/INF.3 (September 16, 2003).

United Nations Security Council. "Report of the Secretary-General to the Security Council on protection for humanitarian assistance to refugees and others in conflict situations." UN Document S/1998/883 (1998).

United Nations Security Council. "Report of the Secretary-General to the Security Council on the Protection of Civilians in Armed Conflict." UN Document S/2001/311 (2001).

———. United Nations Security Council (UNSC), *Small Arms: Report of the Secretary-General*, September 20, 2002, UN Document S/2002/1053.

———. "Resolution 1502 (2003)." UN Document S/RES/1502 (2003) (August 26, 2003).

———. "Report of the UNSG on Ways to Combat Subregional and Cross-Border Problems in West Africa." UN Document S/2004/200 (March 12, 2004).

———. "Rule of Law and Transitional Justice in Conflict and Post-Conflict Societies: Report of the Secretary-General." UN Document S/2004/614.

United Nations, Senior Inter-Agency Network on Internal Displacement. *Mission to Colombia, August 16–24, 2001: Findings and Recommendations* (New York: United Nations, 2001).

———. *Report from the Special coordinator on Internal Displacement: Background.* (New York: UNOCHA, 2001).

United Nations System Emergency Plan for Burundi. *Without Development There Cannot Be Sustainable Peace, From Humanitarian Assistance to Development* (Bujumbura: UN Country Team in Burundi, 2000).

United Nations Treaty Series (UNTS). No. 2545, Vol. 189.

United Nations Treaty Series. No. 8791, Vol. 606.

UNWIRE. 2004. www.unwire.org/News/328_426_11960.asp.

United States Commission on Immigration Reform. *Becoming an American: Immigration and Immigrant Policy*. Washington: U.S. Commission on Immigration Reform, 1997.

United States CIS Asylum Division. "Asylum By Nationality and Deadline FY 1999–2003" (on file with authors).

———. "1 Year Deadline Rejections by Asylum Office FY 1998–2004" (on file with authors).

U.S. Committee for Refugees. "At Fortress Europe's Moat: The 'Safe Third Country' Concept." Washington: USCR, 1997.

———. *World Refugee Survey 1997*. Washington: USCR, 1997.

———. *World Refugee Survey 2002*. Washington: USCR, 2002.

———. "In the Name of Security: Erosion of Refugee Rights in East Africa." USCR, 2002. www.refugees.org/world/articles/wrs00_eafrica.htm (July 21, 2004).

———. "Blame All Around: Sexual Exploitation of West African Refugee Children." USCR Background Analysis, 2002. www.refugees.org/news/press_releases/2002/022802.cfm (November 21, 2004).

———. *World Refugee Survey 2004*. Washington: USCR, 2004.

United States Congress. "HR1414: UN Civilian Police Corps for International Peacekeeping, 108th Congress, 1st Session." U.S. Congress Document. (Washington: U.S. Congress, 2003). www.theorator.com/bills108/hr1414.html (November 21, 2004).

United States Department of Justice, Executive Office for Immigration Review. *Evaluation of the Rights Presentation*. (Washington: Executive Office for Immigration Review, 1998).

United States Department of Justice Executive Office for Immigration Review (EOIR) Office of Planning and Analysis. *FY 2003 Statistical Year Book*. Washington: Executive Office of Immigration Review, 2004.

United States Department of State (DOS)/IIP. "African Crisis Response Initiative." United States Department of State (DOS)/IIP, 2000. usinfo.state.gov/regional/af/acri (November 21, 2004).

———. *African Crisis Response Initiative: Fact Sheet—May 2000*. Washington, D.C.: United States Department of State (DOS), 2000. usinfo.state.gov/regional/af/acri/fact0500.htm (November 20, 2004).

———. *Summary of the African Crisis Response Initiative*. Washington, D.C.: United States Department of State (DOS), 2000. usinfo.state.gov/regional/af/acri/acrisummary.htm (June 21, 2004).

United States Embassy, Bogota, Colombia. "New Visa Requirement for Colombians Transiting the U.S. Enroute to Third Countries." US Embassy, 2001. bogota.usembassy.gov/wwwsvt1e.shtml (November 29, 2004).

U.S. General Accounting Office. *Internally Displaced Persons Lack Effective Protection*. Washington, D.C.: General Accounting Office, 2001.

United States Immigration and Nationality Act (INA).

United States Immigration and Naturalization Service. *Asylum Reform: 5 Years Later*. Washington: U.S. Immigration and Naturalization Service, 2000.

United States Institute of Peace (USIP). *American Civilian Police in UN Peace Operations: Lessons Learned and Ideas for the Future*. USIP Special Report 71 (Washington, D.C.: United States Institute of Peace (USIP), 2001).

———. *Peacekeeping in Africa*. USIP Special Report 66. (Washington, D.C.: United States Institute of Peace (USIP), 2001).

Van Brabant, Koenraad. *Operational Security Management in Violent Environments: A Field Manual for Aid Agencies, Good Practice Review 8* (London: Overseas Development Institute, 2000).

Van Hear, Nicholas, and Darini Rajasingham-Senanayake. "Displacement and the humanitarian regime in Sri Lanka." Working paper for the collaborative project *Complex forced migration: towards a new humanitarian regime*, Copenhagen and Colombo, July 2002.

Van Hear, Nicholas, and Christopher McDowell, eds. *Catching Fire: Containing Complex Displacement in a Volatile World*. Lanham, Md.: Lexington Books, 2005 (forthcoming).

Van Selm, Joanne. *Access to Procedures: 'Safe Third Countries', 'Safe Countries of Origin', and 'Time Limits'* (Geneva: UNHCR Global Consultations on International Protection, 2001).

———. Study of Feasibility of Setting up Resettlement Schemes in EU Member States or at EU Level. Washington D.C.: Migration Policy Institute, 2003.

VENRO (Verband Entwicklungspolitik Deutscher Nichtregierungs-Organisationen e.V.). "Minimum Standards Regarding Staff Security in Humanitarian Aid." VENRO. 2003. www.venro.org/publikationen/archiv/personalsicherheit_engl.pdf (November 22, 2004).

Vincent, Mark, and Birgitte Refslund Sorensen, eds. *Caught Between Borders: Response Strategies of the Internally Displaced*. London: Pluto Press/Norwegian Refugee Council, 2001.

Vogt, Margaret A. "Regional Arrangements, the United Nations, and Security in Africa." Pp. 295–322 in *International Security Management and the United Nations*, edited by Muthiah Alagappa and Takashi Inogushi. Tokyo: United Nations University Press, 1999.

Weidlich, Sabine. "First Instance Asylum Proceedings in Europe: Do Bona Fide Refugees Find Protection?" *Georgetown Immigration Law Journal* 14, No. 3 (2000): 643–672.

Weiss, Thomas G. "Humanitarian Shell Games: Whither UN Reform?" *Security Dialogue* 29, No. 1 (1998): 9–23.

———. "Whither International Efforts for Internally Displaced Persons?" *Journal of Peace Research* 36, No. 3 (1999): 363–373.

Weiss, Thomas G., and Leon Gordenker. *NGO's, the UN, and Global Governance*. Boulder, Colo.: Lynne Rienner, 1996.

Williams, Michael C. *Civil-Military Relations and Peacekeeping—Adelphi Paper 321*. New York: Oxford University Press, 1998.

Women's Commission for Refugee Women and Children. *Out of Sight, Out of Mind*. (New York: Women's Commission, 2000).

World Food Programme (WFP). "Review of Resource Mobilization for World Food Programme Operations Under the Consolidated Appeals Process (CAP)." www .reliefweb.int/cap/CAPSWG/CAP_Policy_Document/ReportsNReviews/ WFPStudyonResourceMobilisationCAP.doc, 6 (November 22, 2004).

World Health Organization (WHO). "The Consolidated Appeals Process." World Health Organization. www.who.int/disasters/repo/7396.html (November 22, 2004).

Zinser, Aldolfo Aguilar. *CIREFCA: The Promises and Reality of the International Conferences on Central American Refugees*. Washington: Georgetown University Hemispheric Migration Project, 1991.

8 U.S.C. Sec. 1101(a)(42).

64 FR 56135 (October 18, 1999).

67 FR 54878 (August 26, 2002).

Index

Index note: page references in *italics* indicate a table; page references in **bold** indicate a figure on the designated page.

About the Author

Susan F. Martin is a Visiting Professor and Director at the Institute for the Study of International Migration at Georgetown University. She is author of *Refugee Women* and coeditor of *Beyond the Gateway: Immigrants in a Changing America*. She is President of the International Association for the Study of Forced Migration and cofounder of the Women's Commission on Refugee Women and Children.

Patricia Weiss Fagen is a Senior Associate at the Institute for the Study of International Migration at Georgetown University. She has worked with the United Nations High Commissioner for Refugees, the UN Research Institute for Social Development, and the Economic Development Institute of the World Bank. Dr. Fagen has a Ph.D. from Stanford University, and has published a number of works related to Latin American history, human rights law and policy, political asylum and refugee issues, and post-conflict reconstruction.

Kari M. Jorgensen is a Program Officer in the Office of Emergency and Transition Programs at CHF International. She holds an M.A. in Arab Studies and a Certificate in Refugees and Humanitarian Emergencies from Georgetown University.

Lydia Mann-Bondat is the Associate Director for Training and Capacity Building at the Institute for the Study of International Migration at Georgetown University. She holds an M.S.F.S. and Certificate in Refugees and Humanitarian Emergencies from Georgetown University, and will be a Sommer Scholar at the Johns Hopkins Bloomberg School of Public Health in 2005–2006.

293

Andrew Schoenholtz is a Visiting Professor and Deputy Director at the Institute for the Study of International Migration at Georgetown University. Dr. Schoenholtz has conducted fact-finding missions in Haiti, Cuba, Germany, Croatia, Bosnia, Malawi, and Zambia to study root causes, refugee protection, long-term solutions to mass migration emergencies, and humanitarian relief operations. Dr. Schoenholtz' most recent publications include *Refugee Protection in the United States Post-September 11th* and *The State of Asylum Representation: Ideas for Change* (coauthored with Jonathan Jacobs).